ROMAN LITERARY CULTURES

PHOENIX

Journal of the Classical Association of Canada
Revue de la Société canadienne des études classiques
Supplementary Volume LV
Tome supplémentaire LV

EDITED BY ALISON KEITH AND
JONATHAN EDMONDSON

Roman Literary Cultures: Domestic Politics, Revolutionary Poetics, Civic Spectacle

UNIVERSITY OF TORONTO PRESS
Toronto Buffalo London

Toronto Buffalo London
www.utppublishing.com

ISBN 978-1-4426-2967-7

Library and Archives Canada Cataloguing in Publication

Roman literary cultures : domestic politics, revolutionary poetics, civic spectacle / edited by Alison Keith and Jonathan Edmondson.

(Phoenix supplementary volume ; 55)
Includes bibliographical references and index.
ISBN 978-1-4426-2967-7 (cloth)

1. Latin literature – History and criticism. I. Keith, Alison Mary, author, editor II. Edmondson, J.C., author, editor III. Series: Phoenix. Supplementary volume (Toronto, Ont.) ; 55

PA6041.R64 2016 870.9 C2016-900031-1

This book has been published with the help of a grant from the Federation for the Humanities and Social Sciences, through the Awards to Scholarly Publications Program, using funds provided by the Social Sciences and Humanities Research Council of Canada.

University of Toronto Press acknowledges the financial assistance to its publishing program of the Canada Council for the Arts and the Ontario Arts Council, an agency of the Government of Ontario.

Canada Council for the Arts Conseil des Arts du Canada

Funded by the Government of Canada Financé par le gouvernement du Canada

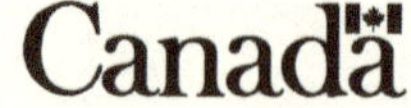

For Elaine,
with love and admiration

Figure 0.1 Roman fresco from Pompeii depicting a woman with stylus and writing tablet and an inquisitive turbaned onlooker behind her. Museo Archeologico Nazionale, Naples. Photo: © Vanni Archive / Art Resource, NY.

CONTENTS

FIGURES

ACKNOWLEDGMENTS

This volume originated in a series of papers presented at a Presidential Panel at the Annual Meeting of the Classical Association of Canada/Société canadienne des études classiques in Québec in 2010, when we honoured Professor Elaine Fantham, sometime Honorary President of the Association, for her manifold contributions to Roman literary cultures over her very distinguished career in Toronto and Princeton. The success of that panel encouraged us to expand the scope of the collection and we invited a group of colleagues and friends of Elaine to reflect further on the intersection between Roman literary texts and Roman social, political, and cultural life. Taking their cue from the literary turn in historical studies and the historical turn in literary studies, the chapters collectively seek to explore the multi-layered texture of Roman literary cultures, from the perspective of domestic politics, poetic revolutions, and civic spectacles. We hope that the volume will thus be of interest both to Roman cultural historians and to literary scholars interested in how Roman texts relate to social and cultural issues.

We would like to express our gratitude to all our contributors, who took up the challenge of the project so readily and were happy to revise their papers to allow them to fit more closely into the overall themes of the volume. The comments of the University of Toronto Press's referees were particularly helpful and we much appreciate the input of these assessors. We are grateful to Susan Dunning and Jen Oliver, graduate students in the Department of Classics at the University of Toronto, for their assistance in ensuring editorial consistency across the entire volume, and to the institutions which have provided, and given permission to use, the images that appear in some of the chapters. We are very pleased to acknowledge the financial support that the Awards to Scholarly Publications Program (ASPP) of the Federation for the Humanities and Social Sciences/Fédération des sciences humaines provided towards the publication costs of this volume. We are especially grateful to the University of Toronto Press and Suzanne Rancourt, Executive Editor, for their enthusiastic support of this volume, and to Barbara Porter and Charles Stuart for their skill and efficiency in seeing it through to publication. Our heartfelt gratitude to the dedicatee is acknowledged elsewhere in the volume.

Alison Keith
Jonathan Edmondson
Toronto, May 2015

R. ELAINE FANTHAM: LIST OF PUBLICATIONS

Books

1 *Comparative Studies in Republican Latin Imagery*. *Phoenix* Suppl. 10. Toronto, 1972.

2 *Seneca's* Troades*: A Literary Introduction, Text, Translation and Commentary*. Princeton, 1982.

3 (co-edited with E. Rummel), *Collected Works of Erasmus* 29. *Literary and Educational Writings* 7. Toronto, 1989. [Responsible for part of the introduction entitled "Erasmus and the Latin Classics" and the annotated translation of *Lingua*.]

4 *Lucan,* De Bello Civili *Book 2*. Cambridge Greek and Latin Classics. Cambridge, 1992.

5 (co-authored with H. Foley, N.B. Kampen, S.J. Pomeroy, and H.A. Shapiro), *Women in the Classical World: Image and Text*. New York and Oxford, 1994 [paperback 1995].

6 *Roman Literary Culture from Cicero to Apuleius*. Baltimore 1996 [paperback 1998; German translation, 1999; expanded 2nd ed. 2012 (#14 below)].

7 *Ovid,* Fasti *Book 4*. Cambridge Greek and Latin Classics. Cambridge, 1998.

8 *Ovid's* Metamorphoses. Oxford Approaches to Classical Literature. New York and Oxford, 2004.

9 *The Roman World of Cicero's* De oratore. Oxford, 2004.

10 *Julia Augusti, the Emperor's Daughter*. Abingdon and New York, 2006.

11 *Latin Poets and Italian Gods*. Robson Classical Lectures 7 (2004). Toronto, 2008.

12 *Seneca, Selected Letters*. Oxford World's Classics. Oxford, 2010.

13 *Roman Readings: Roman Response to Greek Literature from Plautus to Statius and Quintilian*. Berlin and New York, 2011. [Reprint of 31 selected articles on Roman comedy, Roman rhetoric, Ovid's Fasti, Senecan tragedy, Lucan, and Statius.]

14 *Roman Literary Culture, from Plautus to Macrobius* [expanded 2nd ed. of #6 above]. Baltimore, 2012.
15 *Cicero's* pro L. Murena oratio. APA Texts and Commentaries. New York and Oxford, 2013.
16 (translated) *Seneca's* On Tranquility of Mind, in *Lucius Annaeus Seneca, Hardship and Happiness*. Chicago, 2014.
17 (co-edited and translated with B.I. Knott), *Collected Works of Erasmus* 37–8. Apophthegmata. Toronto, 2014.
18 (edited and translated) The Octavia, *attributed to Seneca,* in *Seneca: The Complete Tragedies* 1, ed. and tr. S. Bartsch, S. Braund, A. Dressler, E. Fantham, D. Konstan. Chicago, 2016.

Volumes Edited

1 (co-edited with M. Cropp and S.J. Scully), *Greek Tragedy and Its Legacy: Essays presented to D.J. Conacher*. Calgary, 1986.
2 (co-edited with F. Cairns) *Caesar against Liberty? Perspectives on His Autocracy. PLLS* 11. Cambridge, 2003.
3 (Associate Editor in Chief, with M. Gagarin, Editor in Chief), *The Oxford Encyclopedia of Ancient Greece and Rome*, 7 vols. New York and Oxford, 2010.

Translations

1 G.B. Conte, *The Hidden Author: An Interpretation of Petronius'* Satyricon. Berkeley, 1996.

Online Bibliographies

1 (with E. Fairey) *Quintilian* [electronic resource]. New York and Oxford 2009.
2 (with E. Fairey) *Statius* [electronic resource]. New York and Oxford 2009.
3 (with E. Fairey) *Virgil* [electronic resource]. New York and Oxford 2009.
4 (with E. Fairey), *Roman Religion* [electronic resource]. New York and Oxford, 2010.

Articles and Book Chapters

1 "The *Curculio* of Plautus: An Illustration of Plautine Methods in Adaptation," CQ 15 (1965): 84–100. [Repr. in E. Lefèvre (ed.), *Plautus und Terenz*. Wege der Forschung 236. Darmstadt, 1971.]
2 "Act IV of the *Menaechmi*: Plautus and his Original," *CP* 63 (1968): 175–83. [Repr. in *Roman Readings*, ch. 1, pp. 3–14.]

3 "Terence, Diphilus and Menander: A Reexamination of Terence *Adelphoe*, Act II," *Philologus* 112 (1968): 196–216.

4 "*Hautontimoroumenos* and *Adelphoe*: A Study of Fatherhood in Terence and Menander," *Latomus* 30 (1971): 970–98.

5 "Ciceronian *conciliare* and Aristotelian *ethos*," *Phoenix* 27 (1973): 262–75.

6 "*Aequabilitas* in Cicero's Political Theory, and the Greek Tradition of Proportional Justice," *CQ* 23 (1973): 285–90.

7 "Towards a Dramatic Reconstruction of the Fourth Act of Plautus' *Amphitruo*," *Philologus* 117 (1973): 197–214.

8 "Sex, Status and Survival in Hellenistic Athens; A Study of Women in New Comedy," *Phoenix* 29 (1975): 44–74.

9 "The Trials of Gabinius in 54 B.C.," *Historia* 24 (1975): 425–43.

10 "Virgil's Dido and Seneca's Tragic Heroines," *G&R* 22 (1975): 1–10. [Repr. in J.G. Fitch (ed.), *Seneca*, 372–85. Oxford Readings in Classical Studies. Oxford, 2008.]

11 "Cicero, Varro, and M. Claudius Marcellus," *Phoenix* 31 (1977): 208–13.

12 "Philemon's *Thesaurus* as a Dramatization of Peripatetic Ethics," *Hermes* 105 (1977): 406–21. [Repr. in *Roman Readings*, ch. 3, pp. 32–50.]

13 "Adaptation and Survival: A Genre Study of Roman Comedy in Relation to its Greek Sources," in P.G. Ruggiers (ed.), *Versions of Medieval Comedy*, 297–327. Norman, OK, 1977.

14 "Censorship, Roman Style," *EMC/CV* 21 (1977): 41–53.

15 "Imitation and Evolution: The Discussion of Rhetorical Imitation in Cicero *De oratore* 2.87– 97 and Some Related Problems of Ciceronian Theory," *CP* 73 (1978): 1–16. [Repr. in *Roman Readings*, ch. 11, pp. 243–64.]

16 "Imitation and Decline: Rhetorical Theory and Practice in the First Century after Christ," *CP* 73 (1978): 102–16. [Repr. in *Roman Readings*, ch. 12, pp. 265–84.]

17 "Ovid's Ceyx and Alcyone: The Metamorphosis of a Myth," *Phoenix* 33 (1979): 330–45.

18 "Putting Love in Its Place: A Tribute to Horace," *EMC/CV* 23 (1979): 41–50.

19 "On the Use of Genus-Terminology in Cicero's Rhetorical Works," *Hermes* 107 (1979): 441–59.

20 "Statius' Achilles and his Trojan Model," *CQ* 29 (1979): 457–62. [Repr. in *Roman Readings*, ch. 23, pp. 475–81.]

21 "The Mating of Lalage: Horace, *Odes* 2.5," *LCM* 4 (1979): 47–52.

22 "Plautus in Miniature: Compression and Distortion in the *Epidicus*," *PLLS* 3 (1981): 1–28.

23 "The Synchronistic Chapter of Gellius (*NA* 17.21) and Some Aspects of Roman Chronology and Cultural History between 60 and 50 BC," *LCM* 6 (1981): 7–17. [Repr. in *Roman Readings*, ch. 17, pp. 343–56.]

24 "Seneca's *Troades* and *Agamemnon*: Continuity and Sequence," *CJ* 77 (1981–2): 118–29.

25 "Quintilian on Performance: Traditional and Personal Elements in *Institutio* 11.3," *Phoenix* 36 (1982): 243–63.

26 "*Nihil iam iura naturae valent*: Incest and Fratricide in Seneca's *Phoenissae*," in A.J. Boyle (ed.), *'Seneca Tragicus': Ramus Essays in Senecan Tragedy. Ramus* 12 (1983): 61–76. [Repr. in *Roman Readings*, ch. 24, pp. 482–501.]

27 "Sexual Comedy in Ovid's *Fasti*: Sources and Motivation," *HSCP* 87 (1983): 185–216. [Repr. in *Roman Readings*, ch. 18, pp. 359–92.]

28 "Roman Experience of Menander in the Late Republic and Early Empire," *TAPA* 114 (1984): 299–309. [Repr. in *Roman Readings*, ch. 9, pp. 215–27.]

29 "Orator 69–74," *Central States Speech Journal* 35 (1984): 123–5.

30 "Caesar and the Mutiny: Lucan's Reshaping of the Historical Tradition in *De Bello Civili* 5.237–373," *CP* 80 (1985): 119–31. [Repr. in *Roman Readings*, ch. 25, pp. 502–18.]

31 "Ovid, Germanicus and the Composition of the *Fasti*," *PLLS* 5 (1985): 243–82. [Repr. in P. Knox (ed.), *Oxford Readings in Ovid*, 373–414. Oxford, 2006.]

32 "Women in Antiquity: A Selective (and Subjective) Survey 1979–84," *EMC/CV* 30, n.s. 5 (1986): 1–24.

33 "*Zelotypia*: A Brief Excursion into Sex, Violence, and Literary History," *Phoenix* 40 (1986): 45–57.

34 "Andromache's Child in Euripides and Seneca," in *Essays Presented to D.J. Conacher*, 267–80. Calgary 1986. [Repr. in *Roman Readings*, ch. 22, pp. 457–74.]

35 "Lucan, his Scholia, and the Victims of Marius," *AHB* 1 (1987): 89–96.

36 "*Varietas* and *Satietas*: *De Oratore* 3. 96–103 and the Limits of *Ornatus*," *Rhetorica* 6 (1988): 275–90.

37 "The Growth of Literature and Criticism at Rome," in G.A. Kennedy (ed.), *The Cambridge History of Literary Criticism* I, 220–44. Cambridge, 1989.

38 "Latin Criticism of the Early Empire," in G.A. Kennedy (ed.), *The Cambridge History of Literary Criticism* I, 274–96. Cambridge, 1989.

39 "The Earliest Comic Theatre at Rome: Atellan Farce, Comedy and Mime as Antecedents of the *Commedia dell'Arte*," in D. Pietropaolo (ed.), *The Science of Buffoonery*, 23–32. Toronto, 1989.

40 "Mime: The Missing Link in Roman Literary History," *CW* 82 (1989): 153–63. [Repr. in *Roman Readings*, ch. 10, pp. 228–40.]

41 "Erasmus and the Latin Classics," in E. Fantham and E. Rummel (eds.), *Collected Works of Erasmus 29: Literary and Educational Writings 7*, xxxiv–l. Toronto, 1989.

42 "*Nymphas e navibus esse*: Decorum and Poetic Fiction in *Aeneid* 9.77–122 and 10.215–59," *CP* 85 (1990): 102–19.

43 "*Stuprum*: Public Attitudes and Penalties for Sexual Offences in Republican Rome," *EMC/CV* 35, n.s. 10 (1991): 267–91. [Repr. in *Roman Readings*, ch. 6, pp. 115–43.]
44 "Cato and the Conscience of Imperialism," *Cahiers des études anciennes* 26 (1991): 115–25.
45 "Rhetoric, Tragedy and the Transformation of Pathos," *Proceedings of the Canadian Society for the Study of Rhetoric* 4 (1991–2): 36–63.
46 "Metamorphoses before the *Metamorphoses*: A Survey of Transformations before Ovid," *Augustan Age* 10 (1990–2): 7–18.
47 "The Role of Evander in Ovid's *Fasti*," *Arethusa* 25 (1992): 157–70. [Repr. in *Roman Readings*, ch. 19, pp. 393–408.]
48 "Ceres, Liber and Flora: Georgic and Anti-Georgic Elements in Ovid's *Fasti*," *PCPS* 38 (1992): 39–56. [Repr. in *Roman Readings*, ch. 20, pp. 409–29.]
49 "Ovidius in Tauris (Ovid *Tristia* 4.4 and *ex Ponto* 3.2)," in R.A. Wilhelm and H. Jones (eds.), *The Two Worlds of the Poet: New Perspectives on Vergil*, 268–80. Detroit, 1992.
50 "Lucan's Medusa Excursus: *De Bello Civili* 9.619–99: Its Design and Purpose," *MD* 29 (1992): 95–119.
51 "*Sunt quibus in plures ius est transire figuras*: Ovid's Self-Transformers in the *Metamorphoses*," *CW* 87 (1993): 23–36.
52 "Aemilia Pudentilla or the Wealthy Widow's Choice," in B. Levick and R. Hawley (eds.), *Women in Antiquity: New Assessments*, 221–32. London, 1995.
53 "Recent Readings of Ovid's *Fasti*," *CP* 90 (1995): 367–78.
54 "Rewriting and Rereading the *Fasti*: Augustus, Ovid and Recent Classical Scholarship," M.N. Tod Memorial Lecture, *Antichthon* 29 (1995): 42–59.
55 "The Ambiguity of *Virtus* in Lucan's *Civil War* and Statius' *Thebaid*," *Arachnion* 3 (1995): http://www.cisi.unito.it/arachne/num3/fantham.html.
56 "The Concept of Nature and Human Nature in Quintilian's Psychology and Theory of Instruction," *Rhetorica* 13 (1995): 125–36. [Repr. in *Roman Readings*, ch. 16, pp. 331–42.]
57 "*Religio … dira loci*: Two Passages in Lucan, *De Bello Civili* 3 and Their Relation to Virgil's Rome and Latium," *MD* 37 (1996): 137–53. [Repr. in *Roman Readings*, ch. 26, pp. 519–34.]
58 "Occasions and Contexts of Roman Public Oratory," in W.J. Dominik (ed.), *Roman Eloquence: Rhetoric in Society and Literature*, 111–128. London, 1997.
59 "Images from the City: Propertius' New-Old Rome," in T. Habinek and A. Schiesaro (eds.), *The Roman Cultural Revolution*, 122–35. Cambridge 1997.
60 "'Envy and Fear the Begetter of Hate': Statius' *Thebaid* and the Genesis of Hatred," in S.M. Braund and C. Gill (eds.), *The Passions in Roman Thought and Literature*, 185–212. Cambridge, 1997. [Repr. in *Roman Readings*, ch. 29, pp. 577–606.]

61 "Allecto's First Victim: A Study of Vergil's Amata," in H.-P. Stahl (ed.), *Vergil's* Aeneid*: Augustan Epic and Political Context*, 137–53. London, 1998.

62 "Fighting Words: Turnus at Bay in the Latin Council, *Aen.* 11.234–446," *AJP* 120 (1999): 259–80.

63 "The Role of Lament in the Growth and Death of Roman Epic," in M. Bessinger, J. Tylus, and S. Wofford (eds.), *Epic Traditions in the Contemporary World*, 221–35. Berkeley, 1999.

64 "*Chironis exemplum*: On Teachers and Surrogate Fathers in *Achilleid* and *Silvae*," *Hermathena* 167 (1999): 59–70. [Repr. in *Roman Readings*, ch. 31, pp. 624–34.]

65 "Lucan and the Republican Senate: Ideology, Historical Record and Prosopography," in P. Esposito and L. Nicastri (eds.), *Interpretare Lucano: Miscellanea di studi*, 109–26. Naples, 1999.

66 "Two Levels of Orality in the Genesis of Pliny's *Panegyricus*," in E.A. Mackay (ed.), *Signs of Orality*, 221–37. Leiden, 1999.

67 "The Early Training of the Roman Orator: Principles and Practice," *Paideia* 55 (2000): 197–215.

68 "Meeting the People: The Orator and the Republican *contio* at Rome," in L. Calboli Montefusco (ed.), *Papers on Rhetoric III*, 95–112. Bologna, 2000.

69 "*Domina*-Tricks, or How to Construct a Good Whore from a Bad One," in E. Stark and G. Vogt Spira (eds.), *Dramatisches Waldchen: Festschrift für Eckard Lefèvre*, 287–99. Hildesheim, 2000. [Repr. in *Roman Readings*, ch. 7a, pp. 144–56.]

70 "L'emploi de l'ethos et pathos chez Virgile," in F. Comillat and R. Lockwood (eds.), *Ethos et pathos. Le statut du sujet rhétorique*, 165–75. Paris, 2000.

71 "Production of Seneca's *Trojan Women*, Ancient and Modern," in G.W.M. Harrison (ed.), *Seneca in Performance*, 13–26. Swansea, 2000.

72 "Roman Elegy: Problems of Self-Definition, and Redirection," in E.A. Schmidt (ed.), *L'histoire littéraire immanente dans la poésie latine: huit exposés suivis de discussions*, 183–211. Fondation Hardt: Entretiens sur l'antiquité classique 47. Vandœvres–Geneva, 2001.

73 "Roman Tragedy and the Teaching of Aristotle's *Poetics*," in J. Haarberg and O. Andersen (eds.), *Making Sense of Aristotle: Essays in Poetics*, 109–25. London, 2001.

74 "The *Fasti*: History, Politics, and Religion," in B.W. Boyd (ed.), *Brill's Companion to Ovid*, 197–233. Leiden, 2002.

75 "Quintilian on the Uses and Methods of Declamation," in G. Urso (ed.), *Hispania terris omnibus felicior. Premesse ed esiti di un processo di integrazione: Atti del convegno internazionale, Cividale del Friuli, 27–29 settembre 2001*, 271–80. Pisa, 2002. [Repr. in *Roman Readings*, ch. 15, pp. 320–30.]

76 "The *Fasti* as a Source for Women's Participation in Roman Cult," in G. Herbert-Brown (ed.), *Essays on Ovid's* Fasti, 23–46. Oxford, 2002. [Repr. in *Roman Readings*, ch. 21, pp. 430–53.]

77 "Orator and/et Actor," in P. Easterling and E. Hall (eds.), *Greek and Roman Actors: Aspects of an Ancient Profession*, 362–76. Cambridge, 2002. [Repr. in *Roman Readings*, ch. 13, pp. 285–301.]

78 "Commenting on Commentaries: A Pragmatic Postcript," in R.K. Gibson and C.S. Kraus (eds.), *The Classical Commentary: Histories, Practices, Theory*, 403–22. Leiden, 2002.

79 "Chiron, the Best of Teachers," in A.F. Basson and W.J Dominik (eds.), *Literature, Art, History: Studies on Classical Antiquity and Tradition in Honour of W.J. Henderson*, 111–22. Frankfurt am Main, 2003.

80 "Caesar against Liberty? An Introduction," in F. Cairns and E. Fantham (eds.), *Caesar against Liberty? Perspectives on His Autocracy. PLLS* 11 (2003): 1–18.

81 "Three Wise Men at the End of the Roman Republic," in F. Cairns and E. Fantham (eds.), *Caesar against Liberty? Perspectives on His Autocracy. PLLS* 11 (2003): 96–117.

82 "The Angry Poet and the Angry Gods: Problems of Theodicy in Lucan's Epic of Defeat," in S. Braund and G. Most (eds.), *Ancient Anger: Perspectives from Homer to Galen*, 229–49. *Yale Classical Studies* 32. Cambridge, 2003. [Repr. in *Roman Readings*, ch. 27, pp. 535–58.]

83 "Pacuvius: Melodrama, Reversals and Recognitions," in D. Braund and C. Gill (eds.), *Myth, History and Culture in Republican Rome: Studies in Honour of T.P. Wiseman*, 98–118. Exeter, 2003.

84 "An Appreciation of T.P. Wiseman," in D. Braund and C. Gill (eds.), *Myth, History and Culture in Republican Rome: Studies in Honour of T.P. Wiseman*, 320–5. Exeter, 2003.

85 "Maidens in Otherland, or Broads Abroad: Plautus' *Poenulae*," in T. Baier (ed.), *Studien zu Plautus'* Poenulus, 235–51. Tübingen, 2004. [Repr. in *Roman Readings*, ch. 7c, pp. 176–94.]

86 "Literature in the Roman Republic," in H.I. Flower (ed.), *The Cambridge Companion to the Roman Republic*, 271–93. Cambridge, 2004.

87 "Liberty and the People in Republican Rome [APA Presidential Address, Boston 2005]," *TAPA* 135 (2005): 209–29.

88 "Women of the *Demi-monde* and Sisterly Solidarity in the *Cistellaria*," in R. Hartkamp and F. Hurka (eds.), *Studien zu Plautus' Cistellaria*, 221–38. Tübingen, 2004. [Repr. in *Roman Readings*, ch. 7b, pp. 157–75.]

89 "Terence and the Familiarization of Comedy," *Ramus* 33 (2004): 20–34. [Repr. in *Roman Readings*, ch. 8, pp. 195–214.]

90 "Disowning and Dysfunction in the Declamatory Family," *MD* 53 (2004): 65–82. [Repr. in *Roman Readings*, ch. 14, pp. 302–19.]

91 "*Mater Dolorosa*," *Hermathena* 177–8 (2004–5): 113–24.
92 "Roman Tragedy," in S.J. Harrison (ed.), *Blackwell Companion to Latin Literature*, 116–29. Malden, MA, 2005.
93 "The Family Sagas of the Houses of Aeacus and Pelops: From Ennius to Accius," *Dionisio* 4 (2005): 56–71.
94 "The Perils of Prophecy: Statius' Amphiaraus and his Literary Antecedents," in R. Nauta, H.-J. Van Dam, and J. Smolenaars (eds.), *Flavian Poetry*, 147–62. Leiden, 2006. [Repr. in *Roman Readings*, ch. 30, pp. 607–23.]
95 "'*Dic si quid potes de Sexto Annali*': The Literary Legacy of Ennius's Pyrrhic War," *Arethusa* 39 (2006): 549–68.
96 "Introduction," in P. Fallon (transl.), *Virgil:* Georgics, xi–xxxiii. Oxford World's Classics. Oxford, 2006.
97 "The Image of Woman in Propertius' Poetry," in H.-C. Günther (ed.), *Brill's Companion to Propertius*, 183–98. Leiden, 2006.
98 "Mania e medicina nei 'Menaechmi' e in altri testi," in R. Renato and A. Tontini (eds.), *Lecturae Plautinae Sarsinates* 10. *Menaechmi*, 23–46. Urbino, 2007. [Repr. in English as "The Madman and the Doctor," in *Roman Readings*, ch. 2, pp. 15–31.]
99 "Dialogues of Displacement: Seneca's Consolations to Helvia and Polybius," in J.F. Gaertner (ed.), *Writing Exile: The Discourse of Displacement in Greco-Roman Antiquity*, 173–92. Leiden, 2007.
100 "Introduction," in F. Ahl (transl.), *Virgil: The Aeneid*, xi–xlv. Oxford World's Classics. Oxford and New York, 2007.
101 "Covering the Head at Rome: Ritual and Gender," in J. Edmondson and A. Keith (eds.), *Roman Dress and the Fabrics of Roman Culture*, 158–71. *Phoenix* Suppl. 46. Toronto, 2008.
102 "With Malice Aforethought: The Ethics of *militia* on Stage and at Law," in I. Sluiter and R.M. Rosen (eds.), *KAKOS: Badness and Anti-Value in Classical Antiquity*, 319–34. Leiden, 2008.
103 "Rhetoric and Ovid's Poetry," in P.E. Knox (ed.), *Blackwell's Companion to Ovid*, 26–44. Malden, MA, 2009.
104 "Caesar as an Intellectual," in M. Griffin (ed.), *Blackwell's Companion to Julius Caesar*, 141–56. Malden, MA, 2009.
105 "Telephus at Rome," in J.R.C. Cousland and J.R. Hume (eds.), *The Play of Texts and Fragments: Essays in Honour of Martin Cropp*, 421–32. *Mnemosyne* Suppl. 314. Leiden, 2009.
106 "Caesar's Voice and Caesarian Voices," in N. Hömke and C. Reitz (eds.), *Lucan's* Bellum Civile*: Between Epic Tradition and Aesthetic Innovation*, 53–70. Berlin and New York, 2010.
107 "*Discordia fratrum*," in B. Breed, C. Damon, and A. Rossi (eds.), *Citizens of Discord*, 207–19. Oxford, 2010. [Repr. in *Roman Readings*, ch. 28, pp. 559–76.]

108 "A Controversial Life," in P. Asso (ed.), *Brill's Companion to Lucan*, 3–20. Leiden, 2010.

109 "Two Levels of Orality in the Genesis of Pliny's *Panegyricus*," in R. Rees (ed.), *Latin Panegyric*, 109–25. Oxford, 2012.

110 "Purification in Ancient Rome," in M. Bradley and K.R. Stow (eds.), *Rome, Pollution, and Propriety: Dirt, Disease, and Hygiene in the Eternal City from Antiquity to Modernity*, 59–66. Cambridge, 2012.

111 "The First Book of *Letters*," in H.-C. Günther (ed.), *Brill's Companion to Horace*, 407–30. Leiden, 2013.

112 "The Fourth Book of *Odes*," in H.-C. Günther (ed.), *Brill's Companion to Horace*, 445–66. Leiden, 2013.

113 "The Performing Prince," in M. Dinter and E. Buckley (eds.), *Blackwell's Companion to the Neronian Age*, 17–28. Malden, MA, 2013.

114 "Foreword," in J. Alison, *Change Me: Stories of Sexual Transformation from Ovid*, xxi–xxxi. New York and Oxford, 2014.

115 "Family Finances and the Money-Go-Round of Love," in M.T. Dinter (ed.), *The Cambridge Companion to Roman Comedy*. Cambridge, forthcoming.

ABBREVIATIONS

All abbreviations of literary texts and journal titles in the main follow *OCD*[3] and *L'Année Philologique*, respectively. Note also the following:

AE	*L'Année épigraphique*. Paris, 1888–.
Bruns[7]	C.G. Bruns, ed., *Fontes iuris Romani antiqui*[7]. Tübingen, 1909.
CIL	*Corpus Inscriptionum Latinarum*. Berlin, 1863–.
CLE	F. Bücheler and E. Lommatzsch, eds., *Carmina Latina Epigraphica*. Leipzig, 1895–7.
EAOR	*Epigrafia anfiteatrale dell'Occidente Romano*. Rome, 1988–.
EE	*Ephemeris Epigraphica: Corporis Inscriptionum Latinarum supplementum*. 9 vols. Berlin, 1871–1913.
ELRH	B. Díaz Ariño, ed., *Epigrafía latina republicana de Hispania*. Barcelona, 2008.
FIRA	F. Riccobono and V. Arangio Ruiz, eds., *Fontes iuris Romani anteiustiniani.*[2] 3 vols. Florence, 1940–3.
ICUR	A. Silvagni, A. Ferrua, et al., eds., *Inscriptiones Christianae Urbis Romae*. Rome, 1922–.
IG	*Inscriptiones Graecae*. Berlin, 1903–.
ILLRP	A. Degrassi, ed., *Inscriptiones Latinae liberae rei publicae*. 2 vols. Florence, 1957–63.
ILS	H. Dessau, ed., *Inscriptiones Latinae Selectae*. Berlin, 1892–1916.
Inscr. It.	*Inscriptiones Italiae*. Rome, 1931–.
LGPN	P.M. Fraser, E. Matthews, et al., eds., *A Lexicon of Greek Personal Names*. Oxford, 1987–.
LS	C.T. Lewis and C. Short, eds., *A Latin Dictionary*. Oxford, 1879.
OCT	Oxford Classical Texts

OLD	P.G.W. Glare, ed., *Oxford Latin Dictionary*. Oxford, 1968–82.
ORF	E. Malcovati, ed., *Oratorum Romanorum Fragmenta Liberae Rei Publicae*[4]. Milan, 1976.
PIR[2]	*Prosopographia Imperii Romani. Saec. I. II. III*[2]. Berlin 1933–.
RDGE	R.K. Sherk, ed., *Roman Documents of the Greek East.* Senatus Consulta *and* Epistulae *to the Age of Augustus*. Baltimore, 1969.
RE	*Paulys Real-Encyclopädie der klassischen Altertumswissenschaft*. Stuttgart, 1894–.
RPC	A. Burnett, M. Amandry, and P. P. Ripollès, eds., *Roman Provincial Coinage*. London and Paris, 1992–.
RS	M.H. Crawford, ed., *Roman Statutes*. 2 vols. *BICS* Suppl. 64. London, 1996.
SEG	*Supplementum Epigraphicum Graecum*. 1923–71, 1979–.
SH	H. Lloyd-Jones and P.J. Parsons, eds., *Supplementum Hellenisticum*. Berlin and New York, 1983.
SIG[3]	W. Dittenberger, ed., *Sylloge Inscriptionum Graecarum*[3]. 4 vols. Leipzig, 1915–24.
Suppl. It.	*Supplementa Italica*. Rome, 1981–.
TLL	*Thesaurus Linguae Latinae*. Leipzig, 1904–.

ROMAN LITERARY CULTURES

1

Roman Literary Cultures

ALISON KEITH AND JONATHAN EDMONDSON

It has been twenty years since Elaine Fantham published her groundbreaking social history of Latin literature, *Roman Literary Culture*.[1] The aim of the volume, she explained, was to illuminate the changing production contexts and reading habits of literate Roman society – in part with a view to understanding "the rise and fall of different genres [in the context of] social and political change," and in part to investigate "the cultural equipment and expectations" that the informed Roman reading public brought to bear on individual works of Latin literature.[2] Her emphasis on the importance of socio-political "circumstance and context"[3] to the understanding of authors and their works challenged Latin literary scholars to take explicit account of social class, and the attainments elite status could provide (including an education in Greek and Latin, grammar and rhetoric), not only when considering an author's biography but also when exploring the work's frame of reference and intended audience.

Elaine Fantham's pioneering work proved one of many tectonic shifts in the study of Roman literature and culture over the last several decades; the contours of the field have changed as scholars have sought to continue the development of the traditional practices familiar to classical scholarship, but also to embark upon the study of new kinds of texts, and to practise new approaches to texts both canonical and marginal. The study of Latin literature in particular has seen major upheavals. A sharp separation of "literary" criticism from "historical" analysis of literary works was explicitly promoted by the influence of the so-called New Criticism in the mid-twentieth century; as a result, Latin literature is still frequently discussed in isolation from its multiple contexts of production and circulation.[4] Although the authority of that critical paradigm for classical and modern literary scholarship has waned, other factors have sustained the importance of formalist interpretation of Latin literary texts. Most significantly, of course, classicists

Figure 1.1 Roman fresco from Pompeii depicting piles and a purse of money (above) and writing materials – inkpot and stylus, scroll, wax tablets (below). Museo Archeologico Nazionale, Naples. Photo: © HIP / Art Resource, NY.

lack the abundance of textual, documentary, and material remains available to literary scholars of more recent book cultures, which might more richly illuminate, for example, the economic market for, and material contexts of, our extant corpus of texts as are represented on wall paintings from Pompeii, such as on a still life depicting writing materials, coins, and a purse of money (Figure 1.1).[5] Despite this, scholars such as Alan Bowman, William Johnson, and Kristina Milnor have done much of late to investigate elite reading culture in the Roman Empire by probing not just literary texts, but also the rich harvest of papyri that survive from Roman Egypt and the writing tablets excavated at Vindolanda, not to mention the graffiti of Latin poetry and iconographic representations of bookrolls and writing tablets found at Pompeii.[6] In addition, however, one of the foremost legacies of twentieth-century critical theory to the field of Classics has been the refinement, led by scholars of Latin literature, of a rich and sophisticated theoretical apparatus for genre criticism and the analysis of allusion and intertextuality.[7] As a result, formalist criticism retains significant scholarly authority in the area of Latin literary study.

The papers collected in this volume reflect the continuing commitment to formalist criticism among Latinists, but they also exhibit a renewed engagement with historicist exegesis. Ancient historians have long mined literary texts for nuggets of historical evidence, but it is only recently that they have undertaken sustained readings of a classical author's literary corpus in order to reconstruct the historical context in which it was produced. Thus, for example, Keith Bradley, in *Apuleius and Antonine Rome: Historical Essays* (Toronto 2012), has recently contributed a series of studies of Apuleius' oeuvre for the light his writings shed on a wide variety of sociohistorical problems in the age of the Roman emperors Antoninus Pius and Marcus Aurelius. In so doing, he was following in the pioneering footsteps of Fergus Millar, whose inaugural lecture as Professor of Ancient History at University College London in March 1981 sketched the potential of Apuleius' novel *Metamorphoses*, also known as *The Golden Ass*, for providing us with a deeper understanding of the social and cultural world of the Roman Empire in the mid-second century.[8] Bradley expanded and deepened the scope by probing Apuleius' works for insights into the mechanics of Roman law, magic, and religion; the extent and functioning of the Mediterranean slave trade; and the construction and maintenance of family relationships.[9] T.P. Wiseman's close reading of Catullus' poetry did much to lay bare the violent underpinnings of Roman society that form, he argued, a crucial cultural context for his short poems of love and hate.[10] Similarly, though on a smaller scale, Michele George has recently investigated the representation of the toga in the poetry of Statius, Martial, and Juvenal, in order to illuminate contemporary attitudes towards the official Roman dress code among citizens not belonging to the imperial elite.[11]

While scholars of classical literature have also traditionally been concerned to understand the historical context of the works they study, the critical movement of New Historicism in the late twentieth century has prompted renewed attention to the multiplicity of ways in which classical literary texts participate in ancient civic debates. Vergil's *Bucolics* and *Aeneid*, for example, have always elicited historicizing interpretations, visible already in the ancient commentary tradition on his poetry that circulated under the name of the late antique grammarian Servius. Vergil's Augustan partisanship was widely assumed in antiquity (not least by Augustus),[12] although it has been called into question in the aftermath of the Second World War.[13] However, the stale scholarly debate about Vergil's personal political commitment for or against Augustus has increasingly been superseded by nuanced critical discussion of rather more interesting historical problems raised by Vergil's oeuvre: e.g., the intersection of Epicurean philosophical ideals and republican political commitments in the *Bucolics*[14] and the deployment of themes of ancient political writing (and their implied commitments) in the *Aeneid*.[15] Nor are adherents of historical criticism to be found only among Vergilianists. Such disparate fields of study as Roman comedy and Latin elegy have both witnessed the historicist turn in recent years: for example, Matthew Leigh has devoted a monograph to Roman comedy with the explicit aim "to investigate the comedies of Plautus and Terence in the light of Roman history and Roman history in the light of Plautus and Terence,"[16] while Teresa Ramsby has analysed the Roman elegists' appropriation of epigram and epigraphical conventions in her monograph *Textual Permanence: Roman Elegists and the Epigraphic Tradition*.[17]

In exploring Roman literary *cultures*, contributors to this volume address a variety of Latin texts from the multiple perspectives of domestic politics, poetic revolutions, and civic spectacles. Taking our cue from the literary turn in historical studies, and the historical turn in literary studies, we explore some of the most celebrated (along with some of the most obscure) Latin literary texts, both verse and prose: from Roman drama and Menippean satire through Latin elegy, epic, and novel, to epistles and compilations of laws. The collection of papers offered here draws on the historicizing turn in Latin literary scholarship and extends these exciting new critical methods in dialogue with traditional analysis of genre-blending, allusion, and intertextuality, spanning the Latin literary tradition from mid-republican Roman drama to second-sophistic Latin novel. Analysis of literary genre, especially in Ovidian poetry, proceeds side by side with considerations of the politics of the Roman household (in the sense of both *domus*, "house," and *familia*, "members of the household") and of the civic spectacles in which an engaged citizenry participated.

In Part I, "Domestic Politics," contributors explore the impact of contemporary political debates for our understanding of literary works set in the Roman house and household. Christer Bruun discusses the interpretation of a vexed fragment from Varro's *Menippean Satires* in the context of ongoing Roman moralizing debate about household luxury, in this case of the conspicuous consumption of water in fountains and other aquatic features of the Roman townhouse garden. His attention to the archaeological evidence for the history of luxury aquatic features in elite Roman houses demonstrates how textual problems may be illuminated by socio-historical analysis and material evidence. Thus he contextualizes a textual problem against the relevant archaeological remains and the politically charged debate about increasing luxury in Roman living standards.

The politics of contemporary Roman moralizing discourses also concerns Fanny Dolansky, who analyses the rapes Ovid relates in *Fasti* 2 in the light of Augustus' legislation on adultery and marriage: the *lex Iulia de adulteriis coercendis* of 18/17 BCE and the *lex Iulia de maritandis ordinibus* of 18 BCE, later reinforced by the *lex Papia Poppaea* of 9 CE. Noting Ovid's juxtaposition of Augustus' receipt of the title *pater patriae* ("Father of the Fatherland") with three extended rape narratives in the book (those of Callisto, Lara, and Lucretia), she argues that the poet thereby calls into question both the efficacy and the legitimacy of the *princeps'* moral legislation. Her sophisticated analysis of Ovid's learned poem on the festivals of the Roman calendar reveals the deep interconnection between the politics of the Roman household and the politics of the Roman state at a decisive historical moment.

Alison Keith is also concerned with contemporary Roman sexual morality in her discussion of the overlap between the names of the mistresses celebrated in Latin elegy and the inscriptional evidence for named slave women and freedwomen from the same period at Rome. Her chapter on elegiac onomastics in the Roman *domus* aims to document the contemporary currency of the Greek names of the elegists' mistresses in Augustan Rome, where their names are resonant of Roman imperial conquest. This evidence, she argues, shows that Roman elegy is intimately correlated with Roman imperialism in its celebration of the sexual spoils of military conquest.

The final chapter in this section of the volume, by Sarah Blake, also draws attention to the dynamics of power in the Roman *domus*, with a study of the implications of the phrase *in manus*, which the younger Pliny uses in reference to his epistolary collections but which is more familiar from the contexts of marriage and slave ownership in ancient Rome. In a wide-ranging discussion of Pliny's letters, Blake links the materiality of his production of epistles, quite literally at the hands of his slaves (copyists, carriers, librarians, etc.), with his self-fashioning throughout the collection as a caring husband and slave owner. Her analysis of the slave owner's occluded dependence on his dependents emphasizes the unequal power relations that structure Roman literary cultures and challenges us to recognize the role of slavery at every stage of the production and reception of Latin literature.[18]

The chapters in Part II, "Revolutionary Poetics," focus on the significance of genre, allusion, and intertextuality in Latin literary texts, especially those of Ovid, whose corpus has been a touchstone of shifting critical fashions in Latin literary studies for more than twenty-five years.[19] Barbara Weiden Boyd opens the section, with a chapter on Ovid's revolutionary redefinition of the generic character of both didactic and elegy in the *Remedia Amoris*. She argues that the poem, as the last in a series of books of erotodidaxis, negotiates between continuity and rupture, both continuing the tradition of advice begun in the *Ars Amatoria* and quite literally recanting it. In her chapter, Sarah McCallum discusses the first pastoral episode in the

Metamorphoses, Mercury's account of his invention of the pan pipes after his failed rape of Syrinx. McCallum argues that the Pan and Syrinx episode heralds the revolutionary programmatic importance of the genre of pastoral to the *Metamorphoses* as a whole, which with its wide array of scenes with pastoral significance expands the scope of pastoral far beyond the boundaries set by his poetic predecessors. Ovid's revolutionary poetics in the *Metamorphoses* is also the subject of C.W. Marshall's chapter on narrative transitions in Book 9. His investigation of Ovid's segues in a single book of the *Metamorphoses* illuminates the importance of the technique in a poem that contains more than 250 tales. Comparison with Greek catalogue poetry reveals that segues are a revolutionary component of Ovid's poetic toolkit, for which he is only partially indebted to Hellenistic models.

Cedric Littlewood maintains the focus on the interplay of genres, but moves beyond Ovid to explore Lucan's deployment of elegiac modes, both amatory and funerary, in his epic *Bellum Ciuile*. He finds the familiar opposition of epic and elegy destabilized in Lucan's epic, which mourns what it cannot praise: the death of the Roman Republic and the birth of autocracy. Littlewood's conclusion, that elegiac mourning betokens only political marginalization and enacts republican defeat in Lucan's civil war epic, sheds light on the high political stakes frequently left implicit in Latinists' analyses of genre-blending and intertextuality in literary texts. Elizabeth Kennedy closes this section of the volume, with an exploration of the historical and intertextual dynamics of Aeneas' vengeful murder of Turnus at the conclusion of the *Aeneid* through the prism of Silius' vengeful Hannibal in the *Punica*. She relates the cycles of history and revenge on display in both the *Aeneid* and the *Punica* to the literary practice of typology through the techniques of allusion and intertextuality. Reading the Vergilian Aeneas as the antitype of the Silian Hannibal and the prototype of his Scipio, the conquerer of Carthage at the Battle of Zama in 202 BCE, Kennedy argues that Dido has reason to see Aeneas as a figure pursuing revenge in her dream vision of *Aeneid* 4. While Aeneas himself never seeks revenge on Dido, in Silius' sequel both Hannibal and Scipio bring the cycle of revenge to a conclusion through the destruction of Carthage.

The papers collected in the final section of the volume, Part III, "Civic Spectacle," explore the public ceremonies and political ceremonial that engaged the Roman citizenry en masse both in and through Roman textual culture. Jarrett Welsh discusses a textual problem in a scrap of Roman republican drama by the comic playwright Afranius, whose work survives only in fragments. Welsh examines the language of the fragment for what it can reveal about the performance of the *fabulae togatae* ("comedies in Roman dress"), a kind of comedy distinct from *fabulae palliatae* ("comedies in Greek dress") but, like the latter, produced before enthusiastic crowds on civic holidays at large public festivals in republican Rome. Through careful exegesis, he sets out a nuanced account of how some of Afranius' female characters interacted with the domestic bourgeois society staged in this self-consciously Italo-Roman theatrical form.

In his chapter, Jonathan Tracy examines Lucan's portrayal of the contrasting interactions of Caesar and Cato with their respective armies, which he reads as republics in microcosm. Tracy argues that Lucan represents the traditions of Roman republican government as dependent on the freedom of access to information enjoyed by the full citizen body. Thus, the republican senate-in-exile in Epirus makes decisions publically, after open consultation, rather than (like Caesar) governing tyrannically through acts of censorship and misinformation. He concludes that Lucan understood republicanism to involve not merely civic spectacle but, more importantly, civic participation.

Clifford Ando studies the institutionalization of foreign cult in Roman legal and political documents. He argues that Roman law legislated the continuation of a community's cult practices after their incorporation into the Roman Empire and that this situation had important analogues and precedents in the formal legal acts that comprised surrender and restoration in Roman foreign relations, as attested in the epigraphic record. The continuing participation of the newly Roman community in its pre-Roman ritual practice reflects both the philosophical and practical systems laid out by the Roman jurists and the most characteristic structure of empire as a trans-historical political form, viz., that empires govern through the management and cultivation of difference rather than through the universalization of a supranational culture.

The volume closes with Jonathan Edmondson's study of a specific Roman ritual, the provision of gladiatorial spectacles, in Apuleius' mid-second century CE novel, *Metamorphoses*, otherwise known as *The Golden Ass*. He analyses the rich detail of socio-political dialogue in Apuleius' representation of gladiatorial *munera* as entailing complex rituals of reciprocity between sponsor and local citizenry in the imagined setting of the Roman province of Achaea. More than any other source, Apuleius' novel emphasizes the social motivation that lay behind such acts of euergetism by the local elite and illustrates the important role that ordinary citizens played in the manner in which *munera* were received and remembered in the communities of the Roman Empire.

The contributors to this volume recognize that our collection is by no means exhaustive, and indeed can only sample the multiplicity and complexity of classical Roman literary cultures. Nonetheless, we hope that the rich array of detailed studies offered here, spanning over four hundred years of Latin literature and its contexts, can help to illuminate some of the distinctive sociocultural contexts of Roman literature, exemplify the mutually reinforcing value of combining literary and historical approaches, and will spur further investigation into the fascinating history of Latin letters.

NOTES

1 Fantham 1996, subtitled *from Cicero to Apuleius*. The second edition, Fantham 2013, is subtitled *from Plautus to Macrobius* and significantly expands her discussion to include both republican drama, at the beginning of Roman literary culture, and Christian writings and those of the pagan resistance, in late antiquity.

2 Fantham 2013: xix.

3 Fantham 2013: 1.

4 Even contemporary scholarship on classical aesthetics, an arena that frequently defines itself as transcendental (in opposition to and even beyond socio-historical analysis), however, may be indebted to Fantham's demonstration of the importance of social and political context. Thus Roman 2014, for example, proceeds chronologically through republican and Augustan literature, from Lucilius to Ovid, to offer a historicizing account of the discovery of "aesthetic autonomy" in Roman literary culture.

5 For later periods, see Cavallo and Chartier 1995; Chartier 2005; cf. Howsam 2006.

6 See Bowman 1998; Johnson 2004 and 2010; Milnor 2014. Cf. Beard et al. 1991; Johnson and Parker 2009; more briefly on Egypt, Parsons 2007: 147–58.

7 Both genre criticism and the analysis of allusion and intertextuality (the "arte allusive" of Pasquali's famous phrase) have dominated Latin literary scholarship for at least a century, although both also took on a new momentum as a result of developments in critical theory in the late twentieth century. Landmark studies of genre-blending are those of Kroll 1924 and Harrison 2007; the modern study of allusion and intertextuality begins with Pasquali 1951, and includes Conte 1986; Hinds 1998; and Edmunds 2001.

8 Soon published as Millar 1981.

9 Other exemplary historical studies of classical literature and/or ancient authors are those of Veyne 1961; Cameron 1970, 1993, and 1995; Millar 1993; Bodel 1994; and more recently Citroni 2009.

10 Wiseman 1985.

11 George 2008.

12 [Suet.] *Vita Vergili* 31; cf. ibid. 21: *novissime "Aeneidem" inchoavit, argumentum varium ac multiplex ... in quo, quod maxime studebat, Romanae simul urbis et Augusti origo contineretur* ("Lastly Vergil began the *Aeneid*, a varied and complicated theme ... in which was contained, as he especially desired, the origin

of both the city of Rome and of Augustus"). The late antique commentators Servius and Tiberius Claudius Donatus both assume that Vergil's purpose in the *Aeneid* is to praise Augustus. Servius, for example, attributes the inspiration of the poem to Augustus (Thilo 1881, 2): *postea ab Augusto Aeneidem propositam* [*sc. Vergilius*] *scripsit annis undecim* ("afterwards, Vergil wrote the *Aeneid*, proposed by Augustus, in eleven years"). Cf. Tib. Claud. Don. *incipit* (Georgii 1905–6, 2, lines 20–2): *talem enim monstrare Aenean debuit, ut dignus Caesari, in cuius honorem haec scribebantur, parens et auctor generis praeberetur* ("For he needed to show such an Aeneas that would be worthy of offering to Caesar, in whose honor the poem was written, as ancestor and founder of his lineage").

13 Pöschl 1950.

14 Davis 2004, revised and updated in Davis 2012: 17–39.

15 Hardie 1986; Cairns 1989; Powell 2008.

16 Leigh 2004, 1.

17 Ramsby 2007.

18 See further Fitzgerald 2000; more briefly James 1997. For a historian's analysis of the ancient biographies of Aesop, see Hopkins 1993; cf. Kurke 2012.

19 Landmark studies of Ovidian genre-blending, allusion, and intertextuality include: Conte 1986; Knox 1986 and 2009; Hinds 1987 and 1998; Keith 1992; Newlands 1995; Barchiesi 1994 ; Sharrock 1994; Boyd 1997 and 2002; Hardie 2002; Spentzou 2003; Fulkerson 2005.

WORKS CITED

Barchiesi, A. 1994. *Il poeta e il principe. Ovidio e il discorso augustea*. Rome and Bari. [English translation: *The Poet and the Prince: Ovid and Augustan Discourse*, translated by L.-A. Crowley. Berkeley and Los Angeles, 1997.

Beard, M., et al. 1991. *Literacy in the Roman World*. *JRA* Suppl. 3. Ann Arbor.

Bodel, J. 1994. "Trimalchio's Underworld." In *The Search for the Ancient Novel*, edited by J. Tatum, 237–59. Baltimore.

Bowman, A.K. 1998. *Life and Letters on the Roman Frontier: Vindolanda and Its People*. New York.

Boyd, B.W. 1997. *Ovid's Literary Loves: Influence and Innovation in the* Amores. Ann Arbor.

– ed. 2002. *Brill's Companion to Ovid*. Leiden and Boston.

Cairns, F. 1989. *Virgil's Augustan Epic*. Cambridge.

Cameron, A. 1970. *Claudian: Poetry and Propaganda at the Court of Honorius*. Oxford.

– 1993. *The Greek Anthology: From Meleager to Planudes*. Oxford.

– 1995. *Callimachus and His Critics*. Princeton, NJ.

Cavallo, G., and R. Chartier. 1995. *Storia della lettura nel mondo occidentale*. Rome.

Chartier, R. 2005. *Inscrire et effacer: culture écrite et littérature (XIe – XVIIIe siècles)*. Paris.

Citroni, M. 2009. "*Res publica restituta* et la représentation du pouvoir augustéen dans l'œuvre d'Horace." In *Le principat d'Auguste: Réalités et représentations du pouvoir. Autour de la res publica restituta*, edited by F. Hurlet and B. Mineo, 245–66. Rennes.

Conte, G.B. 1986. *The Rhetoric of Imitation: Genre and Poetic Memory in Virgil and Other Latin Poets*, edited by C. Segal. Ithaca.

Davis, G. 2004. "Consolation in the Bucolic Mode: The Epicurean Cadence of Vergil's First Eclogue." In *Vergil, Philodemus, and the Augustans*, edited by D. Armstrong et al., 63–74. Austin.

– 2012. Parthenope*: The Interplay of Ideas in Vergilian Bucolic*. Leiden.

Edmunds, L. 2001. *Intertextuality and the Reading of Roman Poetry*. Baltimore.

Fantham, E. 1996. *Roman Literary Culture from Cicero to Apuleius*. Baltimore.

– 2013. *Roman Literary Culture from Plautus to Macrobius*. Baltimore.

Fitzgerald, W. 2000. *Slavery and the Roman Literary Imagination*. Cambridge.

Fulkerson, L. 2005. *The Ovidian Heroine as Author: Reading, Writing, and Community in the* Heroides. Cambridge.

George, M. 2008. "The 'Dark Side' of the Toga." In *Roman Dress and the Fabrics of Roman Culture*, edited by J. Edmondson and A. Keith, 94–112. Toronto, Buffalo, and London.

Georgii, H., ed. 1905–6. *Tiberi Claudi Donati Interpretationes Vergilianae*. Leipzig.

Hardie, P.R. 1986. *Virgil's* Aeneid*: Cosmos and Imperium*. Oxford.

– 2002. *Ovid's Poetics of Illusion*. Cambridge.

Harrison, S.J. 2007. *Generic Enrichment in Vergil and Horace*. Oxford.

Hinds, S. 1987. *The Metamorphosis of Persephone: Ovid and the Self-Conscious Muse*. Cambridge.

– 1998. *Allusion and Intertext*. Cambridge.

Hopkins, K. 1993. "Novel Evidence for Roman Slavery." *Past & Present* 138.1: 3–27.

Howsam, L. 2006. *Old Books and New Histories: An Orientation to Studies in Book and Print Culture*. Toronto.

James, S. 1997. "Slave Rape and Female Silence in Ovid's Love Poetry." *Helios* 24: 60–76.

Johnson, W.A. 2004. *Bookrolls and Scribes in Oxyrhynchus*. Toronto.

– 2010. *Readers and Reading Culture in the High Empire: A Study of Elite Reading Communities*. Oxford and New York.

Johnson, W.A., and H.N. Parker, eds. 2009. *Ancient Literacies: The Culture of Reading in Greece and Rome*. Oxford.

Keith, A.M. 1992. *The Play of Fictions: Studies in Ovid's* Metamorphoses *Book 2*. Ann Arbor.

Knox, P.E. 1986. *Ovid's* Metamorphoses *and the Traditions of Augustan Poetry*. Cambridge.
– ed. 2009. *A Companion to Ovid*. Malden, MA.
Kroll, W. 1924. *Studien zum Verständnis der römischen Literatur*. Stuttgart.
Kurke, L. 2012. *Aesopic Conversations: Popular Tradition, Cultural Dialogue, and the Invention of Greek Prose*. Princeton, NJ.
Leigh, M. 2004. *Comedy and the Rise of Rome*. Oxford.
Millar, F.G.B. 1981. "The World of the *Golden Ass*." *JRS* 71: 63–75. [Reprinted in S.J. Harrison, ed., *Oxford Readings in the Roman Novel*, 247–68. Oxford, 1999; and in F. Millar, *Government, Society, and Culture in the Roman Empire*, edited by H.M. Cotton and G.M. Rogers, 313–35. Chapel Hill, 2004.]
– 1993. "Ovid and the *Domus Augusta*: Rome Seen from Tomoi." *JRS* 83: 1–17. [Reprinted in F. Millar, *The Roman Republic and the Augustan Revolution*, edited by H.M. Cotton and G.M. Rogers, 321–49. Chapel Hill, 2002.]
Milnor, K. 2014. *Graffiti and the Literary Landscape in Roman Pompeii*. Oxford.
Newlands, C.E. 1995. *Playing with Time: Ovid and the Fasti*. Ithaca.
Parsons, P. 2007. *City of the Sharp-Nosed Fish. Greek Papyri beneath the Egyptian Sand Reveal a Long-Lost World*. London.
Pasquali, G. 1951. "Arte allusive." In his *Stravaganze quarte e supreme*, 11–20. Venice.
Pöschl, V. 1950. *Die Dichtkunst Virgils, Bild und Symbol in der Äneis*. Wiesbaden. [English translation: *The Art of Vergil: Image and Symbol in the* Aeneid, translated by G. Seligson. Ann Arbor, 1962.]
Powell, A. 2008. *Virgil the Partisan*. Swansea.
Ramsby, T. 2007. *Textual Permanence: Roman Elegists and the Epigraphic Tradition*. London.
Roman, L. 2014. *Poetic Autonomy in Ancient Rome*. Oxford.
Sharrock, A. 1994. *Seduction and Repetition in Ovid's* Ars amatoria 2. Oxford.
Spentzou, E. 2003. *Readers and Writers in Ovid's* Heroides*: Transgressions of Genre and Gender*. Oxford and New York.
Thilo, G., ed. 1881. *Servii Grammatici Qui Feruntur in Vergilii Carmina Commentarii*. 1. *Aeneidos Librorum I – V Commentarii*. Leipzig.
Veyne, P. 1961. "Vie de Trimalchion." *Annales ESC* 16: 213–47. [Reprinted in his *La société romaine*, 13–56. Paris, 1991.]
Wiseman, T.P. 1985. *Catullus and His World: A Reappraisal*. Cambridge.

PART I

Domestic Politics

2

Varro on the Battle against Moisture in the Roman *domus* (A Note on *Men*. Fr. 531–2)*

CHRISTER BRUUN

Introduction

Sometime during the first half of the first century BCE, Marcus Terentius Varro (116–27 BCE) composed his *Saturae Menippeae*, a work containing 150 books according to Jerome. Not much survives of these books, written between ca 80 BCE and (some) as late as close to 50 BCE,[1] for the Teubner edition is a slim volume containing some 590 fragments from about 90 *saturae* for which we have the names.[2] There is thus much that escapes us about the content of the work as a whole, but the general tenor is clear: Varro, to use the succinct expression of Elizabeth Rawson, "contrasted older with modern and corrupt habits."[3]

Two of the preserved fragments, cited below, constitute the subject of this chapter. My discussion will focus on issues that have to do with water and moisture, architecture and banquet spaces in the Roman *domus*, and obviously with that well-known aversion of Varro's to what he deemed "modern luxury."

(531) "in pavimento non audes facere lacunam. at in humu calceos facis elixos"

(532) "sed quae necessitas te iubet aquam effundere domi tuae? si vasa habes pertusa, plumbum non habes? ad quam rem nobis est confluvium? ad quam rem urnarium?"

Not so long ago these lines (translated below) were expertly discussed and placed in context by Jean-Pierre Cèbe in the twelfth instalment of his magisterial multi-volume edition of the *Saturae Menippeae*, which includes a rich commentary. That there may nevertheless be something to add to Cèbe's view obviously follows from the fragmentary nature of the evidence. Simply because there sometimes can be no absolute certainty about how the various fragments belong together and what context they derive from, there have been and will likely continue to be differing interpretations of Varro's text. It is also the case that different readers bring different experiences to bear when studying the meaning of the *saturae*.[4]

In Cèbe's edition, fragments 516–39 are attributed to a Varronian text called Ταφὴ Μενίππου ("The tomb of Menippos"). This work, according to Cèbe's sensible argument, described a banquet celebrating the long-deceased Menippos of Gadara (first half of the third century BCE; the occasion was not his actual funeral, as some have suggested).[5]

It may be helpful to begin by giving a brief synopsis of the content of the various fragments, although only frs. 531–2 can be discussed in any detail here. The order in which Cèbe arranged the fragments is as follows: first the master is honoured by way of funerary games (fr. 516–19), and next a banquet takes place, hosted by a local resident (520–39). This makes the event a "funerary meal," a "περίδειπνον" (for which some literary parallels can be found).[6] There is a reference to moving from the games to the banquet (520), then the group proceeds to table (521–2). Now the participants strike up a dinner conversation. At first there is praise for the frugal ways of the ancients (523); their modesty is recommended, for their abodes were as simple as the tomb of Menippos is unassuming (524–6). They worked hard and idle mockery was absent (527). These characteristics are next compared to present practice. There is luxury at the table (528), and the new ways can clearly be seen in the construction and decoration of houses, specifically in the ways people are attempting to fend off moisture ("techniques pour lutter contre l'humidité des intérieurs," 529–34). There is also cupidity (535) and a problem with dressing too lavishly (536). Things look bad for the future (537), and it is to be hoped that Romans will suffer as punishment for these extravagances (538). The meaning of the last fragment (539) is more difficult to pinpoint.[7]

There are solid foundations for part of the proposed structure. The term *antiqui nostri* appears in fr. 526, and the tense is regularly the imperfect in frs. 523–7, while the present tense is frequently used from fr. 528 onwards.[8] Yet other ways of arranging the fragments could be conceived of and have been adopted in the past.[9] In parentheses Cèbe refers to the order in the old edition by Bücheler (fifth and sixth editions overseen by W. Heräus), which was followed in the recent Teubner edition by Richard Astbury. After agreement on frs. 516–20, the Bücheler-Heräus-Astbury (hereafter B-H-A, with fr. numbers italicized) order has been reworked in the following fashion by Cèbe: B-H-A *522 – 521 – 527 – 525 – 526 – 524 – 528 – 529 – 535 – 536 – 531 – 532 – 533 – 534 – 530 – 538 – 537 – 539 – 523*. Thus, there is almost total agreement on which fragments relate to the first part of the banquet conversation (Cèbe's frs. 521–7), though the order is debated.[10] Next, Cèbe's frs. 527–8 (= B-H-A frs. *528–9*) have an intermediary position. Then we come to what in the current arrangement of the fragments constitutes a central point, "techniques pour lutter contre l'humidité des intérieurs" as it is called,[11] namely, Cèbe's frs. 529–34. These fragments were placed in a somewhat different internal order by previous scholarship. The passages discussed here belong in this section. Before continuing, it is time to look at translation(s) of the relevant fragments (here first given in Cèbe's version), the gist of which is not always easy to comprehend.

(531) "in pavimento non audes facere lacunam" – "at in humu calceos facis elixos"

Here it seems best to begin by quoting Astbury's 1983 explanation (which was basically accepted by Cèbe): "The fragment is part of a discussion of different types of floor; here the contrast is between paving and earth ... a modernist has claimed that the new paving prevents excessive moisture; a *laudator temporis acti* replies that liquid drains away when it is poured on to bare earth, and that the trouble with paving is that any unevenness allows the formation of standing pools when liquid is poured on to it."[12] Based on this understanding Cèbe gave the following translation of what he took to be a dialogue: "tu n'oses pas faire de creux dans le pavé" – "Mais dans la terre tu trempes tes chaussures."

(532) "sed quae necessitas te iubet aquam effundere domi tuae? si vasa habes pertusa, plumbum non habes? ad quam rem nobis est confluvium? ad quam rem urnarium?"

Like his predecessors, Cèbe placed this fragment immediately after the previous one,[13] and gave the following translation: "mais quelle nécessité te force à répandre de l'eau chez toi? Si tu as des vases percés, tu n'as pas de plomb? À quoi nous sert le système d'écoulement, à quoi le meuble à urnes?" To interpret *effundere* as "pour out" and *confluvium* as "drain" are, however, not the only possibilities, and an alternative translation might be:[14] "But out of which necessity do you waste water in your house? If your vessels are broken, do you not have lead with which to mend them? For what purpose do we have a recipient for water?[15] To what use a table on which to stand pitchers of water?" I shall come back to this question below.

Fragment 531

Fr. 531 is particularly vexing and in the past forty years interpretations by at least three scholars have been presented, among whom Astbury and Cèbe are in basic agreement. The fragment is one of several in which we find the verb in the second person singular, which means that the writer/speaker is either addressing an imaginary reader, or is turning to an interlocutor at the banquet. Astbury and Cèbe in fact hold that in fr. 531 we have a dialogue; the case for the "dialogue interpretation" was laid out by Astbury in some detail, as we just saw.[16] The first part is the view of the traditionalist, while the phrase beginning with *at* is the reply of the modernist.

Obviously, we are in the midst of a debate – the particle *at* introducing the second part of the fragment is a clear indication of this – and Astbury's suggestion rightly captures this fact. Yet there are some other problems with this interpretation of fr. 531. For one, there are some doubts as to whether the views of two speakers are presented in the passage. Second, one ought to ascertain how common dirt floors (Ital. "terra battuta" or "battuto di argilla") were in Varro's time. This will, it seems to me, turn out to be a central question.

As for the first issue, to my knowledge no other scholars but Astbury and then Cèbe have held that fr. 531 presents a dialogue. We shall shortly see that the passage functions well enough even if taken as the comment of one individual, as indeed earlier scholars thought. The third/fourth-century CE philologist Nonius Marcellus, whose lexicographical pursuits in his *De compendiosa doctrina* we have to thank for the preservation of this passage, was interested in two words, the form *humu* (instead of *humo*), and the meaning of the word *elixos*.[17] Both appear towards the end of the passage, and one might suggest that if Nonius had been aware that a new speaker began with *at in humu*, he would have copied only the second part.

A weightier argument against splitting up fr. 531 between two speakers derives from a combination of philological and archaeological considerations. It is in fact the case, somewhat paradoxically, that as vexing as some of the fragments of the Ταφὴ Μενίππου are linguistically, scholarly interpretations over the centuries have relied as much on archaeological material, or at least on notions about Roman architecture, to bolster each interpretation.

First it may be noted that Franz Bücheler was dissatisfied with the expression *calceos elixos*, "wet shoes/boots," and suggested the emendation *calces* instead, from *calx* ("lime, limestone"), of which W.M. Lindsay approved.[18] The expression *calces elixos* could then have something to do with the well-known procedure of slaking lime,[19] and there are indeed some passages that could support this view: from *calx viva* (quicklime),[20] after the procedure of *coquere*, the Romans produced *calx exstincta* by adding water. A passage of Nonius Marcellus can also be invoked: *"lixam" namque aquam veteres vocaverunt; unde "elixum" dicimus aqua coctum.*[21]

Bücheler's argument was pondered at length by Werner Krenkel, who ended up refuting it on two grounds. First, he thought, the slaking of lime does not constitute a particularly strong contrast to the first part of the passage (*in pavimento non audes facere lacunam*), and, second, in Latin literature *calx* meaning "lime, limestone" is almost always used in the singular,[22] while Bücheler suggested the plural *calces elixos*.

Krenkel, however, agreed with Bücheler that the explanation involving "wet shoes/boots" was unconvincing, and he instead emendated *calceos* to *alveos*. Setting out from *alveos elixos*, he has over the years presented two interpretations, one in 1971 and one in 2002. The earlier interpretation was discussed, and dismissed, by Astbury and Cèbe, and the latter scholar was not convinced by the more recent contribution either.[23]

Krenkel pointed out that an *alveus* is a vessel for containing liquids (*quidquid aquam recepit, CGL* V, 165.36),[24] and that the word can also be used for bathtubs, and in particular for tubs filled with warm water, which Sergius Orata is said to have introduced to the Romans around 90 BCE (cf. Val. Max. 9.1.1: *C. Sergius Orata pensilia balinea primus facere instituit. quae inpensa a levibus initiis coepta ad suspensa caldae aquae tantum non aequora penetravit*).[25] In Krenkel's view (as argued in 1971), the contrast in Varro then becomes that of the modernist's not allowing some little unevenness in a paved floor, i.e., a *lacuna* (in which water might gather; *id est aquae collectio*, Paul. Fest. p. 104, 14 L.), while at the same time being keen on installing warm water basins (which obviously hold much more water). The background envisaged by Krenkel is the arrival of Hellenistic bathing luxury in Rome. "Traditionalists" looked askance at innovations such as warm water pools in an upper-class *domus*, so the argument goes, and here an innovator is being ridiculed for having all this work done, while he at the same time was very careful *not* to allow any water to gather on his new *pavimentum*. Thus, the argument can be expressed as "it makes no sense to do B (installing warm *alvei*), when you are simultaneously doing A (avoiding *lacunae*)" – the contrast is supposed to denote an absurdity in the innovator's behaviour. The problem here is that a real contrast, and thus the anticipated punch or satirical effect, is absent. Both aspects of human behaviour are precisely in line with each other. Of course an "innovator" wants to avoid small puddles gathering on the *pavimentum*, while part of his love of luxury is to have pools installed.[26] A similar point was already made by Astbury, although briefly ("The contrast between the two parts implied by *at* does not appear to me to be very meaningful if *alveos* is read"), in addition to other objections.[27]

Krenkel's 2002 commentary shares one important feature with his earlier interpretation of the Varronian fragment 531, namely, his attention to the archaeological evidence from Roman Italy. Likewise, in his 2002 presentation of the text of fr. 531, he kept the emendation *alveos*.[28] In one significant regard he had, however, changed his mind, and to my knowledge his work currently represents the last word in the debate.[29] No longer did Krenkel consider *alveos* as referring to bathtubs and fashionable "Badeluxus," but instead to the *impluvium* which collected rainwater in the *atrium* courtyard of a Roman *domus*. On this view, it is an aspect of "Wohnluxus," the modern lavish decoration of Roman houses, which the passage is taken to chastise. Now the contrast is said to be between polishing one's floor so that no water may gather in uneven places and installing a (lavish) *impluvium*.[30]

Here as in his earlier interpretation, Krenkel did not consider *pavimentum* and *humus* as a contrasting pair. This is an unconvincing view.[31] As a consequence, now as before, it is not easy to discern a point of real mockery or satire in the passage. When the "modernist" interlocutor is being criticized for being particular about keeping liquids off his fancy polished floor, while he does not mind filling a large *impluvium* with water, there is really nothing for him to feel upset about. On my understanding, he would be well pleased to counter with a "Just so!" or "That's right!" In addition, the new interpretation does not really include the word *elixos*, which to be sure was accommodated in Krenkel's previous interpretation, involving warm tubs. Finally, there is no way that the presence of *impluvia* in Roman *domus* during the first part of the first century BCE could have been regarded as (offensively) "modernist." The *impluvium* had been a central part of the Roman *atrium* long before that, as the Pompeian and other evidence shows.[32] Krenkel cites a Ciceronian passage about statues decorating an *impluvium* (Cic. *Verr.* 2.1.16), and he refers to some *impluvia* in Pompeii for which marble was used, but at least some of them are later and do not belong in the republican period.[33] In any case, this kind of possibly lavish decoration of the *impluvium* (which in general fulfilled a very useful purpose, because, as Krenkel indeed mentions, the water it collected normally fed into an underground cistern, from which it served the needs of the house)[34] would hardly have been lambasted in the way Varro phrased his fr. 531.

The interpretation of Astbury and Cèbe remains to be discussed. In their scenario, the first part is spoken by the "traditionalist," to which the modernist gives a reply that could be paraphrased thus: "But on bare earth, your shoes will get wet from the mud once liquid is poured onto the ground." It is not clear how one is supposed to understand what the alleged traditionalist has said prior to this. As we saw, Astbury writes that "the trouble with paving is that any unevenness allows the formation of standing pools when liquid is poured onto it." While this is true, it is not evident why this should lead the traditionalist to conclude his retort with the statement (or accusation) "you are not willing to allow an unevenness in the pavement." As we shall see below, this awkwardness disappears if all of fr. 531 is taken as spoken by one person, the traditionalist.

Second, it seems to make sense to take *pavimentum* and *humus* as standing for different features, as the two scholars do. But less compelling is the situation envisaged by them, in Astbury's words: "though liquid drains away into the bare earth, it produces mud which wets the shoes of those who walk upon it (*at in humu calceos facis elixos*)."[35] To be sure, it is true that at Roman banquets guests used to pour wine and perhaps other liquids on the floor. The description of Trimalchio's banquet – *plus vini sub mensa effundebatur, quam aliquis in cella habet* ("more wine was spilled underneath the table than anyone had in his wine-cellar," Petron. 38.15) – is obviously a wild exaggeration, but there are other written sources which confirm that something of the sort was to be expected.[36]

The crucial question for the interpretation of Astbury and Cèbe is the makeup of Roman floors in Varro's time. Did Roman residences in the early first century BCE really have earthen floors? There is literary evidence in Vitruvius (admittedly several decades later than Varro) and above all archaeological evidence to show that one cannot possibly entertain such an idea. Vitruvius dedicates several passages to detailed descriptions of how to construct various types of floors, and it stands to reason that what he wrote was based on experience and would have been common practice somewhat earlier during the first century BCE. The section on the floor of the *triclinium* (in a Greek winter apartment, *hibernacula Graeca*) is worth quoting (Vitr. 7.4.5):

> foditur enim intra libramentum triclinii altitudo circiter pedum binum, et solo festucato inducitur aut rudus aut testaceum pavimentum ita fastigatum, ut in canali habeat nares. deinde congestis et spisse calcatis carbonibus inducitur e sabulone et calce et favilla mixta materies crassitudine semipedali ad regulam et libellam summo libramento cote despumato redditur species nigri pavimenti. ita conviciis eorum, et quod poculis et pytismatis effundetur, simul cadit siccescitque, quique versantur ibi ministrantes, etsi nudis pedibus fuerint, non recipiunt frigus ab eius modi genere pavimenti.

Underneath the level of the dining room one should excavate to a depth of about two feet, and when the soil has been packed down, either lay in a rubble underpavement or a terracotta pavement, sloped so that it has openings [lit. nostrils] onto a channel. Then, onto coals that have been trampled to compactness, a mortar mixed of gravel and lime and ash should be laid to a thickness of half a foot. The topmost layer, planed to the rule and the level by polishing with a whetstone, presents the appearance of black pavement. Thus, during banquets, any wine that is spilled from their cups or spat onto the ground will dry as quickly as possible, and those who do the pouring, even if they serve with bare feet, will not catch cold from this type of pavement.[37]

Astbury rightly pointed out that the Varronian fr. 531 is not explicitly restricted to a *triclinium*.[38] Yet, recommendations for other types of floors in Vitruvius give no more reason to believe in the existence of dirt floors.[39] There is even a hint in Astbury that one might need to consider outdoor spaces here.[40] But the fact that in fr. 536 B (= fr. 530 C) there is a mention of "great peristyles," sand, and promenades[41] does not make it plausible that in fr. 531 the alternatives are between paving and not paving an outdoor walkway. The Romans used outdoor summer *triclinia*, to be sure, which were a sign of great affluence, but I am not aware of any evidence that the permanent setup of couches would have been placed on the bare soil or on a dirt floor. The question is also whether the earliest evidence for this feature of dining luxury can be dated to Varronian times.[42]

There is, finally, also the archaeological evidence for Roman flooring to consider. During the late Republic, the Romans were able to choose between several different kinds of surfaces for their floors.[43] Mosaic floors are found already around 100 BCE in Rome and even earlier at Pompeii,[44] and there were also floors of either cement or mosaic in which pieces of marble or coloured stone of varying size and shape had been inserted, apparently called *pavimenta scutulata* by Pliny (*HN* 36.185) and found in Rome in many houses already during the period 150/100 BCE.[45] Floors of fired brick in various shapes can be found from the early second century BCE onwards.[46]

Above all there were floors of *opus signinum*, sometimes called "cement floors" in English and known as "cocciopesto" in Italian (or "signino"), which were simpler in their decoration. They are common above all in the period ca. 200–80 BCE and consist of mortar or "cement" in which small mosaic cubes (or similar objects) have occasionally been placed to form simple patterns and decorations.[47] There were local variations of this "cocciopesto" technique, depending on what materials were available (like lava in Pompeii).[48] Recent excavations of several *domus* in Rome (on the northern slopes of the Palatine) have shown the technique in use already in the late third century,[49] while work at Fregellae led Filippo Coarelli to argue for a considerably earlier date for the introduction of the *opus signinum* pavement into the Roman cultural sphere (even as early as the late fourth century BCE).[50] Among the advantages of the "cocciopesto" floor, its "impermeabilità" is mentioned,[51] and from what one reads in Vitruvius, it seems clear that there is the intention that there be a very slight slope, in the *triclinium* anyway, so that liquids do not stagnate but run off.[52]

Thus, in Varro's day not even sworn "traditionalists" will have lived in abodes with earthen floors ("la terre nue" in the words of Cèbe), where spilled wine or other liquids made the floor muddy. At a first, and superficial, glance, though, there might seem to be a certain connection between the expression *calceos facis elixos* and the end of Vitruvius' description of the *triclinium* floor cited above (pp. 23–4),[53] for a concern about the feet of the *ministrantes* is voiced there. A closer look reveals the wide difference. The slaves in Vitruvius' *triclinium* are barefoot, and they keep their feet warm (and dry) – just the opposite of how Astbury and Cèbe read Varro, *Men.* fr. 531 – precisely because no liquids gather on the floor: *quod effundetur ... siccescit,* which must mean that anything which is poured out quickly runs off. The floor covering is, after all, made of mortar or "cement": *e sabulone et calce et favilla mixta materies* (Vitr. 7.4.5).

Thus, none of the three recent ways of interpreting *Men.* 531 are particularly satisfying. Bücheler's interpretation runs into problems for linguistic reasons. The merit of Krenkel is to have drawn attention to the archaeological material, but neither of his interpretations hold up to scrutiny because his reading of the text (with the emendation to *alveos*) fails to make proper sense. The hypothesis of Astbury and Cèbe suffers from the fact that the scenario it envisages is in no way supported by archaeological evidence and in fact is strongly contradicted by it. Also, the two scholars set out from the assumption that the fragment contains a dialogue, which makes the line lose much of its sense. It is rather lame for the "traditionalist" to finish off with "you are not willing to suffer a cavity in your paved floor" (the idea being: in your modernist zeal and pursuit of fancy pavements you are forced to avoid any unevenness because puddles of water will form in such cavities), to which the "modernist" is seen as calmly retorting: "well, if you choose earthen floors you will have muddy shoes." If this is the scenario, one must conclude that the logic is on the side of the modernist.

It makes better sense, to assume that the whole line is spoken by the same speaker, as used to be the scholarly consensus. This speaker is a *laudator temporis antiqui,* and he is indeed criticizing the punctiliousness and the softness of the modernist. The speaker is not against the paving of indoor spaces as such (and how could he be?), but he seems to be taking issue with an exaggerated perfectionism and fear of the slightest collection of water on the paved floor, as if it could really harm an active man.[54] What is your worry, he asks, since your shoes get muddy anyway[55] when you walk outside on wet ground? This, then, prompts a somewhat different translation of fr. 531: "you are unwilling to allow any unevenness in your pavement, but walking on the ground do your shoes get wet?!"

Fragment 532

The presence of moisture or water, which we encountered in fr. 531, is certainly the dominating concern in fr. 532. Here there are no textual problems, and, as was already hinted at above, the only difference in recent scholarly interpretations concerns the meaning of the words *effundere* and *confluvium*. Yet the translation of the verb as "répandre" or "pour out" and of *confluvium* as "système d'écolement" or "drain" stems from a particular view of the situation referred to by Varro. This view goes back well over a century to opinions presented by Vahlen and Havet (although the latter candidly admitted that he was not sure exactly what context the fragment belonged to!).[56] In Havet's view, "Une série entière de fragments roule sur la grande question: sable ou dallage?,"[57] that is, "sand or paving" (the first option obviously preferred by the traditionalist). This view was accepted by Cèbe, who, having changed the order of frs. 535–6 B (making them 529–30), begins his commentary on frs. 529–32 by writing: "ces quatre fragments proviennent donc d'un débat relatif à l'architecture et précisément aux mérits respectifs du pavage et du sablage."[58] This, then, in Cèbe's view is a second dominant theme here besides the topic of how to deal with moisture; obviously a connection can be said to exist between these issues.

However, as we have already seen, the case for mud or earthen floors being used by Varro's contemporaries in indoor spaces is extremely dubious. Yet Cèbe may be right that the question of what a suitable pavement is could play a role in fr. 529 C (= 535 B), while in fr. 530 C (= 536 B) the word *sabulum* actually appears, and in fr. 533 C (= 533 B) we find λιθόστρωτα *pavimenta* (this is not the place for a discussion of these passages),[59] but there is nothing explicit in this regard in our fr. 532. As mentioned above, the fragment is part of a series considered to be concerned with humidity, but Cèbe begins his commentary: "après J. Vahlen, nous donnons cette tirade au partisan du sablage";[60] that is, the traditionalist is responsible for the utterance. According to Cèbe, the speaker is on purpose being mildly naive in his "good advice" to the modernist,[61] who finds puddles on his floor because he has had it paved: "But really, why on earth is there water in your house? Don't you have ...?"

Is there any point to this mild irony? What is the context? We are, after all, being treated to a discussion carried on at a banquet. The situation as depicted by Cèbe would seem to work much better in an actual realistic narrative, in which a traditionalist had entered a house with the floors deep in water or at least slippery from moisture. How, in a more or less heated dinner conversation, can the traditionalist "demande plaisamment" of his interlocutor anything that refers to a purely speculative situation? It seems to me that Cèbe's interpretation assumes that the speaker reacts to something that he is observing in the *domus* of the banquet, and must therefore be offered by a modernist. Havet, who wrote after Vahlen, interpreted the tone of the passage very differently, and he assigned it to a modernist: "La discussion était agrémentée par la vivacité de la dispute, car l'avocat du sable trouvait un adversaire ardent qui s'ecriait: Hé! quand votre réservoir fuit, qui vous oblige à laisser couler l'eau?"[62] Surely Havet caught the tone correctly here, and the three rhetorical questions that follow underline a certain vehemence in this interchange. But what was the debate about?

Krenkel chose to translate *effundere* as "to waste,"[63] and he did not translate *confluvium* as "drain," but as something in which to collect water. The latter question is of less importance here, since in my view talking about "wasting water" provides the key to a different understanding of the whole passage. Krenkel's view that the speaker turns against the useless and playful display of water and waterworks has much to recommend itself.[64] He supported his argument with references to mostly literary and some archaeological evidence for lavish Roman water use.[65] Crucial here, however, is the chronological aspect, for Roman water supply underwent a steady development during the later republican period, a development which continued during the first centuries of the Empire. Thus, one cannot automatically assume that something which, say, Frontinus wrote around 100 CE would have applied to the situation almost two centuries earlier, nor that discoveries in Pompeian houses dated to shortly before the eruption necessarily tell us much about the situation when Varro wrote. To put it briefly: while it is true that many elegant Roman *domus* can be seen sporting all kinds of constructions using (and wasting) considerable amounts of water in *nymphaea*, fountains, cascades, pools, and canals (*euripi*),[66] the question is whether this was a feature that could be observed already when Varro wrote.

A private water concession that allowed the owner of a *domus* to install a private conduit that drew water from the public distribution network is important in this regard. We have Frontinus' word that although this was very rare during the Republic, it was something that distinguished members of the elite could hope for in the city of Rome (which by the early first century BCE was supplied by four aqueducts): *aliquid et in domos principum civitatis dabatur concedentibus reliquis* ("Something also was granted to the houses of the leaders of the state with the consent of the rest," Frontin. *Aq.* 94.5). The Roman *domus* and its decorations are of course best studied at Pompeii, where however the water supply was not structured in the same way as in the capital. It is not likely that the situation there will have inspired Varro, but the town is important in so far as that if one can observe water luxury that dates to the first part of the last century BCE in Pompeii, then it seems likely that such features will have been present in Rome too.

It used to be thought that a number of more or less luxurious water features could be observed in Pompeian *domus* as early as in the beginning of the first century BCE, i.e., before Varro. However, since it was then believed that the first aqueduct supplying Pompeii was built only in the Augustan period, the dates for these structures have often been lowered accordingly.[67] However, serving as an argument against such across-the-board revisionism is the *domus* under the Stabian Baths sporting a fountain, which is dated to no later than the middle of the first century BCE.[68] Above all, recent research by Christoph Ohlig has shown that a first aqueduct supplying Pompeii was built long before the Augustan period, probably when the Sullan colonists settled in Pompeii after 80 BCE.[69] Thus, there are no grounds for doubting that a certain "water luxury" was known to the residents of Pompeii by the middle of the first century BCE, and we can infer that the situation in Rome, well known to Varro, must have been similar, if not more lavish. Indeed, the archaeological excavations of a series of *domus* on the slope of the Palatine facing the Via Sacra have shown or made plausible the existence of lavish *nymphaea* and similar structures before the mid-first century BCE.[70]

All of this makes it plausible that someone in Varro's days might have reacted against fashionable new "aquatic luxury." The Menippean fr. 532 then makes perfect sense: "But out of which necessity do you waste water in your house? If your vessels are broken, do you not have lead with which to mend them? For what purpose do we have a receptacle for water? To what use a table on which to stand pitchers of water?" Here, the "traditionalist" is inveighing against wasting a valuable resource such as water on useless display (the water from fountains or *nymphaea* may simply have been allowed to run off into the gutter). Using irony, he professes not to understand the purpose of fountains and cascades: "Surely, there must be a misunderstanding here: when we see water leaking or running off (which is what seems to be happening in your fancy modern *domus*), we mend our vessels and collect the water in appropriate containers!"

As mentioned repeatedly, such has not been the view of most previous scholarship, and one aspect of the view of Cèbe and others was already discussed above (the tone of the comment). More important in regard to their interpretation is the question of why there would be water in the *domus* in the first place. Havet long ago viewed this scenario clearly, as we saw above: "Hé! quand votre réservoir fuit ..." Cèbe did not address the question, so it is not clear if he too thought that a burst (or perhaps merely leaking) cistern was to blame.

But for this explanation to work, one also needs to say something about the location of cisterns in Roman houses in Varronian times. Traditionally, rainwater ended up in the *impluvium* and was then often fed into an underground cistern.[71] This water will not have caused the problems Varro's fr. 532 hints at. The question is whether Roman houses also had cisterns above ground. Some raised domestic cisterns have been identified in the archaeological material in Pompeii and Herculaneum. This reveals relatively small containers, often filled with rainwater, which normally seem to have been used for decorative purposes, such as feeding fountains or streams of water in outdoor *triclinia*.[72] Whether leaks would have been a prominent feature remains uncertain.

Conclusion

The discussion above has argued for a somewhat different understanding, and therefore also for a different translation, of the two fragments *Men.* 531–2. This also has some consequences for the context to which they belong. Jean-Pierre Cèbe placed them both under the heading of "la bataille contre l'humidité," that is, repelling moisture from the Roman *domus*, and moreover he linked them to what he (like other scholars, since at least the mid-nineteenth century) took to be a debate between a modernist and a traditionalist regarding suitable material for indoor pavements. He also thought that he could detect a particular slant in this: "la bataille contre l'humidité des intérieurs est beaucoup plus l'affaire du moderniste."[73]

This approach to the issue of humidity is not wholly convincing. While it is true that the very term *umor*, "humidity," occurs in one fragment of the Ταφὴ Μενίππου (*antiqui nostri in domibus latericiis paululum modo lapidibus suffundatis, ut umorem effugerent, habitabant*,[74] Men. fr. 526 C = 524 B), there is nothing in this passage that necessitates the view that the *antiqui* endured dampness with equanimity (on the contrary, they avoided it when they could, as the passage says!), while only decadent "modernists" aimed to build their houses in ways that minimized the presence of moisture. Yet, every owner of a house, and everyone familiar with the climate of Rome, is aware of the negative consequence of dampness and moisture, which in places can survive even hot summers. Who would not want to reduce *umor* where possible? Barring certain modern Italian experiences, reading Vitruvius will reveal how concerned the Romans were to avoid dampness in buildings.[75] This issue can never have constituted the divide at the banquet in honour of Menippos. There is, however, no doubt that "Wohnluxus" was an issue that divided the company gathered to remember Menippos, and, as we have attempted to show here, in fr. 532 the question of "aquatic luxury" may also have played a role during the discussion at the banquet.

NOTES

* It is with great appreciation that I offer this *opusculum* to Elaine, daring to hope that the topic may be a suitable one. I am not aware of any treatment by our honorand of this particular text, but Fantham 2003: 109–17 provides a discussion of Varro's last decades. I will always remember her hospitality in her Princeton *domus* in October 1996 towards a belated Torontonian colleague, not least the excellent dinner she cooked, while I had the honour of having her as a lunch guest at the Finnish Institute in Rome in 1999 (though in a villa, not a *domus*).

1 Alfonsi 1973: 33.

2 Astbury 2002: xxi for the composition. His Teubner edition contains 591 fragments, among them a few spurious ones. The new edition by Jean-Pierre Cèbe contains the same number of fragments; see Cèbe 1999.

3 Rawson 1975: 235; cf. Alfonsi 1973: 31–5, esp. 35 "Si potrebbe dire di lui che non tanto *castigat ridendo mores,* quanto piuttosto che *castigando deridet mores.*"

4 My own reason for thinking about the passages, which caught my attention long ago, is a paper on Roman luxury and water use, which was delivered at a conference at the École française de Rome in December 2010. I was unable to discuss the Varronian evidence in any detail at the conference.

5 Cèbe 1998: 1980.

6 Cèbe 1998: 1980; *Der Neue Pauly* 9 (2000) 566 s.v. "Perideipnon."

7 Cèbe 1998: 1981–2.

8 No *nunc* ("maintenant") occurs at the beginning of the criticism, although one is led to believe this in Cèbe 1998: 1980.

9 In working on this article I have not consulted every previous edition and commentary on the *Saturae Menippeae*. I was not able to find the work by F. Brunetti and P. Canal (1874), deemed "nullius momenti" by Astbury 2002: xvii, nor the edition and commentary by E. Bolisani (1936), according to Astbury 2002: xvii, "non omnino inutilis."

10 It may be noted that the order is fairly different in some other editions from the twentieth century; see Cèbe 1999: 2146 for a survey of the order of the above fragments in the editions by Bolisani (1936) and Della Corte (1953).

11 Thus Cèbe 1998: 1982, cf. Cèbe 1998: 2006n188: "la bataille contre l'humidité des intérieurs"; and Cèbe 1998: 1996: "les moyens de chasser l'humidité des intérieurs" on frs. 530–2.

12 Astbury 1983: 154; cf. Cèbe 1998: 2003–5.

13 The order was the opposite in Vahlen 1858: 160–1, but the now current one can be found already in Riese 1865 (the previous Teubner edition) and in Bücheler 1871.

14 The translation given here is basically identical to the one in Krenkel 2002: 1037: "aber welche Notwendigkeit heißt dich, das Wasser deines Hauses

verströmen zu lassen? Wenn du undichte Gefäße hast – hast du kein Blei? Wozu haben wir einen Wasserbehälter? Wozu eine Rampe mit Wasserkrugen?"

15 For *confluvium* one finds, in LS, s.v.: "a conflux, confluence (very rare)"; in the *OLD*: "A place where streams (of water or air) meet; (also, app.) a sink or drain"; in the *TLL*: "locus in quem aliquid confluit." Only three instances are cited, the present one and two in the *Aetna*. Cèbe 1998: 2007 adds Palladius, *De re rust.* 1.37.4: *confluvium coquinae fusorium.*

16 Astbury 1983: 154.

17 The text of Nonius is regularly cited by Cèbe in his edition; here see Cèbe 1998: 1976. The passage is quoted at Non. Marc. p. 48 and p. 488 (the traditional numbering of the pages): see Lindsay 1903: 1.69 and 3.783.

18 Bücheler 1871: 209, without apparatus or comment; Bücheler 1882: 218 with the comment "*calceos* paene omnes." *Calces* is printed also in the edition of Nonius Marcellus by Lindsay 1903: 1.69.

19 For this and the rest of the paragraph I am indebted to the argument of Krenkel 1971: 437. Cf. also note 23 below.

20 *Calx* is masculine in Varro, *Men.* 288, but normally feminine.

21 This passage is found in Lindsay 1903: 1.86 (= p. 62 according to the traditional numbering).

22 The exception *calces* is very late, in Gregory of Tours, *Vit. Patr.* 12.3, as pointed out by Krenkel 1971: 437. The issue of *calces* or *calceos* is not discussed in Woytek 1970; for *calx*, cf. Woytek 1970: 34.

23 Astbury 1983: 153–5; Cèbe 1998: 2004–5; Cèbe 2005: 720.

24 As pointed out by Krenkel 1971: 438; Krenkel 2002: 1037. For the passage, see Goetz 1894: 165 l. 36: *alveus quidquid aquam recepit canales fluvii.*

25 Krenkel 1971: 438.

26 Similarly Cèbe 1998: 2005.

27 Astbury 1983: 154–5. His other points of criticism were that Krenkel regarded *in pavimento* and *in humu* as nearly synonymous expressions, that he considered the passage as describing the situation in the *triclinium* only (instead of in the whole *domus*), and that he took his emendation *alveos facere elixos* to mean "lassen Becken mit warmem Wasser vollaufen," which Astbury found unlikely, as did Cèbe 1998: 2005.

28 Krenkel 2002: 1034, with the translation: "im Fußboden wagst du's nicht, die geringste Unebenheit zuzulassen; aber in demselben Boden läßt du dir ganze Becken mit Wasser vollaufen."

29 It has to be said that in his commentary he nowhere addresses the criticism voiced against emending to *alveos*; see Krenkel 2002: 1034–7. Cèbe 2005: 720, in his generally positive review makes a point of remarking of fr. 531 "un sens qui ne convient pas."

30 Krenkel 2002: 1036–7, with a summary at 1036: "Einerseits vermeidet er [*scil.* the modernist who is addressed in fr. 531] ängstlich jede kleine Vertiefung

wegen der Pfützenbildung, läßt alles ganz glatt schleifen – andererseits aber hat er in demselben Fußboden ein ganzes Becken mit Wasser, das *compluvium*."

31 Krenkel 1971: 435 (similarly Krenkel 2002: 1035) cites only one literary example, Quint. *Inst.* 8.3.66, that *humus* also can mean "Fußboden," "indoor floor." Quintilian is quoting a phrase from Cicero's lost *Pro Q. Gallio* which describes a rowdy indoor banquet (a *convivium luxuriosum*, at which one could observe *alios intrantes, alios autem exeuntes*). There is no comment on this matter in Crawford 1994: 152–4, and the *TLL* does not register this meaning.

32 Such structures are ubiquitous in Pompeii, but it is not easy to establish which structures can in fact be securely dated to the pre-Sullan period. For a number of such cases see Pesando 1997: 27–8 and fig. 2 (I.4.5–25, Casa del Citarista), 35 and fig. 3 (I.6.2, Casa del Criptoportico), 47 and fig. 6 (I.7.1, Casa di Cuspius Pansa or Paquius Proculus), 56–7 and fig. 10 (I.15.1), 60 and fig. 11 (V.1.7, Casa del Toro), et passim. See further Coarelli and Pesando 2006, in particular the convenient English summary on pp. 23–5 with evidence for houses with *atrium* and *impluvium* in the *insula* VI.10 down to the end of the second century BCE. For a very early *atrium* house with an *impluvium*, see Coarelli 2000: 93, who mentions an example from the town of Fregellae, dated to the late fourth century BCE. Fregellae was founded by Rome as a Latin *colonia* in 328 (and rebuilt after an initial destruction in 313) and its architecture reflected Roman practices; see Coarelli 2000: 94.

33 Krenkel 2002: 1036.

34 Examples from Pompeii of underground cisterns being fed from the *impluvium* abound in Baldassarre 1990–2003; see, e.g., 2.42 fig. 60; 2.184 fig. 18; 2.423 fig. 2; 2.438 fig. 7; 2.532 fig. 7.

35 Astbury 1983: 154.

36 Krenkel 1971: 435, also cites Juv. 6.425; see also Vitr. 7.4.5 (cited pp. 23–4). Also water could be poured, see Plin. *HN* 28.26: *incendia inter epulas nominata aquis sub mensam profusis abominamur*. Dunbabin 2003 does not discuss this matter, except for the briefest of mentions on p. 64. Water was obviously poured out in the *triclinia* in order to clean the floor, see *Dig.* 8.2.19, 8.2.28.

37 Translation by I. Rowland in Rowland and Howe 1999: 91; cf. p. 269 for a useful illustration (Howe).

38 Astbury 1983: 154–5, echoed by Cèbe 1998: 2005.

39 Vitr. 7.1.4 ends in the recommendation: *item testacea spicata tiburtina sunt diligenter exigenda, ut ne habeant lacunas nec extantes tumulos, sed extenta et ad regulam perfricata. super fricaturam, levigationibus et polituris cum fuerint perfecta, incernatur marmor, et supra loricae ex calce et harena inducantur* ("Pavements in Tiburtine herringbone tile work should be carefully executed so that they have neither protuberances nor ridges, but are uniform and polished on the level. Above this, once the floor has been ground with rough and fine

polish, powdered marble is to be sprinkled over it, and coats of lime and sand laid down over this"; trans. Rowland and Howe 1999: 88). This is type IVc in Morricone 1973b: 604, who gave a Caesarian date for the earliest known instance of this, the most common type of tile floor.

40 Astbury 1983: 155.

41 Varro, *Sat. Men.* 536 B = 530 C: *non vides in magnis peristyliis, qui cryptas domi non habent, sabulum iacere a pariete, aut in xystis, ubi ambulare possint?*

42 For a classic study, see Rakob 1964 on the "Grottentriklinum" in the *praedium* of Julia Felix from Pompeii. This case, like other similar examples and some "Pergolatriklinien" adduced by Rakob all date to the imperial period. See Vitr. 7.1.5 for instructions on how to build outdoor floors (*subdiu*).

43 See in general Morricone 1973b.

44 Morricone 1973a: 504. For a third-century mosaic floor from Pompeii, see Coarelli and Pesando 2011: 53.

45 Morricone 1980, with pp. 9–14 for the term *scutulatum*.

46 Morricone 1973b: 604; cf. note 38 above.

47 Morricone 1970; Morricone 1973b: 603; Adam 1984: 253; cf. Vassal 2006. On the terminology, see Dunbabin 1994: 30–1, who mentions several terms employed for this technique: *(opus) signinum*, "cocciopesto," cement pavement, pavement of aggregate.

48 Morricone 1973b: 603.

49 Papi 1995: 339–42; the author points out that what used to be considered the oldest examples of "cocciopesto" in Italy are found in Lucania and Campania and date to the period 300/250 BCE.

50 Coarelli 1995: 19–20.

51 Morricone 1973b: 603.

52 Vitr. 7.4.5 (above), and cf. Krenkel 2002: 1036: "eine perfekte, von allen Erhebungen und Vertiefungen freie, absolut glatte Fläche, von der jeder Tropfen abrollte."

53 In fact Salza Prina Ricotti (1979: 129n20) seems to entertain such an interpretation of Vitruvius (although she gives the wrong reference, to 7.4.21, while there are only five sections in subchapter 4): "si ricorreva a pavimenti neri e porosi che assorbissero il grasso."

54 *Lacuna* denotes an unevenness in a paved floor in Vitr. 7.1.4.

55 As has been noted before, the use of the verb *facere* in the expression *calceos facis elixos* is not very elegant, but it can be used as a "verbe à tout faire," see Cèbe 1998: 2005.

56 Havet 1882: 67, on fr. 531, which he sees as immediately preceding fr. 532: "J'ai peine à distinguer dans ce dernier passage [*sc.* fr. 531] l'*urbana ironia* que veut y découvrir M. Vahlen et j'ignore si celui qui parle est un *antiqui moris vindex*, comme il le croit, ou un partisan du luxe."

57 Havet 1882: 67.

58 Cèbe 1998: 2000.

59 Cèbe 1998: 2001–3 discusses fr. 530, "ce fragment difficile"; cf. Cèbe 1998: 2007, where the "λιθόστρωτα *pavimenta*" are equated with *opus sectile* pavements.

60 Cèbe 1998: 2006.

61 Cèbe 1998: 2006: "Jouant en quelque sorte les naifs, celui-ci demande plaisamment à son interlocuteur ..."

62 Havet 1882: 67.

63 Cf. *OLD* s.v. *effundo* 11: "To expend, use up: a) money or resources." Cf. *TLL* s.v. *effundo*, B.1.b., which translates "opes, patrimonium, pecuniam publicam, sim; α) i.q. consumere, dissipare, prodigere." *Effundere* appears very commonly with liquids in the meaning of "pour out," but it seems obvious to me that it is possible to construe it as "to waste" in certain circumstances, as Krenkel argues.

64 Krenkel 2002: 1038: "Der Sprecher wendet sich gegen die spielerisch-nutzlose Verschwendung von Wasser."

65 Krenkel 2002: 1038–9.

66 Sundry evidence from various places is cited by, for instance, Salza Prina Ricotti 1979: 102–30; Salza Prina Ricotti 1987; Andersson 1990; George 1997: 8–10; George 1998: 88–93; Broise and Jolivet 1998; Dubois-Pelerin 2008: 81.

67 Summarized in George 1998: 88. Fantham 2009: 160 emphasizes the importance of "both private estates and public parks that provided shady, well-watered spaces for walking and resting."

68 Eschebach 1996: 2.

69 Ohlig 2001: 270–1, in agreement Wilson 2006, esp. 503. Schmölder-Veit 2009: 120–1, 125–7 continues to argue for an Augustan date for the earliest aqueduct.

70 Thus Gualandi and Papi 2004: 112–14, 116. These structures were using piped water.

71 This conclusion is based on the Pompeian evidence; see a brief summary in Jansen 2005: 278, 288–9; cf. Fraioli 2009: 130–2.

72 See above all Dessales 2006: 365–8 (including many late cases and some from outside Italy); also Dessales 2007: 137 on Pompeii; Camardo 2007: 175 on Herculaneum (where the aqueduct seems to have supplied at least one such cistern).

73 Cèbe 1998: 2006n188.

74 "Our ancestors lived in houses of brick, which were supported to a small extent only by stones, so that they might escape dampness." Varro must here refer to mud or sun-dried brick, not to fired brick; for the chronology of Roman brick use, see Rowland and Howe 1999: 12, with earlier literature. Coarelli 2000: 94, who provides good arguments for generally dating the use of fired brick much earlier than previous scholarship, also agrees that Varro refers to sun-dried brick.

75 Vitr. 7.1.5: *contignationes umore crescentes*; 7.3.1: *nec umor possit nocere*; 7.4.1: *quemadmodum umidis locis politiones expediantur* and *Sin autem aliqui paries perpetuos habuerit umores*. In 7.4.2–4 Vitruvius goes on to explain how moisture can be avoided when building in damp places. Not everyone agrees, though, and Salza Prina Ricotti 1979: 130n22 argues strongly that the Romans in fact loved humid and damp spaces: "l'amore che i romani dell'epoca portavano per i luoghi umidi non è una novità per chi si occupa di archeologia"; there is no limit to the number of "Grotte stillanti acqua, ninfei trasudanti umidità, criptoportici sotterranei incrostati di muffa" which the archaeologist encounters. She explains this (alleged) predilection for spaces that today would be condemned as health hazards by the low average lifespan in the Roman world: few Romans ever reached an age at which they would have suffered from rheumatism or arthritis. This demographic claim is not quite correct, and while the frustration of a modern archaeologist undoubtedly is real, one may still doubt that the Romans experienced dampness differently from us.

WORKS CITED

Adam, J.-P. 1984. *La construction romaine: matériaux et techniques*. Paris.

Alfonsi, L. 1973. "Le 'Menippee' di Varrone." *ANRW* I.3: 26–59.

Andersson, E.B. 1990. "Fountains and the Roman Dwelling. Casa del Torello in Pompeii." *JdI* 105: 207–36.

Astbury, R. 1983. "Notes on Varro's Menippeans." *Classica & Medievalia* 34: 141–60.

– 2002. *M. Terentius Varro, Saturarum Menippearum fragmenta.*Munich and Leipzig [1st ed., 1985].

Baldassarre, I., ed. 1990–2003. *Pompei pitture e mosaici*. 9 vols. Rome.

Bolisani, E. ed. 1936. *Varrone menippeo*. Padua.

Broise, H., and V. Jolivet. 1998. "Il giardino e l'acqua: l'esempio degli *horti* Luculliani." In *Horti Romani: Atti del convegno internazionale, Roma, 4–6 maggio 1995*, edited by M. Cima and E. La Rocca, 189–202. Rome.

Brunetti, F.A., and P. Canal, eds. 1874. *M. Terenzio Varrone. Libri intorno alla lingua Latina*. Venice.

Bücheler, F. 1871. *Petronii satirae et liber Priapeorum: adiectae sunt Varronis et Senecae satirae similesque reliquiae*. 2nd ed., Berlin.

– 1882. *Petronii satirae et liber Priapeorum: adiectae sunt Varronis et Senecae satirae similesque reliquiae*. 3rd ed., Berlin.

Camardo, D. 2007. "Ercolano: la gestione delle acque in una città romana." *Oebalus* 2: 167–85.

Cèbe, J.-P., ed. 1998. *Varron, Satires ménippées* 12. Coll. ÉFR 9,12. Rome.
– ed. 1999. *Varron, Satires ménippées* 13. Coll. ÉFR 9,13. Rome.
– 2005. "Review of Krenkel 2002." *Gnomon* 77: 719–21.
Coarelli, F. 1995. "Gli scavi di *Fregellae* e la cronologia dei pavimenti repubblicani." In *Atti del II Colloquio dell'Associazione Italiana per lo studio e la conservazione del mosaico (Roma 1994)*, edited by I. Brigantini and F. Guidobaldi, 17–30. Bordighera.
– 2000. "L'inizio dell'*opus testaceum* a Roma e nell'Italia romana." In *La brique antique et médiévale. Production et commercialisation d'un matériau*, edited by P. Boucheron, H. Broise, and Y. Thébert, 87–95. Coll. ÉFR 272. Rome.
Coarelli, F., and F. Pesando. 2006. *Rileggere Pompei I. L'insula 10 della Regio VI.* Studi della Soprintendenza archeologica di Pompei 12. Rome.
– 2011. "The Urban Development of NW Pompeii: The Archaic Period to the 3rd c. B.C." In *The Making of Pompeii: Studies in the History and Urban Development of an Ancient Town*, edited by S.J.R. Ellis, 37–58. *JRA* Suppl. 85, Portsmouth, RI.
Crawford, J.W., ed. 1994. *M. Tullius Cicero, the Fragmentary Speeches.* Atlanta.
Della Corte, M. ed. 1953. *Menippearum fragmenta.* Genoa and Turin.
Dessales, H. 2006. "*Castella privata.* Water Towers and Tanks in Roman Dwellings." In *Cura Aquarum in Ephesus*, edited by G. Wiplinger, 1.363–70. Dudley, MA.
– 2007. "La distribution de l'eau à Pompéi: un cas hors norme?" In *La norme à Pompéi Ier siècle avant – Ier siècle après J.-C.*, edited by M.-O. Charles-Laforge, 129–41. Rome.
Dubois-Pelerin, E. 2008. *Le luxe privé à Rome et en Italie au Ier siècle après J.-C.* Naples.
Dunbabin, K.M.D. 1994. "Early Pavement Types in the West and the Invention of Tessellation." In *Fifth International Colloquium on Ancient Mosaics (Bath 1987)*, edited by P. Johnson, R. Ling, and D.J. Smith, 26–40. *JRA* Suppl. 9.1. Ann Arbor.
– 2003. *The Roman Banquet. Images of Conviviality.* Cambridge.
Eschebach, L. 1996. "Wasserwirtschaft in Pompeji." In *Cura Aquarum in Campania*, edited by N. de Haan and G.C.M. Jansen, 1–12. Leiden.
Fantham, E. 2003. "Three Wise Men and the End of the Republic." In *Caesar against Liberty? Perspectives on his Autocracy*, edited by F. Cairns and E. Fantham, 96–117. Papers of the Langford Latin Seminar 11. Cambridge.
– 2009. *Latin Poets and Italian Gods.* Toronto, Buffalo, and London.
Fraioli, F. 2009. "*Domus* tardo-repubblicane di Roma tra *Velia* e *Carinae*." *Workshop di Archeologia* 6: 123–35.
George, M. 1997. *The Roman Domestic Architecture of Northern Italy.* BAR Int. S. 670. Oxford.
– 1998. "Elements of the Peristyle in Campanian *atria*." *JRA* 11: 82–100.
Goetz, C. 1894. *Corpus Glossariorum Latinorum.* V. Leipzig.

Gualandi, M.L., and E. Papi. 2004. "Fase 13. Prime modifiche edilizie." In *Palatium e sacra via. L'età tardo-repubblicana e la prima età imperiale (fine III secolo a.C. – 64 d.C.)*, edited by A. Carandini and E. Papi, 101–17. Bollettino d'Archeologia 59–60. Rome.

Havet, L. 1882. "Ταφὴ Μενίππου." *Rev. de philologie, de littérature et d'histoire ancienne* n.s. 6: 52–72.

Jansen, G. 2005. "Water and Water Technology in the Pompeian Garden." In *Omni pede stare. Saggi architettonici e circumvesuviani in memoriam Jos de Waele*, edited by S.T.A.M. Mols and E.M. Moorman, 277–90. Studi della soprintendenza archeologica di Pompei 9. Rome.

Krenkel, W.A. 1971. "Varroniana II. Varro Men. 531 B." *Wissenschaftliche Zeitschrift der Universität Rostock. Gesellschafts- und Sprachwissenschaftliche Reihe* 20, no. 6: 435–41.

– ed. 2002. *Marcus Terentius Varro, Saturae Menippeae*. St Katharinen.

Lindsay, W.M., ed. 1903. *Nonii Marcelli De compendiosa doctrina libros XX*. 3 vols. Leipzig. [Reprinted Hildesheim, 1964.]

Morricone, M.L. 1970. *I pavimenti di signino repubblicani di Roma e dintorni.* Mosaici in Italia, Studi monografici 1. Rome.

– 1973a. "Mosaico." In *Enciclopedia dell'arte antica. Supplemento 1970*, 504–31.

– 1973b. "Pavimento." In *Enciclopedia dell'arte antica. Supplemento 1970*, 601–5.

– 1980. *Scutulata pavimenta. I pavimenti con inserti di marmo e di pietra trovati a Roma e nei dintorni*. Rome.

Ohlig, C. 2001. *De Aquis Pompeiorum. Das Castellum Aquae in Pompeji: Herkunft, Zuleitung und Verteilung des Wassers*. Nijmegen.

Papi, E. 1995. "I pavimenti delle *domus* della pendice settentrionale del Palatino (VI–II secolo a.C.)." In *Atti del II Colloquio dell'Associazione Italiana per lo studio e la conservazione del mosaico (Roma 1994)*, edited by I. Brigantini and F. Guidobaldi, 337–52. Bordighera.

Pesando, F. 1997. *Domus. Edilizia privata e società pompeiana fra III e I secolo a.C.* Rome.

Rakob, F. 1964. "Ein Grottentriklinium in Pompeji." *RM* 71: 182–94.

Rawson, E. 1975. *Intellectual Life in the Late Roman Republic*. London.

Riese, A. 1865. *M. Terenti Varronis Saturarum Menippearum reliquiae*. Leipzig.

Rowland, I., and T. Howe, eds. 1999. *Vitruvius: Ten Books on Architecture*. Cambridge.

Salza Prina Ricotti, E. 1979. "Forme speciali di triclini." *Cronache Pompeiane* 5: 102–49.

– 1987. "The Importance of Water in Roman Garden Triclinia." In *Ancient Roman Villa Gardens*, edited by E.B. Macdougall, 135–84. Washington, DC.

Schmölder-Veit, A. 2009. *Brunnen in den Städten des westlichen Römischen Reichs*. Palilia 19. Wiesbaden.

Vahlen, J. 1858. *In M. Terenti Varronis Saturarum Menippearum reliquias conjectanea*. Leipzig.
Vassal, V. 2006. *Les pavements d'opus* signinum*: technique, décor, fonction architecturale*. BAR Int. S. 1472. Oxford.
Wilson, A.I. 2006. "Water for the Pompeians." *JRA* 19: 501–8. [Review of Ohlig 2001.]
Woytek, E. 1970. *Sprachliche Studien zur Satura Menippea Varros. Wiener Studien* Beiheft 2. Vienna, Cologne, and Graz.

3

Rape, the Family, and the "Father of the Fatherland" in Ovid, *Fasti* 2*

FANNY DOLANSKY

Within the Ovidian corpus, rape looms large. Rapes feature in the *Amores* and *Ars Amatoria*, pervade the *Metamorphoses*, and appear throughout the *Fasti* with eleven distinct narratives and several brief allusions that describe acts ranging from light-hearted foiled attempts to brutal violations. These narratives constitute nearly one-fifth of the *Fasti*'s mythical and legendary passages, and those that recount the rapes of Lucretia (*F.* 2.685–852) and Proserpina (*F.* 4.417–618) are among the longest narratives in the poem.[1] Despite their presence throughout the *Fasti* and prominence in Book 2, with four stories totalling nearly one-third of its content, the rape narratives have garnered only limited interest.[2] The concentration of sombre material in Book 2 is particularly striking given the book's dedication to Augustus and celebration of his title *pater patriae* ("Father of the Fatherland"), and its overall concern with domestic prosperity as descriptions of the Feralia and Caristia, rites that celebrate *pietas* and *concordia*, respectively, clearly reflect. The dating of the book's composition, including possible revision after 8 CE – the year Ovid was exiled for *carmen et error* ("a poem and an error") and Julia, Augustus' granddaughter, ostensibly for sexual misdemeanors – invites additional readings of these narratives that are firmly situated in the politics of the Augustan age.

Ovid relates three completed rapes in Book 2: Jupiter's rape of Callisto (153–92), Mercury's violation of Lara (585–616), and Sextus Tarquinius' assault on Lucretia (685–852). Although these tales differ in various ways, each tells the story of a personal violation that originates with a powerful outsider who seeks to control another's intimate affairs, and culminates in both individual ruin and collective despair as rape and its aftermath disrupt and destabilize the family unit. With this shared theme, I suggest Book 2's rape narratives function in part as social commentary and can be read as responses to Augustus' legislation of 18–17 BCE, some of which was later amended in 9 CE. Relying on a system of rewards and penalties, the Augustan laws aimed at encouraging marriage and reproduction, and punishing adultery among Rome's upper orders. Once matters for the family, these became issues for state concern and regulation as the laws specified whom one could marry and when; set mandatory ages for marriage and remarriage for both sexes, including special conditions for widows and divorcees; and moved adultery from the jurisdiction of the family to public prosecution. Through their juxtaposition with key passages, including commemorations of Augustus as *pater patriae* that highlight his legislative efforts (139, 141), and consistent emphasis on problematic relations, the rape narratives expose the family's vulnerability and compromised self-sovereignty as a result of the Julian laws. Using a network of verbal echoes and allusions, Ovid links these seemingly discrete episodes to keep contemporary concerns about the family foremost in readers' minds. Through a series of grim tales, he offers a subtle critique of the *princeps'* legislative program and his attempts at controlling the domestic sphere.

De Iove crimen habet: The Rape of Callisto

The first completed rape in Book 2 and the poem as a whole explains the appearance of the constellation *Arctophylax* (*Ursa*'s Guard/*Boötes*) on 12 February. Ovid tells the familiar tale of the nymph Callisto, a favourite of Diana. Callisto was to be leader of the goddess's virginal band until Jupiter forced himself upon her (*F.* 2.161–2): *foedera servasset, si non formosa fuisset: | cavit mortales, de Iove crimen habet* ("She would have kept the pledge but for her prettiness. She shunned mortals, Jupiter made her sin"). Once pregnant, Callisto's broken vow of virginity becomes apparent when she undresses to bathe with the goddess and her fellow nymphs, and Diana immediately exiles her from her sacred troupe. Ten months pass; Callisto gives birth to a boy and becomes the victim of Juno's wrath as the goddess punishes her perceived rival by transforming her into a bear. Fifteen years later, Callisto comes face to face with her son who naturally does not recognize his mother in ursine form. He prepares to kill her but both are saved in the nick of time, taken up into the heavens to become the constellations *Arctos* (*Ursa Maior*) and *Arctophylax*.

Callisto's story revolves around ruptured bonds and domestic dysfunction. Her situation exists, however, not because of her own actions (for she wanted to comply with the goddess's wishes) or even Diana's, but, as Ovid repeatedly insists, those of the omnipotent *pater deum*, the father of the gods (*de Iove crimen habet*, "Jupiter made her sin," 162; *invito est pectore passa Iovem*, "she was Jove's unwilling victim," 178).[3] Because Jupiter refuses to restrain his lust, Callisto suffers great personal violation; moreover, others are seriously affected as well, as the rape disrupts normal family dynamics and compromises both the individual and the group. Callisto's breach betrays Diana and her sister nymphs, but soon insecurity and ire are roused in Juno when she discovers Jupiter's infidelity and fears a potential rival. Finally, already exiled from one family group, Callisto is barred from enjoying another as her transformation into a bear keeps her from being a mother to her son and almost effects their mutual destruction, only prevented by the timely and, in this instance, welcome abduction to the skies, presumably at Jupiter's behest (188): *ni foret in superas raptus uterque domos* ("but both were whisked to homes above").[4]

Throughout the episode, family terminology keeps the focus on strained familial relations. Callisto is variously called mother (*mater*, 176, 184) and parent (*parentis*, 186), while the boy is referred to as her son (*nato*, 184). There are other more subtle touches, namely, Diana's address to Callisto as a daughter of Lycaon (*Lycaoni*, 173) and her status as Juno's rival (*in paelice voltus*, 179). Sisters and spouses are betrayed, and "parental" authority is twice disregarded with nearly fatal results. This first occurs when Callisto, unable to abide by Diana's rules, is "expelled from the sisterhood by her sister/mother," forced by the goddess to leave her sister nymphs, then later when her son fails to heed her words and she is almost killed (186–7): *gemitus verba parentis erant. | hanc puer ignarus iaculo fixisset acuto* ("The growl was her parental speech. The ignorant lad would have bedded his honed spike in her").[5] All of these events, set in motion by Jupiter's moment of gratification, reinforce the notion of the family's vulnerability and inability to control its own destiny in the face of a powerful external force.

Iussa Iovis fiunt: The Double Violation of Lara

The second completed rape in Book 2, the violation of Lara, which Feeney calls "the most shattering story in the *Fasti*," may be Ovid's own invention.[6] The story of Lara's misfortune begins not with rape but a foiled attempt. Jupiter, erotic predator *par excellence*, lusted after Lara's sister Juturna, who somehow managed to evade him repeatedly. Frustrated, he enlists the aid of her fellow nymphs to prevent her from eluding him again. Yet Lara, who had a propensity for speaking out of turn, warns Juturna, then informs Juno of her husband's intended adultery, thereby forestalling the assault on her sister while securing her own demise. Jupiter reacts violently: he rips out Lara's tongue and bids Mercury to conduct her to the dead. En route, Mercury finds her pleasing and rapes her as she struggles in silence. Months later she gives birth to the Lares, ever-watchful guardians of the city. From punishment to parturition takes fewer than ten lines (2.607–16):

> Iuppiter intumuit, quaque est non usa modeste
> eripit huic linguam, Mercuriumque vocat:
> "duc hanc ad manes: locus ille silentibus aptus.
> nympha, sed infernae nympha paludis erit."
> iussa Iovis fiunt. accepit lucus euntes:
> dicitur illa duci tum placuisse deo.
> vim parat hic, voltu pro verbis illa precatur,
> et frustra muto nititur ore loqui.
> fitque gravis geminosque parit, qui compita servant
> et vigilant nostra semper in urbe Lares.

Jupiter exploded, rips out the tongue she used indiscreetly, and summons Mercury: "Conduct her to the dead; that place suits the silent. She shall be a nymph, nymph of the hell-pit." Jove's orders are fulfilled. They passed into a grove. They say she aroused her leader, the god. He prepares to rape her. She pleads with looks, not words, her mute lips struggle vainly to speak. She bulges, and bears the twins who guard the crossroads and watch our city always: the Lares.

As Keegan poignantly remarks, focusing on Jupiter's vengeance, which precipitates – and facilitates – Mercury's rape, "[t]he destructive force of tumescent rapine is vivid and excruciatingly visceral. And, once again, the 'Law of the Father' intervenes (611: 'iussa Iovis fiunt')."[7]

In the Juturna-Lara narrative, familial relationships are emphasized throughout, beginning with the *cognatas aquas* ("kindred waters," 588) Juturna leaps into to evade her pursuer.[8] When Jupiter has summoned all the nymphs to help entrap Juturna, he twice refers to her as *vestra soror* ("your sister," 592, 594) as he explains the advantage she will gain from finally succumbing. Once Lara is introduced (599–600), she is quickly associated with kinship terms that further highlight the familial dimension of this drama. We learn that her father, Almo, often urged her to hold her tongue (*"nata, tene linguam,"* 602) where his address of *nata* (daughter) could easily have been replaced by her name instead (Lara or its original Lala, 599–601). The waters Lara goes to hoping to forestall Jupiter's plot are identified as her sister's pools (*Iuturnae stagna sororis*, 603), and after she has reached them, because she takes pity on brides (*miserataque nuptas*, 605), she intimates to Juno what her husband plans to do (*"Naida Iuturnam vir tuus" inquit "amat,"* 606).

The passage treats themes familiar from Callisto's rape: betrayal of sisters and spouses, and a double disregard for parental – and in this case, specifically paternal – authority as Lara defies first Almo, by routinely speaking out of turn, and then Jupiter, by disclosing his plans to Juturna and Juno.[9] Here too Jupiter's desire to control others and failure to respect boundaries, encapsulated in his passion for Juturna as *inmodicus amor* ("limitless love," 585), prove destructive for both individual and group as he initiates a series of unfortunate events. His unrestrained emotions – lust then rage – render the family more vulnerable than before his arrival as the nymphs lose their sister, Almo his daughter, and Juno's conjugal fealty is tested.

The narrative's placement within the larger framework of Book 2 also draws attention to contemporary domestic concerns. The nymphs' story (585–616) stands in stark contrast to the two wholesome family festivals by which it is bracketed: the Feralia (533–70) and the Caristia (617–38). Observed on 21 February and characterized by *pietas*, the Feralia was the final day of the nine-day-long Parentalia festival for commemorating deceased kin. According to Ovid alone, the day also featured magical rites for the goddess Tacita (571–84), the divinized nymph Lara whom both Jupiter and Mercury violated, though in different ways.[10] On the following day, the Caristia shifted the focus to the living; disruptive relatives were forbidden to attend this happy occasion over which Concordia presided. The double rape narrative, in which multiple family bonds are broken, thus seems incongruous between passages promoting domestic unity, but the sharp contrast that emerges offers an opportunity to contemplate the disruption and potential destruction powerful outsiders posed to the family.

Verbal echoes and allusions emanating from the rape narrative further reinforce the family's susceptibility while linking the seemingly disparate episodes of sexual violence throughout the book. Juturna evades her divine tormentor by leaping into *cognatas aquas* (588), a phrase that connects the passage to the Caristia that *cognati* observe (*proxima cognati dixere Karistia kari*, "Dear relatives, *cari*, named the next day Caristia," 617), but also draws the reader back to Callisto, whose rape banished her from *castas aquas* ("pure waters," 174) forever.[11] After treating the festival's focus on the living generations of the family (617–22), Ovid lists those barred from attending, and rehearses a cast of notoriously dysfunctional mythological characters interspersed with figures from real life (623–30) that culminates in his last named offenders: Philomela, Procne, and Tereus (*et soror et Procne Tereusque duabus iniquus*, "Or Procne and her sister, or Tereus their joint foe," 629).[12] Ovid only alludes to what made Tereus hateful to both his sister-in-law and wife, but his audience was surely familiar with the gruesome details he recounts elsewhere (*Met.* 6.401–674). This story of personal and familial violation begins with Tereus secreting Philomela in a hut in the woods where he rapes her and cuts out her tongue. There he imprisons her for a year, raping her repeatedly. Once she escapes and is reunited with Procne, the sisters take revenge by murdering and feeding to Tereus Procne's young son. Simply naming this trio in the *Fasti* thus serves as a powerful allusion to their tragic fates. Tereus' designation as *duabus iniquus* immediately recalls his acts that shattered both Philomela and Procne, and reference to the double violation of Philomela easily associates her with Lara and anticipates the rape of Lucretia.[13]

Hostis ut hospes init penetralia Collatini: The Rape of Lucretia

The book's final rape narrative helps explicate the Regifugium, an obscure festival on 24 February associated with the expulsion of Rome's last king. During the siege of Ardea, the king's son, Sextus Tarquinius, and comrades are discussing the merits of their wives when they decide to pay them a surprise visit to determine whose wife is most virtuous. Upon arrival at the palace, they find their wives banqueting, with the exception of Lucretia, the wife of Collatinus, who sits with her maidservants working wool. Sextus is overcome by desire and a wicked lust soon incites him to have her by any means: *ardet, et iniusti stimulis agitatus amoris | comparat indigno vimque metumque toro* ("He is blazing, and, goaded by immoral love, plots rape and fear on an innocent bed," 779–80). When he comes to Collatinus' house one night, Lucretia welcomes her husband's kinsman and friend. Later he enters her bedchamber, threatens her with a sword and false accusation of adultery, then rapes her. The next day she discloses what transpired to her husband and father then takes her own life, which Brutus, about to become one of Rome's first consuls, vows to avenge. Once their crimes are exposed, the Tarquinii flee.

Patterns evident in the previous rape narratives recur in the book's longest one but with important differences. The familial dimension is similarly patent, yet it is not so much in the events leading up to the rape or the act itself that attention is drawn to family relationships as in the aftermath where Ovid clusters kinship terms to reinforce the impact of Sextus' actions on two different families. The morning after the rape, Lucretia appears as a mother about to go to her son's pyre and summons her father and husband to hear her confession: *ut solet ad nati mater itura rogum, | grandaevumque patrem fido cum coniuge castris | evocat* ("like a mother due to visit her son's pyre. She summons her ageing father and faithful spouse," 814–16). This pairing of father and husband occurs three more times in the passage (*pater ... coniunx*, 821; *genitor coniunxque*, 829; *virque paterque*, 836). It reminds readers that Sextus has violated one man's daughter and another's wife, a fact underscored by the adjectives *patrius* (*et cadit in patrios sanguinulenta pedes*, "and [she] drops, gushing blood, at her father's feet," 832) and *matronalis* (*et matronales erubuere genae*, "and her matronly cheeks flushed," 828) and identification of Lucretia as *animi matrona virilis* ("matron of male courage," 847). But Sextus' crime also has implications for his own family as it adds to the unspeakable deeds Brutus exposes that force the Tarquinii to flee: *regis facta nefanda refert. | Tarquinius cum prole fugit* ("[Brutus] retells the king's untellable crimes. Tarquinius and his line flee," 850–1). His selfish pursuit ultimately damages three family units with fatal results for each.

Like Jupiter and Mercury, Sextus is a powerful outsider who preys on women beyond his domain, intent on satisfying his lust regardless of the costs to others. But he also shares a quality with Tereus that makes him distinct from the divine assailants. As a kinsman of Lucretia's husband, Sextus is an insider of sorts – a fact that makes his crime even worse since familiarity heightens the level of betrayal (785–8):

accipit aerata iuvenem Collatia porta,
  condere iam voltus sole parante suos.
hostis ut hospes init penetralia Collatini:
  comiter excipitur; sanguine iunctus erat.

The bronze door of Collatia welcomes the young man, as the sun prepares to bury its face. The enemy-guest penetrates Collatinus' house; he is welcomed kindly, bound by blood.

Sextus enters Collatinus' *penetralia* – his "innermost parts" – because the initial barrier that could have prevented him has welcomed him instead (785). But then he enters Lucretia's bedchamber without consent.[14] Sextus thus simultaneously violates boundaries of kinship, morality, and space in the course of the rape.[15] And when he arrogates Lucretia's body for himself, he realizes his earlier, proprietary concerns over the chastity of the state's wives that prompted his visit to the palace in the first place: "*ecquid in officio torus est socialis? et ecquid | coniugibus nostris mutua cura sumus?*" ("Are the duties of the marriage bed being observed? Are our wives as solicitous for us?" 729–30).[16]

Violation of boundaries is intrinsic to all stories of rape, but in Ovid's account of the rape of Lucretia it is afforded prominence, especially in comparison with the preceding narratives whose interest in boundaries is less overt. This emphasis comes into even sharper relief when the story's placement is considered. Though a seemingly minor rite, Ovid has chosen to elaborate substantially on the Regifugium with the legend of Lucretia, which follows almost directly after the Terminalia, a feast honouring Terminus, god of spatial boundaries (639–84).[17] In content and tone, the Terminalia passage differs dramatically from the Regifugium. For the former, Ovid presents an idealized portrait of unity and piety as a nuclear family performs rites before the neighbourhood joins in communal celebration (645–78). When the Regifugium begins, readers thus already have the family in view – and possibly its concerns as well, since not far behind the Terminalia's harmonious group lurk the Caristia's banned relations.[18] As soon as the Regifugium ends, we are reminded of personal violation again with an ingenious coda that links the rape of Lucretia back to the Caristia's allusion to Philomela (853–6):

fallimur, an veris praenuntia venit hirundo,
  nec metuit ne qua versa recurat hiems?
saepe tamen, Procne, nimium properasse quereris
  virque tuo Tereus frigore laetus erit.

Are we deceived – or has spring's herald, the swallow, come, unafraid of returning winter? Yet you'll complain often, Procne, of too much haste; your coldness will delight husband Tereus.

Ovid, Augustus, and Stories of Sexual Betrayal

The point of the consistent emphasis on family relations in these narratives lies in its link with Ovid's commemoration of Augustus as Father of the Fatherland (*pater patriae*), a title he received on the Nones of February in 2 BCE and the only title Ovid actually celebrates in Book 2 despite promises otherwise: *at tua prosequimur studioso pectore, Caesar, | nomina, per titulos ingredimurque tuos* ("We still follow your name, Caesar, with conscientious heart, and march forward through your titles," 15–16). Ovid begins his panegyric in earnest by firmly establishing Augustus' paternal supremacy (127–32):

sancte pater patriae, tibi plebs, tibi curia nomen
  hoc dedit, hoc dedimus nos tibi nomen, eques.
res tamen ante dedit: sero quoque vera tulisti
  nomina, iam pridem tu pater orbis eras.
hoc tu per terras, quod in aethere Iuppiter alto,
  nomen habes: hominum tu pater, ille deum.

Holy Father of the Fatherland, the *plebs* gave you this name, the senate gave it and we knights. History gave it first: you received your true names late, you have long been Father of the World. Jupiter's name in high heaven is yours on earth: you the father of men, he of the gods.

Augustus is successively addressed as *pater patriae* (127), *pater orbis* (130), and *pater hominum* (132), and styled as Jupiter's mortal counterpart (131–2).[19] The tribute then shifts abruptly to a striking comparison between Romulus and Augustus.[20] Among the many differences between the *princeps* and his predecessor are their respective attitudes and achievements concerning morality, as an important pair of verses makes clear (139–42):

tu rapis, hic castas duce se iubet esse maritas;
    tu recipis luco, reppulit ille nefas;
vis tibi grata fuit, florent sub Caesare leges;
    tu domini nomen, principis ille tenet;

You rape; as leader he commands brides to be chaste. Your grove harbours sin; he repelled it. Violence pleased you; under Caesar laws thrive. You are named "*dominus*," he "*princeps*."

Ovid accuses Romulus of rape for orchestrating the Sabine abduction, and claims he found *vis* pleasing, the same term he uses in the assaults on Lara and Lucretia (*vim parat*, 613; *comparat vim*, 780).[21] In contrast, the *princeps* enjoins married women's fidelity and under his authority, *leges* – here synonymous with sexual mores – flourish. But in the following verse (142), a hint of scepticism may be detected.

At first glance, the line seems straightforward enough. Romulus took the name "master," which Augustus refused for its associations with ownership and control (Suet. *Aug*. 53.1, Plin. *Ep*. 10.1).[22] Yet although he was not called *dominus*, his attitude concerning citizens' intimate affairs was clearly proprietary. Ovid may also be playing on *nomen* as both "name" and "reputation," inviting readers to question whether Augustus deserved to be called *princeps*, for he certainly was no moral exemplar as stories of his adulteries circulated long after he brought Livia, newly divorced and pregnant, home to be his wife in 39 BCE.[23] With doubt about Augustus' character already introduced, encountering Ganymede a mere two lines later (145–6) only increases suspicions as the young prince abducted from Troy by Jupiter, Augustus' divine complement, is oddly celebrated on a day when his sign may not have actually risen. Boyle is rightly insistent that

[i]t is no accident that the panegyric of Augustus as *pater patriae* and Jupiter on earth in *Fasti* 2 is followed by gratuitous passages on Ganymede and Jupiter's criminal rape of Callisto (*crimen*, 2.162) ... Throughout *Fasti* the politics of *Roma* and

> *Amor* are juxtaposed [and o]ften the violent dimensions of the latter do not simply reflect upon but impregnate the former.[24]

The *pater patriae* passage thus raises questions about Augustus' sexual conduct from comparison with Jupiter, but also about the curious conjunction of his moral legislation and references to rape. If Ovid were signalling discomfort with the *princeps'* measures at this point, it would not be surprising, for Augustus' attempts had already met with resistance from poets, Ovid among them, and discontent was mounting elsewhere too with noblewomen finding ways to evade charges of adultery and equestrians protesting so doggedly that the laws were amended in 9 CE.[25] There is also the elder Julia's defiance of the adultery law that led to her exile the very year her father, now Father of the Fatherland, received tribute.[26]

The concluding lines of the *pater patriae* passage link Augustan legislation with an act of rape, and the subsequent narrative of Callisto immediately furthers this connection. Diana promises Callisto she will be her *comitum princeps* (160), echoing *nomen principis* (142), but when she is prevented from keeping her vow, Diana bids her not to defile chaste waters (*nec castas pollue … aquas*, 174), recalling the statement that Augustus bid brides to be chaste (*hic castas duce se iubet esse maritas*, 139).[27] The *pater patriae* is similarly associated with rape at the end of the Caristia passage with its allusion to Philomela and offering to the Lares, the domestic counterparts to the civic gods that were the focus of Augustus' reorganization of the city and the product of Lara's rape.[28] This association is strengthened additionally by the toast to the feast's participants – as well as the *princeps* – that brings the rites to a close (635–8):

> iamque, ubi suadebit placidos nox umida somnos,
> larga precaturi sumite vina manu,
> et "bene vos, bene te, patriae pater, optime Caesar"
> dicite; suffuso sint bona verba mero.

And now, when dampened night induces peaceful sleep, lift a large wine cup in prayer and say: "Your health, and yours, too, Father of the Fatherland, Caesar Most Good." Pour wine with the fine words.

Some scholars maintain that Augustus's presence at this family festival is intrusive, and McDonough even proposes that it "foreshadows the irruption of Sextus Tarquinius into the *penetralia Collatini* (787), an offensive violation of the private sphere by a public figure."[29] Whether contemporary readers would have agreed is debatable.[30] Yet it is the case, as he notes, that the title *pater patriae* was deeply connected with Augustus' moral legislation, and in this regard he certainly encroached on areas traditionally in the family's domain.[31]

One final instance further places the *pater patriae* in proximity to rape and the domestic dysfunction that ensues. The weather sign concerning Procne and Tereus (853–6) that serves as a coda to the legend of Lucretia, and in a sense to the book's entire series of rape narratives, also facilitates a rupture of textual boundaries as the theme of sexual violence spills over into the opening of Book 3 with Mars' rape of the sleeping vestal Rhea Silvia (3.19–24):[32]

> Seductive peace stole over her languid eyes; her hand becomes limp and slips from her chin. Mars sees her, desires what he sees, takes what he desires; divine power made his rape unfelt. Sleep departs, she lies freighted; there was now, of course, in her guts the Roman city's founder.

Like Jupiter, Mercury, and Sextus Tarquinius, Mars sees what he wants and takes it, regardless of the consequences. From this act, twins will be born (not unlike the outcome of Mercury's rape of Lara), but here the focus is on Romulus alone, the city founder who also earned a reputation for perpetrating rape (2.139; cf. 2.431–4). Surely the designation *conditor urbis* ("city founder") conjured Augustus as well, since he had striven to associate himself with Romulus ideologically. To many, Augustus seemed an *alter conditor* ("second founder") for his restoration of temples and cults, and moral regeneration through the Julian laws, and in their minds the titles *conditor* and *pater patriae* were already linked.[33] With the beginning of Book 3, we are brought back to the celebration on the Nones and the curious conjunction of Rome's leaders and rape, an act that recurs throughout Book 2 with devastating personal and familial effects.

Conclusions

Ovid wrote the *Fasti* from 1 CE until 8 then revised the extant books in exile as datable references, perhaps as late as 17, indicate.[34] By the time Book 2 was deemed "complete," it was the product of a poet who had witnessed decades under a legislative regime that "represent[ed] a massive and deliberate appropriation by the state of a new regulatory sphere: marriage, divorce, and sexuality."[35] The results of this appropriation, however, were not wholly successful. Indeed, in the *princeps'* own household the laws had dramatically failed to achieve their desired aims, as his daughter and granddaughter were both exiled for adultery.[36] Yet the laws were not just ineffective; they were also destructive, eroding the traditional rights of families to manage their own affairs. Perhaps no ancient source states the impact more plainly than Tacitus (*Ann.* 3.25): *omnis domus subverteretur ... legibus laborabatur* ("every household was being undermined ... and was straining under the laws"). Milnor has noted that it is surprising how little overt attention there is to the laws among contemporary literary sources.[37] They did not go unnoticed, however: critics simply had to be careful and creative, and for Ovid the rape narratives proved opportune.

Book 2's three narratives of completed rapes tell of personal violations by powerful outsiders who seek to control the sexuality, and ultimately the destiny, of others without any regard for the repercussions of their acts. In each tale, rape affects not only its immediate victim, but her parents and siblings as well, thereby disrupting and endangering the family as a whole. Callisto's forced breach of virginity betrays Diana and her sister nymphs, and rouses Juno's anger and insecurity; Lara's efforts to protect her sister from rape lead to her own violation and removal to the underworld, which separates her from her kin forever; and the assault on Lucretia prompts her suicide, which deprives a father of his daughter and a husband of his wife.

These dark domestic dramas offer commentary on contemporary social life by subtly critiquing the Augustan laws on marriage, procreation, and adultery, and, more specifically, their encroachment on traditional, familial rights. Placed in proximity to passages on the Nones and the Caristia commemorating Augustus as *pater patriae*, and linked by verbal echoes and allusions to other legendary rapes, these narratives repeatedly draw attention to the family's imperilled autonomy under the Augustan regime. While the juxtaposition of certain passages may be partly the product of the *Fasti*'s calendrical framework, most of the content and emphases within these narratives were the poet's choice. Using these tales of compromised chastity, filial disobedience, conjugal and sororal betrayal, all set in motion by powerful outside forces, Ovid sought to register his concerns about the *princeps*'s moral program and to show readers – perhaps Augustus among them – that Roman families were not stronger as a result.

NOTES

* I am grateful to the audience members at the President's Panel of the Classical Association of Canada's Annual Meeting held in Quebec in May 2010 – not least to the honorand of this volume and its co-editors – for their warm reception of the original presentation from which this paper has developed. My debt to Elaine's scholarship on the *Fasti* is, I hope, evident in these pages, even though our interests in and approaches to the poem diverge. Shadi Bartsch kindly read

an early version of the present contribution and offered helpful suggestions. I owe considerable thanks to Peter White for advice on organization and ways to refine my arguments that have improved the final product significantly.

1 Although my interest differs, I follow Murgatroyd's formulation (2005: 63n1) for identifying a rape narrative: "I include under 'rape' simply the actual or attempted perpetration of sexual intercourse without the other person's consent or willingness, where physical or non-physical coercion is involved ... To qualify as a 'rape narrative' something more substantial than a brief allusion is required, i.e. a passage of more than ten lines that contains at least three 'functions' and two 'stages'." (A "function," in narratological terms, is an action that is significant for the narrative as a whole (e.g., the rapist's attraction to the victim), while the three "stages" are prelude (events immediately prior to the rape that have direct bearing upon it); contact (actual execution of the rape); and aftermath (subsequent events directly related to the rape).) Rape narratives in the *Fasti* occur at 1.391ff (Lotis), 2.153ff. (Callisto), 2.305ff. (Hercules/Omphale), 2.583ff. (Juturna and Lara), 2.685ff. (Lucretia), 3.11ff (Rhea Silvia), 4.417ff. (Proserpina), 5.195ff. (Chloris/Flora), 5.603ff. (Europa), 6.101ff. (Cranaë/Carna), and 6.321ff. (Vesta). Newlands 1995: 159n35 includes Castor and Pollux's rape of Phoebe and her sister, but the rape is only alluded to as a past event at 5.699–700. The edition cited throughout is Alton, Wormell, and Courtney 1997; translations of the *Fasti* are from Boyle and Woodard 2000.

2 The key studies include Fantham 1983; Feeney 1992: 10–12; Richlin 1992 (with an updated version in Richlin 2014); Newlands 1995: 146–74; Johnson 1996; Murgatroyd 2000 and 2005; Keegan 2002; Frazel 2003; Hejduk 2011.

3 Johnson 1996: 17 argues that Diana is complicit in Jupiter's crime since she does not ask Callisto how she came to break her vow or give her an opportunity to defend herself. Diana's possible complicity, however, does not change the fact that Jupiter's rape begins the series of events that result in Callisto's eventual transfer to the skies. It seems significant, too, that whereas the events leading up to the rape and the rape itself are a substantial focus in the *Metamorphoses* (2.401–530), where 17 lines are devoted to how Jupiter disguised himself as Diana to gain Callisto's trust then revealed his true identity as he raped her, Ovid omits all such detail in the *Fasti* and baldly states that Jupiter was the cause of Callisto's fall (*de Iove crimen habet*, 162). In the *Fasti*, he only seems concerned with leaving the lasting impression that Jupiter is ultimately at fault. In contrast, though, see Robinson 2011 *ad loc.* 2.162 who proposes that *crimen* "suggests guilt on Callisto's part. She is, of course, innocent (assuming events proceeded as per other accounts of the myth)."

4 Johnson 1996: 17–18 offers cogent reasons why it is most likely Jupiter who conveys them to the skies.

5 Johnson 1996: 20.

6 Feeney 1992: 11; cf. Keegan 2002: 143–5, whose reading deftly exposes many of the episode's disturbing elements. Newlands 1995: 160 proposes that Ovid modelled this myth on the story of Procne, Tereus, and Philomela and cites Le Bonniec 1969: 90 who believes it is entirely the product of Ovid's "erotic imagination."

7 Keegan 2002: 145.

8 I treat this as a single narrative since Jupiter's plot to rape Juturna forms the critical prelude to the punishment and eventual rape of Lara.

9 McDonough 2004: 361, who discusses "the multiplicity of tensions between family members" in this episode, notes that it has not received much critical attention.

10 For the emphasis on *pietas*, see Littlewood 2001: 921 and Dolansky 2011. McDonough 2004: 359n5 discusses theories regarding Ovid's possible invention of Lara as well as Muta as an alternate name for Tacita, but ultimately proposes that *dea muta* may actually be an epithet for Tacita (i.e., "the unspeaking goddess").

11 Callisto's connection with water might draw the reader back even farther to the reference to Ganymede where *aquas* takes the same final position in the pentameter line (*iam puer Idaeus media tenus eminet alvo,* | *et liquidas mixto nectare fundit aquas,* "Already Ida's boy emerges to mid-belly and pours streaming water nectar-mixed," 145–6), adding to the conjunction of Jupiter with rape, on which see below.

12 For the logic in including such a long list of colourful characters and incongruities, see Miller 1991: 93–5.

13 Cf. McDonough 2004: 364 for the link to Lara, and Robinson 2011 *ad* 2.603, who proposes that Ovid's emphasis on the sororal relationship between Juturna and Lara helps to tie the narrative more closely to the myth of Procne, Tereus, and Philomela. Newlands 1995: 162–8 discusses points of commonality between the stories of Lucretia and the myth of Procne, Tereus, and Philomela and suggests (163) the brief reference to the latter at *F.* 2.853–6 forms a coda to the story of Lucretia's rape; cf. Pavlock 1991: 37, proposing that it "acts almost as an epilogue."

14 To me, the phrase *penetralia Collatini* seems able to admit two readings that can operate concurrently: a literal one in which the phrase refers to the inner rooms of Collatinus's house, and a transferred meaning in which it signals Lucretia's violation by conjuring both the physical space where the act takes place (the bedchamber Collatinus and Lucretia share) and the emotional location of its impact (i.e., the rape strikes at the very core of both Lucretia and Collatinus, though in different ways and for different reasons): see *OLD penetrale* 1c for its figurative sense of "innermost or secret parts, depths, recesses" of the heart or mind; *penetrale* was not used to refer to "private parts" in the sense of the

genitals, nor was *penetrare* used in a sexual sense in the classical period: see Adams 1982: 151. When Sextus arrives at the palace the night of the rape, he does not simply enter Collatinus's house, but first his bedchamber and then his wife. The reader, however, is already aware at 2.779–80 of his intentions regarding what is most private and intimate for Collatinus. Thus when the reader learns a few lines later that Sextus has entered *penetralia Collatini*, it is not unreasonable that he or she might think of both literal and transferred meanings of the phrase. Moreover, an Augustan audience may well have been familiar with the story from Livy and Dionysius of Halicarnassus, and so potentially more receptive to double meanings. Others have similarly suggested there might be more than meets the eye in Ovid's choice of *penetralia*, for Richlin 1992: 171 translates "the house/innards of Collatinus," while Fox 1996: 215 renders it "private quarters" and comments on the sexual overtone to Sextus's entrance through the use of *ineo*.

15 Cf. Newlands 1995: 162–3, who similarly notes his violation of kinship bonds. The description of Sextus's initial approach draws attention to his hostile intent and pending appropriation of Lucretia's space (793–6):

surgit et aurata vagina liberat ensem
   et venit in thalamos, nupta pudica, tuos.
utque torum pressit, 'ferrum, Lucretia, mecum est'
   natus ait regis, 'Tarquiniusque loquor.'

(He rises and frees his sword from its golden sheath, and enters your bedchamber, modest bride. Mounting the bed, the king's son declares, "I've my sword, Lucretia; it's Tarquinius speaking.")

Fox 1996: 215 cites line 793 among instances of sexual symbolism combining with military imagery in this narrative, but there is also a definite interest in space in the lines that follow. The physical spaces Sextus encroaches upon – Lucretia's bedchamber and bed – foreshadow his encroachment on her body, which he likewise enters unbidden.

16 Murgatroyd 2005: 192–3 suggests that compared to Livy's version, Ovid has enhanced the irony by having Sextus make the men's contest specifically about their wives' fidelity, whereas Livy does not identify a particular quality.

17 Scullard 1981: 81 proposes that Romans of the late Republic would have regarded the Regifugium as a kind of Independence Day to mark the expulsion of Rome's last king, but the festival's origins relate to a rather different king – the *rex sacrorum* instead. Ancient sources on the festival are few and there is no scholarly consensus about its significance. See also Boyle and Woodard 2000: 203–4.

18 In her study of the myth of Procne, Tereus, and Philomela in the *Metamorphoses*, Joplin 2002 [1984]: 280n12 also draws a connection between

the *Fasti*'s narratives of the Terminalia and the rape of Lucretia but does not develop it further. Perhaps the reader is actually already primed for boundary violation when the Regifugium begins due to the Terminalia's final couplet, which refers to overstepping boundaries as a Roman prerogative (683–4): *gentibus est aliis tellus data limite certo: | Romanae spatium est Urbis et orbis idem* ("For other nations the earth has fixed boundaries: Rome's city and the world are the same space"). Robinson 2011 *ad* 2.684 remarks that this line "could be thought to resonate oddly with a passage praising the importance of boundaries." Interestingly, he also suggests that among the line's positive references is evocation of the opening of Augustus's *Res Gestae*: *rerum gestarum divi Augusti, quibus orbem terrarum imperio populi Romani subiecit* ("[A copy] of the achievements of the divine Augustus, by which he brought the whole world under the *imperium* of the Roman people"). Yet a cynical, or as Robinson prefers, "suspicious" reader might be reminded of some of Augustus's other achievements regarding boundaries, including his encroachment on those formerly afforded to families to manage their own affairs.

19 Keegan 2002: 139 calls him the "super-Father" in this passage.

20 Views vary considerably: e.g., Herbert-Brown 1994: 43–54 concludes that contemporary audiences would have found the portrayal of Romulus amusing rather than offensive and the contrast unproblematic, while others regard the *synkrisis* as deflating and damaging to Augustus: see Wallace-Hadrill 1987: 228, Hinds 1992: 132–4, and Boyle 1997: 9, 11.

21 Robinson 2011 *ad* 2.613 notes the rarity of the phrase *vim parat* outside Ovid and cites a number of examples for its use in the *Metamorphoses*.

22 For Augustus's resistance to the term, see Suet. *Aug*. 53 and Hinds 1992: 134 with n. 29 on the *princeps*'s sincerity.

23 Cf. Harries 1989: 166 regarding 2.131–2, who comments on "*nomen* here easily extending from the 'name' *pater* to a shared 'reputation'." Suetonius (*Aug*. 69) reports on Augustus's notorious womanizing, and according to Dio (54.16.3), knowledge of his affairs was raised by some senators at the introduction of the Julian laws in 18 BCE and rumours of one liaison continued to plague him the following year (Dio 54.19.3). Robinson 2011 *ad* 2.139 suggests that "suspicious readers" might think about Augustus' reputation even earlier, especially in regard to his marriage to Livia, and read 139 differently: "for them, Augustus, rather than encouraging *maritas* to be *castas*, seems to be behaving more like Romulus and encouraging *castas* to be *maritas*, setting the example himself (*se duce*)." He goes on to note that for some, Augustus and Romulus were also linked as "wife-snatchers," citing Caligula's remark that he was acting "by the example of Romulus and Augustus" (*exemplo Romuli et Augusti*, Suet. *Cal*. 25.1) when he took Calpurnius Piso's wife, Livia, for himself on the night of their wedding banquet.

24 Boyle 1997: 9, and cf. Harries 1989: 166–7 for a similar conclusion about the Ganymede reference, though his focus differs. Others do not regard the placement as damaging or purposeful: e.g., Fantham 1995: 54, Barchiesi 1997: 81–3. Similarly, there is disagreement over Ovid's astronomical knowledge in terms of the identification of Ganymede with Aquarius (on which see Robinson 2011: 157–9) and the question of his rising (e.g., some place his true rising on 22 January: see Boyle and Woodard *ad* 2.145–6 and Gee 2000: 174).

25 Poets: e.g., Prop. 2.7; Ov. *Am.* 3.4.37–8, *Ars* 2.157–8 (and several of the *Amores* and much of the *Ars* mock the adultery law). See also Williams 1962, Wallace-Hadrill 1985, and Syme 1978: 189–92. Evasion: Treggiari 1991: 297 (294–8 on the effectiveness of the law in general) and Cohen 1991: 109–12. Both discuss the case of Vistilia, a woman of praetorian rank who was convicted of adultery in 19 CE despite having had her name inscribed on the aedile's list of public prostitutes. Her case prompted a *senatus consultum* that closed the loophole she had exploited by ruling that no woman whose father, grandfather, or husband had been a Roman knight could prostitute herself (Tac. *Ann.* 2.85). By Tiberius's reign, such circumvention of the law had apparently become a problem: Suet. *Tib.* 35.2. See also Csallig 1976: 200–1 for examples of "sham marriages and sham adoptions" under Tiberius. Equestrian protest: Suet. *Aug.* 34, Dio 56.1–10.

26 The year began well with Augustus' receipt of the honourific title and featured the dedication of his new forum in August, but the condemnation of Julia soon followed. Severy 2003: 158–86 tracks the year's events.

27 Robinson 2011 *ad* 2.160 remarks that the use of *princeps* to describe Callisto "is striking so soon after its celebration at 2.142," but does not see a connection between the uses of *castas* in proximity. He does, however, introduce a further link between Callisto and Augustus as *principes*: according to Suetonius (*Aug.* 80), Augustus had seven birthmarks on his torso that were arranged exactly in the form, order, and number of the stars of *Ursa Maior*.

28 In 7 BCE, Augustus reorganized Rome into 14 districts and 265 wards (*vici*). Consequently, the existing cults of the Lares Compitales (or Praestites), present at crossroads shrines in every ward, were restructured as well, transformed into cults of the Lares Augusti and Genius Augusti.

29 Littlewood 2001: 921, McDonough 2004: 365. Libations had been made to the *princeps* at private banquets since Actium (Hor. *Od.* 4.5.35–6, Dio 51.19.7), but a toast to the *paterfamilias* of the household somehow seems more fitting here.

30 Miller 1991: 98, for instance, suggests that the toast to the *pater patriae* recalls the invocation on the Nones, but the Caristia's solemn tone "corrects" that passage with its "latent irony" and "outrageous syncrisis" of Romulus and Augustus.

31 This is particularly true regarding adultery as the Julian law restricted a father's ability to take action and denied a husband the right to kill his wife

with impunity. See further Treggiari 1991: 293–4 and Cohen 1991: 123–5. The marriage legislation also interfered with the traditional prerogatives of a *paterfamilias* who no longer had the right to prevent a son or daughter's marriage or refuse to provide a daughter with a dowry.

32 Although not interested in boundary issues, Newlands 1995: 163 notes how the weather sign functions as a coda to Lucretia's rape and anticipates the rape of Rhea Silvia/Ilia. Mention of Ilia at 2.598 (*quaeque colunt thalamos, Ilia diva, tuos*, "and those tending your bedchamber, divine Ilia") in the midst of the Juturna-Lara narrative perhaps also looks ahead to her rape.

33 Hinds 1992: 127–9 offers many examples of Augustus' efforts to align himself with Romulus. Suetonius (*Aug.* 7.2) reports that some senators wanted him to be called Romulus as a second founder of the city, but the proposal for "Augustus" held sway. An excellent instance of the association of *conditor* and *pater/parens patriae* can be found in Livy 5.49.7 concerning the praise Camillus received from his soldiers: *Romulus ac parens patriae conditorque alter urbis haud vanis laudibus appellabatur* ("with justified praise he was being called another Romulus, father of his country and a second founder of Rome"). Ogilvie 1965 *ad loc.* suggests this would have resonated with his audience for its "contemporary force." For Augustus as *alter conditor* in *Fasti* 2, see Littlewood 2001: 917–25.

34 *F.* 1.63–4 may refer to Germanicus' award of a triumph in 17 CE to which *F.* 1.285–8 does with certainty. On revision, see in particular Fantham 1986, who offers several instances of both revision and new composition during exile, and Herbert-Brown 1994: 173–212 on the rededication to Germanicus and his relationship to the text.

35 Cohen 1991: 124.

36 Scholars have long suspected the charges of adultery for both Julias were merely pretexts for serious political crimes: e.g., Syme 1939: 426–7, 432 and more fully in 1978: 194–8 with bibliography; Raaflaub and Samons 1990: 428–32. In her recent biography of the elder Julia, however, Fantham 2006: 86–8 makes a good case for giving the charges of adultery due consideration.

37 Milnor 2005: 142.

WORKS CITED

Adams, J.N. 1982. *The Latin Sexual Vocabulary*. London.

Alton, E.H., D.E.W. Wormell, and E. Courtney, eds. 1997. *P. Ovidi Nasonis Fastorum libri sex.* Leipzig.

Barchiesi, A. 1997. *The Poet and the Prince: Ovid and Augustan Discourse.* Berkeley and Los Angeles.

Boyle, A.J. 1997. "Postscripts from the Edge: Exilic *Fasti* and Imperialized Rome." *Ramus* 26: 7–28.

Boyle, A.J., and R.D. Woodard. 2000. *Ovid,* Fasti. Harmondsworth.

Cohen, D. 1991. "The Augustan Law on Adultery: The Social and Cultural Context." In *The Family in Italy from Antiquity to the Present,* edited by D.I. Kertzer and R.P. Saller, 109–26. New Haven.

Csallig, P. 1976. *The Augustan Laws on Family Relations.* Budapest.

Dolansky, F. 2011. "Honouring the Family Dead on the Parentalia: Ceremony, Spectacle, and Memory." *Phoenix* 65: 125–57.

Fantham, E. 1983. "Sexual Comedy in Ovid's *Fasti.* Sources and Motivation." *HSCP* 87: 185–216.

– 1986. "Ovid, Germanicus, and the Composition of the *Fasti.*" *Papers of the Liverpool Latin Seminar* 5: 243–81.

– 1995. "Rewriting and Rereading the *Fasti*: Augustus, Ovid and Recent Classical Scholarship." *Antichthon* 29: 42–59.

– 2006. *Julia Augusti: The Emperor's Daughter.* New York and London.

Feeney, D.C. 1992. "*Si licet et fas est*: Ovid's *Fasti* and the Problem of Free Speech under the Principate." In *Roman Poetry and Propaganda in the Age of Augustus,* edited by A. Powell, 1–25. Bristol.

Fox, M. 1996. *Roman Historical Myths.* Oxford.

Frazel, T. 2003. "Priapus' Two Rapes in Ovid's *Fasti.*" *Arethusa* 36.1: 61–97.

Gee, E. 2000. *Ovid, Aratus, and Augustus.* Cambridge.

Harries, B. 1989. "Causation and the Authority of the Poet in Ovid's *Fasti.*" *CQ* 39: 164–85.

Hejduk, J.D. 2011. "Epic Rapes in the *Fasti.*" *CP* 106.1: 20–31.

Herbert-Brown, G. 1994. *Ovid and the Fasti: An Historical Study.* Oxford.

Hinds, S. 1987. "Generalising about Ovid." *Ramus* 16: 4–31.

– 1992. "*Arma* in Ovid's *Fasti.*" *Arethusa* 25: 81–149.

Johnson, W.R. 1996. "The Rapes of Callisto." *CJ* 92: 9–24.

Joplin, P.K. (Original work published 1984) 2002. "The Voice of the Shuttle Is Ours." In *Sexuality and Gender in the Classical World. Readings and Sources,* edited by L.K. McClure, 259–86. Malden, MA. [Originally published in *Stanford Literature Review* 1.1: 25–53.]

Keegan, P.M. 2002. "Seen, Not Heard: *feminea lingua* in Ovid's *Fasti* and the Critical Gaze." In *Ovid's Fasti – Historical Readings at Its Bimillennium,* edited by G. Herbert-Brown, 129–54. Oxford.

Le Bonniec, H. 1969. "Les *Fastes* d'Ovide." *Orpheus* 16: 3–24.

Littlewood, R.J. 2001. "Ovid among the Family Dead: The Roman Founder Legend and Augustan Iconography in Ovid's *Feralia* and *Lemuria.*" *Latomus* 60: 916–35.

McDonough, C.M. 2004. "The Hag and the Household Gods: Silence, Speech, and the Family in Mid-February (Ovid Fasti 2.533–638)." *CP* 99: 354–69.

Miller, J.F. 1991. *Ovid's Elegiac Festivals*. Frankfurt am Main.

Milnor, K. 2005. *Gender, Domesticity, and the Age of Augustus*. Oxford.

Murgatroyd, P. 2000. "Plotting in Ovidian Rape Narratives." *Eranos* 98: 75–92.

– 2005. *Mythical and Legendary Narrative in Ovid's Fasti*. Leiden.

Newlands, C. 1995. *Playing with Time: Ovid and the* Fasti. Ithaca and London.

Ogilvie, R.M. 1965. *A Commentary on Livy Books 1–5*. Oxford.

Pavlock, B. 1991. "The Tyrant and Boundary Violations in Ovid's Tereus Episode." *Helios* 18: 34–48.

Raaflaub, K., and L.J. Samons, II. 1990. "Opposition to Augustus." In *Between Republic and Empire: Interpretations of Augustus and his Principate*, edited by K. Raaflaub and M. Toher, 417–54. Berkeley.

Richlin, A. 1992. "Reading Ovid's Rapes." In *Pornography and Representation in Greece and Rome*, edited by A. Richlin, 158–79. Oxford.

– 2014. *Arguments with Silence*. Ann Arbor.

Robinson, M. 2011. *Ovid*, Fasti *Book 2*. Oxford.

Scullard, H.H. 1981. *Festivals and Ceremonies of the Roman Republic*. Ithaca.

Severy, B. 2003. *Augustus and the Family at the Birth of the Roman Empire*. New York and London.

Syme, R. 1939. *The Roman Revolution*. Oxford.

– 1978. *History in Ovid*. Oxford.

Treggiari, S. 1991. *Roman Marriage*. Oxford.

Wallace-Hadrill, A. 1985. "Propaganda and Dissent? Augustan Moral Legislation and the Love-Poets." *Klio* 67: 180–4.

– 1987. "Time for Augustus: Ovid, Augustus, and the *Fasti*." In *Homo Viator: Classical Essays for John Bramble*, edited by M. Whitby, P. Hardie, and M. Whitby, 221–30. Bristol and Oak Park, IL.

Williams, G. 1962. "Poetry in the Moral Climate of Augustan Rome." *JRS* 52: 28–46.

4

Naming the Elegiac Mistress: Elegiac Onomastics in Roman Inscriptions*

ALISON KEITH

Anglo-American scholars of Latin elegy enjoy a rare consensus in their current agreement that the stock character of the mistress in Latin elegy reflects that of the high-priced Greek courtesan familiar from new comedy, Hellenistic epigram, and Greek biography, a figure both literally and literarily available to the Roman elites as a result of the expansion of their military empire into Greece.[1] The elegiac mistress herself must thus be counted another luxury import from the eastern Mediterranean, like the silks, gems, and perfumes in which she conventionally dresses.[2] Certainly, the Greek names of the Roman elegists' mistresses imply their foreign provenance. Indeed, Ovid explicitly informs his readers in *Ars* 1 that Rome provides an abundance of foreign women from whom to choose a mistress (*Ars* 1.171–6):[3]

quid, modo cum belli naualis imagine Caesar
   Persidas induxit Cecropiasque rates?
nempe ab utroque mari iuuenes, ab utroque puellae
   uenere, atque ingens orbis in Vrbe fuit.
quis non inuenit turba, quod amaret, in illa?
   eheu, quam multos aduena torsit amor!

Why, did Caesar not recently bring on Persian and Athenian ships in the guise of a naval engagement? Surely youths and maidens came from either sea, and the whole huge world was in the City. Who did not find something to love in that crowd? Alas, how many men did a foreign love overthrow!

This claim is borne out by the inscriptional evidence of slave women and freedwomen in Rome in the late republican and early imperial period who bore the Greek names ascribed by the elegists to their mistresses and the other sexually available characters celebrated (and/or reviled) in this body of poetry, such as hairdressers, maids, and even bawds (who are often assumed to be retired courtesans). Recent scholarship on Greek courtesans has examined the onomastic conventions preserved in Athenaeus and his sources on literary and historical Greek *hetairai,* but scholars of Latin elegy have only rarely taken the contemporary inscriptional evidence from Rome into account in their discussions of the elegiac mistress.[4]

One of the most significant markers of social status in classical Rome was undoubtedly onomastic, and the Roman epigraphic dossier clearly documents the importance of both Greek and Latin names to the construction of female (and male) identity in the early principate. In an influential study of 1971, the Finnish scholar Heikki Solin argued that a Greek name indicated a servile background, whether of the bearer of the Greek name herself or of a close ancestor, although it did not necessarily prove the bearer's Greek ethnicity.[5] In this study, I set out the inscriptional evidence for the presence in early imperial Rome of slave women and freedwomen bearing the names of the celebrated courtesans of classical Greece, situating this material in the context of the textual evidence for their nomenclature in extant elegy.[6] I then focus on the overlap between the names of the mistresses in Latin elegy and the inscriptional evidence we have for slave women and freedwomen bearing precisely these Greek names in the same period at Rome. My study aims to document the contemporary currency of the Greek names of the elegists' mistresses in Augustan Rome, where their names are resonant of Roman imperial conquest, and thereby to show that Roman elegy is intimately correlated with Roman imperialism in its celebration of the sexual spoils of military conquest.

Professor Solin, in his two indispensable compilations of Greek and slave personal names in Rome (respectively 2003 [1982] and 1996), collects the inscriptional evidence for women bearing the names of famous Greek courtesans at Rome: Thais, Cytheris, Lais, Lycoris, and Phryne.[7] We may note the significance of the specifically Greek provenance of the names of these famous prostitutes for, as Juvenal implies, prostitutes were often from the east (Juv. 3.62–6):[8]

iam pridem Syrus in Tiberim defluxit Orontes,
et linguam et mores et cum tibicine chordas
obliquas nec non gentilia tympana secum
uexit et ad circum iussas prostare puellas.

Now for a long time has the Syrian Orontes flowed into the Tiber, bringing the language, customs, slanting strings along with the flute player, and the tambourine belonging to the same race, and girls bidden to prostitute themselves in the Circus.

Thomas McGinn has collected the abundant evidence of importation into Rome of female slaves from the eastern empire for prostitution and we may also note, in this connection, the Roman association of sex with Greek luxury imports.[9]

The most frequently attested such name for slave women and freedwomen at Rome, in all periods, is that of Lais, which was borne by (at least) two Greek courtesans: the earlier (b. 422 BCE) earned the soubriquet "the Corinthian" after the Athenian general Nicias installed her there (Plut. *Nic.* 15; Paus. 2.2.5; Athen. 13.574e–576c), while her later Sicilian namesake was active in the mid-fourth century BCE (Athen. 13.570b–589c).[10] The two Greek courtesans entered the annals of Greek literature early, memorialized in a series of funerary epigrams spanning the late classical period (*AP* 6.1, by "Plato"), through the Hellenistic era (*AP* 7.218–19, by Antipater of Sidon and Pompeius, respectively, both from a cycle on the death of famous courtesans at *AP* 7.217–23), to late antiquity (*AP* 6.18–20, by Julianus). At Rome, the name is widely preserved epigraphically, with 52 attestations for slave women and freedwomen dating from the late Republic (2) to the high Empire (6),[11] and a total of 97 attestations altogether, the rest for women of uncertain social status.[12] The most significant concentration of datable references for slave women and freedwomen of the name, moreover, falls in the early empire, with five datable to the reign of Augustus,[13] 14 to the rest of the Julio-Claudian emperors,[14] and another 26 to the first century CE more broadly.[15]

While none of the Roman elegists employ the name Lais for any of their mistresses, hairdressers, maids, or bawds, both Propertius and Ovid explicitly compare their mistresses to this most famous of Greek courtesans. Indeed, in his elegy 2.6, Propertius compares Cynthia to the three most celebrated Greek courtesans (2.6.1–6):

Non ita complebant Ephyraeae Laidos aedis,
  ad cuius iacuit Graecia tota fores;
turba Menandreae fuerat nec Thaidos olim
  tanta, in qua populus lusit Ericthonius;
nec quae dele[c]tas potuit componere Thebas,
  Phryne tam multis facta beata uiris.

Corinthian Lais' house was not so thronged, though all Greece lay at her doors; nor was Menandrian Thais' crowd of admirers so large, in whom the Athenians took pleasure; nor was Phryne, who could have rebuilt shattered Thebes, made wealthy by so many men.

Ovid echoes Propertius when he compares Corinna, on her named entry into his *Amores*, to both Lais and Semiramis, the legendary queen of Babylon (*Am.* 1.5.9–12):

ecce, Corinna uenit tunica uelata recincta,
candida diuidua colla tegente coma,
qualiter in thalamos formosa Semiramis isse
dicitur et multis Lais amata uiris.

Look, Corinna comes, clad in unbelted tunic, her plaited hair covering her shining neck, just like beautiful Semiramis is said to have entered bedchambers and Lais, loved by many men.

Like the name Lais, the name Semiramis also appears in the epigraphic record, if much less frequently.[16] By comparing their mistresses to the most celebrated courtesans of classical Greece, both Propertius and Ovid would seem to invite speculation concerning the social standing of their mistresses.

The next most popular courtesan's name for slave women and freedwomen in early imperial Rome was Thais, the name of the mistress of Alexander the Great and Ptolemy I (Athen. 13.567, 585c).[17] She shared her name with the stock comic character of the *blanda meretrix* ("seductive courtesan") in Menander, who even named a play after her (cf. Prop. 4.5.43), and her name therefore resonates widely in Graeco-Roman new comedy (cf., e.g., the courtesan "Thais" in Terence's *Eunuchus*).[18] Professor Solin reports a total of 23 slave women and freedwomen attested epigraphically at Rome,[19] out of 57 attestations of the name Thais altogether;[20] and they span the reigns of Augustus (4)[21] and the Julio-Claudians (11),[22] through the rest of the first century CE (6)[23] to the high Empire (2),[24] again with a significant concentration in the early imperial period (21 of 23). As we have seen, Propertius makes explicit reference to Thais, along with Lais and Phryne, at the opening of elegy 2.6 (quote above); and he also alludes to the new comic courtesan of that name in elegy 4.5 (lines 41–4):

nec te Medeae delectent probra sequacis
(nempe tulit fastus ausa rogare prior),
sed potius mundi Thais pretiosa Menandri,
cum ferit astutos comica moecha Getas.

Nor take delight in the insults of Medea, who followed her man (of course she was scorned for having dared to ask the man first), but rather in the costly Thais of elegant Menander, when the comic courtesan tricks the clever Scythian slaves.

Ovid too mentions the new comic courtesan, in both the *Ars amatoria* (3.604, *ut sis liberior Thaide, finge metus*, "though you be freer than Thais, feign fear") and the *Remedia amoris* (383–6):

quis ferat Andromaches peragentem Thaida partes?
  peccat, in Andromache Thaida si quis agat.
Thais in arte mea: lasciuia libera nostra est.
  nil mihi cum uitta: Thais in arte mea est.

Who would put up with Thais playing Andromache's role? She would be wrong to play Thais in Andromache. Thais belongs to my *Art*: my playfulness is free from restrictions. I have nothing to do with the matron's fillets: Thais belongs to my *Art*.

All three references to Thais by the Latin elegists confirm the literary background in new comedy of the figure of the expensive Greek courtesan, and suggest a Hellenizing socio-cultural context for contemporary conventions of slave onomastics at Rome.

The least popular Greek courtesan's name at Rome in our period is that of Phryne, a courtesan of Boeotian provenance active in Athens in the mid-fourth century BCE.[25] She was the subject (perhaps even the author) of an epigram recorded by Athenaeus (*Deipn.* 13.591d).[26] Like Thais, she figured in Greek new comedy (Athen. *Deipn.* 13.591d) and, like Lais, in epigram and biography (in the works *On Courtesans* by both Apollodorus and Callistratus, Athen. *Deipn.* 13.591e). She also appeared in forensic oratory both Athenian and Roman, having been attacked by Aristogeiton in his speech *Against Phryne* (Athen. *Deipn.* 13.591e) and defended by Hyperides (Quint. *Inst. Or.* 2.15.19), in a speech translated into Latin by Messalla (Quint. *Inst. Or.* 10.5.2), from which scant fragments survive (*ORF* 1967 [3] 1 p. 533). Professor Solin records only two certain examples of the name for slave women and freedwomen at Rome, again both of early imperial date,[27] although he reports two more of uncertain status, both datable to the first century CE.[28] But hers is also the only such name to be borne by an elegiac character in Augustan Latin elegy, for Tibullus gives the name to Nemesis' bawd in the final poem of his second collection (2.6.44–50):

  lena nocet nobis; ipsa puella bona est.
lena uetat miserum Phryne, furtimque tabellas
  occulto portans itque reditque sinu.
saepe ego cum dominae dulces a limine duro
  agnosco uoces, haec negat esse domi.

saepe ubi nox mihi promissa est, languere puellam
  nuntiat aut aliquas extimuisse minas.

The bawd harms me; my girl herself is good. Phryne the bawd forbids me entrance in my misery, and slyly comes and goes bearing in her bosom secret messages. Often on the cruel threshold I recognize the sweet voice of my mistress when Phryne says she's out. Often, when a night was promised, Phryne brings me word my girl's unwell or victim of intimidation.

Phryne is also the name of Horace's freedwoman mistress in *Epode* 14 (lines 15–16): *me libertina nec uno | contenta Phryne macerat* ("the freedwoman Phryne, not content with one alone, torments me").[29] Horace's most recent commentator observes that her name "does not seem to have been current in real life in Rome (*RE* XX 893–4)"[30] but, as we have seen, Professor Solin's dossiers now make widely available the evidence for the contemporary currency of the name precisely among women of this class in Augustan Rome.

Professor Solin's most noteworthy evidence, however, is contained in his dossiers of the epigraphical attestations of the names Lycoris[31] and Cytheris,[32] borne by slave women and freedwomen at Rome in the late republican and early imperial periods. For independent textual evidence attests to the name Lycoris as that of the mistress celebrated in Gallus' amatory elegies, and to the name Cytheris as that of the courtesan who was reportedly her inspiration (Serv. ad *Buc.* 10.1, 6).[33]

Gallus, ante omnes primus Aegypti praefectus, fuit poeta eximius; nam et Euphorionem, ut supra <VI 72> diximus, transtulit in latinum sermonem, et amorum suorum de Cytheride scripsit libros quattuor ... hic autem Gallus amauit Cytheridem meretricem, libertam Volumnii ... SOLLICITOS sollicitatos, plenos sollicitudinis post Cytheridis abscessum, quam Lycorin uocat.[34]

Gallus, the first prefect of Egypt, was an outstanding poet; for, as we said above on *Buc.* 6.72, he translated Euphorion into the Latin language, and wrote four books of his *Amores* about Cytheris ... Moreover this same Gallus loved the courtesan Cytheris, the freedwoman of Volumnius ... TROUBLED 'tormented', full of anxiety after the departure of Cytheris, whom he calls Lycoris.

Solin identifies 14 Lycorides in the Roman epigraphic record,[35] a number considerably lower than that of women bearing the name Thais (57) and Lais (97), but significantly higher than that of women named Phryne (4). He reports eight Lycorides of uncertain status, one probably freed, and five slave women and freedwomen. All date from the principate (early 1st c.–3rd c. CE), with the majority (nine of 14) from the first century CE.[36] In the report of their nomenclature, epigraphic conventions suggest that the nine Lycorides datable to the first century CE were originally slaves who gained their freedom. Of particular interest are the first-century Lycoris Augustae li[b.] (*CIL* VI 8888) and Saenia C. l. Lycoris (VI 25748), whose status as freedwomen is clearly marked by the onomastic formula "li[b(erta)] / l(iberta)" ("freedwoman") that appears on their inscriptions. The Roman patron of the former, Augusta (whether Augustus' wife Livia or a later Julio-Claudian princess), is also telling in its association of the freedwoman with the leading household of the early principate. Similarly august early imperial gentilician names are borne by the (probable) freedwomen Statilia Lychoris (VI 6571) and Claudia Lycoris (VI 8554), both datable to the reigns of Augustus' Julio-Claudian successors (Tiberius to Nero) and from households associated with the imperial palace.[37]

Attestations of the name Lycoris in Rome are concentrated in the first century CE, a temporal distribution that may also be significant, as a reflection of the continuing popularity of Gallus' elegiac verse in the century after his death. Of course it is well known that there was an explosion of the Roman epigraphic habit from the Augustan age onwards; as a result, republican women of these names stand a far lesser chance of appearing in the epigraphic record. Nonetheless, the most commonly reported courtesan's name, Lais, occurs in the Roman epigraphic record as early as the late republican period.[38] However that may be, and it must be acknowledged that the evidence does not allow us to draw firm conclusions, it is surely significant that we can securely date all the extant references to Gallus' *amores* in Latin literature to a little over a hundred years following his death.

It is to the late antique grammarian Servius that we owe the information that Gallus "wrote four books of his love poems about Cytheris" (*amorum suorum e Cytheride scripsit libros quattuor*, Serv. ad *Buc.* 10.1), "whom he called Lycoris" (*quam Lycorin uocat*, Serv. ad *Buc.* 10.6).[39] In Cicero's correspondence with Atticus we hear something of the mime-actress Volumnia Cytheris (Cic. *Att.* 15.22), the freedwoman of P. Volumnius Eutrapelus (*RE* IX A, 883 #17), and there is ample attestation of the name Cytheris among slave women and freedwomen in the early principate: especially notable are Rusticelia M.l. Cytheris (*CIL* VI 25617), Memmiae (*mulieris*) l. Chiterini (*CIL* VI 7802), and Sulpicia P.l. Cytheris (*AE* 1980, 84), all of Julio-Claudian date. Professor Solin marshals nineteen women of the name from the Roman epigraphic record: six of uncertain status,[40] one probably freed, and twelve freed former slaves.[41] The name proves durable, being attested from the late Republic (i.e., Volumnia Cytheris herself) all the way down to late antiquity (third- or fourth-century CE); again, however, attestations cluster in the first century CE (fifteen of nineteen). Given the associations of the name with

Venus, it is perhaps not surprising to find women of the name memorialized as *Cytetris delicium*, "darling Cytheris" (*RAL* 1984, 294 Nr. 165),[42] and *Cytheri dulcis*, "sweet Cytheris" (*ICUR* 23507);[43] both may have been slave "pets."[44] The affectionate tone in which both are named confirms the erotic propriety of the name Cytheris for Volumnius' freedwoman, mime-actress-cum-courtesan, and implies their sexual availability.

Especially notable is a Rusticelia Cytheris of Augustan date, for on her tombstone were inscribed six elegiac couplets in two blocks of three couplets each (*CIL* VI 25617 = *CLE* 965):[45]

RUSTICELIA M. L. CYTHERIS

debitum reddidit X K. Sept. Maluginense et Blaeso cos.

Quandocumque leuis tellus mea conteget ossa
   incisum et duro nom[en] erit lapide,
quod si forte tibi [fuerit] fatorum cura meorum,
   ne graue sit tumulum uisere saepe meum,
et quicumque tuis umor labetur ocellis,
   protinus inde meos defluet in cineres.
Quid lacrumis opus est, Rusticeli carissime coniunx,
   extinctos cineres sollicitare meos?
una domus cunctis nec fugienda uiris,[46]
   ut quae uolui, tempore tempus habet
nondum (bis) uic[e]nos annos compleuerat annus,
   supremum Parcae sorte dedere mihi.

Rusticelia Cytheris, freedwoman of Marcus Rusticelius

died ten days before the Kalends of September in the consulship of Ser. Cornelius Lentulus Maluginensis and Q. Junius Blaesus [= 23 August 10 CE].

Whenever the light earth will cover my bones and my name be inscribed on hard stone, if perchance you will feel concern for my fate, let it not be painful to visit my tomb often, and whatever moisture slips from your little eyes, will drip thence immediately down into my ashes.

What need is there Rusticelius, dearest husband, to trouble my dead ashes with your tears? One house [*sc.* Hades] cannot be avoided by all men, though what I wanted, time has provided over time. Not yet had a year filled up twice twenty years each, when the Fates gave me the last by lot.[47]

By contrast to Gallus' silent mistress Lycoris, who occasions his elegiac verses, and Volumnia Cytheris, who appears in the letters and invectives of Cicero, Rusticelia Cytheris has something to say and does so in elegiac couplets at that. It is instructive, therefore, to consider both the similarities and differences between these two distinct Cytherides, separated by at least a generation, but both memorialized in elegiac verse, one under the name Lycoris by the first practitioner of love elegy at Rome, the other (presumably) by her husband in the conventional language of Latin funerary epigram.

Spoken in the dead woman's voice, the elegiac verses that adorned her tomb were, in all likelihood, not only composed by someone other than the speaker herself but also probably commissioned by someone other than her – perhaps by her widower, M. Rusticelius, or by the supplier from whom he purchased the gravestone.[48] Traditional conceits of Roman funerary commemoration appear in references to the light earth covering her bones (*leuis tellus mea conteget ossa*, 3), the incised gravestone (*incisum et duro nomen … lapide*, 4), and the one house (i.e., Hades), which receives all comers (*una domus cunctis nec fugienda uiris*, 11).[49] Also conventional is the reference, before the elegiacs even begin, to death as payment of a debt (*debitum reddidit*, 2).[50]

Like the late-republican Volumnia Cytheris, the Augustan Rusticelia Cytheris was a freedwoman legally bound to her patron. But unlike Volumnia Cytheris, who circulates among Roman magnates in the notices of Cicero, Servius, and others (even, perhaps, under the name Lycoris, in the verse of Gallus and Vergil), Rusticelia Cytheris appears to speaks for herself on her tombstone, addressing her patron as her husband (*coniunx*, 9) and reserving the affective language of love for her relationship with him (*cura*, 5; *carissime*, 9).[51] Throughout the text, in fact, the speaker expresses sentiments that conform closely to Roman ideals of conjugal affection in the formulaic clichés of Roman funerary epitaphs.[52] Thus Rusticelia Cytheris addresses her patron/husband Rusticelius (whose metrically intractable name is included, unmetrically, in a hexameter line) as "dearest husband" (*Rusticeli carissime coniunx*, 9). She assumes that he will be saddened at her death (*quod si forte tibi [fuerit] fatorum cura meorum*, 5) and find visiting her tomb so painful (*ne graue sit tumulum uisere saepe meum*, 6) that he will weep (*quicumque tuis umor labetur ocellis*, 7; *lacrumis*, 9). Her concern for his grief may well reflect his sorrow, but also shows her to advantage as she focuses from beyond the grave on her husband's emotional well-being. Although the speaker has gone to join "all men" in the house of Hades (*cunctis uiris*, 11), her husband fills her thoughts (*tibi*, 5; *tuis ocellis*, 7; *Rusticeli carissime coniunx*, 9), as she assures him that time has brought all that she wanted (*ut quae uolui, tempore tempus habet*, 12).

This "picture of an ideally happy family"[53] is consistent with the funerary conventions of classical antiquity, and stands in striking contrast to the portraits of Volumnia Cytheris and Gallus' Lycoris on display in Latin literature. From another perspective, however, the apparently divergent representation of Rusticelia Cytheris admits of some reconciliation with that of her more famous theatrical namesake and her elegiac avatar. Richmond Lattimore observes that "we must allow for a good deal of falsification in inscriptions composed, for the most part, by owners and patrons who were anxious to pose as benefactors."[54] This formulation invites us to attend to the "ventriloquization" of the dead woman's voice on her tombstone[55] and to recognize, in the masculine composition and circulation of this woman's words on her tombstone, the traffic in women that subtends and supports the patriarchal heterosexual economy of classical Rome, realized in this case quite literally with the freedwoman's marriage to her patron.

Like her literary sisters, Gallus' Lycoris and Volumnia Cytheris, Rusticelia Cytheris is constructed within the homosocial economy of desire that grounded the social relations of patriarchy in classical antiquity and contributed to Rome's military hegemony over the Mediterranean littoral in this period. Her bicultural name testifies not only to her slave provenance and probable Greek lineage (Cytheris), but also to her achievement of manumission and Roman citizenship (Rusticelia), and her social standing was further elevated by legal marriage to her Roman patron Rusticelius. Her social mobility may be interpreted as having outstripped that of Gallus' literary mistress Lycoris, who remains a Greek courtesan in Gallan elegy and its literary reception (in Vergil, Propertius, Ovid, and Martial), and even that of Volumnia Cytheris, who remained socially disreputable as a mime-actress and courtesan (in Cicero's correspondence and the invective *Philippics*) although she gained her freedom and, with it, limited legal rights.

The confrontation of the Gallan Lycoris with Volumnia Cytheris and Rusticelia Cytheris may recall the practice of the ancient critics who sought to establish the historical identity of the elegists' mistresses (Apul. *Apol.* 10; cf. ps. Acro ad Hor. *Sat.* 1.2.64).[56] Indeed, it is informative to consider the evidence of Apuleius in the context of this study of slave women and freedwomen bearing the names of the mistresses on display in Latin elegy (Apul. *Apol.* 10):

eadem igitur opera accusent C. Catullum, quod Lesbiam pro Claudia nominarit, et Ticidam similiter, quod quae Metella erat Perillam scripserit, et Propertium, qui Cunthiam dicat, Hostiam dissimulet, et Tibullum, quod ei sit Plania in animo, Delia in uersu.

But in the same manner let my opponents accuse Gaius Catullus because he named Lesbia for Clodia; and Ticidas, similarly because he wrote Perilla when she was

Figure 4.1 Fragmentary funerary inscription from Rome, including part of the name Cynthia (*CIL* VI 33672). J.B. Speed Art Museum, Louisville, Kentucky. Photo: © USEpig.04.03.

> Metella; and Propertius, who says Cynthia to conceal Hostia; and Tibullus because he loved Plania in his heart, Delia in his verse.

Apuleius, a second-century CE philosopher and rhetorician, documents his knowledge of the identity of some (though not all) of the Roman elegists' mistresses by juxtaposing a series of Greek pseudonyms with the native Latin names of purportedly historical women. Although Apuleius identifies the Roman women beloved by the elegists by their supposed elite Roman gentilicia, his practice aligns suggestively with the inscriptional evidence from early imperial Rome of freedwomen commemorated by both their original Greek name and the Latin gentilician that was their badge of freedom. An especially ironic onomastic juxtaposition of this kind appears in Professor Solin's 1996 register of the nineteen examples of slave women and freedwomen by the name of Lesbia,[57] one of whom bears the name Clodia Lezbia.[58]

Despite Apuleius' identification of the elegists' mistresses as elite Roman women, their Greek pseudonyms bear a servile valence from contemporary attestation in the Roman epigraphic record. Thus, for example, the name Delia, which Apuleius identifies as concealing a Plania in Tibullus' elegies, is attested as the name of a freedwoman at Rome: *L(ucius) [A]elius Flaesc[- - -] | Delia T(iti) et (mulieris) l(iberta) Me[- - -]* (Ferrua 1966, Nr. 51).[59] Interestingly, the name Cynthia is the least frequently attested in the epigraphic dossier, though there is a tantalizing reference to a Cynthia in a fragmentary epitaph from Rome (*CIL* VI 33672; Figure 4.1).[60] By contrast, the name of the mistress celebrated in Ovid's *Amores*, Corinna, is attested in the inscriptional record of Rome and occurs in our period, borne by (1) a *libraria*, a female copyist or storeroom clerk (*ollam [dat] | Corinnae | libr(ariae)*, *CIL* VI 3979),[61] of Augustan date; as well as by (2) a slave of Julio-Claudian date (*CIL* VI 7332); (3) a freedwoman of the same period (Fabiae Corinnae l., *CIL* VI 17588); and (4) a likely freedwoman of the first century CE (Corinnae Argentariae, *AE* 1988, 157).[62]

Ovid himself denies that Corinna was his mistress' real name (*Tr.* 4.59–60): *nouerat ingenium totam cantata per urbem | nomine non uero dicta Corinna mihi.* ("Corinna, celebrated throughout the whole city, knew my talent, though I didn't call her by her real name.") Indeed, it may be doubted whether she existed at all. Already in the *Amores* he jokes of knowing someone who claims to be Corinna (2.17.28–30): *et multae per me nomen habere uolunt. | noui aliquam, quae se circumferat esse Corinnam. | ut fiat, quid non illa dedisse uelit?* ("Many want to have a name in my poetry. I know someone who puts it about that she is Corinna. What wouldn't she give for it to happen?") Moreover in the *Ars*, he reports contemporary speculation about her identity (3.536–8): *nomen habet Nemesis: Cynthia nomen habet. | Vesper et Eoae nouere Lycorida terrae. | et multi, quae sit nostra Corinna, rogant.* ("Nemesis has a name, and so does Cynthia. West and East know Lycoris. And many ask who my Corinna is.") Her absence from Apuleius' notice in *Apologia* 10 concerning the mistresses celebrated in Latin amatory verse is no doubt significant in this regard. But it is significant that the name was current in contemporary Rome for slave women and freedwomen.[63]

Perhaps not surprisingly, however, Nemesis ("retribution") is the most frequently reported name in the Roman epigraphic record, with thirteen attestations, again primarily for slave women and freedwomen.[64] Particularly noteworthy are the Julio-Claudian dancing girl (*saltatrix*) Iulia Nemesis (*CIL* VI 10143) and the freed maid (*ancilla*) Nemesis Nicenis Tauri l. (*CIL* VI 6490).[65] Again too, the bulk of the attestations date to the early principate[66] (nine of thirteen, with another three in the second century CE, and the last dating to either the second or the third century CE).[67] In addition to the abundant epigraphical evidence for the contemporary currency of the name Nemesis for slave women and freedwomen in Rome, however, there is also the rich evidence of Hellenistic epigram, in which the haughty beloved often bears the name.[68] As Kirby Flower Smith well remarked, the name "typifies the idea of retaliation, of repayment in kind for injuries received, of which we hear so much in the Anthology … and which Tibullus himself expresses in 1.9.79."[69]

But the inscriptional evidence offers a particularly compelling social context for assessing the significance of the Tibullan Nemesis' association with an ex-slave in 2.3,[70] to say nothing of her predilection for expensive clothing and gems from the Greek east (Tib. 2.3.51–62):

at tibi laeta trahant Samiae conuiuia testae
  fictaque Cumana lubrica terra rota.
eheu diuitibus uideo gaudere puellas:
  iam ueniant praedae si Venus optat opes,
ut mea luxuria Nemesis fluat utque per urbem
  incedat donis conspicienda meis.
illa gerat uestes tenues quas femina Coa
  texuit, auratas disposuitque uias.
illi sint comites fusci quos India torret,
  Solis et admotis inficit ignis equis.
illi selectos certent praebere colores
  Africa puniceum purpureumque Tyros.

For you let Samian ware extend a merry party and cups of clay turned on the wheels of Cumae. Alas, there's no denying that girls adore the rich. Then welcome Loot if Love loves affluence. My Nemesis shall float in luxury and strut the Roman streets parading gifts of mine. She shall wear fine silks woven by women of Cos and patterned with paths of gold. She shall have swart attendants, scorched in India, stained by the Sun-god steering near. Let Africa with scarlet and with purple Tyre compete to offer her their choicest dyes.

In the contrast between the Italian simplicity of the speaker's tastes (2.3.51–2) and the exotic dress of his mistress (2.53–62), Tibullus projects the Roman rapacity for foreign luxury items onto his elegiac mistress, implicitly representing it as characteristic of her gender and ethnos, and denouncing her on both counts. The vignette of Nemesis parading like the strumpet she is through the great city evokes the rich spoils of empire but frames Roman wealth and luxury as a reproach to the foreign mistress, whose diaphanous dress of "Coan" silk, rich dyes of scarlet and purple, and exotic Indian attendants, all expensive eastern luxury imports at Rome, advertise their wearer's sexual availability and thereby leave her open to the familiar denunciations of the Roman moralizing tradition.[71] The elegy locates both mistress and love poet in the metropolitan centre of Roman power, and illustrates the flow of luxury products into Rome from the eastern periphery of empire, in a move that ostensibly overturns the class, ethnic and gender hierarchies operative in Roman society (2.3.81–4):

nunc, si clausa mea est, si copia rara uidendi,
  heu miserum laxam quid iuuat esse togam?
ducite. ad imperium dominae sulcabimus agros:
  non ego me uinclis uerberibusque nego.

But if my girl's a prisoner now and I can rarely see her, what good to me, alas, is a toga flowing free? Lead on. I'll plough the furrows at the bidding of a mistress and cheerfully accept the leg irons and the lash.

The dossier of contemporary epigraphic evidence from Rome underlines the cruel ironies inherent in this insouciant disavowal of *imperium* (83).

Many of the other Greek names that appear in Latin elegy, borne by the female slaves and attendants of the elegiac mistress, were also current among the ranks of slave women and freedwomen in ancient Rome. Pholoe, the name of the Tibullus' female rival for Marathus' attentions in elegy 1.8 (line 69: *oderunt, Pholoe, moneo, fastidia diui,* "I warn you, Pholoe, the gods hate arrogance"), appears in contemporary poetry in Horace's ode to Albius (probably the elegist Tibullus) as the name of the cruel girl who spurns Cyrus (*C.* 1.33.6–7: *Cyrus in asperam | declinat Pholoen,* "Cyrus turns his attention to haughty Pholoe"), and elsewhere also describes a girl who shuns love (*C.* 2.5.17, *Pholoe fugax*) and a nymph who flees Pan (Stat. *Silv.* 2.3.8–11). Nisbet and Hubbard noted in 1970 that the name "is not attested outside poetry" but Professor Solin's dossiers show the name recorded of a *verna,* or slave born in the household, on an inscription from the high Empire (*CIL* VI 24166, second or third century CE).[72]

In addition, many of the incidental mistresses in Propertius' elegiac poems bear names that are considerably better attested in the Roman epigraphic record than Cynthia. Thus Professor Solin reports twelve slave women and/or freedwomen of the name Arethusa, borne by the speaker of Propertius' elegy 4.3, with one of Augustan date, the two-year-old Aretusa Scariphi Neronis (*bima, CIL* VI 6031) and five of the first century CE.[73] Even the name Propertius ascribes to the bawd of elegy 4.5, Acanthis, is recorded on an inscription of Augustan date as belonging to a freedwoman (*Appuleia L.L. l. Acantis, CIL* VI 34494).[74] Moreover, the two women who join Propertius for a drinking party in the absence of his mistress in elegy 4.8 also bear names attested in the epigraphic record. Phyllis (4.8.29, 57) is especially widely attested of slaves and freedwomen at Rome in the early principate,[75] but Teia (4.8.31, 58) is attested only in the Greek epigraphic corpus (*SEG* XLVIII 508, Messene, second century BCE; *IG* II^2 7787, of a family from Ancyra, of imperial date).[76]

Other servile names in the Propertian corpus relevant to this study appear in elegy 4.7 of Cynthia's slaves Petale and Lalage, and of Cynthia's successor and rival, Chloris. The name Petale (Prop. 4.7.43) is especially interesting in this context, for it is widely attested of slave women and freedwomen in the epigraphic record at Rome.[77] Of particular interest is the funerary plaque for a freedwoman of this name belonging to (and apparently commemorated by) a certain Sulpicia, who has been plausibly identified as the contemporary female elegist (*BullCom.* 53 [1925] 229 = *AE* 1928, 73).[78]

Sulpiciae cineres lectricis cerne viator
  quoi servile datum nomen erat Petale.
ter denos numero quattuor plus vixerat annos
  natumque in terris Aglaon ediderat.
omnia naturae bona viderat, arte vigebat
  splendebat forma, creverat ingenio.
invida fors vita longinquom degere tempus
  noluit hanc: fatis defuit ipse colus.

Passerby, look at the ashes of the female reader named (belonging to/commemorated by) Sulpicia, to whom the slave name Petale had been given. She had lived for three times ten years plus four in number, and she had produced a son, Aglaon (Gk, "gleaming") while on earth. She had seen all good things of nature, she was flourishing in art, she was glittering in beauty, she had grown in talent. Envious Fortune was unwilling for her to spend a long time in life. Their own distaff failed the Fates. (Trans. Hallett 2009)

While Cynthia's aged slave Petale loyally brings garlands to her grave (Prop. 4.7.43: *nostraque quod Petale tulit ad monumenta coronas*), Sulpicia Petale received from her mistress the tribute of a funerary epitaph in elegiac verse that commemorates her as flourishing in beauty and talent. Both sets of elegiac verses, moreover, suggest the mistress' concern for the slave woman/freedwoman with whom she lives on intimate terms.

Like the Propertian Petale, Cynthia's slave Lalage is represented as loyal to her dead mistress and punished for her loyalty (Prop. 4.7.45–6): *caeditur et Lalage, tortis suspensa capillis, | per nomen quoniam est ausa rogare meum.* ("Lalage too is beaten, hung up by her plaited hair, because she dared to ask for something in my name.") The name Lalage occurs with some frequency in Hellenistic epigram (Meleager, *AP* 5.148.1, 5.149.1, 5.171.2, etc.) as well as in contemporary Latin lyric (Hor. *C.* 2.5.16). In addition, several Lalages are attested in the epigraphic record of Rome, including a freedwoman of

Augustan date (*Livia Lalage l., CIL* VI 3940).[79] Even Cynthia's rival and apparent successor in this poem, Chloris (4.7.72, *si te non totum Chloridos herba tenet,* "if Chloris' poison does not completely hold you"), bears a name that is attested in the epigraphic record.[80]

Likewise, both the hairdressers in Ovid's *Amores,* Nape (*Am.* 1.11–12) and Cypassis (2.7–8), have names attested in the inscriptional record at Rome. Professor Solin (2003, 1218) reports eighteen women by the name of Nape: two freeborn, nine uncertain, and seven probably slaves and/or freedwomen.[81] Of Augustan date are the freedwomen Nape Liviae l. (*CIL* VI 4015),[82] Vaticia C. l. Nape (*CIL* VI 6134), and Nape Antonia Drusi l. (*CIL* VI 22868). Of Julio-Claudian date are Nape, the maidservant (*ancilla*) of Mucia Nysa (*CIL* VI 22869); the probable freedwomen Seia Nape (*CIL* VI 37450), Numeria Nape (*CIL* VI 27933), Statilia Nape (*CIL* VI 13724),[83] Detelia Nape (*CIL* VI 16820), Afra[ni]a Nape (*CIL* VI 17751), Fabia Nape (*CIL* VI 27618), and Titiena Nape (*CIL* VI 21938); and the freeborn Sellia C. f. Nape (*CIL* VI 26142) and Trebonia L. f. Nape (*CIL* VI 27618). Also early Julio-Claudian in date is the probable freedwoman Annaea Cypasis (*Arch. Class.* 23 [1971] 242, Nr. 2),[84] who shares her name with the second of the two hairdressers in Ovid's *Amores.*

These findings can be extended to include the names not only of mistresses but also of the boy beloveds, or *pueri delicati,* of Latin love elegy. Thus the name Marathus, borne by the *puer delicatus* of Tibullus' Marathus cycle (1.4, 1.8, 1.9), was also borne by Augustus' freedman, the historian Julius Marathus (*PIR*[2] I 402),[85] while the name Lygdamus, that of a slave apparently belonging to Cynthia in Propertian elegy (Prop. 3.6, 4.7, 4.8) is attested as the nom de plume of the author of six elegies included in the Tibullan corpus ([Tib.] 3.1–6), as well as on an undatable inscription where it belongs to a slave (*Lygdami ser., CIL* XV 2438).[86] Similarly Cerinthus, the name of the male beloved in the elegies by and about the contemporary female elegist Sulpicia ([Tib.] 3.8–18), was current in early imperial Rome, attested of a doorkeeper and two other slaves.[87]

The inscriptional evidence amassed here offers vivid illustration of the contemporary currency of the Greek names of the elegists' girlfriends (and boyfriends) in early imperial Rome, where their names are resonant of the Romans' hegemony over the wealthy Greek eastern Mediterranean, and the resulting flow of slaves into the metropolitan centre. The contrast between the native Italian names of the Roman elegists (including Sulpicia, who signs a poem with her *gentilicium,* [Tib.] 3.16)[88] and the exotic Greek names of the beloveds (including the *pueri delicati,* Marathus [Tib. 1.4, 8–9] and Cerinthus [(Tib.) 3.9–11, 13–18]) documents the class and ethnic entitlements of Roman elite over immigrants, freed persons, and slaves, which is buttressed by the hierarchy of gender on display in the work of the male elegists (although undoubtedly troubled by its disruption in the *eligidia* of Sulpicia).[89] The programmatic invocation of elite male addressees bearing Latin or Italian names throughout the elegists' poetry (Messalla in Tibullus and Sulpicia; Messallinus and Cornutus in Tibullus; Macer in Tibullus and Ovid; Tullus, Bassus, and Maecenas in Propertius) brings out all the more starkly the corresponding lack of Latin or Italian female names in their verse, with the exception of Sulpicia herself ([Tib.] 3.8.1, 16.4) and the legendary criminal Tarpeia (Prop. 4.4; cf. Prop. 1.16.2). Moreover, even when the Roman elegists address men whose cognomina are foreign – such as Gallus (Prop. 1.5, 10, 13, 20), Ponticus (Prop. 1.7, 1.9), Lynceus (Prop. 2.34), Atticus (Ov. *Am.* 1.9), and Graecinus (Ov. *Am.* 2.10) – there is evidence to suggest that their addressees belonged to the Italian equestrian elite, like the elegists themselves.[90] This onomastic and epigraphic study thus illuminates the Latin elegists' participation in, and benefit from, the larger Roman imperial project that is otherwise occluded in an ostensibly non- or anti-political presentation of elegiac themes.[91] Whether or not our elegists had served on the staffs of Roman generals or provincial governors (as Catullus, Gallus, and Tibullus undoubtedly had, and Propertius was apparently invited to do), their poems bear witness to their enjoyment of the sexual (and other) spoils of contemporary Roman hegemony of the Mediterranean.

NOTES

* This paper is dedicated Elaine Fantham and was inspired by her groundbreaking work on women in classical literature and ancient society, especially Fantham 1975, 1995, 2006, and Fantham et al. 1994, and her pioneering accounts of the complex relationship between Latin literature and Roman culture, especially Fantham 1996 and 2013. Her scholarship has been a model of intellectual openness and philological rigour to me and countless other colleagues and students in Canada and around the world, and her friendship is a source of ongoing pleasure. I am also grateful to Elaine for discussing the translation of *CIL* VI 25617 (= *CLE* 965) with me at the beginning of this project. Versions of this paper were presented at the Annual Meeting of the American Philological Association in Philadelphia and the Biannual Meeting of the Accademia Properziana del Subasio in Assisi, both in 2012. I am grateful to the two audiences for their comments, and especially to Megan Drinkwater, Ellen Greene, Laurel Fulkerson, Sharon James, Luciano Landolfi, Allen Miller, Teresa Ramsby, Thea Thorsen, and Tara Welch. An earlier version of this paper appeared in Italian under the title "Le *Puellae* nelle elegie di Properzio e le loro omonime nei reperti epigrafici," in Bonamente and Santini 2014, 371–88.

1 James 2003.

2 Bowditch 2003, 2006, 2009, 2011, 2012; Keith 2008: 86–165.

3 I cite the text of Ovid's *Ars Amatoria* and *Remedia Amoris* from Kenney 1994; the text of the *Amores* from McKeown 1987; the text of Propertius from Fedeli 1984; and the text of Tibullus (and Sulpicia) from Lee 1990. Translations are my own except for those of Tibullus, which are from Lee 1990 (rev. Maltby).

4 Exceptions, all discussing Cynthia/Hostia, include Boucher 1965; Knox 2004; and Coarelli 2004, the latter of whose excesses may have warned off others. See also, more recently, Keith 2008: 86–114 and 2011; and cf. McGinn 2004, index s.v. Ovid, Propertius, and Tibullus. On Greek courtesans, see Henry 1985 and 1995; Davidson 1997; Kurke 1997 and 2002; McClure 2003; Faraone and McClure 2006; Glazebrook and Henry 2011; and on the literature concerning courtesans, see also Griffin 1986, 37–8.

5 Solin 1971: 146–58; cf. Bruun 2013, who confirms the preference for Latin names over Greek ones when naming *vernae* in Rome and also a tendency to move away from Greek names to Latin ones when we can identify onomastic practice over at least two generations of freed persons. On Roman nomenclature, see Solin 2002; the standard discussion of Latin cognomina is Kajanto 1965. I am grateful to Christer Bruun and Jonathan Edmondson for discussion of both the onomastic and epigraphic issues.

6 On Greek courtesans' names, see McClure 2003: 59–78.

7 Solin 2003: 272–6, § I.8: Thais (272–3), Lais (274), Lycoris (275), and Phryne (276). Contrast Solin 1996, 263–4, which includes the name Cytheris in addition to the four cited above. It is worth noting that Solin 2003 is the revised second edition of Solin 1982, and that Solin 1996 was a by-product of that earlier work.

8 The text of Juvenal is cited from Clausen 1959; translations are my own.

9 McGinn 2004: 55–71; cf. Dalby 2000: 125–33. Hallett 2011 discusses an Athenian prostitute in Plautus' *Pseudolus* whose name, *Phoenicium*, implies a Semitic/Carthaginian background.

10 On Lais I and II, see McClure 2003: 187–8 (in Appendix III, "Named Courtesans and Prostitutes in Book 13 of Athenaeus' *Deipnosophistae*") and 239, Index s.v. "Lais II." The name is also widely preserved epigraphically in the Greek-speaking world, including in Magna Graecia (i.e., southern Italy and Sicily): see *LPGN* s.v. Λαίς; the editors record forty-nine women of the name altogether (including the two famous *hetaerae*), with eighteen from southern Italy and Sicily (*LPGN* IIIA 265 s.v.).

11 Solin 1996: 263–4.

12 Solin 2003: 274–5.

13 Aemiliae l. meae Laini (*CIL* VI 11038); Aquillia Lais l. (*CIL* VI 5891); Lais lib. (*CIL* VI 6038); Lais L.l. (*CIL* VI 23822); Pollia M.l. Lais (*CIL* VI 926).

14 ***Augustus – Nero***: Gallonia L.l. Laais (*CIL* VI 18874); Lais l. Coponi *sarcinatrix* (*CIL* VI 9881); Aemilia P.l. Lais (*CIL* VI 11105); Sempronia P.l. Lais (*CIL* VI 11383); Iulia C.l. Lais (*CIL* VI 33132); Octavia M.l. Lais (*CIL* VI 35975); Cornelia L.l. Lais (*CIL* VI 38247); Marcia (*mulieris*) l. Lais (*Bull. Com.* 51 [1923 (1924)]: 120 Nr. 2); Mussia P. et C.l. Lais (*Forma Italiae, reg.* I, *vol.* X, *Collatia* [1974]: 345; cf. *Arctos* 9 [1975]: 101); Pinaria (*mulieris*) l. Lais (*NSA* 1914: 391 Nr. 59). ***1st half 1st c. CE***: Laidi (VI 14661); [- - - Se]x. (*mulieris*) l. Lainis (*CIL* VI 21073). ***Tiberius – Nero***: Iunia (*mulieris*) l. Lais (*CIL* VI 4504); Antistia (*mulieris*) l. Lais (*CIL* VI 6672).

15 ***1st c. CE***: Herennia (*mulieris*) l. Laeis (*CIL* VI 28019); Sentiae C.l. Laidi (*CIL* VI 13572); Iuliae C.l. Laidi (unpublished from the Museo Nazionale Romano alle Terme); Laini (*CIL* VI 9807); [- - -] C.l. Laini (*NSA* 1914: 379 Nr. 8); [Iul]-iae D.l. Laini (*NSA* 1923: 369); Fadena C.l. Lais (*CIL* VI 17647); Lais (*CIL* VI 21067); Lais (*CIL* VI 21068); [- - -]atumennia Gallae l. Lais (*CIL* VI 21070); [- - -] (*mulieris*) l. Lais (*CIL* VI 21072); Lais Pothi (*CIL* VI 21074); Lucretia C.l. Lais *nutrix* (*CIL* VI 21661); Manlia L.l. Lais (*CIL* VI 21978); Orcia A.l. Lais (*CIL* VI 23575); Pupia (*mulieris*) l. Lais (*CIL* VI 25238); Servilia M.l. Lais (*CIL* VI 26444); Sextilia L.l. Lais (*CIL* VI 26499); Turpilia P.l. Lais (*CIL* VI 27779); [Fulvia A.]l. Lais (*CIL* VI 33919); Elctoria Q.l. Lais (*CIL* VI 37656); Pacilia (*mulieris*) l. Lais (*CIL* VI 37822 *a*); Cornelia (*mulieris*) l. Lais (*CIL* VI 38254); [- - -]a L.l. Lais (*AJA* 96 [1992]: 95 *Nr.* 12); Lais (*NSA* 1914: 389 Nr. 41).

16 For the currency of the name Semiramis among slave women and freedwomen in the early imperial period, see Solin 2003, 605, who reports five altogether, of whom two are of uncertain status, and three are slave women and/or freedwomen. ***Julio-Claudian***: Corneliae Samiramidi (*CIL* VI 3352); ***1st c. CE***: Simirami (*CIL* VI 35751); ***50–150 CE***: Claudiae Samiramidi (*CIL* VI 15581); ***2nd c. CE***: Ragonia Sameramis (*ZPE* 125 [1999]: 249 *Nr.* 1); [S]amerami (*Bull. Com.* 43 [1915 (1916)]: 311 = *NSA* 1916: 99 Nr. 38; cf. *Arctos* 11 [1977]: 123).

17 On the historical Thais, see Traill 2001: 289–90; on attestations of the name Thais in Athens, see Traill 2001: 290n25. For attestations of the name in the Greek world, see *LGPN*, s.v. Θαίς, where there are recorded twenty-two attestations, including seven from southern Italy and Sicily (*LGPN* IIIA, 197).

18 On Thais in Latin literature see Traill 2001.

19 Solin 1996: 263.

20 Solin 2003: 272–4.

21 ***Augustus***: Grania Q.l. Thaeis (*CIL* VI 34659); Sutoria M.l. Thais (*CIL* VI 1892); Servilia Thais l. (*CIL* VI 26375); Thais Philarguri (*CIL* VI 32307).

22 ***Augustus – Nero***: Furia A.(*mulieris*) l. Thais (*CIL* VI 18822); Iust<u>leia (*mulieris*) l. Thais (*CIL* VI 20922); Vipsania M.l. Thais (*CIL* VI 33281); Thais (*CIL* VI 22324); Gelliae (*mulieris*) l. Taini [*sic*] (*CIL* VI 35370); Alliae Thaidi vernae (*CIL* VI 11495); Antistiae L.l. Thaidi (*CIL* VI 11938); Thaidi (*CIL* VI

27317); Herennuleiae Thaidi libertae (*CIL* VI 35444); Seia Thais (*CIL* VI 26111). ***Tiberius – Nero***: Volusia Thais (*CIL* VI 7323).

23 ***1st c.*** ***CE***: Larniae C. et Musa[e] l. Thaidi (*CIL* VI 26008); Avienia Sex. L. Thais (*CIL* VI 12898); Numiotira (*mulieris*) l. Thais (*CIL* VI 22292); Sertoria M.l. Thais (*CIL* VI 26361); Orchivia L.l. Thais (*CIL* VI 38702); [- - -]a L.l. Thais (*AJA* 96 [1992]: 95 Nr. 12).

24 ***50–150 CE***: Taidi (*CIL* VI 38464); Thaidi lib. (*Epigraphica* 51 [1989]: 237 Nr. 5).

25 On Phryne, see Cooper 1995; McClure 2003: 191–2 (Appendix III, s.v.) and 241 (Index s.v.). The name is less well attested in the Greek world than Lais and Thais: *LGPN* IIIA 468, s.v., reports seven occurrences, including a Latin inscription from Abella in Campania recording the freedwoman Orfia Phryne.

26 ἐπλούτει δὲ σφόδρα ἡ Φρύνη καὶ ὑπισχνεῖτο τειχιεῖν τὰς Θήβας, ἐὰν ἐπιγράψωσιν Θηβαῖοι ὅτι «Ἀλέξανδρος μὲν κατέσκαψεν, ἀνέστησεν δὲ Φρύνη ἡ ἑταίρα.» (Athen. *Deipn.* 13.591d, "Phryne was very wealthy and used to promise to build Thebes' walls, if the Thebans inscribed in an epigram that 'Alexander destroyed the city but Phryne the courtesan restored it'.")

27 Caesilia P.l. Prhyne [*sic*] (*CIL* VI 7195), of Augustan date; and Phryne Tertullae (*serua*) *quasillaria Africana* (Van Buren 1927: 21 Nr. 7), datable to the first century CE.

28 Solin 2003, 276: Vibia Phryne (*CIL* VI 28877) and Atilia Pryne (*CIL* VI 12637), both datable to the first century CE.

29 The text of Horace is cited from Klingner 1962; translations are my own.

30 Mankin 1995: 233.

31 It is odd that Solin includes his register of Lycorides under the heading "Hetären," in both his *Namenbücher*, in sections that gather the names of historical persons and literary characters (2003: 272–6 § I.8; 1996 II.1.7, 263–4), when neither Athenaeus nor Lucian records a hetaera named Lycoris (nor Cytheris). It was presumably her appearance in Gallus' elegiac poetry that led Solin to include Lycoris along with her putative inspiration, Cytheris, amongst the famous Greek hetaerae. (I am grateful to Allison Glazebrook for the information about Athenaeus.) The name is attested epigraphically in Greek in Tegea (*IG* V.2, 233) and Magna Graecia in Calabria, where it appears on a Latin inscription of imperial date, of a freedwoman (Terraea Lycoris): see *LPGN* IIIA 281 s.v. Λυκωρίς.

32 ***Sulla – Caesar***: Volumnia Cytheris (*RE* IX A: 883 Nr. 17). ***Augustus***: Rusticelia M.l. Cytheris (*CIL* VI 25617). ***Augustus – Nero***: Memmiae (*mulieris*) l. Chiterini (*CIL* VI 7802); Sallustia Citheris (*CIL* VI 8187); Sulpicia P. l. Cytheris (*AE* 1980, 84); Iulia Citheris (*CIL* VI 24024); Cytetris *delicium* (*RAL* 1984: 294 Nr. 165); Durdenae P. l. Cytheridi (*CIL* VI 1818). ***Tiberius – Nero***: Attiae Cytheridi (*CIL* VI 9817). ***1st c.*** ***CE***: Manlia Cytheris (*CIL* VI 21973); Cominia Cytheris (*CIL* VI 34991); Macriana (*mulieris*) L. Chiteris [*sic*] (*CIL* VI 33602); Citharis [*sic*] libert. (*Bull. Com.* 43 [1915(1916)]: 307); [- - -]a Citheris [- - -]aes.

lib. (*CIL*. VI 16712); Marcia (*mulieris*) l. Cytheris (*CIL* VI 22130). The name is attested epigraphically in southern Italy on two Latin inscriptions from Puteoli, both apparently of freedwomen (-vidia Cytheris, *CIL* X 2037; and Pompeia Cytheris, *CIL* X 2049), but there are no Greek attestations of the name: see *LPGN* IIIA s.v. Κυθηρίς.

33 Cf. Gallus fr. 145 Hollis; Verg. *Buc.* 10; Prop. 2.34.91; Ov. *Am.* 1.15.30, *Ars* 3.537; Mart. *Epigr.* 8.73.6; *Vir. Ill.* 82.2. On Cytheris/Lycoris, see *RE* IX A: 883 Nr. 17; Mazzarino (1980–1); Traina 2001[1994]; Keith 2011.

34 The text of Servius is cited from Thilo and Hagen, 1961; translations are my own.

35 Solin 2003: 275–6; cf. 1996: 264. ***Julio-Claudian***: [- - - H]agnes lib. Lucoridi (*CIL* VI 8764); Fabiae Lycoridi (*CIL* 6.17548). ***Tiberius – Nero***: Statilia Lychoris (*CIL* VI 6571); Claudia Lycoris (*CIL* VI 8554). ***1st c. CE***: Lycoris Augustae li[b.] (*CIL* VI 8888); Saenia C. l. Lycoris (*CIL* VI 25748); Vigelliae Lycoridi (*CIL* VI 7851); Seviae Lycoridi (*CIL* VI 20849); Arria Lycoris (*CIL* VI 28349). ***2nd–3rd c. CE***: Titiniae Lycoridi (*CIL* VI 32510); Volusiae Lycoridi (*CIL* VI 29559); Lycoris (*CIL* VI 11296).

36 Solin 2003: 276.

37 On the funerary monument in the gardens of the Statilii that housed the remains of the family's slaves and freed slaves, the findspot of Statilia Lychoris' epitaph (*CIL* VI 6571), see Edmondson 2011: 337.

38 Solin 2003: 274, identifies two freedwomen of the name Lais from the late Republican period (Sulla – Caesar): Auruncleia D. l. Lais (*CIL* I^2 3002) and Fabia C. l. Lais (VI 21230 = I^2 1326); as well as five freedwomen of the name, of Augustan date: Aemilia l. meae Laini (VI 11038), Aquillia Lais l. (VI 5891), Lais lib. (VI 6038), Lais L. l. (VI 23822), and Pollia M. l. Lais (VI 926).

39 The identification is commonly accepted: see, e.g., Hollis 2007: 242–3.

40 Sallustia Citheris (*CIL* VI 8187), Iulia Citheris (VI 24024), Attiae Cytheridi (VI 9817), Manlia Cytheris (VI 21973), and Cominia Cytheris (VI 34991), all dated to the first century CE.

41 Memmiae (*mulieris*) l. Chiterini (VI 7802) and Sulpicia P. l. Cytheris (*AE* 1980, 84), both of Julio-Claudian date; Durdenae P. l. Cytheridi (*CIL* VI 1818), of the first or second century CE; Macriana (*mulieris*) l. Chiteris (VI 33602), Citharis [*sic*] libert. (*Bull. Com.* 43 [1915 (1916)]: 307), Marcia (*mulieris*). l. Cytheris (*CIL* VI 22130), and –a Citheris [- - -]aes. lib. (VI 16712), all dated by Solin to the first century CE.

42 *RAL* 1984: 294 Nr. 165, first- or second century CE.

43 *ICUR* 23507, third or fourth century CE.

44 *OLD* s.v. *delicium*; cf. *OLD* s.v. *dulcis* 7; and on "*delicia* children," see Nielsen 1990 and Laes 2003. Of course, the women named Cytheris in the second, third, and fourth centuries CE are more likely to have been named for their charm and beauty (or if so named as children, rather than renamed as adults, for

their hoped-for charm and beauty) than with reference to Volumnia Cytheris. Nonetheless, the name speaks to their sexual availability as slaves.

45 I quote the corrected version of the text, rather than the original, from *CIL* VI 25617. My discussion of Rusticelia Cytheris follows Keith 2011.

46 Line 11 of the inscription (= line 9 of the elegiacs) is not a hexameter, but a pentameter: see Galletier 1922: 287–8. This is only one of a number of metrical problems presented by the text. Others include: *nomine*, corrected to *nomen*, in line 4; otiose *fuerit*, in line 5; the unmetrical addition of vocative *Rusticeli carissime*, in line 9; otiose *coniunx* at the opening of line 10 (whose removal turns the line into a regular pentameter); unmetrical *uoluī* (from *uōlō*), which must be scanned *uōlūī* for the metre, in the first hemiepes of line 12; otiose *bis* in line 13; and the spelling *uicinos* for *uicenos*, in line 14. See Bücheler 1972: 445 ad *CLE* 965.

47 I am grateful to Elaine Fantham, Judy Hallett, Sharon James, and Hugh Mason for discussion concerning the translation of the elegiac couplets, especially the penultimate couplet, though they do not necessarily agree with the translation I offer here.

48 On the *carmina epigraphica*, see Galletier 1922; Lissberger 1934; Lattimore 1962; Chevallier 1972; Mayer, Miró, and Velaza 1998; Cugusi 2003 and 2007; Schmidt 2015.

49 For references to the gravestone, see Lattimore 1962: 81; for references to the house of Hades, see id. 168; for the sentiment that death comes to all, see id. 255, with n. 313, which cites line 11 of our inscription (= 9 of the elegiacs, *CE* 965.9).

50 Lattimore 1962: 171, who cites it as the earliest instance of this figure in a Latin inscription.

51 Lattimore 1962: 284, notes that "the *liberta* may also be *coniunx*," citing *CIL* III 5563, 7868; V 580; VI 2584. See also Treggiari 1991: 572, "Index of Subjects" s.v. *libertae*, – *liberta et coniunx*.

52 See Treggiari 1991: 243–9 on the formulaic expression of *coniugalis amor* in Latin inscriptions.

53 Lattimore 1962: 299.

54 Lattimore 1962: 285.

55 The title of Harvey 1992, a study of early modern English literature. She notes (5) that "ventriloquizations of women in the Renaissance achieved the power they did partly because so few women actually wrote and spoke."

56 By contrast, we moderns have laboured to construe the literary significance encoded in their names: see, e.g., Randall 1979; Wyke 2002.

57 ***Augustus***: Trebia M.l. Lesbia (*Tituli* 2 [1980]: 135 Nr. 47); Lezbiae (*CIL* VI 4135). ***Augustus – Nero***: Spur(iae) Sex. l. Lesbiae (*CIL* VI 6809); Avennia (*mulieris*) l. Lezbia (*CIL* VI 14453); Manlia (*mulieris*) l. Lezbia (*CIL* VI 21979).

1st half of the 1st c. CE: Lesbia (*CIL* VI 21200); Clodiae (*mulieris*) l. Lezbiae (*NSA* 1922: 414 Nr. 31). ***Tiberius – Nero***: [Stat]ilia Sisennae [aug]uris l. Lesb[ia] (*CIL* VI 6570). ***1st c. CE***: Postumia (*mulieris*) l. Lesbia (*CIL* VI 24882); Sentia L.l. Lesbia (*CIL* VI 26216); Lesbia l. (*CIL* VI 28023); [- - -]a (*mulieris*) l. Lesbia (*CIL* VI 38462; [- - -] (*mulieris*). l. Lesbia (*Bull. Com.* 51 [1923(1924)]: 106 Nr. 150); Livia L. (*mulieris*) l. Lezbia (*CIL* VI 25772), whose findspot is reported as "*tabula ex lapide Tiburtine in villa Crostarosa*"; Lezbia *lanipend.* Aucti lib. (*Rend Istit Lomb.* 103 [1969]: 94 Nr. 10); Curtiae C.l. Lezbiae (*CIL* VI 16662). ***50–150 CE***: Lesbiae Caes. (*CIL* VI 35672). ***2nd half of the 1st c. CE***: Salvidena (*mulieris*) l. Lesbia (*Epigraphica* 28 [1966(1967)]: 23 Nr. 6).

58 *NSA* 1922: 414 Nr. 31: Clodiae (*mulieris*) l. Lezbiae. On Clodia Metelli, see Hejduk 2008 and Skinner 2011.

59 There is also a single attestation of the Greek name Δηλία on a Hellenistic inscription probably from Athens (*IG* II^2 1534 B, c. 259/8 BCE): see *LGPN* II 102 s.v. Δηλία.

60 I have found no attestations of the name Κυνθία in the Greek epigraphic record.

61 The worker is tentatively defined by the *OLD*, s.v. 1, as "(prob.) A female secretary or copyist," while Treggiari 1976: 78, identifies her as "a store-room clerk, perhaps working under a storekeeper, *cellarius*." The inscription, in the epigraphic collection of the Capitoline Museums in Rome, has been re-edited: see *AE* 1992, 92, no. 22.

62 *Argentaria | Albana fecit | Corinnae | Argentariae matri | quae u(ixit) a(nnis) L.* Mother and daughter share the same gentilician, but their *praenomina* are Greek (Corinna) and Latin (Albana), respectively, which may imply either the daughter's free birth and the mother's marriage to her patron, or the daughter's birth as a *verna* to her enslaved mother and then the pair's manumission by the same patron; cf. Bruun 2013, on Latin names for *vernae*.

63 The name is attested epigraphically in the Greek world, on a Latin inscription from Pompeii, datable to the late Republic or early Principate, of the freedwoman Poppaea Corinna: see *LGPN* IIIA 255. The name is also used of a Greek *hetaera* by Lucian, in his *Dialogue of Courtesans* 6.

64 Solin 2003: 469–70. The name is also widely attested in the Greek epigraphic record: *LPGN* records nine examples of the name, with one each from Crete (*IC* 3 p. 71 no. 49), Cyrene (*BMI* 1060), Leuctra (*IG* V.1, 1330) and Macedonia (*SEG* XLIX 699), and five from southern Italy (four of the five in Latin), including the freedwoman Furia Nemesis (*PdelP* 33 [1978] 64 no. 8): see *LPGN* IIIA 312 s.v. Νέμεσις.

65 On female slaves in elite Roman households, see Treggiari 1976: 76–80 on *ancillae*, 90–2 on entertainers.

66 ***1st half 1st c. CE***: [I]ulia Nemesis *saltatrix* (*CIL* VI 10143); Nemesidi (*CIL* VI 38463a); Domatia Nemesis (*CIL* VI 16910); Sextia Nemesis (*CIL* VI 26532). ***Tiberius – Nero***: Claudia Nemesis (*CIL* VI 8961); Nemesis Nicenis Tauri

l. *ancilla* (*CIL* VI 6490). ***1st c.*** CE: Nemesis (VI 22900); Ussienia Nemesis (*CIL* VI 29606); Nemesidi (*CIL* VI 7912); cf. *vern.* Nemesine (*CIL* VI 15561).

67 ***2nd c.*** CE: Cannutiae Nemesi (*CIL* VI 23787); Aeiatia Nemesis (*CIL* VI 10608); Nemesis (*CIL* VI 16275). ***2nd/3rd c.*** CE: [N]emesis (*Bull. Com.* 88 [1982–1983]: 137 Nr. 62).

68 *AP* 5.273 (Agathias); 9.260 (Secundus of Tarentum), 405; 11.326 (Automedon); 12.193, 229 (Strato), 140 (anon.), 141 (Meleager).

69 Smith 1913: 53.

70 2.3.59–60: *uota loquor: regnum ipse tenet quem saepe coegit | barbara gypsatos ferre catasta pedes* ("My words are day-dreams. King is the very man whom often | a foreign scaffold forced to mark time with chalked feet").

71 On the eastern provenance of the articles of Nemesis' luxurious toilette, see Miller 1969: 104–5, 108; Dalby 2000: 168–72 and 184; and Maltby 2002: 408–10 *ad loc.*, with further bibliography. On the moralizing tradition against the luxury associated with "effeminacy" (*mollitia*), see Edwards 1993: 63–97. On luxurious dress and its association with Greek licence, see Griffin 1986: 10.

72 Nisbet and Hubbard 1970: 373, ad *C.* 1.33.7; Solin 2003: 690.

73 Solin 1996: 309. Afrania Areth[usa] (*CIL* VI 11207), Julia Ti. liberta Arethusa (*CIL* VI 20378), Arethusa [I]asonis (*RPAA* 63 [1990–1991(1993)]: 265 Nr. 107 *fig.* 1 *c*), Fufiae C.l. Arethusae (*CIL* VI 18591), and Arethusae (*CIL* VI 22341). The name is widely attested epigraphically in the Greek world as well, with seven occurrences, including two in Latin from southern Italy, Venusia (Lat. Arethusa, *CIL* IX 520) and Puteoli (Lat. Pullia Arethusa, *CIL* X 2901) respectively: see *LGPN* II 49, IIIA 53, IV 57, and VA 59 s.v. Ἀρέθουσα.

74 For the durability of the name, cf. *CIL* VI 10471, *Acanthidi*, from the 2nd or 3rd c. CE. The name is attested epigraphically in the Greek world from Cyrene (*SEG* IX, 45.7, 5th c. BCE; *SEG* IX, 49.12, 4th c. BCE) and Leukas (*IG* IX.1, 553, probably of Hellenistic date): see *LGPN* I 22 and IIIA 21, s.v. Ἄκανθις.

75 Solin 2003: 606 and cf. Hutchinson 2006: 195 ad Prop. 4.8.29. On the possible Gallan resonance of the name Phyllis (cf. Verg. *Buc.* 10.37–41), see Fabre-Serris 2008: 65n34. Of Augustan date are Phylis (*CIL* VI 4304), probably a slave, and Iulia Phyllis (VI 26608), presumably a freedwoman; and of Julio-Claudian date are Aurelia M. l. Phyllis (VI 38076) and Claudia Phyllis *liberta* (VI 15178), both clearly freedwomen; Antoniae Phyllidi (VI 12064), Domitia Phyllis (VI 35359), Viselliae Phyllidi (VI 29033), and Phyllis l. (VI 16308), presumably freedwomen; and two other Phyllides (VI 6501, 8834), both probably slaves. Phyllis Statiliae *sarcinatr(ix)* (VI 6351), of Tiberian to Neronian date, was a "mender of clothes," perhaps a slave attached to the household of the Statilii. On lower-class women's jobs in grand households, see Treggiari 1976, 1979.

76 Hutchinson 2006: 196, ad Prop. 4.8.31.

77 ***Julio-Claudian***: Caeciliae Petale (*CIL* VI 13840); Iulia Petale (*CIL* VI 20601); Furiae Petale (*CIL* VI 5238). ***1st c.*** CE: Papiria Petale (*CIL* VI 23792); Furiae A.l. Petale

(*NSA* 1920: 283); Petalenis (*CIL* VI 5457); Sulpicia C.l. Petale (*LIKM* 81), probably the same woman commemorated in an inscription, quoted in the text, of Augustan date (*Bull. Com.* 53 [1925]: 229 = *AE* 1928, 73). ***2nd or 3rd c.*** CE: [- - -]tiae Peta[le?] (*CIL* VI 23970); Pontiae Petale (*CIL* VI 24750). ***4th or 5th c.*** CE: Πετάλη (*ICUR* 4039 = *IG* XIV 2103). On the attestation of the name Petale in the Greek world (five from Athens, and one each from Paros and Tenos), including southern Italy (from Neapolis, *CIL* X 8172: Lat. Octavia Petale, presumably a freedwoman), see *LGPN* I 371, II 367, IIIA 361 s.v. Πετάλη; and cf. Knox 2004: 166–7.

78 Hallett 2009, with further bibliography.

79 Solin 1996: 563; cf. Solin 2003: 615. ***Augustus***: Liviae Lalage l. (*CIL* VI 3940a); the findspot of the epitaph was the *Monumentum Liviae*, so we may assume that she was a freed slave from the household of Augustus' wife Livia. ***Julio-Claudian***: Claudiae Lalage (*Epigraphica* 5–6 [1943–1944 (1945)]: 19 Nr. 103); Iun[ia] Lalage *pediseq[ua]* (*CIL* VI 9778); Iulia Lalage (*CIL* VI 20547). ***1st c.*** CE: Terent[- - -] Lalage[- - -] (*CIL* VI 27242); Statiae Lalageni (*CIL* VI 13726); Lalage (Mart. 2.66.3, 5; cf. *PIR*[2] L 75. ***2nd c.*** CE: Claudia Lalage (*CIL* VI 4865). On the attestation of the name Lalage in Latin verse (Hor. *C.* 1.22.10, 23; 2.5.16; Mart. 2.66.3, 5; *Priapea* 4.3) and in southern Italian inscriptions from Canusium and Pompeii (Lat. Vellaea Lalage, a freedwoman, *CIL* IX 406; and three slave Lalage, all commemorated in Latin, *CIL* IV 1507, 4391, 3041–2), see Knox 2004, 166. *LGPN* reports no occurrences of the name in the Greek epigraphic record beyond southern Italy.

80 ***1st c.*** CE: Chloridi (*CIL* VI 27687). On the attestation of the name Chloris in classical literature (Hor. *C.* 2.15.18; Ov. *F.* 2.195–8), and the suggestion of the name's popularity in the genre of mime, see Knox 2004: 167–8. *LGPN* reports no occurrences of the name in the Greek epigraphic record.

81 The name is also attested epigraphically in southern Italy, from Canusium (Lat. Dastidia Nape, a freedwoman), but elsewhere in the Greek-speaking world only in [Longus]' *Daphnis and Chloe* (1.6.3, etc.): see *LGPN* I 323, IIA 310 s.v. Νάπη.

82 The findspot of the epitaph commemorating Nape Liviae l. (*CIL* VI 4015) was also the *Monumentum Liviae*, and we may assume that, like Liviae Lalage l. (*CIL* VI 9340a: see n. 79 above), she too was a freed slave from the household of Augustus' wife.

83 The epitaph on which her name is preserved (as *Statilia Nape mater*) commemorates the death of a certain M. Caecilius Diomedes, presumably her son; the findspot is reported as "*in domo Pauli Pini, regione Columnae.*"

84 Solin 2003: 615, notes the possibility that the inscription is from Sutrium, however, citing *AE* 1979, 228.

85 Solin 1996: 376. *LGPN* reports two attestations of the name in the Greek epigraphic record, at Apollonis in Lydia (*TAM* V.2, 1203; V.2, 18; first century BCE) and from Kition in Cyprus (*RDAC* 1968: 78 Nr. 11; of imperial date): see *LGPN* I 298 and VA 280, s.v. Μάραθος.

86 Solin 1996: 261. *LGPN* reports four occurrences of the name in the epigraphic record of the Greek-speaking world, all from southern Italy and in Latin (*CIL* IX 816; X 8059, 240; X 1403g I, 6; and *Inscr. It.* III.1, 286), including two freedmen and the freeborn son of a freedman: *LGPN* IIIA 277 s.v. Λύγδαμος.

87 Solin 1996, 365. ***Augustus – Nero***: Cerinthus C. Caesaris *ostiarius* (*CIL* VI 3996); Cerint[hus] L. Volusi Saturnini (*CIL* VI 34812). ***1st c.*** **CE**: Cerinthus (*CIL* XV 6366). The name is widely attested in the epigraphic record of the Greek-speaking world, with seven Greek occurrences (four over several generations in Lydian Hypaipa, and one each from Ephesus, Klazomenai, and Karystos) and five Latin occurrences from southern Italy (*CIL* IV 4371, X 1920; *Suppl. It.* 5: 67 Nr. 21: three freedmen and two slaves): see *LGPN* I 255, IIIA 241, VA 245 s.v. Κήρινθος.

88 Propertius "signs" eight poems with his *nomen* (2.8.17, 2.14.27, 2.24.35, 2.34.93, 3.3.17, 3.10.15, 4.1.71, 4.7.49); Tibullus two (1.3.55, 1.9.83); Sulpicia one, as *Serui filia Sulpicia* ([Tib.] 3.16); Ovid many more, though with his cognomen Naso (*Am. Epigr.* 1; *Am.* 1.11.27, 2.1.2, 2.13.25; *Ars* 2.744, 3.812; *Rem.* 71, 72, 558), including several of the poems from exile; cf. Catullus' practice in his lyric (e.g., 8.1, 12, 19; etc.) and elegiac poems (68.27, 135; 72.1; 76.5; 79.2, 3; 82.1).

89 On the different roles women can play in the imperial contest (e.g., mother/wife/daughter of the imperial adventurer; his sexual spoils; his racialized domestic servant or slave), see the large transnational feminist literature about the widely varying relationships of women to nineteenth-century European imperialism as evidenced in art, advertising, literature, and politics: e.g., McClintock 1995; Cooper and Stoler 1997; McClintock, Mufti, and Shohat 1997; and Stoler 2002.

90 On the aristocratic lineage of Propertius, see Cairns 2006: 1–69 and Keith 2008: 1–18, both with further bibliography and comparative evidence for the class background of his contemporaries Vergil, Horace, Tibullus, and Ovid. On Gallus, see Boucher 1966, and Cairns 2006: 70–249. On Lynceus as a pseudonym for L. Varius Rufus, see Boucher 1958; Cairns 2006: 295–319; and Hollis 2006: 102. On historical individuals addressed by Ovid, see Syme 1978. It seems impossible, however, to account for Demophoon (the addressee of Prop. 2.22) or Horos (the addressee of Prop. 4.1) in this way, given the current state of the evidence: see Fedeli 2005: 626–30, ad 2.22 init.; Hutchinson 2006: 60, ad 4.1 init.

91 *Contra* Sullivan 1973.

WORKS CITED

Bonamente, G., and C. Santini. 2014. *Atti Convegno Properziano Assisi 2012.* Turnhout.

Boucher, J.-P. 1958. "L'oeuvre de L. Varius Rufus d'après Propèrce II, 34." *RÉA* 60: 307–22.

– 1965. *Études sur Properce. Problèmes d'inspiration et d'art.* Paris.

– 1966. *Caius Cornélius Gallus.* Paris.

Bowditch, L. 2003. "Propertius 2.10 and the Eros of Empire." In *Being There Together: Essays in Honor of Michael C. J. Putnam on the Occasion of His Seventieth Birthday,* edited by P. Thibodeau and H. Haskell, 163–80. Minneapolis.

– 2006. "Propertius and the Gendered Rhetoric of Luxury and Empire: A Reading of 2.16." *Comparative Literature Studies* 43.3: 306–25.

– 2009. "Palatine Apollo and the Imperial Gaze: Propertius 2.31 and 2.32." *AJP* 130: 401–38.

– 2011. "Tibullus and Egypt: A Postcolonial Reading of Elegy 1.7." *Arethusa* 44: 89–122.

– 2012. "Roman Love Elegy and the Eros of Empire." In *A Companion to Roman Love Elegy,* edited by B. Gold, 119–33. Malden, MA.

Bruun, C. 2013. "Greek or Latin? The Owner's Choice of Names for Vernae in Rome." In *Slavery and Material Culture,* edited by M. George, 19–42. Toronto, Buffalo, and London.

Bücheler, F., ed. 1972. *Carmina Latina Epigraphica,* 2 vols. Leipzig; repr. Amsterdam [1895–7].

Cairns, F. 2006. *Sextus Propertius: The Augustan Elegist.* Cambridge.

Chevallier, R. 1972. *Épigraphie et literature à Rome.* Faenza.

Clausen, W.V., ed. 1959. *A. Persi Flacci et D. Iuni Iuvenalis Saturae.* Oxford.

Coarelli, F. 2004. "Assisi, Roma, Tivoli. I luoghi di Properzio." In *Properzio tra storia arte mito. Atti convegno internazationale,* edited by C. Santorini and F. Santucci, 99–115.

Cooper, C. 1995. "Hyperides and the Trial of Phryne." *Phoenix* 49.4: 303–18.

Cooper, F., and A.L. Stoler, eds. 1997. *Tensions of Empire: Colonial Cultures in a Bourgeois World.* Berkeley, Los Angeles, and London.

Cugusi, P. 2003. "Per una nuova edizione dei Carmina Latina Epigraphica. Qualche osservazione metodologica." *Epigraphica* 65: 197–213.

– 2007. *Per un nuovo corpus dei Carmina Latina Epigraphica. Materiali e discussioni, con un appendice sul lusus anfibiologico sugli idionimi.* Edited by M.T. Sblendorio Cugusi. Roma.

Dalby, A. 2000. *Empire of Pleasures: Luxury and Indulgence in the Roman World.* London and New York.

Davidson, J. 1997. *Courtesans and Fishcakes.* London.

Edmondson, J. 2011. "Slavery and the Roman Family." In *The Cambridge World History of Slavery.* 1. *The Ancient Mediterranean World,* edited by K. Bradley and P. Cartledge, 337–61. Cambridge.

Edwards, C. 1993. *The Politics of Immorality in Ancient Rome.* Cambridge.

Fabre-Serris, J. 2008. *Rome, l'Arcadie et la mer des Argonautes*. Lille.
Fantham, E. 1975. "Sex, Status, and Survival in Hellenistic Athens: A Study of Women in New Comedy." *Phoenix* 29.1: 44–74.
– 1995. "Aemilia Pudentilla: or The Wealthy Widow's Choice." In *Women in Antiquity: New Assessments*, edited by R. Hawley and B.M. Levick, 221–32. London.
– 1996. *Roman Literary Culture from Cicero to Apuleius*. Baltimore.
– 2006. *Julia Augusti: the Emperor's Daughter*. Abingdon, New York.
– 2013. *Roman Literary Culture from Plautus to Macrobius*. Baltimore.
Fantham, E., et al. 1994. *Women in the Classical World: Image and Text*. New York and Oxford.
Faraone, C.A., and L.K. McClure, eds. 2006. *Prostitutes and Courtesans in the Ancient World*. Madison, WI.
Fedeli, P., ed. 1984. *Propertius: Bibliotheca Scriptorum Graecorum et Romanorum Teubneriana*. Stuttgart.
– 2005. *Properzio. Il libro secondo*. Cambridge.
Ferrua, A. 1966. "Antiche iscrizioni inedite di Roma." *Epigraphica* 28: 18–49.
Galletier, E. 1922. *Étude sur la poésie funéraire romaine d'après les inscriptions*. Paris.
Glazebrook, A., and M.M. Henry, eds. 2011. *Greek Prostitutes in the Ancient Mediterranean, 800 BCE–200 CE*. Madison, WI.
Griffin, J. 1986. *Latin Poets and Roman Life*. Chapel Hill.
Hallett, J.P. 2009. "Absent Roman Fathers in the Writings of Their Daughters." In *Growing Up Fatherless in Antiquity*, edited by S. Huebner and D.M. Ratzan, 175–91. Cambridge.
– 2011. "Ballio's Brothel, Phoenicium's Letter, and the Literary Education of Greco-Roman Prostitutes: The Evidence of Plautus's *Pseudolus*." In Glazebrook and Henry 2011, 172–96.
Harvey, E.D. 1992. *Ventriloquized Voices*. London.
Hejduk, J.D. 2008. *Clodia: A Sourcebook*. Norman, OK.
Henry, M. 1985. *Menander's Courtesans and the Greek Comic Tradition*. Frankfurt.
– 1995. *Prisoner of History: Aspasia of Miletus and Her Biographical Tradition*. New York.
Hollis, A.S. 2006. "Propertius and Hellenistic Poetry." In *Brill's Companion to Propertius*, edited by H.-C. Günther, 97–125. Leiden.
Hollis, A.S. ed. 2007. *Fragments of Roman Poetry c. 60 BC–AD 20*. Oxford.
Hutchinson, G.O., ed. 2006. *Propertius: Elegies Book IV*. Cambridge.
James, S.L. 2003. *Learned Girls and Male Persuasion: Gender and Reading in Roman Love Elegy*. Berkeley.
Kajanto, I. 1965. *The Latin Cognomina*. Helsinki.

Keith, A.M. 2008. *Propertius, Poet of Love and Leisure.* London.

– 2011. "Lycoris Galli/Volumnia Cytheris: A Greek Courtesan in Rome." *EuGeStA* 1.

Kenney, E.J., ed. 1994. *P. Ovidi Nasonis Amores, Medicamina Faciei Femineae, Ars Amatoria, Remedia Amoris.* Oxford.

Klingner, F., ed. 1962. *Horatius,* Opera. Leipzig.

Knox, P. 2004. "Cynthia's Ghosts in Propertius 4.7." *Ordia Prima* 3: 153–69.

Kurke, L. 1997. "Inventing the 'Hetaira': Sex, Politics and Discursive Conflict in Archaic Greece." *CA (Edinburgh)* 16: 106–50.

– 2002. "Gender, Politics and Subversion in the *Chreiai* of Machon." *PCPS* 48: 20–65.

Laes, C. 2003. "Desperately Different? *Delicia* Children in the Roman Household." In *Early Christian Families in Context,* edited by D. Balch and C. Osiek, 298–324. Grand Rapids, MI.

Lattimore, R. 1962. *Themes in Greek and Latin Epitaphs.* Urbana, IL.

Lee, G., ed. 1990. *Tibullus: Elegies.* Leeds.

Lissberger, E. 1934. *Das Fortleben der römischen Elegiker in den Carmina Epigraphica.* Diss. Tübingen.

Maltby, R. 2002. *Tibullus: Elegies: Text, Introduction and Commentary.* Leeds.

Mankin, D., ed. 1995. *Horatius,* Epodes. Cambridge.

Mayer, M., M. Miró, and J. Velaza. 1998. *Litterae in titulis, tituli in litteris. Elements per a l'estudi de la interacció entre epigrafia i literatura en el món romà.* Barcelona.

Mazzarino, S. 1980–1. "Contributo alla lettura dei Nuovo Gallus (*JRS,* 1979, 157 ss) e alla storia della mima 'Lycoris'." *Helicon* 21–2: 3–26.

McClintock, A. 1995. *Imperial Leather: Race, Gender, and Sexuality in the Colonial Contest.* New York and London.

McClintock, A., Mufti, A., and Shohat, E., eds. 1997. *Dangerous Liaisons: Gender, Nation, and Postcolonial Perspectives.* Minneapolis and London.

McClure, L.K. 2003. *Courtesans at Table: Gender and Greek Literary Culture in Athenaeus.* New York and London.

McGinn, T.A.J. 2004. *The Economy of Prostitution in the Roman World.* Ann Arbor.

McKeown, J.C., ed. 1987. *Ovid:* Amores. *Text, Prolegomena and Commentary in Four Volumes.* Vol. 1. Liverpool.

Miller, J.I. 1969. *The Spice Trade of the Roman Empire, 29* B.C. *to* A.D. *641.* Oxford.

Nielsen, H.S. 1990. "*Deliciae* in Roman Literature and the Urban Inscriptions." *ARID* 19: 79–88.

Nisbet, R.G.M., and M. Hubbard, eds. 1970. *A Commentary on Horace* Odes, *Book I.* Oxford.

Randall, J.G. 1979. "Mistresses' Pseudonyms in Latin Elegy." *LCM* 4: 27–35.

Schmidt, M.G. 2015. "Carmina Latina Epigraphica." In *The Oxford Handbook of Roman Epigraphy*, edited by C. Bruun and J. Edmondson, 764–82. Oxford and New York.

Skinner, M.B. 2011. *Clodia Metelli: The Tribune's Sister.* Oxford.

Smith, K.F. ed. 1913. *Tibullus, the Elegies.* Oxford.

Solin, H. 1971. *Beiträge zur Kenntnis der griechischen Personnenamen in Rom* I. Helsinki.

– 1982. *Die Griechischen Personennamen in Rom.* 3 vols. Berlin.

– 1996. *Die Stadtrömischen Sklavennamen: Ein Namenbuch.* 3 vols. Stuttgart.

– 2002. "Zur Entwicklung des Römischen Namensystems." In *Person und Name,* Ergänzungsband zum Reallexikon der Germanischen Altertumskunde 32, edited by H. Beck et al., 1–17. Berlin and New York.

– 2003. *Die Griechischen Personennamen in Rom.* 2nd ed. 3 vols. Berlin.

Stoler, A.L. 2002. *Carnal Knowledge and Imperial Power: Race and the Intimate in Colonial Rule.* Berkeley, Los Angeles, and London.

Sullivan, J.P. 1973. "The Politics of Elegy." *Arethusa* 5: 17–34.

Syme, R. 1978. *History in Ovid.* Oxford.

Thilo, G., and H. Hagen, eds. 1961. *Servii Grammatici.* 3 vols. Hildesheim.

Traill, A. 2001. "Menander's *Thais* and the Roman Poets." *Phoenix* 55.3-4: 284–303.

Traina, G. 2001. "Lycoris the Mime." In *Roman Women,* edited by A. Fraschetti, 82–99; translated by L. Lappin. Chicago. [Originally published in Italian as *Roma al femminile.* Rome and Bari, 1994.]

Treggiari, S. 1976. "Jobs for Women." *AJAH* 1: 76–104.

– 1979. "Lower Class Women in the Roman Economy." *Florilegium* 1: 65–86.

– 1991. *Roman Marriage:* Iusti Coniuges *from the Time of Cicero to the Time of Ulpian.* Oxford.

Van Buren, A.W. 1927. "Inscriptions from Rome." *AJP* 48: 18–28.

Wyke, M. 2002. *The Roman Mistress: Ancient and Modern Representations.* Oxford.

5

In Manus: Pliny's Letters and the Arts of Mastery*

SARAH BLAKE

Pliny the Younger introduces his collected letters with a casual air; although he composed each individual epistle with some care (*paulo curatius scripsissem*), he asserts that the collection as a whole has been put together randomly (Plin. *Ep.* 1.1.1): *collegi non servato temporis ordine, neque enim historiam componebam, sed ut quaeque in manus venerat* ("I have now assembled them without maintaining chronological sequence, for I was not compiling a history, but as each happened to come to hand"). Pliny's arrangement of the collection has been much discussed; it seems quite clear now that the letters were not in fact arranged at random, but put together with some care and for particular effect.[1] And just as there is more to the story of Pliny's art of anthology, there is more to the story of the phrase *in manus*. A seemingly innocuous expression, the phrase gestures towards an obscured social fact at the core of the collection, namely, that both Pliny's composition practices and his self-portrait as an exemplary Roman man in letters depend intimately on what lay to and under Pliny's hand: his slaves.

The Roman word for hand, *manus*, is used in an enormously wide variety of idiomatic phrases and figures of speech; these expressions might be grouped very generally into several broad conceptual categories: those conveying (1) nearness and proximity; (2) possession or control; (3) technical skill, usefulness or force; (4) authenticity or authorship. Each one of these categories also provides a way to think about slave labour and the role of slaves in the life of elite Roman men like Pliny: slaves (and to some extent freed people) are often physically proximate to the master; they are legally possessed by the master and fall under his control; they perform all manner of tasks from the mundane to those requiring specialized training; they are subject to physical force or violence at any time; they often serve as agents of masterly authority, e.g., as proxies or business agents.[2] What is "to hand," therefore, for Pliny is his slaves. Understanding the polyvalence of his slaves-to-hand has an interesting relevance for the authorial persona created by Pliny in his letter books. In the following discussion, I will argue that Pliny's use of his slaves and sometimes freedmen is as intimate and as easy for him as the use of his own hand; from a phenomenological or experiential perspective it might be more accurate to say that the use of his slaves *is* the use of his own hand. Beginning with expressions built around the term *manus*, this essay aims to illuminate the role of slavery at the core of Pliny's letter collection, and at the core of "Pliny" himself as a master and an author.[3]

The prepositional phrase *in manus* with the verb *venire* conveys the sense of randomness and happenstance proximity that Pliny is aiming for in *Epistles* 1.1, but it also indicates the transfer of something, some object, from the possession of one person to another. So, a person might fall into someone else's hands, *incidere in manus*, i.e., to fall into captivity.[4] In legal language, to be *in manus* is to be under some form of control, as we see in the technical terms for marriage and also for manumission.[5] In Pliny's epistolary world, however, to take something up into one's hands (*sumere in manus*) or to be in another's hands (*in manibus esse*) primarily means to read or be read.[6] The *manus* has a place in both literal and figurative manipulations of bodies and texts.

Pliny's practice of circulating his texts among his friends, primarily his speeches but also his poetry, is a common topic in the letters; in *Ep.* 8.19.2 he puts it succinctly: *est autem mihi moris, quod sum daturus in manus hominum, ante amicorum iudicio examinare* ("It is my practice, before consigning a work to the hands of the public at large, to try it out first on the judgement of friends").[7] Perhaps Pliny's fullest description of this practice is in *Ep.* 7.17, in which he lays out methodically his practice of sending round written versions of his speeches to friends to seek emendations, then revising his work again in response, and then seeking the advice of friends yet again. He is motivated, as he says, by fear, and he must balance out his apprehension, calibrate his audiences, and prepare himself for the reactions both of individuals known to him and of the larger unknown public who looms beyond his inner circle (7.17.15):[8]

> nihil enim curae meae satis est. cogito quam sit magnum dare aliquid in manus hominum, nec persuadere mihi possum non et cum multis et saepe tractandum, quod placere et semper et omnibus cupias.

> There is no limit to my concern. I ruminate on the weight of entrusting something to men's hands, and I cannot persuade myself that I am not to discuss often, and with many, writings which one wishes will gain lasting and universal approval.[9]

For Pliny, the delivery of his writings into the hands of other unknown men is a serious undertaking not to be done lightly. It marks the moment at which an author may win eternal *gloria* but it also marks the author's loss of control of the text, and its submission to the judging audience of anonymous others. It is also the moment, for Pliny, of the creation of a fixed text, one that cannot be recalled and revised. As Sean Gurd has shown, the instability of the circulating text is socially generative for Pliny;[10] once perfected, fixed, and gone, the text ceases to play a productive role in maintaining socio-literary networks of reciprocal friendship. Pliny's letter to Arrianus Maturus in which he asks for editorial assistance with a new speech (*hunc rogo ex consuetudine tua et legas et emendes*) ends with this observation (*Ep.* 1.2.6):

edendum autem ex pluribus causis, maxime quod libelli quos emisimus dicuntur in manibus esse, quamuis iam gratiam nouitatis exuerint; nisi tamen auribus nostris bibliopolae blandiuntur.

Several reasons prompt my need to publish, above all the fact that the works which I have already issued are said to be in men's hands, though they have lost the glamour of being new. But perhaps the booksellers are flattering me.

The published text has moved out of Pliny's hands, the protected circle of his trusted friends and into the hands of unknown men; something new is now demanded.[11]

The metaphor of the publication of the book as a manumission is relevant here: in Horace's *Epistle* 1.20, the published book leaving its master-author's protection and going out into the wide world is figured as a freed or runaway slave.[12] The moment of transition as the book (*liber*) leaves, becomes free (*liber*), and passes out of the hands of the author into the hands of an unknown audience often prompts expressions of anxiety and loss.[13] The work itself may take on a new identity; it will at the very least have a changed relationship with the author to whose reputation it will contribute.[14]

Pliny's concerns about the afterlives of his texts and the future of his reputation recur throughout the *Letters*. The letters themselves, however, do not provoke the same degree of fear. The collection was probably intended as a complement to the speeches and was therefore ancillary to Pliny's really valuable literary work, as he saw it.[15] Pliny's ability to control the content of his letters (particularly through revision for publication) seems to outweigh any concern he might have about sending his epistolary texts out into the world. Whether as a literary convention of epistolarity or as a piece of real-world communication, the letters are predicated on the assumption that they will go forth into the hands of other men.[16]

The letter is surely the literary form most salient to the dynamics of mastery and authority. T.N. Habinek has discussed the long-standing connection in Roman literary history between writing of all forms and material presence, and the opportunities for mastery that arise from this connection. In tracing the development of writing practices in Roman culture as an effective means to assert status, he notes that "writing amplifies the persona of the writer, extending his reach as it were; and it constitutes a mode of ritualization that generates new agencies and new opportunities for mastery."[17] The written word and its circulation allow the masterful presence to be extended. This is particularly the case with letters, which foreground the author and work to enact his presence or his will in his absence. Pliny's corpus is full of examples of purposeful letters.[18]

In this guise, the letter itself is masterly; it possesses and wields a circumscribed measure of the distributed authority of the master, and is therefore functionally like a slave who carries out his master's will or who represents his master's authority by proxy.[19] At the same time, the letters themselves are slave-like in that they are passive conveyances for masterly authority and presence over distance.[20] There is an ambivalence in mastering through the letter: Pliny's letters are written by his "hand" and carried out into the world by his messengers, a copy remaining with him, *in manus*. At the same time "he" is written down in them, made material and thus subject to damage, then passively carried and delivered into other men's hands.

Let us now examine the dynamics of authorship and authority in a selection of Pliny's letters to and about his domestic subordinates, i.e., those most obviously to hand. In these letters we can see aspects of the constitution of "Pliny" as a master-and-author. Consider the role of the letter in two of Pliny's letters to his wife Calpurnia, beginning with *Ep.* 6.7:

scribis te absentia mea non mediocriter adfici unumque habere solacium, quod pro me libellos meos teneas, saepe etiam in uestigio meo colloces. gratum est quod nos requiris, gratum quod his fomentis adquiescis; inuicem ego epistulas tuas lectito atque identidem **in manus** quasi nouas sumo. sed eo magis ad desiderium tui accendor: nam cuius litterae tantum habent suauitatis, huius sermonibus quantum dulcedinis inest! tu tamen quam frequentissime scribe, licet hoc ita me delectet ut torqueat. uale.

You write that my being absent from you causes you no little sadness and that your one consolation is to grasp my writings as a substitute for my person, and that you often place them where I lie next to you. I am happy that you are missing me, and that my books console you as you rest. I in turn keep reading your letters, repeatedly fingering them as if they had newly arrived. But this fires my longing for you all the more, for when someone's letter contains such charm, what sweetness there is in conversing face to face! Be sure to write as often as you can, even though the delight your letters gives me causes me such torture.

Pliny takes his absent wife's letters *in manus* not only to read and reread them, but also as an act of intimacy between them. Though they are physically separated from each other, each one takes the writings of the other as a material substitute; note that Pliny mentions touching and fondling the letters while we hear that Calpurnia places his books in the place left by Pliny, *in uestigio meo*, a phrase indicating the physical closeness of the bed or couch. This eroticized exchange becomes epistolophilia: the physical letter replaces the erotic object, the touch of the spouse.[21]

In another letter to his wife while she is absent, the exchange of physical letters again serves to alleviate the pain of physical separation, but also to substitute for physical presence for the purpose of observation (6.4):

> numqum sum magis de occupationibus meis questus, quae me non sunt passae aut profiscentem te ualetudinis causa in Campaniam prosequi aut profectam e uestigio subsequi. nunc enim praecipue simul esse cupiebam, ut oculis meis crederem quid uiribus quis corpusculo adparares ... quo impensius rogo, ut timori meo cottidie singulis uel etiam binis epistulis consulas. ero enim securior dum lego, statimque timebo cum legero.

> Never have my routine tasks caused me to complain so much, since they have not allowed me either to accompany you when you departed for your convalescence in Campania, or to follow hot on your heels once you had set out. At this time I long to be with you, to witness with my own eyes what you are taking to build up your physical strength ... So with greater urgency I beg you to relieve my apprehension with one or even two letters each day. I shall be free of anxiety as I read them, and fear again as soon as I have finished reading.

Note that the absence of Calpurnia, gone to convalesce in Campania, causes Pliny to remark not only on his discomfort at being absent from her, but almost as importantly, his concern that she be following a regimen of health recovery overseen by him. In her physical absence from him, Calpurnia has, to some measure, passed out of his control. The near-constant exchange of letters (twice a day) goes some way towards maintaining his continued oversight of her behaviour, as the letter aims carefully to show.[22] Certainly Pliny's wife occupies a position in his physical and epistolary world as both a close proximal presence and also as subordinate, a body and a mind, to be mastered. Her absence provides him with a rich literary vein to mine, but Pliny's poeticized desire for his wife goes hand in hand with his interest in her program of education and the regulation of her activity.[23]

As we see in *Ep.* 4.19, Calpurnia has become integrated somewhat into his literary production (4.19.2–4):

accedit his studium litterarum, quod ex mei caritate concepit. meos libellos habet lectitat ediscit etiam. qua illa sollicitudine cum uideor acturus, quanto cum egi gaudio adficitur! disponit qui nuntient sibi quem adsensum quos clamores excitarim, quem euentum iudicii tulerim. eadem, si quando recito, in proximo discreta uelo sedet, laudesque nostras auidissimis auribus excipit. uersus quidem meos cantat etiam formatque cithara non artifice aliquo docente, sed amore qui magister est optimus.

These qualities [intelligence, thrift, and chastity] are enhanced by her enthusiasm for literature, which her love for me has fostered. She possesses and repeatedly reads and even memorizes my books. What concern she shows when I am due to speak in court! And what delight, once the speech is finished! She posts individuals to report to her the assent and the applause which I have received, and the outcome which I have imposed on the judge. Whenever I am giving a recitation, she sits close by, concealed by a curtain, and listens most avidly to the praises heaped on me. She also sings my verses and adapts them to the lyre, with no schooling from a music-master, but with affection, which is the best possible teacher.

Calpurnia's involvement in his literary activities, her way of shadowing him and amplifying his achievements, is a point of pride for Pliny. He has, like Pompeius Saturninus, whom he praises ardently in *Ep.* 1.16.6, "moulded the girl he married into so learned and elegant a wife" (*uxorem quam uirginem accepit, tam doctam politamque reddiderit*).[24]

The creation and maintenance of certain slaves and freedmen useful to his literary pursuits was also a point of pride for Pliny. He famously praises his own mildness, generosity, and care for his domestic slaves, especially during their illnesses and after their death.[25] His concern for Calpurnia's health finds a parallel in his concern for his freedman Zosimus, a highly trained reader (5.19.3–7):

homo probus officiosus litteratus; et ars quidem eius et quasi inscriptio comoedus, in qua plurimum facit. nam pronuntiat acriter sapienter apte decenter etiam … idem tam commode orationes et historias et carmina legit, ut hoc solum didicisse uideatur. haec tibi sedulo exposui, quo magis scires, quam multa unus mihi et quam iucunda ministeria praestaret. accedit longa iam caritas hominis, quam ipsa pericula auxerunt. est enim ita natura comparatum, ut nihil aeque amorem incitet et accendat quam carendi metus; quem ego pro hoc non semel patior. nam ante aliquot annos, dum intente instanterque pronuntiat, sanguinem reiecit atque ob hoc in Aegyptum missus a me post longam peregrinationem confirmatus rediit nuper; deinde dum per continuos dies nimis imperat uoci, ueteris infirmitatis tussicula admonitus rursus sanguinem reddidit. qua ex causa destinaui eum mittere in praedia tua, quae Foro Iulii possides.

He is an honest and dutiful man, and well educated. His specialization and selling-point, so to speak, is as a reciter of comedies, at which he is most adept, for his delivery is clear, correct, appropriate and in good taste as well … He also reads speeches, histories, and poetry so expertly that he gives the impression that this is the sole skill that he has learnt. I have carefully explained all this to you to make you more aware of the numerous and pleasing roles he alone plays for me. Moreover, I have long had an affection for him, and this has increased by reason of these very dangers confronting him. It is a rule of nature that nothing rouses and ignites love so much as fear of loss, and I have more than once entertained this fear, for a few years ago, when in the course of recitation he was straining himself to the utmost, he vomited blood. For this reason I sent him to Egypt, and after a lengthy sojourn abroad, he recently returned restored to health. But subsequently he put too much strain day after day on his vocal chords, and a cough gave him warning of his former weakness, and he again vomited blood. For this reason I have decided to send him to your estate which you own at Forum Iulii.

We learn that Pliny has long cared for Zosimus which means, perhaps, a long period of education and cultivation.[26] This concern for his reciter leads him to send Zosimus, much like one sends a letter, first unsuccessfully to Egypt for recuperation, and then to the household owned by his friend Valerius Paulinus.

In *Ep.* 8.1, Pliny again details the illness of his *lector*, Encolpius, the interruption to his work, and his care for Encolpius' recovery:

iter commode explicui, excepto quod quidam ex meis aduersam ualetudinem feruentissimis aestibus contraxerunt. Encolpius quidem lector, ille seria nostra ille deliciae, exasperatis faucibus puluere sanguinem reiecit. quam triste hoc ipsi, quam acerbum mihi, si is cui omnis ex studiis gratia inhabilis studiis fuerit! quis deinde libellos meos sic leget, sic amabit? quem aures meae sic sequentur? sed di laetiora promittunt. stetit sanguis, resedit dolor. praeterea continens ipse, nos solliciti, medici diligentes. ad hoc salubritas caeli, secessus quies tantum salutis quantum otii pollicentur.

I have accomplished the journey successfully, though with the one snag that one of my servants fell ill in the most oppressive heat. In fact, my reader Encolpius, mainstay of my serious studies and joy of my relaxation, coughed up blood when his throat was irritated by the dust. How grim this will be for him, and what a harsh blow to me, if this disqualifies him for intellectual work, when his entire charm lies in it! Who then will read and savour my books as he does? To whom will my ears be pinned as they are to him? But the gods give promise of a happier outcome. The discharge of blood has stopped, the pain has diminished; then, too, he is a self-controlled patient, we are exercised about him, and the doctors are attentive. Moreover, the healthy climate, the retirement, and the relaxation give promise of a cure as much as of leisure.

Pliny's distress for Encolpius is unabashedly self-interested and again a source of pride for him (worth writing about!), contributing to his self-portrait as a benevolent master.[27] These two letters show Pliny at his paternalistic, solipsistic best, "swallowing up the action, voice, thought and dreams of his slaves," as Sandra Joshel has observed:[28]

> The actions, thoughts and feelings of the ailing Zosimus and Encolpius concern Pliny – only Pliny .... The slave exists in his services to Pliny, his feelings of loss that mirror Pliny's, and his interests that are identified with – and as – his master's.[29]

We might also include Calpurnia in this category of mirrors-to-Pliny, integral parts of the practices through which he produces himself in literature, but in no measure existing as persons or independent agents outside of this relation.

Pliny writes about his slaves as much or more than any other Roman author.[30] These discussions of slaves and slavery, however, primarily serve his program of exemplarity.[31] He describes his practices of slave owning not so much to indicate anything about slavery as an institution, or about specific and real interactions with slaves, but rather to delineate himself as a certain kind of master, and to find both connection to and distinction from other kinds of masters.[32] As his dependents appear in his letters, both travelling away from him and yet remaining with him *in manus*, these epistolary figures, like those in the other letters, form part of a hall of mirrors reflecting back Pliny-the-Master-the-Author to himself.

In the final section of this essay, I wish to examine Pliny's art of mastery more closely and to propose a different model for understanding the ways in which Pliny's authorial mastery came to be and is maintained. The model, drawn from critical sociology, phenomenology, and cognitive archaeology, is necessarily speculative, but offers a chance to see Pliny from a different angle.

In each of the cases I discussed above, Pliny recorded the experience of separation from a person ordinarily to hand: Calpurnia, Zosimus, and Encolpius each fell ill, which created a physical distance between their bodies and the body of their husband, patron, and master. Ordinarily there would exist an unremarkable harmony or even symbiosis among these figures, but the failure of the subordinate body (here the wife, freedman, and slave) creates a fissure, a fault line in the organism I have called Pliny-the-Master-the-Author. Illness as rupture here has made visible aspects of the physical world that typically go unnoticed.[33] And Pliny, as Joshel describes, seizes the moment to display his powers of care: "Pliny, like paternalism itself, makes slaves visible only to make disappear important components of their condition, either by consuming their agency or by rendering it invisible."[34]

Consider again the "illness" of Zosimus and Encolpius. They both sustain injuries from reciting for Pliny: Zosimus too frequently and Encolpius while travelling dusty roads. Pliny used their throats as if they were his own, until it was no longer possible to do so. At these moments of rupture through illness, we see Pliny practising what Bruno Latour might call a form of purification, a separation of himself as *patronus, dominus,* and *uir* as an ontological being distinct from the collective assembly of the *familia.*[35] These moments are marked; the rest of the time these other bodies are unmarked. This act of purification creates two distinct elements out of an undifferentiated whole and retrojects these categories. In daily practice, however, Pliny is not a purified self, but a hybrid self, a person composed of a man and his servile apparatus.[36]

As Horsfall notes, the Roman master's use of readers and secretaries

> in the baths or during a journey is not a matter of antiquarian curiosity. They really do help to spare the eyes of the ophthalmia-prone Roman senator. They really do enable him to continue his work ... and twenty-four hours per day are available for work, if their owner so wishes.[37]

This is the everyday. We know that Pliny was surrounded almost constantly by personal slaves. We know also that the majority if not all of his literary composition was done through and with slave labour: the readers, the secretaries, the trained editors, the copyists, the performing readers, the couriers, the archivists, the grammarians, the researchers, the librarian, the book technicians, in addition to the ones that fetched food and water, plumped pillows, changed chamber pots.[38] To this we may add the rest of the slaves and freed persons near and far who made up the *mei* of Pliny's daily life (e.g., *Ep.* 1.4). Rex Winsbury has called slavery the "enabling infrastructure of Roman literature."[39] It might be more critically true, however, to say that slavery is the enabling infrastructure of the Roman master-author itself.

The status quo is not purification but incorporation, that is, smoothly functioning slaves are not remarkable; they are simply *to hand.* And in this very proximity and ubiquity slaves become integrated so fully into the *corpus* of the Roman master that they cannot be conceptually separated out. From this perspective, slaves are legible only as prosthetic limbs of the master, extensions that serve to amplify not just his *ego* but his *corpus.* The Roman master must then be understood to be a special kind of *persona,* an amplified person who consists in multiple bodies including slave bodies, and whose authorial presence is distributed through these bodies and, in Pliny's case, epistolary bodies.[40]

As has been observed, the great dependence of Roman writers upon slave contributions provoked an anxiety that perhaps explains the many caricatures of slaves and freedmen found throughout Roman literature.[41] It is worth remembering, however, that nearly all Roman literature was produced by master-authors. If the slaves are not legible, as they are almost always not, we must find ways to read them. To this end, I suggest here a handful of methods for fleshing out the *corpus* of the Roman master: first, tracing; second, practising suspicion; and finally, optimistically speculating.

In order to read the illegible slave apparatus, it is necessary to look for traces of the agentic forces at play in the assemblage of slaves subsumed into the "body" of the master, that is, to look for traces of the purification process described above;[42] this can sometimes be done only through unfashionably literal readings of the letters. Consider, for example, the following letter to Tacitus from early in Book 1 (1.6.1–3):

ridebis, et licet rideas. ego, ille quem nosti, apros tres et quidem pulcherrimos cepi. "ipse?" inquis. ipse; non tamen ut omnino ab inertia mea et quiete discederem. ad retia sedebam; erat in proximo non uenabulum aut lancea, sed stilus et pugillares; meditabar aliquid enotabamque, ut si manus uacuas, plenas tamen ceras reportarem.

You will laugh at this and your laughter is in order. This acquaintance of yours has captured three boars, and most handsome ones at that. "What, you yourself?" you ask. Yes, but without totally abandoning my idle and restful life. I would sit by the nets, armed not with hunting spear or lance, but with pen and tablets. I would contemplate some subject and jot it down, so that if I returned empty-handed, my tablets would be full.

Pliny boasts to his friend Tacitus that he himself has captured three boars while hunting and underlines his solo achievement: *"ipse?" inquis. ipse!*[43] On the surface this warm little letter serves to further an intimacy with Tacitus, and to play with one of Pliny's recurring themes, idleness (*otium*) and literary productivity in various settings, here, specifically, woodland.[44] Writing is compared to hunting, and the instruments required for each are cleverly compared. Note, however, in this letter the total integration and incorporation of slave labour into Pliny's activity. When Pliny says *ipse*, he includes the slaves who accompanied him and who assisted in carrying the equipment, setting the nets, killing the boar and protecting Pliny, and carrying the fruits of the hunt back home again.[45]

An essential element of Pliny's creativity is the restful solitude of the woods: *iam undique siluae et solitudo ipsumque illud silentium quod uenationi datur, magna cogitationis incitamenta sunt* ("The woodland all around, the solitude, and the silence imposed by the hunt are great incentives to thought," 1.6.2).

Was Pliny truly alone in the sense that we understand? It seems clear that he was not, for he was accompanied at the very least by *uenatores*. And even when we accept that Pliny may have written this letter without ever venturing near the woods, intending perhaps only an ironic comment on Tacitus' *Dialogus*, it is still the case that the letter was produced in the company of and with the collaboration of slaves.[46] The important point here is that for Pliny, "alone" means "alone with slaves"; and solitude means solitude from other *uiri*, such as Tacitus, whose status gives them legibility to our modern eyes.

Pliny's idea of silence and solitude includes the presence of slaves. In his villa at Laurentum, for example, there is a degree of *silentium* that Pliny carefully underlines as extraordinary (2.17.22). He describes an unusual feature of the house, a special chamber built deep inside the house in which he can sleep undisturbed (2.17.22):

iunctum est cubiculum noctis et somni. non illud uoces seruolorum, non maris murmur, non tempestatum motus non fulgurum lumen, ac ne diem quidem sentit, nisi fenestris apertis. tam alti abditique secreti illa ratio, quod interiacens andron parietem cubiculi hortique distinguit atque ita omnem sonum media inanitate consumit.

Attached to it is a chamber for sleeping at night. There, nothing is heard of the voices of confidential slaves, or the gentle sound of the sea, or the lashings of storms; nothing is seen of lightning flashes or even of daylight unless the windows are open. The reason for this dense and buried seclusion lies in the intervening passage which separates the bedroom wall from that of the garden; thus the empty space absorbs all the noise.

It is here – entombed – that Pliny is in total silence, without the sound of his slaves in conversation; note that this sound is compared to the murmuring of the sea, a natural constant. Note also that Pliny means here only that his slaves do not speak to him or to each other. This kind of silence does not preclude Pliny speaking to his slaves (as one speaks to oneself), or of communicating with his slaves non-verbally.[47] Slaves may yet be present. *Silentium* and *solitudo* are contingent upon the context.

A second method for reading illegible slaves is to practise suspicion. I present an example of a suspicious archaeology of language. In his description of the role of slaves and the question of authorial autography (*sua manu*), Myles McDonnell reminds us of the possibilities of causative verb use:[48]

Transitive active verbs are used with a causative sense not infrequently in Latin, but only when it is clear from the context that the subject him or herself does not perform the action. So a Latin author would write … *describo*, I copy, when what he meant was "my slave copies," much as a professor might tell a colleague "I am photocopying your article" when in reality the job is being done by a student.[49]

The hybridity of action in literary production can be disguised even in simple language. In this light, consider the following snippet from a letter Pliny wrote for his friend Ursus (8.9.1):

olim non librum in manus, non stilum sumpsi, olim nescio quid sit otium quid quies, quid denique illud iners quidem, iucundum tamen nihil agere nihil esse.

It is some time since I held a book or pen, and for some time I have known no leisure or relaxation – in short, that sluggish but blessed life of doing nothing and being nothing.

Pliny describes picking up the pen himself, taking up the book, but perhaps we should be suspicious of his use of the first person to indicate only his unique body. The issue cannot be resolved, but the possibility of hybrid Pliny+slave action must be invoked here. McDonnell raises the question of context; Pliny's *ego* is one man in second-century CE Rome, but it is possible that in a modern context, this *ego* should be understood to be a hybrid, constituted in the bodies of multiple men and women.

In the face of these potentially dead ends, let us turn finally to the practice of optimistic speculation, or, trying to look at the evidence from a different perspective, in the hope that the practice of trying itself may bring about development. To this end, I adduce here some basic theory from the world of cognitive science. Recent work in cognitive science and archaeology has shown that the human mind does not only exist in the brain, but has always been to some degree constituted in the body and in the environment. The tools and other objects that surround us do in fact extend the functional architecture of the human cognitive system.[50] From the beginning of the human species, human cognition has only been possible through material engagement. As philosophers of the embodied mind have argued, our humanity is fundamentally cyborg; we are "shifting coalitions of tools."[51] The human mind, the human sense of self, includes and is structured by both social and physical aspects of our environment; these human selves are historically contingent. As the cane of the blind man becomes part of his personhood, as "digital natives" live through their smartphones, so too slave apparatus was the enabling technology of the Roman master and his performance of self.[52] Roman masters were cyborgs; it remains to speculate about the degree of this hybridity, how it functioned, how it was expressed, and how it was experienced by either "master" or "slave." It is not possible to know fully, but neither should it be possible to ignore the dynamics of this hybridity in the study of Roman literary culture.

This argument does not intend to deny humanity, self, subjectivity, or agency to ancient slaves, or, in so far as it does, it seeks also to deny the humanity of Roman masters; Roman masters are amplified personae, monstrous perhaps as the Hundred-Handed Giants of Greek mythology. Nor does the argument seek to conceal the abusive exploitation and loathsome violence intrinsic to slave societies. Rather it is a call to historicize the concepts of agency and personhood.[53] Reading "Pliny" in and into his letters should prompt us to think harder about the texts we have to hand.

NOTES

* It is a great honour to contribute an essay to a volume dedicated to Elaine Fantham, whose body of work has been profoundly influential for me, as for so many scholars of the world of Roman literature. This essay is written in gratitude and admiration.

1 Barchiesi 2005: 330–2; Marchesi 2008; Gibson 2012: 67–8. On the letters as personal history, see Gibson and Morello 2012: 9–19.

2 On the historical realities of slavery at Rome, see Bradley 1987 and 1994. On freedpeople, Mouritsen 2011.

3 On Pliny's letters as self-fashioning or self-portraiture from a variety of theoretical perspectives, see Leach 1990; Riggsby 1995 and 1998; Roller 1998; and Henderson 2002 and 2003.

4 Sen. *Ep.* 4.9.1.

5 Gaius, *Inst.* 1.108 on *manus* marriage; 1.17 on *manumission.*

6 E.g., *Ep.* 1.16.3, 7.30.5, 8.3.3. Cf. Hor. *Ep.* 2.1.53: *Naevius in manibus non est* ("is not Naevius read?").

7 Starr 1987 on the general patterns of text circulation amongst elite Romans.

8 Gurd (2012: 106–26) shows how Pliny creates multiple audiences with differing social relevance for his text both in this letter and elsewhere.

9 The text of Pliny's letters used here is Mynors 1963. Translations of these letters are by P.G. Walsh (2006), unless otherwise noted. The translation here has been slightly adapted.

10 Gurd 2012. See also Riggsby 1998.

11 Cf. *Ep.* 9.11 in which Pliny records learning that his books have sold out in Lyons (9.11.2). He notes that he considers his work "as quite the finished article when the opinions of people scattered over such widely different regions are as one about it" (*incipio enim satis absolutum existimare, de quo tanta diversitate regionum discreta hominum iudicia consentiunt*).

12 Oliensis 1995; Dupont 2009: 152–6.

13 E.g., Ov. *Tristia* 1.1.1–4; Martial 1.2.

14 See Roman 2006 on the dynamics of authorial presence played out in poetry about lost or absent tablets and, from a different angle, Seo 2009 on plagiarism in the texts of Martial.

15 See, among other discussions of this topic, Fitzgerald 2007. On Pliny's relationship to his epistolary models Cicero and Seneca, with bibliography of previous scholarship, see Gibson and Morello 2012: 74–103.

16 On the conventions of ancient epistolography generally, see Malherbe 1988; Rosenmeyer 2001; Trapp 2003; Poster 2007; Ebbeler 2010.

17 Habinek 2009: 121–2; Woolf 1996; Habinek 2005a and 2005b.

18 It has been observed that generally the letters are devoid of the practical details that would have made them truly efficacious. The issue arises in discussions of revision in the letters and the degree to which the published letters differ from their "real" counterparts; See Bell 1989. One could argue, to the contrary, that stripping the letters of practical details in the revision process leaves *only* the authoritative component of the communication; in this light, Pliny is performing an abstraction of authority to highlight the strength of his influence.

19 See Fitzgerald 2000 on slaves as proxies and go-betweens in Roman literature, especially 55–68.

20 See McCutcheon 2013 for an insightful analysis of the material culture of Cicero's epistolography, including slaves as couriers, amanuenses, etc. The classic example of letter-as-slave is in Hdt. 5.35: the scalp of the slave is tattooed with a secret message, his hair is regrown, and he travels safely through enemy lines, where his head is shaved again to reveal the message. DuBois 2003: 3.

21 Separation itself is rarely an issue in Pliny's letters but these letters are exceptions (Edwards 2005: 281). Pliny's letters to friends often complain of the time between letters, but less of physical distance and separation.

22 Pliny's inclusion of the detail that Calpurnia has gone to Campania makes it clear that the letter was intended to be read by an outside audience, as an "opened letter" (Henderson 2003; de Pretis 2003). Presumably Calpurnia would know that she was, in fact, in Campania, having received his letter there.

23 On Pliny as the creator of an ideal wife as part of his own self-image, see Carlon 2009: 138–85; on Pliny and wives in general, Shelton 2013: 93–176. An interesting comparison can be made here with the letters of Cicero to Terentia: Gunderson 2007.

24 Gunderson 1997 on the erotic poetics of letters like *Ep.* 1.16; in this letter Pliny's intense amatory feelings about Pompeius Saturninus are reined in somewhat by this reference to the appropriate object of passion for men like Pliny, the proper education of a proper wife.

25 *Ep.* 8.16 is the fullest discussion of Pliny's principles of slave management.

26 Note the dual sense of *caritas* as affection and costliness, approximated by the English "dearness" perhaps.

27 Playful echoes of Catullus 8 in Plin. *Ep.* 8.1.3 suggest that Pliny found some literary delight in his account of Encolpius' troubles.

28 Joshel 2011.

29 Joshel 2011: 235; 237. See also Stewart 2012 on paternalism and manumission in Plautus for a similar argument.

30 On the invisibility of slaves in Roman literature, Fitzgerald 2000; Reay 2003; 2005; Habinek 2005b; Joshel 2011. See Gonzalès 2003 for a complete review of the slaves and freedmen mentioned in Pliny's letters. Gonzalès 2007: 308 for a distinction in Pliny's discussions of slaves as *servi* and as the household, *mei* or *tui*, e.g., in *Ep.* 1.4.

31 Bradley 2010.

32 *Ep.* 1.4, 1.21 and 3.14 are standout examples of this. See Hoffer 1999: 45–55; Gonzalès 2003 and 2007.

33 In Heideggerian or phenomenological terms, Pliny's equipment or tools of himself (wife, trained slaves, and freedmen) have gone from ready-to-hand to present-at-hand (Heidegger 2010 [1953]).

34 Joshel 2011: 234.

35 Latour 1993, 2005.

36 Blake 2012.

37 Horsfall 1995: 54. Cf. Pliny's bout of eye disease, requiring him to travel in a dark shuttered carriage and be read to, presumably by some slave with the special ability to see in the dark: *hic non stilo modo uerum etiam lectionibus difficulter sed abstineo, solisque auribus studeo. Cubicula obductis uelis opaca nec tamen obscura facio* ("Here I renounce not only my pen, but also my sight-reading, and am confining myself to listening. I keep the rooms in shadow by drawing the curtains but without totally excluding the light," 7.21.1).

38 Starr 1991; Horsfall 1995; McDonnell 1996; Houston 2002.

39 Winsbury 2009.

40 Habinek 2005b; Blake 2012. On the anthropological theory of distributed personhood, key texts are Strathern 1988 and Gell 1998.

41 Habinek 2005b: 385.

42 Latour 2005 on tracing out the associations of agents in the performance of an action.

43 Cf. *Ep.* 9.10.

44 Gibson and Morello 2012: 162–3. Hoffer 1999 on villas as literary factories. Leach 2003 on *otium*.

45 Ancient hunting technique: see Anderson 1985. Cf. *Dig.* 32.99.1 (Paulus): *venatores et aucupes utrum in urbanis an in rusticis contineantur, potest dubitari: sed dicendum est, ubi pater familias moraretur et hos alebat, ibi eos*

numerari ("Doubts may arise about whether slaves used for hunting or fowling should be included amongst the urban or the rural slaves. They should be listed as belonging there where the head of the household kept them and fed them," trans. Wiedemann 1981: 117–18, no. 126).

46 Edwards 2008.

47 As Pliny describes in 9.36 (about his Tuscan villa this time), he is wont to lie in bed alone in darkness for the first hour of the day, after which he calls in his secretary to let in the light, to open the windows (9.36.2).

48 McDonnell 1996: 483.

49 McDonnell suggests (1996: 489n76) that this use of the causative verb in actions relating to literary production is influenced by the Greek middle, since Roman literature was deeply Greek.

50 Malafouris 2013; Knappett and Malafouris 2008; Menary 2010.

51 Malafouris 2013; Clark 2003 and 2008; Clark and Chalmers 1998.

52 Prensky 2001.

53 An issue particularly when "self" is used as shorthand for a kind of subjectivity or humanity that scholars seek (on good principle) to grant retroactively to the oppressed peoples of the past, e.g., Knapp 2011: 169: "Slavery deprived the slave of self-determination, but it did not deprive him of self-identity. He remained a thinking, feeling, acting human being, and lived with slavery coping as best he could." See Johnson 2003 on the discourse of "agency" in American slave studies.

WORKS CITED

Anderson, J.K. 1985. *Hunting in the Ancient World*. Berkeley.

Barchiesi, A. 2005. "The Search for the Perfect Book. A P.S. to the New Posidippus." In *The New Posidippus: A Hellenistic Poetry Book*, ed. K. Gutziller, 320–42. Oxford.

Bell, A. 1989. "A Note on Revision and Authenticity in Pliny's Letters." *AJP* 110.3: 460–6.

Blake, S. 2012. "Now You See Them: Slaves and Other Objects as Elements of the Roman Master." *Helios* 39.2: 193–211.

Bradley, K. 1987. *Slaves and Masters in the Roman Empire: A Study in Social Control*. Oxford and New York.

– 1994. *Slavery and Society at Rome*. Cambridge.

– 2010. "The Exemplary Pliny." In *Studies in Latin Literature and Roman History XV*, edited by C. Deroux, 384–422. Collection *Latomus* 323. Brussels.

Carlon, J. 2009. *Pliny's Women: Constructing Virtue and Creating Identity in the Roman World*. New York.

Clark, A. 2003. *Natural Born Cyborgs: Minds, Technologies, and the Future of Human Intelligence*. Oxford.

Clark, A. 2008. *Supersizing the Mind: Embodiment, Action, and Cognitive Extension*. Oxford.

Clark, A., and D. Chalmers. 1998. "The Extended Mind." *Analysis* 58.1: 7–19.

de Pretis, A. 2003. "'Insincerity,' 'Facts' and 'Epistolarity': Approaches to Pliny's Epistles to Calpurnia." *Arethusa* 36.2: 127–46.

DuBois, P. 2003. *Slaves and Other Objects*. Chicago and London.

Dupont, F. 2009. "The Corrupted Boy and the Crowned Poet." In Johnson and Parker 2009: 143–63.

Ebbeler, J. 2010. "Letters." In *The Oxford Handbook of Roman Studies*, edited by A. Barchiesi and W. Scheidel, 464–76. Oxford.

Edwards, C. 2005. "Epistolography." In Harrison 2005: 270–83.

Edwards, R. 2008. "Hunting for Boars with Pliny and Tacitus." *CA* 27: 35–58.

Fitzgerald, W. 2000. *Slavery and the Roman Literary Imagination*. Cambridge.

– 2007. "The Letter's the Thing (in Pliny, Book 7)." In *Ancient Letters: Classical and Late Antique Epistolography*, edited by R. Morello and A.D. Morrison, 191–210. Oxford.

Gell, A. 1998. *Art and Agency: An Anthropological Theory*. Oxford.

Gibson, R.K. 2012. "On the Nature of Ancient Letter Collections." *JRS* 102: 56–78.

Gibson, R.K., and R. Morello. 2012. *Reading the Letters of Pliny the Younger: An Introduction*. Cambridge.

Gonzalès, A. 2003. *Pline le Jeune. Esclaves et affranchis à Rome*. Paris.

– 2007. "Peur des affranchis impériaux et compassion envers les affranchis privés dans l'oeuvre de Pline le Jeune." In *Fear of Slaves, Fear of Enslavement in the Ancient Mediterranean*, edited by A. Serghidou, 307–24. Besançon.

Gunderson, E. 1997. "Catullus, Pliny, and Love-Letters." *TAPA* 127: 201–31.

– 2007. "S.V.B.; E.V." *CA* 26.1: 1–48.

Gurd, S. 2012. *Work in Progress: Literary Revision as Social Performance in Ancient Rome*. New York.

Habinek, T.N. 2005a. *The World of Roman Song: From Ritualized Speech to Social Order*. Baltimore.

– 2005b. "Slavery and Class." In *A Companion to Latin Literature*, edited by S.J. Harrison, 385–93. Malden, MA.

– 2009. "Situating Literacy at Rome." In Johnson and Parker 2009: 114–40.

Heidegger, M. 2010 [1953]. *Being and Time*. Albany, NY.

Henderson, J. 2002. *Pliny's Statue: The Letters, Self-Portraiture, and Classical Art*. Exeter.

– 2003. "Portrait of the Artist as a Figure of Style: P.L.I.N.Y's Letters." *Arethusa* 36.2: 115–25.

Hoffer, S.E. 1999. *The Anxieties of Pliny the Younger*. Atlanta.

Horsfall, N. 1995. "Rome Without Spectacles." *G&R* 42.1: 49–56.

Houston, G.W. 2002. "The Slave and Freedman Personnel of Public Libraries in Ancient Rome." *TAPA* 132: 139–76.

Johnson, W. 2003. "On Agency." *Journal of Social History* 37.1: 113–24.

Johnson, W.A., and H.N. Parker, eds. 2009. *Ancient Literacies: The Culture of Reading in Greece and Rome*. New York.

Joshel, S. 2011. "Slavery and Roman Literary Culture." In *The Cambridge World History of Slavery.* 1. *The Ancient Mediterranean World*, edited by K. Bradley and P. Cartledge, 214–40. Cambridge.

Knapp, R.C. 2011. *Invisible Romans*. Cambridge, MA.

Knappett, C., and L. Malafouris, eds. 2008. *Material Agency: Towards a Non-Anthropocentric Approach*. New York.

Latour, B. 1993. *We Have Never Been Modern*. Cambridge, MA.

– 2005. *Reassembling the Social: An Introduction to Actor Network Theory*. New York.

Leach, E.W. 1990. "The Politics of Self-Presentation in Pliny's Letters and Roman Portrait Sculpture." *CA* 9: 14–39.

– 2003. "*Otium* as *Luxuria*: Economy of Status in the Younger Pliny's Letters." *Arethusa* 36.2: 147–65.

Malafouris, L. 2013. *How Things Shape the Mind: A Theory of Material Engagement*. Cambridge, MA.

Malherbe, A.J. 1988. *Ancient Epistolary Theorists*. Atlanta.

Marchesi, I. 2008. *The Art of Pliny's Letters: A Poetics of Allusion in the Private Correspondence*. Cambridge.

McCutcheon, R. 2013. *An Archaeology of Cicero's Letters: A Study of Late Republican Textual Culture*. PhD diss. University of Toronto.

McDonnell, M. 1996. "Writing, Copying and Autograph Manuscripts in Ancient Rome." *CQ* 46.2: 469–91.

Menary, R., ed. 2010. *The Extended Mind*. Cambridge, MA.

Mouritsen, H. 2011. *The Freedman in the Roman World*. Cambridge.

Mynors, R.A.B., ed. 1963. *C. Plini Caecili Secundi Epistularum Libri Decem*. Oxford.

Oliensis, E. 1995. "Life after Publication: Horace's *Epistles* 1.20." *Arethusa* 28: 209–24.

Poster, C. 2007. "A Conversation Halved: Epistolary Theory in Greek and Roman Antiquity." In *Letter-Writing Manuals and Instructions from Antiquity to the Present*, edited by C. Poster and L.C. Mitchell, 21–51. Columbia, SC.

Prensky, M. 2001. "Digital Natives, Digital Immigrants." *On the Horizon* 9.5: 1–6.

Reay, B. 2003. "Some Addressees of Virgil's Georgics and Their Audience." *Vergilius* 49: 17–41.

– 2005. "Agriculture, Writing and Cato's Aristocratic Self-Fashioning." *CA* 24: 331–61.

Riggsby, A. 1995. "Pliny on Cicero and Oratory: Self-Fashioning in the Public Eye." *AJP* 116: 123–35.
– 1998. "Self and Community in the Younger Pliny." *Arethusa* 31.1: 75–97.
Roller, M. 1998. "Pliny's Catullus: The Politics of Literary Appropriation." *TAPA* 128: 265–304.
Roman, L. 2006. "A History of Lost Tablets." *CA* 25: 351–88.
Rosenmeyer, P. 2001. *Ancient Epistolary Fictions: The Letter in Greek Literature*. Cambridge.
Seo, J.M. 2009. "Plagiarism and Poetic Identity in Martial." *AJP* 130.4: 567–93.
Shelton, J.-A. 2013. *The Women of Pliny's Letters*. New York.
Starr, R.J. 1987. "The Circulation of Literary Texts in the Roman World." *CQ* 37.1: 213–23.
– 1991. "Reading Aloud: *Lectores* and Roman Reading," *CJ* 86: 337–43.
Stewart, R. 2012. *Plautus and Roman Slavery*. Malden, MA.
Strathern, M. 1988. *The Gender of the Gift: Problems with Women and Problems with Society in Melanesia*. Berkeley.
Trapp, M.B. 2003. *Greek and Latin Letters: An Anthology with Translation*. Cambridge.
Walsh, P.G. 2006. *Pliny the Younger, Complete Letters*. Oxford.
Wiedemann, T.E.J. 1981. *Greek and Roman Slavery: A Sourcebook*. London and New York.
Winsbury, R. 2009. *The Roman Book: Books, Publishing, and Performance in Classical Rome*. London.
Woolf, G. 1996. "Monumental Writing and the Expansion of Roman Society in the Early Empire." *JRS* 86: 22–39.

PART II

Revolutionary Poetics

6

Ovid's Circe and the Revolutionary Power of *carmina* in the *Remedia amoris*

BARBARA WEIDEN BOYD*

for Elaine, with gratitude and affection –
hoc tibi, quod potui, confectum munus pro multis redditur officiis

Ovid's *Remedia amoris* has long been read as, and thus has long suffered the fate of, most sequels: its fundamentally secondary character, as a poem that exists only – at least ostensibly – to undo the work of the poems that preceded it, gives it a somewhat murky literary identity, located somewhere between parody and palinode. And the opening scene of the poem, involving Cupid's defensive response to the title (*Legerat huius Amor titulum nomenque libelli: | 'bella mihi, uideo, bella parantur' ait*, "Amor had read the title and name of this little book; | 'wars,' he said, 'wars against me, I see, are being readied'," *Rem.* 1–2), together with Ovid's quick and lengthy reassurance that Cupid's worries are groundless, only adds to the confusion: if Ovid is not turning his back on love elegy, what *is* he doing writing a poem the bold oxymoron of whose title seems poised to undo the entire tradition of erotic elegy beginning with Gallus? And how does the intricate generic shell game that Ovid proceeds to play in the *Remedia* reflect the tension between tradition and revolution that informs his work's elegiac identity?

In this essay, I shall look at the internal contradiction that lies at the heart of this poem from a slightly different perspective from that taken by other recent critics. Conte, Fulkerson, Hardie, and Rosati have all discussed some of the features of the *Remedia's* relentless deconstruction of its own raison d'être.[1] Noteworthy, however, is the tendency exhibited in these and other studies to frame the "meaning" of the *Remedia* in negative terms, and to read the poem as an ambivalent attempt to undo the work of the *Ars*, an attempt that may itself reflect the political mood of the times. Instead, I want to use the poem's relentless interest in questions of genre to consider how the poem reflects on the nature of the didactic, asserting its simultaneous futility and utility in love and in love poetry, and so offers a revisionist model for elegy. My particular focus will be on the polarization of *medicina* and magic in the *Remedia*: Ovid's oppositional treatment of these two otherwise complementary approaches to managing the disease of love is an important indication of his revolutionary attitude towards the conventionally understood boundaries of genre. Furthermore, this is a poem, I suggest, that perfectly captures the spirit of an era in which the *princeps*, through the patronage of Apollo, can exploit imagery associating a ruler with the healer of the state;[2] Ovid's appropriation of this identity for himself may well be thought to transgress yet another boundary.

In appropriating the trope of *medicina amoris* ("cure for love") for his own anti-love elegy, Ovid suggests that the curative powers of his *ars* will be in use in the *Remedia*. His repeated emphasis on his *ars* ("art"), furthermore, is consistent with the idea that erotodidaxis is a *technê* ("skill") like medicine – for so the Hippocratic Oath styles medicine, quite prominently[3] – and so adapts itself easily to the theme of *medicina amoris* that appears to have originated with Gallus' *Amores* and that then becomes a unifying thread running through the work of all the Augustan elegists.[4] And the medical imagery, such as it is, to be found in the *Remedia* supports the curative implication of the title: the importance of *tempus* ("time, timing") and *modus* ("method, moderation") in diagnosis and treatment is given regular attention (see especially *Rem.* 79–134); and Telephus, Philoctetes, and Venus, characters famously wounded and then healed, turn up predictably in *exempla* (Telephus: 47–8; Philoctetes: 111–14; Venus: 5–6, 159–60). Magic, on the other hand, a central motif of erotic elegy before Ovid, is portrayed in the *Remedia* as an "anti-*medicina*," a technique for luring lovers that is non-scientific and therefore doomed to fail.

Yet the same Ovid who so conspicuously rejects magic as an alternative to the *technê* of medicine is well aware of its essential duality, a duality inherent, as Sharrock has shown in her study of *Ars* 2, in the duality of *carmen* ("poem, charm, song") itself.[5] The *carmen* of a sorcerer or witch has the power both to cause lovesickness and to cure the disease, just as the *carmen* of a poet has the power both to enthral its listeners and to liberate them from their thrall. Ovid's productive assimilation of the two meanings of *carmen* is clear from his assertion of the magical powers of his poetry in *Amores* 2.1.23–8:

carmina sanguineae deducunt cornua lunae
  et reuocant niueos solis euntis equos;
carmine dissiliunt abruptis faucibus angues
  inque suos fontes uersa recurrit aqua;
carminibus cessere fores, insertaque posti,
  quamuis robur erat, carmine uicta sera est.

Songs draw down the horns of the blood-red moon
  And call back the snow-white horses of the sun as it travels;
On account of song, snakes split, their jaws torn open,
  And water runs backward, turned towards its source;
To songs, doors have yielded; and, even when inserted into a doorpost,
  The bolt, though oak, has been overpowered by a late-night song.

We see here that a number of the tropes conventionally associated with magic[6] – drawing down the moon; reversing the path of the sun; rupturing the jaws of snakes; making water flow backwards; opening the lover's door – illustrate the power of Ovid's *carmina* in love. His later rejection of magic's power in love must not only, therefore, be taken with a grain of salt, but also itself underscores Ovid's interest in exploring both sides of *carmina*, especially as they invite play around the generic boundaries of theme and subject matter.

Here I focus on a single episode in the *Remedia*, in which the dual nature of *carmina*, and of Ovid's *carmen* in particular, is the unifying theme. It is in this duality that the primary metaphor that structures the *Remedia* lies, and that gives this poem its strongly closural character. I shall also use this episode to suggest some ways in which the *Remedia*, even as it perpetuates the ethos of elegy, offers a revolutionary redefinition of the generic character of the didactic. The *Remedia* is ideally, if not uniquely, suited to this investigation: because of its position as last in a series of books on erotodidaxis, and because of its delicate negotiation between continuity and rupture – between continuing the tradition of advice begun earlier and quite literally recanting it – it invites consideration as a reflection, even a commentary, on the traditions that shape it. I suggest that we consider the *Remedia* as a comprehensive metatext in which Ovid uses didactic elegy to instruct his reader about the fluidity of genre boundaries, in the process writing a poem that presents didactic elegy as a totalizing discourse about the experience of literary tradition.

The *exemplum* under discussion constitutes a rejection of magic as a means for allaying the harmful effects of love. Ovid uses this *exemplum* in the first place, I suggest, to assert the power of his own didactic poetry. In so doing, he also does for didactic poetry something similar to what Rosati has observed regarding metadiegesis (i.e., embedded narrative) in the *Metamorphoses*: "the serial reproduction of narratives in miniature within the main narrative provides us with a method for the analysis and interpretation of the main narrative."[7] In other words, the *exemplum* that is my focus here can, I suggest, be seen as a miniature model for the poem as a whole, and interpretive insights about it can therefore have a correspondingly broad application. At the same time, Rosati's suggestion, appropriate as it is to a densely narrative hexameter poem, requires some modification in the case of the *Remedia*, where the combination of occasional mythological narratives – often included through brief allusion rather than extended development – with the discursive style typical of didactic, sets up a constant tension between continuity and fragmentation. I therefore find it useful to supplement Rosati's approach to the miniature narrative with Foley's description of an "omnibus genre," i.e., a genre that opportunistically appropriates other genres.[8] Foley uses this concept to describe epic, seeing it as a master genre that has room in the abundant folds of its variegated garment to enclose all the other "smaller" genres. In applying Foley's view of epic narrative to Ovidian didactic, I suggest much the same thing, noting also that didactic has a long tradition of what I would call not generic indeterminacy precisely, but generic fluidity, moving with ease from one genre to another as its subject matter requires. The range and variety of Hesiod's two great didactic poems stand at the beginning of this long tradition, whose exfoliation in Latin has been illustrated well by Katharina Volk;[9] while I shall not rehearse in any detail post-Hesiodic developments, I think it is clear that any tradition that can include both Empedocles and Nicander, Callimachus and Lucretius, is one that can easily be seen as an omnibus, taking on all types of passengers for at least a brief journey along the path of song. I turn now to a few of these travellers in the excursus on magic at *Remedia* 249–90.

Whereas, as we have seen, Ovid equates the power of his erotic elegy in the *Amores* to the power of magic, in his didactic works the worthlessness and ineffectiveness of magic are recurring motifs. He rejects *fortes herbae* ("powerful plants"), *hippomanes* (a magic philtre made with a secretion from mares), and other magical remedies, asserting their inefficaciousness, at *Medicamina* 35–42, and in *Ars* 2.99–106 he similarly dismisses the sham claims of magic as fundamentally opposed to his own "scientific" advice. In the *Remedia*, however, he gives the subject much fuller treatment than previously: he embellishes the catalogue of magical ingredients and rituals to which he will not resort (249–60) with an *exemplum* (263–88) involving Circe, the archetypal witch.[10] The ostensible point of this *exemplum* is to demonstrate that, for all Circe's devising, her magic was ultimately useless in love; the implicit comparandum throughout is the *medicina amoris* that "Doctor Love," as Sharrock calls Ovid, dispenses in this poem.

This is a curious episode for a number of reasons. First of all, while the characters are ostentatiously Homeric, the plot is decidedly not: no trace of this story is to be found in Homeric, or later, epic. Again, while Horace, in the midst of a moralizing interpretation of Ulysses' adventures, suggests that Circe is to be considered a *meretrix* ("prostitute," *Epistle* 1.2.25), that does not seem to be the sort of reading Ovid is suggesting here.[11] The visual record is similarly unhelpful: it is clear from the famous "*Odyssey* landscapes" found on the Esquiline and usually dated to the mid-first century BCE[12] that the Homeric version of their encounter was well known in its details. In Panel 6 of this series, Ulysses can be seen approaching Circe's palace, and then compelling her to kneel to him as he threatens her with his sword; the scene is carefully modelled on the encounter of the two at *Od.* 10.321–4.[13] And Ovid himself elsewhere shows himself intimately familiar with the details of the Homeric Circe: in *Metamorphoses* book 14, she is featured as both a voracious lover (more often rejected than not, as in the stories involving Glaucus and Picus) and a vindictive wielder of powerful magic (as in her transformations of Scylla and Picus) in the inset narrative of Macareus, who thankfully recalls Ulysses' success in controlling her and thereby restoring his men to themselves (14.293–307).[14]

The Circe of Ovid's *Remedia* is similarly at the mercy of Ulysses, but that is where the similarity ends. In fact, her unrequited love for Ulysses makes her resemble more closely Homer's Calypso – a memorable character whose desire to delay Ulysses is revisited elsewhere in Ovid's didactic elegy. At *Ars* 2.119–44, shortly after that book's dismissal of magic, Ovid follows Homer reasonably closely in an *exemplum* depicting Calypso's love for Ulysses, using the episode to demonstrate the relatively greater importance in a love affair of eloquence as opposed to good looks (*Ars* 2.123): *non formosus erat, sed erat facundus Vlixes* ("Ulysses was a good talker, albeit not good-looking"). The seductiveness of Ulysses' rhetoric takes a generically precise form: much as he had played the role of Homeric bard in *Odyssey* books 9–12, so here with Calypso he narrates episodes of the Trojan War, illustrating them as he does so with pictures drawn in the sand. As Galinsky has noted, this Ulysses is something like Ovid himself, in his ability to tell the old stories yet again but to make them new in the process (*Ars* 2.128): *ille referre aliter saepe solebat idem* ("one and the same Ulysses would tell the same story differently each time").[15] Calypso invites Ulysses to tell her his stories as a delaying tactic, and her response to his narrative, though not explicitly described by Ovid, is likely to have been much like Dido's response to Aeneas' retelling of the Trojan War (*Aen.* 4.77–9): *nunc eadem labente die conuiuia quaerit, | Iliacosque iterum demens audire labores | exposcit pendetque iterum narrantis ab ore* ("now as the day fades she seeks the same festive gatherings, and madly demands to hear again the Trojan struggles and again hangs on the lips of the storyteller"). The similarity, though not captured in a particular word or phrase, is embedded in the emphasis on repetitiousness that permeates both scenes, as well as in the identical subject matter of Aeneas' and Ulysses' stories.[16] There is also an important difference between Vergil's Aeneas and Ovid's Ulysses, however, which will have implications for the Circe *exemplum* of the *Remedia*: in *Ars* 2, Ulysses' volubility is as effective in ensnaring him as it is in charming Calypso, who realizes that he is so enthralled with the Trojan war narrative that, so long as she renews her request for a story, he will remain to tell it again.[17] It is clear in the *Aeneid* scene that Aeneas seduces Dido, not vice versa, with words; Ovid's rewriting of this verbal seduction in *Ars* 2 plays with the seductive power of language, suggesting that the storyteller – Ulysses, or even Ovid himself – is as susceptible to the power of a well-wrought *carmen* as are his listeners, perhaps even more so.

When we return to the Circe and Ulysses *exemplum* in the *Remedia,* on the other hand, Ulysses' susceptibility to the power of language is gone, and he more closely resembles Vergil's Aeneas than his voluble self as depicted in *Ars* 2. Circe's abandonment, too, closely corresponds to that of Dido by Aeneas (as opposed to anything in Homer). In fact, almost every detail of Circe's speech in this episode, with the exception of her self-identification as a goddess and daughter of Sol (*Rem.* 276), recapitulates the central themes of Dido's speeches in *Aeneid* book 4, sometimes even implying a (chronologically impossible) awareness of Dido's arguments and their rebuttal by Aeneas – arguments that the reader has already seen in the *Aeneid,* but that Circe herself cannot know, given the relative mythical relationship of the *Odyssey* and the *Aeneid.*[18] Circe alludes to the marriage between them that she had once desired, but of which she now only asks him to deem her worthy (273–6) in terms that recall – or anticipate – Dido's assertion of a promise of marriage by Aeneas, his refusal to acknowledge it, and her eventual abandonment of the claim (*Aen.* 4.314–19, 338–9, 431); Circe's request for only the gift of a little more time with Ulysses (*spatium pro munere posco,* "I ask for time as a gift," 277) briefly recalls for the reader Dido's far more ominous wish for some time to come to terms with her loss (*Aen.* 4.433–4): *tempus inane peto, requiem spatiumque furori, | dum mea me uictam doceat fortuna dolere* ("I ask only for time, a rest and release from my madness, until fate can teach me how to grieve in defeat"). Similarly, Circe's repeated mention of Ulysses' eagerness to leave (266, 271, 277) closely parallels Dido's sense that Aeneas is acting in haste (*properas ... ?*, "do you hurry?," *Aen.* 4.310; *quo ruit?*, "where does he rush?," 4.429), and, like Dido, Circe uses the stormy seas to argue for delay (279–80 ≈ *Aen.* 4.309–10, 428–30). Circe assures Ulysses that her land is a place of peace and love, where she alone has suffered harm (*in qua male uulneror una*, "where I alone am grievously wounded," 283), thereby employing the image of love as a wound (*uulnus*) so closely associated with Dido (*Aen.* 4.1–2); and she offers Ulysses the opportunity to be its sole ruler (283–4), unaware of the fact that Dido's offer of joint rule is not enough to keep Aeneas in Carthage (*Aen.* 4.374; cf. 1.572–4).[19] With the pointed imperfect of *illa loquebatur* ("she was speaking," *Rem.* 285) at the close of Circe's speech, Ovid reminds us how much longer Dido's speeches were in the *Aeneid*; and the other half of that line, *nauem soluebat Vlixes* ("Ulysses was unfastening the ship"), summarizes in three words both the uselessness of Circe's talk and the determined intransigence of Ulysses, who here has nothing whatsoever to say in response to her pleas (unlike *facundus Vlixes* of the Calypso episode in *Ars* 2). The general effect is of a Ulysses who provides a "precedent," in epic chronology, for Aeneas' taciturnity and evasiveness. Finally, we should recall that a major episode of *Aeneid* 4 is devoted to Dido's vain resort to magic (4.504–21). Dido thus provides a model for Ovid's Circe that itself looks back to Homer's Circe, but with a disconcertingly defamiliarizing result: through the mediation of Dido, the Ovidian Circe becomes almost the antithesis of the Homeric Circe. The revolutionary poetics of Ovidian didactic simultaneously confirm Circe's epic provenance and transform her almost beyond recognition.

Ovid's treatment of Circe in the *Remedia*, particularly his assignment of six couplets of direct speech to her (273–84) – the first such intrusion into the generally relentless authority of the *praeceptor* – recalls other models besides epic prototypes. Both Barchiesi and Casali have discussed aspects of the ways in which Circe's speech – complemented by Ulysses' silence – resembles nothing so much as a mini-*Herois*, especially the seventh, in which Dido addresses Aeneas at length even as he scurries away to his ships.[20] To be sure, Ulysses is actually present for Circe's speech in the *Remedia*, but only just. And his lack of response – when his talkativeness was a central feature of the Ulysses-and-Calypso scene in *Ars* 2 – adds to the *Heroides*-like quality of the episode; we may compare, for example, Dido's address to the evanescent Aeneas in *Heroides* 7, implying that he is still in Carthage (*facta fugis, facienda petis; quaerenda per orbem | altera, quaesita est altera terra tibi*, "you flee what you have done, but seek new things to do; you have already sought around the world for one land, and now must find another," *Her.* 7.13–14), and her words at *Her.* 7.167–80, where she uses the same argument about the dangers of wind, weather, and storms at sea to delay him that Circe employs in the *Remedia*. At the same time, the transformation of Circe into an elegiac lover undermines the epic aspirations of the scene: stripped of speech, Ulysses is also stripped of the elaborate narrative that sustains his heroic identity and makes him desirable in the first place (recall, again, that in the Calypso episode in *Ars* 2, it was Ulysses' talent as Homeric bard that served to keep him and Calypso enthralled with each other). There is no Mercury here to give Ulysses *moly*, no men for him to lead safely home. There is no *catabasis* to undertake, no advice from Circe about how to navigate Scylla, Charybdis, the Sirens, and so forth; Ulysses simply becomes a bored lover, eager to escape now that the thrill is gone.

It is easy, on the other hand, to put this Ulysses into the frame of erotodidactic elegy, and to see his escape from Circe as a model of the successful escape from love recommended throughout the *Remedia*. I suggest that we read Ovid's Circe and Ulysses episode as an ironically successful model of the transformative power of *carmina* in the *Remedia*. In this poem, Ovid uses the familiar didactic trope of the journey – in particular, the voyage – as a metaphor for the successful escape from love that he teaches; and as several other passages in the *Remedia* suggest, Ulysses' success at evading capture during his journey is never far from Ovid's mind: he promises success at escaping Scylla and Charybdis (737–40), and Lotus-eaters and Sirens (789–90), to those who allow him to captain their ship as if he were Ulysses himself (69–70).[21] In the Circe *exemplum*, the journey of Ulysses exists solely so that Ulysses can meet and then abandon her; the *telos* of Homeric narrative disappears in the process, and Ulysses finally does become *Oûtis*, "Nobody" – and everybody (or at least every male pupil of Ovid's erotodidaxis). Ovid miniaturizes both the Homeric prototype for his narrative and its Vergilian variant, enclosing them both literally and symbolically in the embrace of didactic. The *Remedia* thus proposes a revolutionary reshuffling of generic hierarchies. The almost intolerable intimacy between elegy and epic that results is at the heart of the *Remedia*'s lesson: this Circe is not an authoritative guide to magic, not to mention the underworld, and this Ulysses, though just recognizable, is neither an emotionally vulnerable nor a sexually insatiable hero. Didactic thus trumps both the native genre of these two characters, epic, and their adopted one, elegy, subordinating their experience to the lesson to be learned by Ovid's reader.

In considering Ovid's transformation of the Homeric tale through a Vergilian lens, we might also use the metaphors of "mixing" and "splitting" to characterize the omnibus nature of the poem. The mixing of singular substances and the splitting of objects and creatures otherwise unified are recurring motifs in the language of magic, as illustrated in some of the Ovidian passages to which I have already referred: magic entails the mixing of potions (*mixto ... suco, Med.* 37) and rhymes (*mixtaque cum magicis nenia Marsa sonis,* "Marsian charms mixed with magic sounds," *Ars* 2.102), the splitting of snakes (*dissiliunt ... angues, Am.* 2.1.25; *funduntur ... angues, Med.* 39), and the splitting of the earth (*rumpet humum, Rem.* 254). Ovid displays his own exceptional ability with such combinations and divisions elsewhere in the *Remedia,* when he caps a list of great poets neatly categorized by the genres in which they excelled with a statement ostensibly asserting his respect for and adherence to generic decorum (*Rem.* 395–6): *tantum se nobis elegi debere fatentur, | quantum Vergilio nobile debet epos* ("elegiac verses confess that they owe as much to me as lofty epic owes to Vergil"). Like the two lines on the page that constitute this couplet, the trope of "parallelism" entails separation: i.e., even as Ovid asserts equality with Vergil, he draws a boundary line between the two genres that the two poets represent, *elegi* and *epos*. Yet as Morgan has observed, Ovid's couplet simultaneously models an ironic challenge to its contents: the monumental hexameter is used to characterize Ovid and elegy, the lighter pentameter, to characterize Vergil and epic.[22] The blurring of boundaries enacted by this couplet, as it simultaneously pronounces and undoes the logic of generic distinctions, is a function of the power of *carmina* to mix and to split in a single moment – or a single poem. I began this discussion with a suggestion that, in appropriating the imagery of healer for his own purposes, Ovid effectively incorporates contemporary political rhetoric into his self-definition as a poet; yet the "medicinal" mixture that Ovid produces also turns back upon itself, embodying as it does so the very confusion – disorderly, even irrational – that it proposes to resolve. Thus, the revolutionary poetics of the *Remedia* also at least hints at the ability of the poet to match even the *medicina* of the *princeps,* and in so doing to assert his own poetic hegemony, crossing boundaries in a world in which the rule of law and the rigid organization of society within carefully controlled boundaries have otherwise become the order of the day.

But my final thoughts here are focused not so much on Ovid's political performance in the *Remedia* – however suggestive it may be – as on the poetic revolution it helps to create. The conundrum of the *Remedia* is not the poem's failure, then, but just the opposite: success. If we extend the logic of the double-edged nature of *carmina* to the *Remedia,* the relevance of the Circe *exemplum* is immediately, even blatantly, apparent: the magical *carmina* she controls have little power when held up against the didactic *carmina* of Ovid. But this blatant meaning, both obvious and superficial, conceals a second and more interesting layer of meaning: if we see Circe as the anti-*exemplum,* i.e., the character for whom the wrong kind of *carmina* must necessarily fail, then the most important positive *exemplum* here is the vanishing one, Ulysses, who like Ovid's best pupils listens unmoved to Circe's pleas and, in escaping her, escapes from the world of the *Remedia* entirely; the Ulysses enthralled by Calypso – and by epic – in *Ars* 2 has finally gotten away. And yet the reader is not entirely like this Ulysses, for, unlike him, she is not quite finished with the *Remedia*. Conversely, Ovid is less unlike Circe than his deconstruction of magic might suggest, for he does after all manage to keep his reader reading; he continues to charm her with his revolutionary *carmen*.

NOTES

* Elaine Fantham has played a central role in bringing scholarship on Ovid to the forefront of contemporary classical studies; for this alone I would be grateful, did I not also have her leadership of women in the profession to admire and to emulate and her personal kindnesses to recall. But my gratitude must be shared as well by the editors of this volume, Alison Keith and Jonathan Edmondson, who have shepherded this collection of papers from its inception several years ago and have improved my paper, such as it is, in innumerable ways. Any mistakes or infelicities that remain are of course mine alone.

1 Conte 1989 [1986]; Fulkerson 2004; Rosati 2006; Hardie 2006.

2 See especially Wickkiser 2005 (although she does not consider the *Remedia* in her discussion); and cf. Miller 2009: 28–9 and 170–9.

3 von Staden 1996.

4 For Gallus' influential role in particular, see Ross 1975: 66–8; O'Hara 1993.

5 Sharrock 1994: 50–67.

6 McKeown 1998 on *Am*. 2.1.23–8; Tupet 1976: 385–6 and passim; Fauth 1980.

7 Rosati 2002: 286.

8 Foley 2004: 181–2.

9 Volk 2002.

10 My discussion is indebted throughout to Brunelle 2002, although the focus of his essay lies elsewhere.

11 Horace's Ulysses is a product of a long tradition of philosophical readings of the *Odyssey*: see Rutherford 1986. For a survey of the influence and reception of the *Odyssey* in ancient writers, see Kaiser 1964.

12 For images and a description of the "*Odyssey* landscapes," see Biering 1995 (for the Circe panel, 81–90 and plates 13–15); for detailed discussions and interpretation, see Leach 1988: 27–49; Ling 1991: 107–11; and O'Sullivan 2007; and cf. Vitr. 7.5.2, mentioning Ulysses' travels as likely subjects for painters.

13 For a Pompeian fresco depicting Circe's obeisance to Ulysses, see Schefold 1962: pl. 171.1. The scene also appears on the Tabula Iliaca Rondinini: Weitzmann 1970: 40–1 and fig. 8.
14 For a detailed collection and discussion of the Homeric echoes in this episode, see Myers 2009 on 14.243–307 and passim.
15 Galinsky 1975: 4.
16 I am indebted to one of the editors of this volume for this excellent observation.
17 For a discussion of the episode, Sharrock 1987; Sharrock 1994: 78–82.
18 On Ovid's predilection for such chronological play, see especially Barchiesi 2001a (1993).
19 See also Casali 2009: 345–6, observing the irony in Circe's comment that there is no need for Ulysses to flee since there is no new Troy here (*non hic noua Troia resurgit*, 281): Circe "inadvertently anticipates with extreme precision the (intertextual) future in the exact moment when her situation of ignorance is most acute."
20 Barchiesi 2001b: 12–18 (1984: 82–93); Casali 2009: 345–6.
21 Boyd 2009: 116–18.
22 Morgan 2000: 111–12; Morgan 2010: 21–2; Boyd 2009: 115–18.

WORKS CITED

Barchiesi, A. 2001a [1993]. "Future Reflexive: Two Modes of Allusion and Ovid's *Heroides*." In *Speaking Volumes: Narrative and Intertext in Ovid and Other Latin Poets*, edited and translated by M. Fox and S. Marchesi, 105–27. London. [Reprinted from *HSCP* 95 (1993): 333–65.]

– 2001b [1984]. "Continuities." In *Speaking Volumes: Narrative and Intertext in Ovid and Other Latin Poets*, edited and translated by M. Fox and S. Marchesi, 9–28. London. [English translation of "Problemi d'interpretazione in Ovidio. Continuità delle storie, continuazione dei testi," *MD* 16 (1984): 77–107.]

Biering, R. 1995. *Die Odysseefresken vom Esquilin*. Munich.

Boyd, B.W. 2009. "*Remedia amoris*." In *A Companion to Ovid*, edited by P.E. Knox, 104–19. Oxford.

Brunelle, C. 2002. "Pleasure, Failure and Danger: Reading Circe in the *Remedia*." *Helios* 29: 55–68.

Casali, S. 2009. "Ovidian Intertextuality." In *A Companion to Ovid*, edited by P.E. Knox, 341–54. Oxford.

Conte, G.B. 1989 [1986]. "Love without Elegy: The *Remedia amoris* and the Logic of a Genre." *Poetics Today* 10.3: 441–69. [English translation of "L'amore senza elegia: I 'Remedia amoris' e la logica di un genere." In *Ovidio, Rimedi contro l'amore*, edited by C. Lazzarini, 9–53. Venice, 1986.]

Fauth, W. 1980. "*Venena amoris*: Die Motive des Liebeszaubers und der erotischen Verzauberung in der augusteischen Dichtung." *Maia* 32: 265–82.

Foley, J.M. 2004. "Epic as Genre." In *The Cambridge Companion to Homer*, edited by R. Fowler, 171–87. Cambridge.

Fulkerson, L. 2004. "*Omnia uincit amor*: Why the *Remedia* Fail." *CQ* 54.1: 211–23.

Galinsky, K. 1975. *Ovid's* Metamorphoses*: An Introduction to the Basic Aspects*. Oxford.

Hardie, P. 2006. "*Lethaeus Amor*: The Art of Forgetting." In *The Art of Love: Bimillennial Essays on Ovid's* Ars Amatoria *and* Remedia Amoris, edited by R. Gibson, S. Green, and A. Sharrock, 166–90. Oxford.

Kaiser, E. 1964. "Odyssee-Szenen als Topoi." *MH* 21: 109–36, 197–224.

Leach, E.W. 1988. *The Rhetoric of Space: Literary and Artistic Representations of Landscape in Republican and Augustan Rome*. Princeton, NJ.

Ling, R. 1991. *Roman Painting*. Cambridge.

McKeown, J.C., ed. 1998. *Ovid:* Amores, *Volume III: A Commentary on Book Two*. Leeds.

Miller, J.F. 2009. *Apollo, Augustus, and the Poets*. Cambridge.

Morgan, L. 2000. "Metre Matters: Some Higher-level Metrical Play in Latin Poetry." *PCPS* 46: 99–120.

– 2010. Musa Pedestris*: Metre and Meaning in Roman Verse*. Oxford.

Myers, K.S., ed. 2009. *Ovid:* Metamorphoses *Book XIV*. Cambridge.

O'Hara, J.J. 1993. "Medicine for the Madness of Dido and Gallus: Tentative Suggestions on *Aeneid* 4." *Vergilius* 39: 12–24.

O'Sullivan, T.M. 2007. "Walking with Odysseus: The Portico Frame of the *Odyssey* Landscapes." *AJP* 128: 497–532.

Rosati, G. 2002. "Narrative Techniques and Narrative Structures in the *Metamorphoses*." In *Brill's Companion to Ovid*, edited by B.W. Boyd, 271–304. Leiden and Boston.

– 2006. "The Art of *Remedia Amoris*: Unlearning to Love?" In *The Art of Love: Bimillennial Essays on Ovid's* Ars Amatoria *and* Remedia Amoris, edited by R. Gibson, S. Green, and A. Sharrock, 143–65. Oxford.

Ross, D.O. 1975. *Backgrounds to Augustan Poetry: Gallus, Elegy, and Rome*. Cambridge.

Rutherford, R.B. 1986. "The Philosophy of the *Odyssey*." *JHS* 106: 145–62.

Schefold, K. 1962. *Vergessenes Pompeji*. Bern, Munich.

Sharrock, A. 1987. "*Ars amatoria* 2.123–42: Another Homeric Scene in Ovid." *Mnemosyne* 40.3: 406–12.

– 1994. *Seduction and Repetition in Ovid's* Ars Amatoria *II*. Oxford.

von Staden, H. 1996. "'In a Pure and Holy Way': Personal and Professional Conduct in the Hippocratic Oath?" *Journal of the History of Medicine and Allied Sciences* 51.4: 404–37.

Tupet, A.-M. 1976. *La magie dans la poésie latine. 1. Des origines à la fin du règne d'Auguste*. Paris.

Volk, K. 2002. *The Poetics of Latin Didactic: Lucretius, Vergil, Ovid, Manilius*. Oxford.

Weitzmann, K. 1970. *Illustrations in Roll and Codex: A Study of the Origin and Method of Text Illustration*. Princeton, NJ.

Wickkiser, B.L. 2005. "Augustus, Apollo, and an Ailing Rome: Images of Augustus as a Healer of State." In *Studies in Latin Literature and Roman History XII*, edited by C. Deroux, 267–89. Brussels.

7

Primus Pastor: The Origins of Pastoral in Ovid's *Metamorphoses**

SARAH L. MCCALLUM

In the opening lines of the *Metamorphoses*, the poet declares his intention to provide a comprehensive treatment of changed forms from the beginning of the world to his own time (*Met.* 1.3–4): *ab origine mundi | ad mea … tempora* ("from the origin of the world to my own times").[1] Throughout the opening book of the *Metamorphoses*, Ovid self-consciously plays with the concept of "beginnings." After the programmatic opening lines (*Met.* 1.1–4), Ovid presents the cosmogony (*Met.* 1.5–88), the *origo* of his stated project. But this episode is merely the first of a number of "firsts," as the remainder of the book stands as a collection of anthropogonies, aetiologies, and even a "second" cosmogony after Jupiter inflicts a devastating flood upon the world to punish humanity (*Met.* 1.262–312).[2]

Episodes within this catalogue of beginnings showcase the generic program of the poem as a whole. As noted by Joseph Solodow, Ovid at one place or another handles the themes and employs the tone of virtually every species of literature,[3] and the first book provides a preview of the types of genres that will be in dialogue throughout the tales of transformation. The first erotic episode of the *Metamorphoses*, Apollo's love for Daphne (*Met.* 1.452–567), opens with the phrase *primus amor*, a striking lexical cue of both the episode's "firstness" and its generic provenance in Ovid's elegiac *Amores*, his earliest literary work.[4] Apollo's pursuit of Daphne signals the programmatic importance of elegiac themes and generic conventions to the entire project of the *Metamorphoses*.[5]

In this paper, I argue that the story of Pan and Syrinx (*Met.* 1.689–712) has a similar programmatic function within Book 1, indicating that pastoral contributes significantly to the generic polyphony of the *Metamorphoses*.[6] Pan's amatory pursuit of Syrinx follows the narrative pattern seen in the tale of Apollo and Daphne.[7] But the former episode exhibits a predominantly pastoral generic "voice" that stands in sharp contrast to the erotic elegiac tone of the latter. As I will show, the heightened presence of bucolic or pastoral elements lends distinctive generic *color* to the two main sections of the episode: the encounter of Mercury and Argus; and the inset aetiological narrative about the origins of the syrinx. Ovid uses pastoral expressions to depict Mercury and Argus as shepherd and cowherd, respectively, and stages the scene between these two agents of Jupiter and Juno as a rustic encounter between herdsmen. Through the aetiology of the syrinx, the symbolic instrument of pastoral verse, Ovid contemplates the origins of the genre and its importance within his own epic program.

Setting the Pastoral Stage

In the scene immediately preceding the story of Mercury and Argus, Juno hands over Io, transformed into a lovely heifer (*bos … formosa*, 612), to the guardianship of Argus.[8] Equipped with one hundred eyes, Argus can keep a constant watch over Io, the rival of his divine mistress. But the role of Argus extends beyond that of mere sentinel (630–1): *luce sinit pasci; cum sol tellure sub alta est | claudit et indigno circumdat uincula collo* ("By daylight he permits her to graze; when the sun is beneath the deep earth, he shuts her in and puts fetters around her undeserving neck"). The lingering pause created by the penthemimeral caesura emphasizes the infinitive *pasci*, thereby prompting us to consider its special significance (*lūcĕ sĭn|īt pās|cī; || cūm | sōl tēl|lūrĕ sŭb | āltā est*). In Vergil's first *Bucolic*, the phrase *pascere boues* appears in the response of the divine youth to the entreaty of Tityrus (*Buc.* 1.45):[9] "*pascite ut ante boues, pueri; summittite tauros.*" ("Drive the cattle to pasture, boys, as before; rear the bulls.") Within this programmatic endorsement of the pastoral world, *pascere boues* (to drive cattle to pasture, to nourish cattle) signals Vergil's engagement with the poetry of Theocritus and his successors: the Latin phrase can be read as an etymologizing translation of βουκολεῖν (to nourish cattle, to tend cattle),[10] and therefore functions as a generic marker of τὰ βουκολικά.[11] In *Metamorphoses* 1, the verb *pascere* likewise associates the Ovidian story of Io with the genre of herding poems produced by Theocritus and Vergil. Argus, monitoring the grazing habits of Io, the *bos formosa* (612), assumes the characteristic behaviour of the Theocritean βουκόλος and recalls the programmatic directive (*pascite … boues*) from Vergil's first *Bucolic*. The pastoral description of Argus adds to the bathos and situational humour of the episode, as the awe-inspiring and divinely appointed guardian performs the mundane duties of a βουκόλος while tending his herd of one. In generic terms, the characterization of Argus as a guardian-cum-herdsman initiates an engagement with the bucolic tradition that endures until his eventual destruction at the hands of Mercury.

The description of Argus as the *custos Iunonius* (*Met.* 1.678) further underscores his double role as sentinel and bucolic herdsman. On one level, the word *custos* refers to Argus' duty as the guard appointed by Juno to keep close watch over Io.[12] But the specific context of the Io myth activates the other sense of *custos*, "keeper (of animals)" or "herdsman," given that Argus is the guardian of the *bos formosa*.[13] This usage appears in a significant passage from Vergil's *Bucolics*,[14] when Mopsus recites the epitaph of Daphnis, the archetypal herdsman and legendary inventor of bucolic song (*Buc.* 5.43–4): "*Daphnis ego in siluis, hinc usque ad sidera notus, | formosi pecoris* ***custos****, formosior ipse.*" ("I, Daphnis, was well known in the forests, from here all the way to the stars, the guardian of the beautiful cattle, more beautiful myself.") Vergil here reinterprets Daphnis' proclamation regarding his status as a herdsman of cattle in the programmatic first *Idyll* of Theocritus (*Id.* 1.120–1): Δάφνις ἐγὼν ὅδε τῆνος ὁ τὰς βόας ὧδε νομεύων, | Δάφνις ὁ τὼς ταύρως καὶ πόρτιας ὧδε ποτίσδων ("I am that Daphnis who put the cattle to graze here, the Daphnis who watered the bulls and young heifers here").[15] Furthermore, Vergil incorporates into Mopsus' epitaphic verses a second allusion to the figure of Daphnis from the *Idylls*, as the phrase *pecoris custos* ("guardian of the cattle," *Buc.* 5.44) is a Latin translation of Menalcas' opening address of Daphnis as ἐπίουρος βοῶν ("guardian of the cattle," [Theoc.] *Id.* 8.6).[16] In *Metamorphoses* 1, the bucolic pedigree of *custos* creates an association between Argus and the Theocritean and Vergilian incarnations of Daphnis, thereby connecting Ovid's version of the Io myth to the poetic realm of the *Idylls* and *Bucolics*. By depicting Argus in language reminiscent of Daphnis, Ovid also capitalizes on the inherent humour of the monstrous *custos Iunonius* adopting the guise of the principal hero of bucolic verse. The resulting image exemplifies Ovid's playful manipulation of Vergilian and Theocritean poetry throughout the Io episode.

In similar fashion, Ovid transforms the god Mercury into a suitably pastoral opponent for the "βουκόλος" Argus. When Mercury sets out to slay the *custos Iunonius* as ordered by Jupiter, he dons his characteristic winged sandals, sleep-inducing staff, and cap (*Met.* 1.671–2). But after descending to the earthly realm, Mercury lays aside all but the staff, which he wields like a shepherd's crook to drive along a stolen herd of goats (*Met.* 1.676–7): *hac agit* ***ut pastor*** *per deuia rura* ***capellas*** *| dum uenit* ***abductas*** *et* ***structis*** *cantat* ***auenis*** ("with this [staff], as if he were a shepherd, he drives through the remote countryside she-goats which were stolen along the way, and he plays upon reed pipes").[17] The phrase *ut pastor* is an unmistakable generic signpost, which indicates that the encounter between Mercury and Argus will proceed along pastoral lines. When Mercury steals a herd of goats (*capellas ... abductas*) and fabricates rustic pipes (*structis ... auenis*), he completes his herdsman disguise; the image of a piping goatherd is particularly reminiscent of the most talented musicians of the *Idylls*.[18] Herding and making music figure prominently in the *Idylls* and the *Bucolics*, being the central preoccupations of the rustic personalities who populate each collection. Furthermore, the term *auena* identifies Mercury's newly acquired pipes with the programmatic "slender reed" played by Tityrus in the first *Bucolic* (*tenui ... auena, Buc.* 1.2) and the "pipe of the Sicilian shepherd" which emblematizes Gallus' generic shift from elegy to pastoral (*pastoris Siculi ... auena, Buc.* 10.51).[19] Through the description of Mercury's pastoral masquerade, Ovid dramatizes his own generic experimentation; the god's theft of goats and acquisition of pipes, both symbolic of the genre of pastoral, emblematize the poet's appropriation of material from the pastoral tradition. Mercury, now equipped with the accoutrements of a piping goatherd, advances to kill Argus, the monstrous βουκόλος.

Ovid's self-conscious engagement with the pastoral genre intensifies in the initial dialogic exchange between Argus and Mercury (*Met.* 1.678–81). The first speech of Argus functions as the programmatic *exordium* of Ovid's first pastoral episode within the *Metamorphoses*: it has clear affiliations with the conventional discourse and landscape of the *Idylls* and *Bucolics*, and may be read as a statement regarding Ovid's generic experimentation. Argus, captivated by the piping and taken in by Mercury's herdsman disguise, cordially invites him to sit in the shade while the goats enjoy the lush grass (*Met.* 1.678–81):

uoce noua captus custos Iunonius "at tu,
quisquis es, hoc poteras mecum **considere** saxo,"
Argus ait; "neque enim pecori fecundior ullo
herba loco est, aptamque uides pastoribus umbram."

Captivated by the new sound, Juno's guardsman Argus says "You there, whoever you are, you might sit down with me on this rock, for in no place is there more abundant grass for your flock, and you see a shade fit for herdsmen."

The key features of Argus's speech are an invitation to sit (*poteras ... considere*, 679) and an emphasis on the natural surroundings, particularly the foliage (*herba ... umbram*, 681). Ovid borrows this formula directly from the discourse of Theocritean and Vergilian herdsmen who encounter one another in the pastoral landscape and share in a musical exchange. Compare, for example, Argus's words to those spoken by Palaemon and

Menalcas in the *Bucolics* (3.55): *Dicite, quandoquidem in molli* ***consedimus*** *herba* ("Sing, seeing that we are sitting on soft grass"); and (5.1–3): *Cur non, Mopse … | … hic corylis mixtas inter* ***consedimus*** *ulmos?* ("Why, Mopsus, don't we sit here among the elms mingled with hazels?").[20] Specific lexical and thematic parallels are evidence of the intertextual connections between the speech of Argus and its Vergilian pastoral models: the use of the verb *considere*; the lush grass of the setting (*fecundior herba* ≈ *mollis herba*); and the shade provided by trees (*umbra* ≈ *coryli, ulmi*). The term *umbra* (shade) also has special significance within the *Bucolics*; in the opening passage of the collection (*in umbra, Buc.* 1.4), it signifies the ideal *locus* for pastoral convening and poetic composition[21]. The formula of these Latin examples may be traced further back to Theocritus (*Id.* 1.12–14, 21–3; 5.31–2):

λῇς ποτὶ τᾶν Νυμφᾶν, λῇς, αἰπόλε, τεῖδε **καθίξας,**
ὡς τὸ κάταντες τοῦτο γεώλοφον αἵ τε μυρῖκαι,
συρίσδεν;

"Are you willing, by the Nymph, are you willing, goatherd, to sit here, where this sloping hill and tamarisks are, and play the syrinx?"

δεῦρ' ὑπὸ τὰν πτελέαν **ἑσδώμεθα** τῶ τε Πριήπω
καὶ τᾶν κρανίδων κατεναντίον, ᾇπερ ὁ θῶκος
τῆνος ὁ ποιμενικὸς καὶ ταὶ δρύες.

"Come, let us sit beneath the elm opposite Priapus and the springs, where the seat of that shepherd and the oaks are."[22]

ἅδιον ᾀσῇ
τεῖδ' ὑπὸ τὰν κότινον καὶ τἄλσεα ταῦτα **καθίξας.**

"You will sing more sweetly if you sit here beneath the wild olive and these groves."[23]

Argus, it seems, has become a βουκόλος in both deeds and words, shepherding Io through an idealized pastoral landscape featuring grass for the flock (*pecori fecundior … | herba*, 680–1) and shade suited to herdsmen (*aptam … pastoribus umbram*, 681). Ovid's obvious homage to the conventional discourse of the *Bucolics* and *Idylls* within the initial dialogic exchange has a programmatic function; it identifies the episode as an experiment in the pastoral genre, the first of its kind within the *Metamorphoses*. Furthermore, the comparative phrase *fecundior herba* (680–1) may be read as playfully agonistic; i.e., the "more richly abundant" grass of Ovid's pastoral landscape signifies his superior treatment of the genre. The stage is now set for the encounter between Argus, the monstrous βουκόλος, and Mercury, the divine *pastor*.

Mercury's Piping and Pastoral "Firstness"

In the encounter proper, Ovid's generic experimentation with pastoral fulfils the programmatic promise of Argus' invitation. Ovid continues to associate Argus and Mercury with the conventional herdsmen of the *Idylls* and *Bucolics* who convene in the wilderness to exchange pastoral songs. In the attempt to sedate Argus, Mercury plays rustic pipes and sings of the invention of the syrinx. The two aspects of his musical performance recall the pastoral program of *Bucolic* 6 and its aetiological narrative, which serves as a poetic blueprint for Ovid's collection of metamorphic aetiologies.[24] Through repeated references to the "newness" of Mercury's music and the invention of the pipes, Ovid also emphasizes the generic "firstness" of his own pastoral episode within the *Metamorphoses*.

In response to Argus's invitation, Mercury sits down, engages the *custos Iunonius* in conversation, and attempts to lure him to sleep by playing rustic strains (*Met.* 1.683–4): ***iunctis****que canendo | uincere* ***harundinibus*** *seruantia lumina temptat* ("and he tries to subdue his watchful eyes by playing a song on joined reeds"). Ovid refers to Mercury's reed pipes, previously called *structae auenae* (677), as *iunctae harundines* (683–4). The word *harundo*, much like *auena* (677),[25] associates the instrument played by the god with the symbolic pipes of Vergil's *Bucolics*. In particular, *harundo* recalls the opening lines of *Bucolic* 6, in which Vergil claims that he prefers to compose pastoral verse, rather than laudatory martial epic (*Buc.* 6.6–8): *nunc ego … | <u>agrestem</u>* ***tenui*** *<u>meditabor</u>* ***harundine*** *<u>Musam</u>* ("Now I will study the rustic Muse with a slender reed").[26] Vergil's programmatic *recusatio* introduces the second half of the collection with an intratextual echo of its pastoral beginnings in the first *Bucolic* (1.2): *<u>siluestrem</u>* ***tenui*** *<u>Musam</u> <u>meditaris</u>* ***auena*** ("you study the woodland Muse with a slender reed").[27] In *Metamorphoses* 1, Mercury's pipes of "joined reeds" (*iunctis … harundinibus*, 683–4) intertextually recall the "slender reed" taken up by the poet of the sixth *Bucolic* (*tenui … harundine*, 6.8). The god's possession of the symbolic *harundines* identifies him as a pastoral singer, the first of the *Metamorphoses*, whose pipes programmatically prefigure those played by the poem's other rustic personalities, namely, Pan, Marsyas, and Polyphemus.[28] Unlike the typical herdsmen of Theocritus or Vergil, however, Mercury wields the pipes as a weapon against Argus, his bucolic foe.

But the god's soporific piping fails to vanquish Argus, who fights valiantly against sleep and remains ever watchful (*Met.* 1.682–5). Argus then asks Mercury to tell him how the reed pipe (*fistula*) came to be invented (*Met.* 1.687–8): *quaerit quoque (namque reperta | fistula nuper erat) qua sit ratione reperta* ("And he asks (for the pan pipe had been discovered recently) how it had been discovered"). Like the other musical instruments already discussed (*auena, harundo*), the *fistula* has a strong association with the poetics of the pastoral genre: it is used variously as a term for shepherd's pipes and the pipes of the rustic deity Pan; and it acts as the Latin synonym for the Greek σῦριγξ, the programmatic instrument of the Theocritean *Idylls*.[29] The shepherd's pipe, as denoted by *fistula* or σῦριγξ, features prominently in both Theocritean bucolic and Vergilian pastoral poetry.[30] In Theocritus, for example, the syrinx (σῦριγξ) embodies the clear, sharp sound of bucolic poetry itself,[31] and appears in musical exchanges between rustic musicians as either a symbolic gift or a wager.[32] Throughout the *Bucolics*, the *fistula* is likewise "the principle, symbolic instrument of pastoral music,"[33] played and exchanged by herdsmen in scenes of musical rivalry and amoebaean banter.[34] The elegist Gallus even uses the *fistula* to refer metonymically to the pastoral genre and Arcadian poetics in juxtaposition with his own elegiac *amores* (*Buc.* 10.33–4): *o mihi tum quam molliter ossa quiescant, | uestra meos olim si fistula dicat amores!* ("Oh, how softly then would my bones rest, if only your pipes would sing my love poetry!")[35] Ovid also acknowledges the generic significance of the *fistula* in his pastoral experimentation elsewhere in the *Metamorphoses*, particularly in his depiction of Apollo as the archetypal herdsman in Book 2,[36] and his description of Polyphemus' enormous epic reed pipes in Book 13.[37] The god Mercury, as discussed above, acquires and performs upon the *fistula*, the symbolic instrument of pastoral, as part of his herdsman disguise (*structis … auenis*, 677; *iunctis … harundinibus*, 683–4).[38] When Argus asks Mercury to switch from playing the pipes to providing an account of the instrument's invention, he effectively challenges his rustic companion to sing a pastoral song, the first of Ovid's epic poem.

The Pastoral Aetiology of the Syrinx

Complying with Argus' request, Mercury recounts the tale of Pan's pursuit of the nymph Syrinx and the resulting discovery of the pastoral pipes (*Met.* 1.689–712). Mercury sets the tale of Pan and Syrinx in Arcadia, the archetypal pastoral environment of Vergil's *Bucolics*.[39] Syrinx, one of the wood nymphs who dwell on the Arcadian mountain Nonacris, is much pursued by the satyrs and other pastoral deities who inhabit "the shady woods and fertile countryside" (692–4): *non semel et Satyros eluserat illa sequentes | et quoscumque deos umbrosaque silua feraxque | rus habet* ("and many times she had escaped from pursuing Satyrs and all of the gods who inhabit the shady forest and fertile countryside"). To the well-educated Roman audience, her name would immediately recall the σῦριγξ of Theocritean bucolic,[40] the shepherd's pipe which serves in various places as the instrument and/or wager of bucolic singing contests, and which the dying Daphnis dedicates to Pan in the programmatic first *Idyll*.[41]

After his introduction of Syrinx, Mercury depicts Pan's first glimpse of the nymph with further language evocative of pastoral verse. Pan observes Syrinx returning from Mount Lycaeus (*redeuntem colle Lycaeo | Pan uidet, Met.* 1.698–9), a geographical feature found in the landscape of both the *Idylls* and the *Bucolics*. In the opening poem of the Theocritean corpus, Thyrsis names the "high hills of Lycaeus" (ὤρεα μακρὰ Λυκαίω, *Id.* 1.123–4) as one of the pastoral deity's characteristic haunts. The mountain, one of the highest in Arcadia, also figures prominently in Vergil's tenth *Bucolic* as part of the landscape mourning Gallus in a scene of pathetic fallacy (*Buc.* 10.15).[42] Moreover, Pan's personal adornment, a wreath of pine (*pinuque caput praecinctus acuta, Met.* 1.699), recalls the πίτυς, which acts as the locus and model of Theocritean verse.[43] Through his depiction of the setting and appearance of Pan, Mercury hints at the generic *color* of the episode he is about to recount.

But just as soon as it has begun, Mercury's tale of Pan and Syrinx comes to an abrupt conclusion – Argus, it seems, has been put to sleep by the god's pastoral song. Not wishing to disturb the slumber of his soon-to-be victim, Mercury leaves it to Ovid's narrative voice to complete the story of Pan's pursuit. In an abbreviated account of a mere thirteen lines, the pastoral imagery continues. Fleeing to the river Ladon,[44] Syrinx implores her sisters to prevent her rape through transformation. Pan finds himself embracing, not his desired nymph, but the reeds of the marsh (*calamos … palustres, Met.* 1.706). Through her transformation, Syrinx becomes both an element of the pastoral landscape,[45] and the reeds with which Pan invents his emblematic pipes.

As Pan discovers the lovely sound produced by the reeds and fashions them into his instrument, Ovid playfully evokes a Vergilian reference to the deity's invention in the eighth *Bucolic*.[46] In Vergil's pastoral poem, Damon sings of Pan as the first to awaken the "idle reeds" (*calamos … inertis, Buc.* 8.24). Ovid plays with his Vergilian model through the inherent double meaning of *iners*, which can convey both "idleness" and "artlessness." Through his exhalation, Pan stirs up winds (*motos uentos, Met.* 1.707), which set the once "idle" reeds in motion. The swaying reeds, no longer *iners*, produce a uniquely artful and sweet sound that captivates Pan (*Met.* 1.709): *arte noua uocisque deum dulcedine captum*. The term *dulcedo* recalls the programmatic sweetness of Theocritus's verse implicit in the first word of his corpus (ἁδύ, *Id.* 1.1).[47] Subtly alluding to the Vergilian image of Pan awakening the *calamos inertis* (*Buc.* 8.24), Ovid depicts Pan transforming the idle reeds into the swaying and artful producers of pastoral song. In similar vein, a wall painting showing a confident Pan playing his new instrument to an attentive audience of nymphs features in a trio of mythological scenes of metamorphosis in a *cubiculum* of the House of Jason at Pompeii (Figure 7.1).

Figure 7.1 Fresco from the House of Jason (*cubiculum* g), Pompeii, showing Pan holding a syrinx, flanked by Nymphs. Museo Archeologico Nazionale, Naples. Photo: © Scala / Art Resource, NY.

Finishing the tale with a pastoral flourish, Ovid describes Pan binding reeds to create his emblematic pipes (*Met.* 1.711–12): *atque ita disparibus calamis compagine cerae | inter se iunctis nomen posuisse puellae* ("and so when he had fastened together reeds of different lengths with a joining of wax he named them after the girl"). The depiction of Pan joining the reeds with wax recalls similar images of the construction of pipes in pastoral verse, most notably Vergil's portrayal of the invention in his second *Bucolic* (*Buc.* 2.32–3): *Pan primum calamos cera coniungere pluris | instituit* ("And Pan first began the practice of joining together many reeds with wax").[48] In the Ovidian aetiology, Pan's pipes of "joined reeds" (*iunctis calamis*, 711–12) simultaneously recall those of his Vergilian predecessor (*calamos ... [coniunctis] pluris*, *Buc.* 2.32) and those played by the "shepherd" Mercury in the surrounding narrative (*iunctis harundinibus*, *Met.* 1.683–4).[49] When Pan bestows the name of the nymph upon his newly made pipes, the aetiology is complete and the predominantly pastoral episode draws to a close.

Conclusion

Within the catalogue of "firsts" that opens the *Metamorphoses*, the Pan and Syrinx episode indicates the revolutionary programmatic importance of pastoral to Ovid's entire epic project. Other passages promise to provide additional evidence for Ovid's ongoing experimentation with pastoral in the *Metamorphoses*. In the second book, an Ovidian experiment in "seconds," echoes, and repetitions, we find a doublet for the programmatic pastoral encounter of herdsmen from Book 1 in the exchange between Mercury and Battus (2.676–707). The opening address to Apollo that precedes the encounter between Mercury and Battus further suggests the pastoral character of the episode. Apollo, who denied his association with the pastoral world during his elegiac pursuit of Daphne (*non ego sum pastor*, 1.513), appears in Book 2 wearing the guise of the archetypal herdsman of pastoral (2.680–2): *illud erat tempus, quo te pastoria pellis | texit onusque fuit baculum siluestre sinistrae, | alterius dispar septenis fistula cannis* ("that was the time when the shepherd's hide covered you and the burden of your left hand was a woodland staff, while that of the other hand was a pipe of seven unequal reeds").[50] In Book 3, moreover, the foundation myth of Boeotia playfully alludes to the pastoral genre, when the prophesied heifer leads Cadmus to the future site of Thebes and pastoral gives way to foundation epic.[51] Pastoral landscapes, personalities, and motifs also permeate the musical victories of Apollo over Marsyas and Pan in Books 6 and 11, respectively (*Met.* 6.382–400; 11.146–93). And just as Apollo's *primus ardor* finds its closural match in the *ultimus ardor* of the Pomona and Vertumnus episode of Book 14,[52] Ovid's programmatic engagement with pastoral culminates in the Polyphemus episode of *Metamorphoses* 13. The influence of pastoral may also extend beyond passages that feature its characteristic landscapes and personalities.[53]

The abundance of significant pastoral episodes throughout the *Metamorphoses* fulfils the programmatic promise of the Pan and Syrinx episode. When Mercury, the poem's *primus pastor*, tells the tale of Pan's love for Syrinx, Ovid effectively declares his intention to include pastoral among the constituent genres of the *Metamorphoses*. This inclusion marks a revolutionary departure from the relationship between epic and pastoral in earlier Greek and Latin literature. Though we may detect "proto-pastoral" elements in the Homeric and Hesiodic epics and echoes of Vergilian pastoral in the *Aeneid*,[54] Ovid expands the scope of pastoral far beyond the boundaries set by his poetic predecessors. As he experiments with the pastoral language and themes of his predecessors, Ovid engages in a self-reflexive contemplation of poetic production in the swiftly changing artistic landscape of Augustan Rome. With characteristic innovation, Ovid creates a complex network of inter- and intratextually related pastoral episodes, which contribute to the aesthetic appeal and deeper significance of his epic endeavour.

NOTES

* I would like to express my gratitude to Elaine Fantham, whose contributions to the study of Latin literature are an enduring inspiration. Many years ago I had the privilege of studying Roman satire under Elaine's tutelage, and I would like to use this opportunity to thank her properly for her wisdom, encouragement, and kindness. I am also grateful to Zoa Alonso, Lauren Curtis, Alison Keith, and Naomi Weiss for providing valuable and generous comments on earlier versions of this paper.

1 All excerpts from Ovid's *Metamorphoses* are taken from Tarrant 2004.

2 Myers 1994a: 43–5, 61.

3 Solodow 1988: 18.

4 Myers 1994a: 125; Keith 2002: 247. On the significance of *primus amor*, see also Barchiesi 2005: 206–7 *ad Met.* 1.452.

5 Nicoll 1980: 176–8.

6 For the concept of generic polyphony within Ovid's *Metamorphoses*, see Farrell 1992: 238–40.

7 Konstan 1991: 15–30; and Rosati 2002: 274–5.

8 It is perhaps worth noting that the adjective *formosus* (beautiful, handsome) appears frequently in Vergil's *Bucolics* (1.5; 2.1, 17, 45; 3.57, 79; 4.57; 5.44, 86, 90; 7.38, 55, 62, 67; 10.18), but is virtually absent from the poet's other works,

appearing only once in the *Georgics* of a lovely heifer (*pascitur in magna Sila formosa iuuenca*, *G*. 3.219): see Barchiesi 2005: 218 *ad Met*. 1.612.

9 All excerpts from Vergil's *Bucolics* are taken from Mynors 1969.

10 Wright 1983: 116–17 suggests that Vergil's *pascere boues* is a bilingual translation that reflects the ancient etymology of βουκόλος (e.g., Ath. 6.262a: κόλον γὰρ ἡ τροφή, ὅθεν καὶ ὁ βουκόλος). See also: *uitulam ... pascite* (*Buc*. 3.85); and *pascite taurum* (*Buc*. 3.86).

11 Gutzwiller 2006: 308–404 discusses the semantic range of the verb βουκολεῖν and the use of *bucolic* (τὰ βουκολικά) as "the standard ancient term for both the Greek and the Latin poetry that we now connect with the pastoral genre."

12 For *custos* as a term for "one employed to keep persons in confinement or under observation, guard," see *OLD*[2] s.v. *custos* 3. See also Plaut. *Aul*. 555–6: *Argus ... | quem quondam Ioni Iuno custodem addidit*.

13 See *OLD*[2] s.v. *custos* 1.c.

14 Elsewhere in the *Bucolics*, cf. 3.5: *hic alienus ouis custos bis mulget in hora*; 10.36 *aut custos gregis aut maturae uinitor uuae*.

15 All excerpts from the Theocritean corpus are taken from Gow 1965a. On the connection between *Buc*. 5.43–4 and Theoc. *Id*. 1.120–1, see Gow 1965b: 26 on *Id*. 1.120–1; Coleman 1977: 164 on *Buc*. 5.43–4; Clausen 1995: 153 on *Buc*. 5.43–4; and Hunter 1999: 99–100 on *Id*. 1.120–1.

16 Though the authorship of *Idyll* 8 is uncertain, the poem was familiar to Vergil and much imitated by him: see Gow 1965b: 170–1. The phrase βοῶν ἐπίουρος occurs also at [Theocr.] *Id*. 25.1 to depict an old ploughman watching over a herd of cattle. It should also be noted that the term ἐπίουρος also occurs twice in the *Odyssey* to signify the role of swineherd (ὑῶν ἐπίουρος, *Od*. 13.405, 15.39): see Gow 1965b: 442 on 25.1.

17 Mercury's retention of the staff as part his shepherd's attire may recall the κορύνη ("stick, staff") of Lycidas in the *Idylls* (Theoc. *Id*. 7.43) and the *pedum* (crook) of Mopsus in the *Bucolics* (5.88).

18 Segal 1981: 119–20 points out the rarity and musical distinction of goatherds who play the syrinx, and cites Lycidas and the anonymous goatherd of *Idyll* 1 as the only examples in Theocritus.

19 See Coleman 1977: 72 on *Buc*. 1.2 and 289 on *Buc*. 10.50–1; and Clausen 1995: 36 on *Buc*. 1.2.

20 Clausen 1995: 105 on *Buc*. 3.55: "The pastoral musician is usually seated while performing." See also the description of Daphnis that precedes an invitation to rest (*Buc*. 7.1): *Forte sub <u>arguta</u>* ***consederat*** *<u>ilice</u> Daphnis* ("By chance Daphnis had taken a seat beneath the rustling oak").

21 On the pastoral significance of *umbra*, see Alpers 1986: 18, 49; Barchiesi 2005: 224 on *Met*. 1.681; and Davis 2012: 19, who discusses both the prologic and epilogic significance of the term within the *Bucolics*.

22 Hunter 1999: 74 on *Id.* 1.21 connects this passage to *Buc.* 5.3.

23 For other seated herdsmen in Theocritus, see also: *Id.* 6.3–4; and *Id.* 11.17.

24 Knox 1986: 10–14.

25 See p. 127, above.

26 The word *harundo* also denotes the reeds on the banks of the river Mincius in *Bucolic* 7 (12–13): *hic uiridis tenera praetexit harundine ripas | Mincius.* ("Here Mincius fringes his verdant banks with the tender reed.")

27 See Clausen 1995: 175, 181 on *Buc.* 6.8.

28 As discussed in greater detail below, Pan's exhalation in the reeds inspires him to invent the syrinx (*in harundine, Met.* 1.707). See also the pastoral figures Marsyas and Pan playing the *harundo* in musical competitions against Apollo (*harundine, Met.* 6.384; *harundine,* 11.154); and Polyphemus' gargantuan pastoral pipes made from one hundred joined reeds (*harundinibus compacta … fistula centum, Met.* 13.784).

29 See *fistula OLD*[2] s.v. 2; and *TLL* 6.1.828.73–829.4.

30 As Keith 1992: 113 observes.

31 See Hunter 1999: 68–9 on *Id.* 1.1–11 and 71–2 on *Id.* 1.3 (συρίσδες).

32 See, for example: the dying Daphnis offering his fine, honey-sweet syrinx to Pan (σύρριγγα, *Id.* 1.129); Damoetas giving his syrinx to Daphnis (σύρριγγ', *Id.* 6.43); and Daphnis and Menalcas each wagering a set of pipes (σύρριγγ', *Id.* 8.18–24). On the construction, invention, and uses of the σῦριγξ in the *Idylls,* see Gow 1965b: 3, 27, 83, 175, 190, and 215.

33 Clausen 1995: 36 on *Buc.* 1.2. Coleman 1977: 232 on *Buc.* 8.21 observes that *fistula* has more "specifically pastoral associations" than *tibia.*

34 For example, Corydon gives his *fistula* to Damoetas (*Buc.* 2.37); Damoetas discusses with Menalcas his victorious performance on the *fistula* (*Buc.* 3.22, 25); Corydon says he will hang up his *fistula,* (i.e. retire) if bested by Codrus (*Buc.* 7.24); the goatherd Damon complains of Nysa's disdain for his *fistula* (*Buc.* 8.33).

35 Harrison 2007: 66 discusses the metageneric implications of Gallus's statement.

36 Apollo's *fistula,* together with his skin garment (*pastoria pellis, Met.* 2.680) and sylvan staff (*baculum siluestre, Met.* 2.681), marks him as a conventional pastoral herdsman: see Barchiesi 2005: 294 *ad Met.* 2.680–2. This image of Apollo-as-*pastor* bears striking similarity to the figure of Lycidas in Theocritus' seventh *Idyll* (*Id.* 7.13–19), as noted by Williams 1971: 141; and Keith 1992: 113. For discussion of Lycidas and his identity, see Segal 1981: 110–66; and Gutzwiller 1991: 158–71.

37 See note 28, above.

38 Coleman 1977: 72 on *Buc.* 1.2 discusses the various materials from which *fistula* (pan pipes) may be constructed, including hemlock, marsh reeds (*harundo, calamus*), and, in the Vergilian pastoral tradition, the oaten reed (*auena*).

39 Coleman 1977: 22, 32; Hubbard 1998: 45–6; Barchiesi 2005: 225 *ad Met.* 1.689; and Breed 2006: 26.

40 Anderson 1997: 215.

41 See Gow 1965b: 619 *ad* σῦριγξ.

42 Coleman 1977: 279 *ad Buc.* 10.15.

43 Wright 1983: 109.

44 The mention of this river creates a subtle correlation between the stories of Syrinx and Daphne, as varying traditions cite Ladon as the father of Daphne in place of Peneus: see Servius *ad Aen.* 3.91.

45 The term *calamus* appears throughout the *Bucolics* (*Buc.* 1.10, 2.32, 5.2, 5.48, 6.69, 8.24), signifying the reeds of landscape and the instrument of pastoral poetic composition.

46 Coleman 1977: 232.

47 Hunter 1999: 70 *ad* 1.1: "'sweetness' is to be the key quality of Theocritus's bucolic verse."

48 For the image of pipes constructed with wax, see [Theocr.] *Id.* 8.18–24. The honey-sweet fragrance emanating from the pipes Daphnis offers to Pan in the first *Idyll* (*Id.* 1.128–9) is attributed to wax, presumably that used in the construction of the instrument. Aside from the passage in the second *Bucolic*, waxen pipes also appear in Vergil's third *Bucolic* (3.25–6): *aut umquam tibi fistula cera | iuncta fuit?* ("Or did you ever have pipes joined together with wax?").

49 Coleman 1977: 75 *ad Buc.* 1.10 notes that the term *calamus* is a Greek loan word, which may be used interchangeably with the normative Latin term *harundo*.

50 Keith 1992: 113. This image of Apollo-as-*pastor* bears striking similarity to the figure of Lycidas in Theocritus's seventh *Idyll*, a parallel that has been elsewhere observed: see Williams 1971: 141; and Keith 1992: 113.

51 Prominently placed at first position in the first line of Apollo's speech, *bos* recalls both the generic term bucolic, and the name of the land itself (*Met.* 3.10): *"bos tibi" Phoebus ait "solis occurret in aruis ..."* ("'A cow' said Phoebus 'will meet you in solitary fields'.") Ovid's use of *antrum* for the cave from which the cow descends (*Met.* 3.14) also recalls Vergil's inventive Latinization of the Greek word ἄντρον in the *Bucolics*; see Coleman 1977: 88 *ad Buc.* 1.75.

52 Myers 1994a: 113–27; and Myers 1994b: passim.

53 For example, the numerous *loca amoena* that appear throughout the poem as sites of rape and violence are also saturated with pastoral language and imagery; see Parry 1964.

54 For discussion of the bucolic or proto-pastoral significance of the Homeric and Hesiodic epics and their influence on Theocritus's *Idylls*, see Segal 1981: 41–3, 115–16, 156–8, 172–4, 211–12; Halperin 1983: 174–6, 218–48; Gutzwiller

1991: 23–44; and Hunter 1996: 90–7. For discussion of intertextual interaction between Vergil's *Bucolics* and the *Aeneid,* see: Klingner 1956: 256–74; Alpers 1979: 240–9; Boyle 1993: 102–3. On the pastoral resonance of Vergil's description of Evander's realm in *Aeneid* 8, see: Putnam 1965: 105–50.

WORKS CITED

Alpers, P. 1979. *The Singer of the Eclogues: A Study of Virgilian Pastoral.* Berkeley.

– 1986. "Community and Convention in Vergilian Pastoral." In *Vergil at 2000: Commemorative Essays on the Poet and His Influence,* edited by J.D. Bernard, 43–65. New York.

Anderson, W.S., ed. 1997. *Ovid's* Metamorphoses *Books 1–5.* Norman, OK.

Barchiesi, A., ed. 2005. *Ovidio: Metamorfosi, Vol. I (Libri I–III).* Milan.

Boyd, B.W., ed. 2002. *Brill's Companion to Ovid.* Leiden.

Boyle, A.J., ed. 1993. *Roman Epic.* London.

Breed, B.W. 2006. *Pastoral Inscriptions: Reading and Writing in Virgil's* Eclogues. London.

Clausen, W. 1995. *A Commentary on Virgil,* Eclogues. Oxford.

Coleman, R., ed. 1977. *Vergil:* Eclogues. Cambridge.

Davis, G. 2012. Parthenope*: The Interplay of Ideas in Vergilian Bucolic.* Leiden and Boston.

Farrell, J. 1992. "Dialogue of Genres in Ovid's 'Lovesong of Polyphemus' (*Metamorphoses* 13.719–897)." *AJP* 113.2: 235–68.

Gow, A.S.F., ed. 1965a. *Theocritus.* I. Cambridge.

– 1965b. *Theocritus.* II. Cambridge.

Gutzwiller, K.J. 1991. *Theocritus' Pastoral Analogies: The Formation of a Genre.* Madison, WI.

– 2006. "The Bucolic Problem." *CP* 101.4: 380–404.

Halperin, D.M. 1983. *Before Pastoral: Theocritus and the Ancient Tradition of Bucolic Poetry.* New Haven.

Harrison, S.J. 2007. *Generic Enrichment in Vergil and Horace.* Oxford.

Hubbard, T.K. 1998. *The Pipes of Pan.* Michigan.

Hunter, R. 1996. *Theocritus and the Archaeology of Greek Poetry.* Cambridge.

– ed. 1999. *Theocritus: A Selection.* Cambridge.

Keith, A.M. 1992. *The Play of Fictions: Studies in Ovid's* Metamorphoses *Book 2.* Ann Arbor.

– 2002. "Sources and Genres in Ovid's *Metamorphoses.*" In Boyd 2002: 235–69.

Klingner, F. 1956. *Römische Geistewelt.* 3rd ed. Munich.

Knox, P.E. 1986. *Ovid's* Metamorphoses *and the Traditions of Augustan Poetry.* Cambridge.

Konstan, D. 1991. "The Death of Argus, or What Stories Do: Audience Response in Ancient Fiction and Theory." *Helios* 18: 15–30.

Mynors, R.A.B., ed. 1969. *P. Vergili Maronis Opera*. Oxford.

Myers, S. 1994a. *Ovid's Causes: Cosmogony and Aetiology in the* Metamorphoses. Ann Arbor.

– 1994b. "*Ultimus Ardor*: Pomona and Vertumnus in Ovid's *Met.* 14.623–771." *CJ* 89: 225–50.

Nicoll, W.S.M. 1980. "Cupid, Apollo, and Daphne (Ovid, *Met.* 1. 452 ff.)." *CQ* 30.1: 174–82.

Parry, H. 1964. "Ovid's *Metamorphoses*: Violence in a Pastoral Landscape." *TAPA* 95: 268–82.

Putnam, M.C.J. 1965. *The Poetry of the* Aeneid*: Four Studies in Imaginative Unity and Design*. Cambridge.

Rosati, G. 2002. "Narrative Techniques and Narrative Structures in the *Metamorphoses*." In Boyd 2002: 271–304.

Segal, C. 1981. *Poetry and Myth in Ancient Pastoral: Essays on Theocritus and Virgil*. Princeton, NJ.

Solodow, J.B. 1988. *The World of Ovid's* Metamorphoses. Chapel Hill, NC.

Tarrant, R.J., ed. 2004. *P. Ovidi Nasonis* Metamorphoses. Oxford.

Williams, F. 1971. "A Theophany in Theocritus." *CQ* 21.1: 137–45.

Wright, J.R.G. 1983. "Virgil's Pastoral Program." *PCPS* 29: 107–47.

8

Narrative Transitions in Ovid's *Metamorphoses* 9*

C.W. MARSHALL

Introduction

The development of narratalogical approaches to classical literature has, among other things, described ways that narrative structures mark how an author or a genre chooses to begin or end. This can reveal underlying patterns that show something about the author's compositional process.[1] Similar tools can discuss how works make their middles, a more nebulous but still informative enquiry. For such analyses, there can be no text richer than Ovid's *Metamorphoses*, the self-consciously constructed assembly of so many mythological narratives divided over fifteen books, which yet also constitutes a single unified work, the *carmen perpetuum* (1.4) – the song that never ends.[2]

In *Metamorphoses*, something is always beginning, and something is almost always ending: *omnia mutantur, nihil interit* (15.165).[3] The programmatic proem promises a universal history in hexameter verse (1.1–4) and the inconclusive conclusion steadfastly refuses to end, since the poet will live (15.879 *uiuam*). The poem begins and ends; each of the fifteen books begins and ends; and operating at a level between these two, the poem can helpfully be understood as a triptych, with groupings of five books each constituting a meaningful structural unit.[4] Readers notice the sequence of the Muses in Book 5, Orpheus in Book 10, and Pythagoras in Book 15, as Ovid at each point associates his poetic art with his cosmological history. We do so in part because of the structural factors as each of Books 5, 10, and 15 make gestures towards an ending, but never quite achieve it.

One reason for this apparent failure is that the overt structural divisions are undermined by further divisions operating at the narrative level.

Metamorphoses contains over 250 separate stories, each of which begins, reaches a middle, and ends. Many of these sequences cross other structural divisions with a frequency that must be seen as intentional: Phaethon straddles Books 1 and 2, Thebes books 3 and 4, Perseus Books 4 and 5, and so forth; Book 10 ends with the finish of Orpheus's song – a strong and unmistakable closural gesture – and yet Orpheus' end is postponed until the beginning of Book 11. The many stories themselves are patterned into sequences, as with the several separate stories concerning Medea (7.1–403).

There exist structural elements in *Metamorphoses* (such as the book architecture) that meaningfully divide the poem and enable the reader to navigate it in manageable chunks, and there exist narrative elements (stories and sequences) that meaningfully divide the poem along other criteria and equally enable the reader to navigate the poem in other, complementary, manageable chunks. Given this, and the sheer quantity of divisions, one may be left wondering whether beginnings and endings can have any meaningful application in a poem where everything continually seems to be coming to be or passing away. When so much of the poem is either an implicit *incipit* or an explicit *explicit*, then any start or finish is only a transient change as Ovid's *animus fert dicere mutatas formas in noua corpora* (1.1–2).

Paradoxical and polemical, I believe all this to be part and parcel of Ovid's poetical plan: the work frustrates attempts to articulate the nature of its compositional structure, because the poem aspires to describe too much, with too much sophistication. While I do not want to deny Ovid his literary ambitions, I think it is possible to isolate a component of his compositional technique that resides outside of these structural elements: how does Ovid facilitate transitions from one story to the next? By asking this question, I hope to approach the nature of *Metamorphoses* sideways, and perhaps come to understand a component of Ovid's poetic practice that has not received sufficient scholarly attention.[5]

The division between structural organization and narrative organization establishes independent and complementary lenses with which the whole poem may be viewed: the political dimension (however it is perceived) remains, as do the extensive engagements with previous literature in Greek and Latin. One kind of transition exists in the negative space between book divisions: the blank space that exists on the page for the reader (representing the pause experienced by a Roman listener as one roll is replaced and another is opened) constitutes a real gap that is experienced by the audience. Whatever actual amount of time is represented by this break, the pause allows the poet a new beginning, even when it occurs in the middle of a story. This negative space created at book divisions is limited in two respects. First, however effective it might be, the pause created only exerts itself through absence, in the silence of the blank space at the end of the roll. Second, the pause created is governed by performance factors that extend beyond the immediate control of the poet. Given these limits, transitions at a structural level must operate with less nuance than those that exist at the narrative level. The gaps between stories can occur at any point in the poem (not simply at book ends or where a *coronis* exists in the papyrus margin), and when they do occur, their length, content, and form remain under the poet's control. These transitions, as the poet navigates from one story to the next, lie outside of the principle narrative sections of the poem but still remain an integral part of Ovid's *carmen perpetuum*: "the transitions are intrinsic."[6]

Not everyone has felt this way, of course. Quintilian criticizes the nature of Ovid's transitions, though he does forgive them (*Inst. Orat.* 4.1.77):

illa uero frigida et puerilis est in scholis adfectatio, ut ipse transitus efficiat aliquam utique sententiam et huius uelut praestigiae plausum petat, ut Ouidius lasciuire in Metamorphosesin solet, quem tamen excusare necessitas potest res diuersissimas in speciem unius corporis colligentem.

That is indeed a weak and childish affectation found in schools, when the transition itself employs some *bon mot* [*sententia*], and by this virtual legerdemain seeks approval. Ovid likes to play this way in the *Metamorphoses*, but he can be excused since he must draw together the most diverse subjects into the appearance of a single work.

As will be seen, the use of *sententiae* does not always feature, and Quintilian's counter-example to good transitions in oratory is not intended to constitute a direct criticism of Ovid.[7] There is an element of playfulness, however – *puerilis, lasciuire* – and that suggests a commitment to an aspect of artistry in Ovid that can to some extent be measured. My hope here is to examine and begin to quantify these narrative transitions, or "segues," to discover something about the dense interworkings of Ovid's poem. As a representative example, I will consider *Metamorphoses* 9.

Sophocles' *Trachiniai* in *Metamorphoses* 9

Metamorphoses 9 opens with a sequence of narratives concerning Hercules that appears to draw specifically on Sophocles' *Trachiniai*. The structural break from Book 8 to Book 9 is smoothed with the continued presence of Achelous, who had been introduced at 8.547, following the story of Meleager and the Calydonian Boar, which concludes at 8.878. That is not the end of the speech itself, however, as Achelous continues: "*Quid moror externis?*" ("Why do I delay you with outsiders?," 8.879). This begins a segue. The end of Erysichthon's autophagy (8.877–8) is being described by Achelous, a story that creates a negative counterpoint to the preceding story of Baucis and Philemon.[8] Achelous is telling his tale to his dinner companions, who include Theseus and Pirithous. There is a literary pedigree to the scene too, as Ovid draws upon Callimachus' poem of storytelling to Theseus on a journey home, *Hecale* (and the Callimachean reference redoubles as the story of Erysichthon draws upon *Hymn* 5).[9] Ovid's story ends with a paradox about *corpora,* as Erysichthon feeds his body by making it smaller, which causes Achelous to break off (8.879, quoted above). Achelous' body becomes a figure for Ovid's shape-shifting stories, since he himself is capable of assuming three forms (8.879–82).[10] But then he breaks off again, lingering over the word *cornua,* for the plural is no longer appropriate, since he now has but a single horn (8.883–4). "Groans followed his words," we are told, and the text breaks off, since this is the end of the roll.

The poet's intentional pause forces the reader to take a break, as the *cornua* (s.v. *OLD* 7d) of one book's roll are replaced and the *cornua* of another are removed and opened up, so we can hear the story of the lost horn. However long the pause for this change (does it begin a few minutes later? the next day? several months later? – if only we knew about the context for the original performances of Roman epic!), so long the listener to the poem waits in silence with the sullen river god. When Theseus speaks (described oceanically as *Neptunius heros,* as the river feeds the story to his sea of listeners), he breaks the silence of the god, breaks that of the audience, breaks that of the narrator of the poem, as Book 9 begins, recapitulating the groan (*gemitus,* 9.1). Grabbing the tale by the horns, Theseus asks sylleptically for the cause of the groan and the break on the river's brow, which is presently obscured by reeds (9.1–3). This unusual garland blurs the fluvial forms Achelous can take. The reed has become a byword for pliancy, as Achelous bends to Theseus' wishes, to tell the tale of the one thing that would not bend, when his horn was snapped. As Achelous again begins to speak, he promises a story (cf. 9.5 *commemorare* and *referam*), yet it is a tale of defeat and of humiliation, with the god triply vanquished (*uictus, uinci, uictor,* 9.4–7). And then he begins, with the name Deianira (9.8–9), which serves as an introduction to the story he does tell, of how Hercules broke off his horn, and created the horn of plenty, Cornucopia – a label given brokenly at the end of his speech, with the phrase *Bona Copia cornu est* (9.88), about which there is plenty to say.

These thirteen lines, *Met.* 8.879–9.7, constitute a narrative segue from the story of Erysichthon to the story of Achelous' horn, linking two apparently unrelated stories. While both tales are told by the same internal voice, the frame narrative provided by the segue accomplishes several things.

It moves the narrative from the remote to the personal (*quid moror externis?*, 8.879). It bridges one book to the next and provides a meta-narrative basis for the silence of sighs (*gemitus*, 8.884). It talks of changed bodies, and of what persists through changes. Its reed imagery (*harundine*, 9.3) creates a malleable contrast to the inflexibility of the horn. In becoming increasingly personal for Achelous, Ovid telegraphs an emotional quality for the story to pursue. Of course, whether the audience finds the story as sad as does the river (and whether Ovid expects us to do so) is a separate question.

The end of Achelous's speech presents another transition (9.89–102). As the embedded narrative closes, the narrator begins again in an authorial voice (9.89): *Dixerat* ... ("He had spoken ...").[11] *Dixerat* might be seen as a marker of closure, reintroducing the nature of the frame, but the lines that follow seem determined to continue the same story: the nymph in 9.89 recalls the Naiads in 9.87 who originally held the horn;[12] her dishevelled hair (*fusis ... capillis*, 9.90) recapitulates that of Achelous (*crines*, 9.3). The horn in the dramatic present (*cornu*, 9.91), as then (*cornu*, 9.88), is filled with fruit (*pomis*, 9.87; *poma*, 9.92). Verbal echoes in lines 89–92 serve as a transition out of direct speech, while insisting on lexical continuity. That this is meant as a closural gesture is clear from what follows. A night passes in silence (9.92), but as dawn breaks (*lux subit*, 9.93), the narrative remains with the *iuuenes* as they set out (9.94). The river that had halted their journey (8.549–50), now known to be a god and not merely a natural phenomenon, continues unabated, and so Theseus and his companions walk out of the poem, leaving Achelous to drown himself in his tears (9.94–7). Again a story ends, except that the narrator editorializes, assessing the grandeur of Achelous' grief (9.98–100), in which the image of the horn is physically set against reeds on Achelous' brow. The editorializing narrator addresses the subject of the next story directly (*at te, Nesse ferox*, 9.101), but this story will also concern Hercules and Deianira and will draw on Sophocles' *Trachiniai* for its primary literary material (9.101–2 anticipate the story that follows, but are functionally separate from it). Indeed, the only indication that there exists material preceding the Nessus story is the initial *namque* at 9.103.

Given Ovid's closural games, it is hard to say exactly when the story ends, and consequently when the segue begins. Is the recapitulation of the end of Achelous' speech part of the transition, in the same way that the address of Nessus anticipates the story to come? If so, then the segue (introducing the frame) comprises all of 9.89–102; others might choose to see the transition beginning at 9.93, or 9.98, or even 9.101 – it would certainly be possible to define the segue in such a way as to make any of these the obvious choice.

The book's third segue provides a transition of a different sort. The passage at 9.103–33 provides an account of the death of Nessus (described at 9.121 as *biformis* to complement the three-bodied Achelous, with *terga sagitta* at 9.127 echoing the same words that also end 9.102). Time passes (9.134–7):

Longa fuit medii mora temporis, actaque magni
Herculis implerant terras odiumque nouercae.
uictor ab Oechalia Cenaeo sacra parabat
uota Ioui …

There was a long intervening lapse of time, and the deeds of great
Hercules had filled the lands and the hatred of his stepmother.
The victor at Oechalia was preparing a sacred offering
to Cenaean Jove …

Line 136 has brought us to the time presented in Sophocles' play (which Ovid and some of his readers know), though Ovid focuses not on Deianira but on Hercules (cf. *Heroides* 9), as he foregrounds the sacrifice, a story which continues until the metamorphosis of lithic Lichas at 9.225. Is it therefore right to see 9.134–5 as a two-line segue? I think it is. Like the book's first two stories, this one bears a specific relationship to Sophocles' *Trachiniai*. Since this is the only passage set during the play's action, it makes sense to view it as a discrete unit; the passage of time (*longa … mora*) supports this. This is also the first time Hercules is named in Book 9; the next will come when Jupiter is addressing the gods about Hercules' apotheosis, at 9.256 and 9.264 (cf. 9.278, 286). Having been named in passing at 7.364 as a means for establishing the chronology of a minor bovine metamorphosis soon after the first Trojan war, Hercules's name has been absent from the epic, and in this book periphrases have been used instead, particularly "Alcides" (9.13, 51, 110, 217), or simply *ille*. Hercules' name at the beginning is unnecessary: *uictor ab Oechalia* offers a rock-solid identification.

After the *aition*, the poet continues, and offers an affirmation that sailors still see the stone (9.226–9):

nunc quoque in Euboico scopulus breuis eminet alto
gurgite et humanae seruat uestigia formae,
quem, quasi sensurum, nautae calcare uerentur
appellantque Lichan. At tu, Iouis inclita proles … 229

Even now there is a low protruding rock in the deep Euboean
flood which keeps traces of its human form,
and which sailors fear to tread on as if it would feel them,
and they call it Lichas. But you, famed offspring of Jupiter …

Does the *nunc quoque* clause complete the *aition* (and therefore constitute the final closural gesture), or is it part of the poet's segue to the next story, which, while anticipated in *Trachiniai*, is set after it (and, like so much else, is a variant from the Sophoclean version, using Philoctetes and not Hyllus as the agent of immolation)? I think it is probably best to see the story extend until the caesura at 9.229, with the sonorous *appellantque Lichan* serving as the conclusion. What follows is a direct address of Hercules, who becomes the subject of the story of the pyre on Mt Oeta (9.229–72). The segue itself, then, falls within the hexameter, as under-articulated as can be. The poet varies his technique, cutting his tale at the caesura, and uses the inceptive vocative to begin a new story mid-line, as he returns from the present day to Hercules.

This is the end of Ovid's rendering of Sophocles' *Trachiniai*, though the presence of Hercules continues to be felt. Apotheosis promises Hercules new life, and anticipates the apotheoses of Romulus in Book 14 and Caesar in Book 15.[13] Ovid's choice of what follows, however, deftly takes a step back: rather than continuing with Hercules' new life, he provides an account of his birth. So far in *Met*. 9.1–272, there have been four stories, all allusively related to Sophocles' *Trachiniai*: Achelous (9.8–88; cf. *Trach*. 6–30), Nessus (9.103–33; cf. *Trach*. 497–530, 555–81), Lichas (9.136–229; cf. *Trach*. 756–82), and the Pyre on Mt Oeta (9.229–72; cf. *Trach*. 1191–215).[14] Together these stories constitute a Sophoclean sequence, and we perceive part of Ovid's structural intention for the book. Each is comprehensible on its own: segues provide associated information, but never anything indispensable. Ovid employs first, second, and third person narration, and this in turn can be absorbed into our methodology.[15]

The Functions of Narrative Transitions

Determining what is not a segue has helped identify the book's first stories; the reverse process might identify segues as those sections of the poem that are not-a-story. If we accept the structure of the stories seen so far (each with a distinguishable beginning, middle, and end, capable of standing alone without reference to the surrounding text), there are five more stories in Book 9: the birth of Hercules, with the metamorphosis of Galanthis (9.285–323), Dryope (9.334–93), Iolaus and Callirhoe's sons (9.397b–449), Byblis (9.454–665), and Iphis and Ianthe (9.669–797). If this is coherent, then we should be able to see the passages not prescribed by these stories as segues: the five passages are 9.273–84, 324–33, 394–7a, 450–3, and 666–8. Segues are used to provide a frame narrative for the stories they contain. The first three of these segues provide another frame in which Alcmene and Iole converse following Heracles's apotheosis.

Alcmene delivers the story of Hercules' birth to a pregnant Iole (9.273–84): *Sensit Atlas pondus* ... ("Atlas felt his weight ..."). The passage begins with a disjunctive image, a momentary transition to Atlas, first introduced in Book 2, who amid the African waste feels the extra weight imposed on the sky by Hercules' accession (the sky Hercules himself once bore; cf. *Her.* 9.17–18). The next three lines (9.273–5) indicate that Eurystheus will continue to pursue the Heraclidae: Eurystheus had been mentioned in passing by the dying Hercules at 9.203, and so this too is part of a gesture of closure. The same might be said for the following reference to Alcmene, who also has been mentioned at 6.112, where she is Tirynthia (cf. 8.544, 9.23), but has not been a character in the poem so far. Indeed, it is only with the mention of Iole at 9.278 that the audience is aware that the influence of the *Trachiniai* persists: lines 278–80 describe Hyllus (not mentioned previously) taking her into his bed and into his heart (apparently in that order) according to his father's wishes, and now she has been impregnated *generoso semine* (9.280; cf. Soph. *Trach.* 1216–51, where Heracles exacts a promise from Hyllus).

Alcmene wishes Iole a smoother birth than that she had with Hercules. Interestingly, *Alcmene incipit* (9.281) is not the beginning of Alcmene's story: the phrase lies enjambed after *cui sic* (9.280), and so does not quite stand alone as a beginning should; second, the identity of the addressee (*tibi,* 9.281) cannot be deduced from the context of the story, and so is dependent upon the frame narrative provided by the segue; third, though of less weight, is *namque* (9.285), which had begun the book's second story at 9.103, and now begins the next. While maintaining contact with the previous sequence, both through character continuity and fleeting allusion to *Trachiniai,* this segue introduces a new narrative voice to provide a first-hand account of the birth of Hercules.[16] Surprisingly for a mother in the throes of labour (9.289 ends with *labores,* providing an painful echo of Hercules' *labores* at 9.277), Alcmene's suffering serves simply as scene setting for the metamorphosis of Galanthis, *una ministrarum* (9.306, a phrase that had been used of the Nymph holding the Cornucopia at 9.90). Changed to a weasel, Galanthis *ore parit* ("gives birth through her mouth," 9.323), and so at least is spared the particular pains Alcmene has undergone.[17]

Following this speech, the frame narrative returns (9.324–33): *Dixit et admonitu ueteris commota ministrae* | *ingemuit* ("She spoke and, much moved by the warning given by her former serving girl, | she groaned ..."). The names of the speakers are not mentioned as one stops and the other begins, the groan echoing that in 9.1. Following the birth story, Iole calls Alcmene *genetrix* (326), but raises the stakes for the tale she tells, since its subject is going to be a blood relation (albeit a half-sibling). As she begins, she also provides a précis of the story to follow, yet it introduces no material required to understand the story itself. The story proper begins (*est lacus*, 9.334) with the tranquil setting of a *locus amoenus* (indeed, a *lacus amoenus*, 9.334–5), which Dryope habitually would visit (9.336). The relationship to the speaker established in the segue adds pathos but offers no essential information.

As Alcmene dries Iole's tears, the next segue is filled with characteristic Ovidian touches (9.394–7):

> Dumque refert Iole factum mirabile, dumque
> Eurytidos lacrimas admoto police siccat
> Alcmene (flet et ipsa tamen), compescuit omnem
> res noua tristitiam. nam…

> And while Iole told of the amazing event, and while
> Alcmene was using her thumb to dry the tears
> of Eurytus' daughter (and yet she wept herself), a new affair
> subdued all their sadness. For…

The tableau of the two women is suspended mid-line, as a new subject is introduced. They never leave this comforting embrace and the final image of mutual consolation and sadness extends indefinitely. The story that follows, though ostensibly tied to the Herculean sequence, does not involve the women, and does not refer to them. These three segues place the women's speeches within the larger Herculean context: though they have nothing to do with Hercules himself, the very fact that their narrators exist within his sphere continues the larger sequence begun at 9.1. The segue at 9.273–84 embeds the story within the character speeches; lines 324–33 switch narrators from Alcmene to Iole; lines 394–7a allow them to share their mutual sorrow.

The next segue embodies both geographical and genealogical continuity (9.450–6):

> Hic tibi, dum sequitur patriae curuamina ripae,
> filia Maeandri totiens redeuntis eodem
> cogita Cyanee praestanti corpora forma,
> Byblida cum Cauno, prolem est enixa gemellam.
> Byblis in extemplo est ut ament concessa puellae,
> Byblis Apollinei correpta cupidine fratris.
> [non soror ut fratrem nec qua debebat amebat.]
> illa quidem primo …

Here, while Meander's daughter, Cyanee, was following the windings
of her father's bank as it returned so many times to the same place,
she was known by you; and children of surpassing beauty,
Byblis and Caunis, twin offspring, were borne by her.
Byblis is a warning that girls should love what is permitted,
Byblis was seized with desire for her Apolline brother.
[She was loving, not as a sister towards a brother, nor as she ought.]
At first, indeed, she …

After a wandering account of Iolaus, which transitions into a description of Callirhoe's sons and then Miletus, the vagabond Miletus encounters the daughter of Maeander, Cyanee, and they become the parents of Byblis and Caunis. Geographical continuity is weakly motivated, but the genealogical link ties the stories together, as the segue recapitulates on the meandering Maeander, mentioned in a simile in the previous book (8.162–6a) and *en passant* at 2.246. As Heraclitus knew, however, you cannot step into the same river twice, and the return of Maeander means something different than it had previously. The introduction of Miletus might be seen as the introduction of the segue, starting as early as 9.441b (*qui, dum fuit …*). The Byblis story, as a stand-alone narrative, begins only after the triple use of her name (9.453–5) and lasts until she melts into a mountain spring (9.659–65). It is only in this transition that there is anything approaching the *sententiae* disparaged by Quintilian in the *Institutio Oratoria* (4.1.77, quoted, p. 142): but buried among the Byblical anaphora, lines 454–5 hardly suggest themselves for wide applicability. The segue extends from 9.450 to 6 (seven lines, six if 9.456 is deleted),[18] and it might arguably start as early as 9.441b.

The final segue in Book 9 is of a type already seen – the comparison (9.666–8):[19]

Fama noui centum Creteas forsitan urbes
implesset monstri, si non miracula nuper
Iphide mutata Crete propiora tulisset. 668

The story of this strange marvel would perhaps have filled the hundred
Cretan cities, if Crete had not recently,
With Iphis' transformation, borne miracles closer to home.

Crete has not been mentioned by name, though it is clear from 9.147–9 that Miletus, Byblis' father, has come from there. This recapitulation provides some hint of continuity from one story to the next, but it also provides an authorial cue to the magnitude of what is to follow: Crete seems to beget abnormal passions. Ovid raises the stakes for his audience again, as he had at the book's opening. Even if the listener does not think immediately of Pasiphae (she is mentioned by name at 8.136, though Tarrant accepts Mendner's deletion of these lines; she is also referred to indirectly at 8.122) and the reader will soon be reminded of her at 9.735–40. In this final segue Ovid promises something more salacious than incest and bestiality. That story, Iphis and Ianthe, occupies the remainder of the book (9.669–797), and exhibits its geographical continuity on Crete with what has preceded.

Transitional sequences in Book 9 connect stories to each other in many ways: Ovid's interest lies in the ongoing variation of the effects, offering his reader *poikilia*. The *Trachiniai* sequence, itself part of Ovid's engagement with *Hecale*, represents the variety possible: lines 1–8 introduce personalizing details, and raise the narrative stakes; lines 89–102 introduce a comparison; lines 134–5 introduce time passing; the caesura at 9.229 returns the reader to a previous narrative fork – a path untravelled. The next three segues offer different functions: lines 273–84 embed the story within character speeches; lines 324–33 switch narrators from Alcmene to Iole and offer a summary; lines 394–7a disembed the juxtaposed speeches, before the arrival of Iolaus. This does not exhaust the possibilities for how Ovid connects his narratives. Indeed, there are at least three major types to be added to the examples so far: geographical continuity (*hic*), chronological continuity (*nunc*), and genealogical continuity. Though *Met.* 9 does not offer an example of a segue emphasizing chronological continuity (two events happening at the same time), there are three examples in *Met.* 8, where the transition is marked by the use of *interea* (8.6, 183, 567). Solodow offers two more types, a transition through absence and a transition through contrary-to-fact condition.[20] Any given segue may serve more than one function.

Counting Segues

There is admittedly something artificial in this procedure of isolating segues: for example, at 9.274–84, the passage itself included both the introduction to *oratio recta* and the opening words themselves. The process can however isolate a series of stand-alone narratives that are thematically connected. The first four narratives all drew on the same intertext, Sophocles' *Trachiniai*:

9.8–88	Achelous
9.103–33	Nessus

9.136–229a	Lichas
9.229b–72	Pyre on Mt Oeta

The next three tie together figures particularly close to Hercules:

9.285–323	Alcmena and the birth of Hercules
9.334–93	Iole and her sister Dryope
9.397b–449	Iolaus and Callirhoe's sons (or 397b–441a)

The last two stories offer a geographical connection to Crete (where both Miletus and Iphis originate) which reinforce the thematic link of unnatural sex:

9.457–665	Byblis
9.669–797	Iphis

The remainder of the book can be seen as segues: 9.1–7, 89–102, 134–6, the penthimimeral caesura in 229, 273–84, 324–33, 394–7a, 450–6, and 666–8; i.e., 59.5 lines of *Met.* 9 (7.4% of the whole) are dedicated to transitions.

This is comparable to the totals in the surrounding books: 64 of 884 lines in *Met.* 8 (7.2%);[21] 58.5 of 739 lines in *Met.* 10 (8.0%);[22] 57 of 795 lines in *Met.* 11 (7.2%).[23] While one might question the specifics of individual passages, the overall picture will remain unaffected:[24] on average, just over 7% of *Met.* 8–11 are segues. Though some books might possess fewer such passages (e.g., *Met.* 7, for no particular reason), the average is stable. Further, segues typically serve one of the functions already identified: e.g., *Met.* 10.162–6 offers another example of summary, serving as a précis to the Hyacinthus story told more fully at 10.167–219.

Thinking in terms of segues requires a reassessment of the way Ovidian narrative is often seen to operate. Segues are a process, not a moment. They are more amorphous than a simple paragraph break, since they connect disparate stories with narrative (and, rarely, with nothing, as with the midline transition at *Met.* 9.229). Published texts of the *Metamorphoses* typically mark paragraphs, and these can be compared with the passages identified here as segues: Anderson's Teubner text (1998) for *Met.* 9 contains 19 paragraph breaks; Tarrant's OCT (2004) contains 22 (or 23, if we assume one at line 1); 15 of these are shared between them.[25] Of these 15, six coincide with the beginning of a passage identified here as a segue (9.134, 273, 324, 394, 450, and 666).[26]

Still, three of the passages identified here as segues do not correspond to paragraph breaks shared by Anderson and Tarrant. The first is *Met.* 8.879–9.7, a segue that straddles the book division and is one of the ways the poet stitches these books together. Both commentators do mark a paragraph at 8.879, but the addition of breaks at 9.1 and (in Tarrant) at 9.4 demonstrate something of the abrupt nature of the narrative here. The same is true of the next segue, 9.89–102. Anderson marks paragraphs at 9.93 (where his commentary also has a section heading) and 9.98; Tarrant has them at 9.89 and 9.98. Again, the function of the overall passage as a transition is made clear by the places where the editors differ in their placement of paragraph breaks. The solution in both cases is not to add paragraph breaks at 9.8 and 9.103 (the end of the segue, as I see it). Rather, it becomes possible to perceive the overall process of transition in these places, taking place through a passage and not simply between lines. The remaining segue is at the penthemimeral caesura at 9.229. This is marked by Tarrant, but not by Anderson, who does note the abrupt shift: "Brusquely at the central caesura Ovid abandons Lichas and … turns our attention back to the hero."[27] There can be no firm rules, obviously, but the process of thinking about segues may reveal underlying anxieties felt by editors who must work counter to the transitional process sculpted by the poet.

Segues exist alongside other techniques as the poet integrates disparate stories into the smooth flow of his narrative. They can be contrasted with the arresting function of the *locus amoenus*, which slows the progress of the narrative allowing the reader to linger over a natural image: for example, 9.334–5 (*est lacus…*), 10.86–105 (*collis erat …*), 11.229–37 (*est sinus …*), and 11.592–615 (*est … mons cauus …*). There remains a sense, though, in which the resulting stories – all that is not a segue – still do not stand alone: a story might begin with a pronoun that refers to a character named in the segue, or might begin with a conjunction. For example, in Book 9, *nam* or *namque* begins stories four times (9.103, 285, 397b, 669; cf. *at*, 9.229b). Rather than see this as dependence on what has preceded, *nam* in this position may almost be understood as a marker for the beginning of a new tale.[28]

At work as well, as always in Ovid, is the poet's extensive engagement with earlier poetry, much of which we can only begin to perceive, because so many of the Greek models exist only in fragments. A single example can complement the preceding discussion of Sophocles' *Trachiniai*. Callimachus' *Hecale* is clearly important for Ovid: Hollis identifies it as a primary source for the Crow in *Met.* 2,[29] for Theseus and Aegeus in *Met.* 7, and for Baucis and Philemon who occupy the midpoint of the poem's central book (8.626–720). I suggest, however, that the influence of *Hecale* lingers into Book 9, interweaving with the *Trachiniai* stories. Achelous' reception of Theseus in Ovid establishes as a parallel to Hecale's reception of him in Callimachus. The influence of the association extends beyond the initial story of hospitality, and it does so by replicating a literary move also made by Catullus. The echo of Hecale fr. 165 (Hollis) in Catullus 64.111 has the Roman poet transfer Theseus' Marathonian bull to the Cretan bull.[30] In inventing Theseus' encounter with Achelous, Ovid creates a third Thesean bull in the triform Achelous. Achelous evokes the bull of Marathon in *Hecale*, and (if only by its absence) he reminds the reader of Catullus' description of the Minotaur, whom Ovid's Theseus had dispatched earlier at 8.155–73 (cf. 8.122–4, 131–3).

Conclusion

The division of a book of *Metamorphoses* into stories and segues is a tool for understanding Ovid's techniques of narrative structure. The exercise allows us to imagine what *Metamorphoses* would look like if the segue passages were absent.[31] Without the segues, the poem would comprise a series of self-contained narratives in hexameter verse. There would still be distinct beginnings and ends to each story, and the possibility of a sequence (such as that drawing on Sophocles' *Trachiniai*) remains. Indeed, we know of a number of poems with this very structure: in hexameter verse, Nicander's *Heteroioumena* (?130 BCE) almost certainly possessed it, as did the poem represented in *P. Oxy.* 4711, an elegiac *Metamorphoses* that has been tentatively identified as that of the first-century poet Parthenius, whom Macrobius says was Vergil's Greek tutor (*Sat.* 5.17.18).[32] On one side is "the story of Adonis (1–6) and, following without connection, that of Asteria (7ff.)";[33] on the other side is a Narcissus story. As the editor of the papyrus observes, "metamorphosis is mentioned in the first two and may confidently be supplied in the last," and "[t]he stories of Narcissus and Adonis both conclude with transformations into flowers."[34] The papyrus, however, does not mark any formal division between the Adonis and Asteria stories. The editor hypothesizes that a *coronis* once existed in the margin,[35] but even this is speculative. Similarly, it has been suggested that in Callimachus' *Aetia* each story might be "followed in the papyrus by a *paragraphos*, which may mark the end of an episode or of a particular aetiological subject."[36] Rather, the poem in *P. Oxy.* 4711 appears to continue uninterrupted: the end of one story and the beginning of the next would then be marked in the text only by verbal elements within the poetry itself, either gesturing towards closure (such as the concluding couplet containing an explicit metamorphosis, as is found in lines 5–6 of the papyrus) or to beginnings (as in Hesiod's *Ehoiai*).

Segues are not then a necessary component of a catalogue poem of metamorphoses. Indeed, a deliberate structure did exist in the arrangement of Books 3 and 4 of Callimachus' *Aitia*: "We can tell that he alternated longer poems with shorter ones. Occasionally we can glimpse patterns of thematic variation, changes in focus, and contrasts of tone."[37] We would be mistaken, however, to think of these books as accumulations of shorter poems, as has been done by those who look to *Aitia* as a programmatic source underlying the organization of Propertius' fourth book, for instance. Callimachus instead provides a clear precedent for seeing such collections of stories as a single literary work, a perspective apparently shared by *P. Oxy*. 4711. Ovid has chosen to include segues, and in doing so evokes other Callimachean precedents, the most obvious examples of which are *Hecale* and *Aitia* 1 and 2. In *Hecale*, embedded stories describe the antecedent action to Theseus' encounter with the old woman, describing, for example, Theseus' boyhood and Hecale's meeting of her husband. Following its magnificent prologue, *Aitia* 1 and 2 provided a frame narrative in which Callimachus dreams he is a young shepherd on Helikon who engages in a question-and-answer game with the Muses. Origin stories (many of which are adapted by Ovid in *Metamorphoses*) are presented embedded within these answers.

The sophistication with which Ovid embeds, layers, and interweaves his stories allows us to perceive these narrative transitions as arguably the most significant innovation Ovid makes in his presentation of the poetic material (which may, admittedly, be modelled on other non-extant Hellenistic poems). "There is an old and venerable tradition of censuring Ovid's transitions as trivial, frivolous, and self-indulgent";[38] if nothing else, *P. Oxy*. 4711 shows that the transitions represent a choice by the poet. Within the elaborate and tangled web of narratives that comprises Ovid's *Metamorphoses*, hundreds of stories jostle for position as they vie for the reader's attention. Yet the audience is expected to navigate these passages with carefree ease. How this is accomplished is through the poet's use of segues, those transitional passages that slide the reader from one tale to the next. Segues are the stitching that hold the quilt of *Metamorphoses* together, and by examining them and their function, we achieve an increased appreciation of narrative structure in Ovid's poem.

NOTES

* The paper is offered in sincere gratitude for the continued kindness and support Elaine has offered to me and to many others over the years, and whose scholarship has contributed so much to our understanding of Ovid. I am grateful to the editors, to †Jim Butrica, and to Susanna Braund. This research has been supported in part by SSHRC.

1 Endings: Smith 1968; Fowler 1989; Dunn 1996; Roberts, Dunn, and Fowler 1997; Kermode 2000. Beginnings: Said 1975; Dunn and Cole 1992.

2 See Rosati 2002 for an overview of this approach.

3 I cite Tarrant's OCT (2004), preserving capitalization, and making minor punctuation changes to indicate when speeches are not excerpted complete. Throughout this paper, a and b are sometimes added to line references to identify the points before and after a penthemimeral caesura. The translation is that of Hill 1999, and is used because of its clarity and efforts to preserve the Latin lineation; at times my translation and the text will differ. In both text and translation, paragraph indents have been removed (except at 229, for clarity).

4 Holzberg 1998.

5 Previous studies include Miller 1921: 464–76; Wilkinson 1958: 231–41; Frécaut 1968; Solodow 1988: 41–6; Wheeler 1999: 122–39. All of these are selective, and do not focus on a single book or offer the quantification attempted here. Keith (1992: 22–8, 39–47, 63–7, 92–6, 114–23, 133–4) discusses transitions in Book 2.

6 Wilkinson 1958: 235.

7 See *contra*, Elliot 1985: 10–11; Morgan 2003: 71, 86.

8 See Gamel 1984; Myers 1994: 92–3.

9 On the influence of Callimachus in *Met.* 8 and 9, see Gamel 1984: 117; Myers 1994: 90–2; Crabbe 1981: 2288–90, etc.; more generally, with an emphasis on Vergil, see Thomas 1993. Hinds (1988: 19) notes the paradox of the river swollen by rains (*imbre tumens*, 8.550) being the conduit for Callimachus' slender muse; cf. Barchiesi 1989: 57–64. Crabbe (1981: 2315–18) also notes that the Achelous stories recapitulate the themes of *Met.* 1.

10 These details are drawn from Sophocles, *Trach.* 9–14. *Hecale* fr. 67–9, and his description of Theseus' fight with the Bull of Marathon, during which he breaks off a single horn; cf. Hollis 2009: 214–25, esp. 219, where he suggests in an understatement that *Met.* 8.883–4 "may owe something to Call[imachus]."

11 Solodow (1988: 42) describes Ovid's "sleight of hand to get from Achelous to Nessus."

12 It also recalls 8.579–80: *Dianae | Niades.*

13 The infamous anachronism that has Heracles still alive in *Met.* 11 (see Wilkinson 1958: 234; Wheeler 1999: 135–8; O'Hara 2007: 122) conceivably reflects the uncertainty of the apotheosis in Sophocles' play.

14 While it is likely that Deianira did appear in *Aetia*, it was a pre-Sophoclean warrior woman Callimachus depicted: see Nisetich 2001: 75.

15 Additional axes of course exist along which Ovid can introduce variation: Rosati (2002: 282–6) discusses narrative voices, for example.

16 Solodow 1988: 43.

17 For this unusual story, see also Plut. *Mor.* 381A and the early Christian *Letter of Barnabas* 10:8.

18 Tarrant (2004) deletes line 456, which makes the threefold echo of Byblis' name even more resonant as a transitional device into her story.

19 Solodow (1988: 45–6) uses this as an example of a "transition through contrary-to-fact condition."

20 Solodow 1988: 43–6.

21 Segues in *Met.* 8: 1–5, 152–4, 236–40, 260–72, 611–25, 721–37, 879–84, with no formal segue at the line breaks at 182/3 and 546/7.

22 Segues in *Met.* 10: 1–3, 106–8, 143–54, 162–6, 220–3, 298–314a (note that the break comes late, at the end of the fourth foot), 519–26, 558–9, 705–9, with no formal segue at the line breaks at 85/6, 243/4, and 502/3.

23 Segues in *Met.* 11: 1–2, 67–70, 85–90a, 194–6, 221–8, 266–73, 289–90, 346–52a, 379–81, 749–63, and the line breaks at 409/10 and 572/3.

24 For example, in Book 11, one could suggest that though they use *interea* as a transitional device, two passages (11.410–14, 573–6) function as segues, which would bring the total number of segues in Book 11 to 66 lines, or 8.3%.

25 Anderson (1998) marks paragraphs at lines **1**, 93, **98, 134, 211, 239**, 259, **273, 324, 394, 418, 450, 517**, 523, **564, 630, 666**, 702, and **764**. Tarrant (2004) marks them at lines **(1)**, 4, 35, 62, 89, **98, 134**, 152, **211**, 229b, **239, 273, 324**, 356, **394, 418, 450, 517, 564, 630, 666**, 714, and **764**. Shared paragraph breaks are marked in bold.

26 Paragraphs serve other purposes, too, such as marking the end of major speeches (as at 9.517, 564, and 630, which are printed as paragraph breaks within the Byblis story). Comparison can also be made helpfully to the organization of commentaries, since that reveals the structure the commentator perceives in the poem. Anderson (1972) divides *Met.* 9 into sections that begin at the following points: lines 1, 93, 134, 273, 324, 394, 418, 450, and 666. All but the first two of these correspond to shared paragraphs as reckoned in the previous note. Further, only half of Anderson's paragraph breaks coincide with structural units in his commentary. The structural breaks in Bömer's commentary (1977) operate at a number of hierarchical levels, and it is consequently much more difficult to derive his sense of a book's organization.

27 Anderson 1972: 432; cf. Bömer 1977: 364, beginning a new section here.

28 Cf. Hesiod's genealogical poem *Ehoiai*, where the same two words marked each new entry in the poetic catalogue. Ziogas 2011 considers "Ovid as a Hesiodic poet" (his title) as he discusses the representation of Atalanta in *Ehoiai* and *Met.* 10.560–707.

29 Hollis 2009: 33–4, 390; cf. Keith 1992: 9–20, 43–5. As has been noted, other links exist between Book 2 and Books 8 and 9 in the mention of Maeander and Atlas.

30 Hunter 2006: 97–100.

31 Implicitly, Wilkinson (1958: 234) considers this when he suggests that transitions are provided "[i]n order not to break the spell of continuity."

32 This attribution is supported in Hutchinson 2006, but argued against in Bernsdorff 2007. Reed (2006: 76) expresses doubt about the attribution to

Parthenius, but suggests another possible Hellenistic metamorphosis poem by Theodorus (*SH* 749 and 750 are particularly relevant to the papyrus).

33 Henry 2005: 47.

34 Henry 2005: 47, 51.

35 Henry 2005: 52.

36 Fantuzzi and Hunter 2004: 81, describing fr. 50.17 M.

37 Nisetich 2001: 130.

38 Wheeler 1999: 122.

WORKS CITED

Anderson, W.S. 1972. *Ovid's* Metamorphoses *Books 6–10*. Norman, OK.

Anderson, W.S., ed. 1998. *Ovidius* Metamorphoses. Stuttgart and Leipzig.

Barchiesi, A. 1989. "Voci e instanze narrative nelle *Metamorfosi* di Ovidio." *MD* 23: 55–97.

Bernsdorff, H. 2007. "*P. Oxy*. 4711 and the Poetry of Parthenius." *JHS* 127: 1–18.

Bömer, F. 1977. *P. Ovidius Naso, Metamorphosen. Buch VII–IX*. Heidelberg.

Boyd, B.W., ed. 2002. *Brill's Companion to Ovid*. Leiden.

Crabbe, A. 1981. "Structure and Content in Ovid's *Metamorphoses*." *ANRW II* 31.4: 2274–327.

Dunn, F.M. 1996. *Tragedy's End: Closure and Innovation in Euripidean Drama*. Oxford.

Dunn, F.M., and T. Cole, eds. 1992. *Beginnings in Classical Literature*. Yale Classical Studies 29. Cambridge.

Elliott, A.G. 1985. "Ovid and the Critics: Seneca, Quintilian and 'Seriousness'." *Helios* 12: 9–20.

Fantuzzi, M., and R. Hunter. 2004. *Tradition and Innovation in Hellenistic Poetry*. Cambridge.

Fowler, D. 1989. "First Thoughts on Closure: Problems and Prospects." *MD* 22: 75–122.

Frécaut, J.-M. 1968. "Les transitions dans les *Métamorphoses* d'Ovide." *REL* 46: 247–63.

Gamel, M.-K. 1984. "Baucis and Philemon: Paradigm or Paradox?" *Helios* 11: 117–31.

Harder, A.M., R.F. Regtuit, and G.C. Wakker, eds. 1993. *Callimachus* (Hellenistica Groningana 1). Groningen.

Henry, W.B., ed. 2005. "*P. Oxy*. 4711: Elegy (Metamorphoses?)." *P. Oxy*. 69: 46–53.

Hill, D.E. 1999. *Ovid,* Metamorphoses *IX–XII*. Warminster.

Hinds, S. 1988. "Generalising about Ovid." In *The Imperial Muse: Ramus Essays on Roman Literature of the Empire* (= *Ramus* 16 [1987]), edited by A.J. Boyle, 4–31. Berwick and Victoria.

Hollis, A.S., ed. 2009. *Callimachus:* Hecale. Oxford.

Holzberg, N. 1998. "*Ter quinque volumina as carmen perpetuum*: The Division into Books in Ovid's *Metamorphoses*." *MD* 40: 77–98.

Hunter, R. 2006. *The Shadow of Callimachus: Studies in the Reception of Hellenistic Poetry at Rome*. Cambridge.

Hutchinson, G.O. 2006. "The Metamorphosis of Metamorphoses: P. Oxy. 4711 and Ovid." *ZPE* 155: 71–84.

Keith, A.M. 1992. *The Play of Fictions: Studies in Ovid's* Metamorphoses *Book* 2. Ann Arbor.

Kermode, F. 2000. *The Sense of an Ending: Studies in the Theory of Fiction with a New Epilogue*. Oxford. [Originally published 1967.]

Miller, F.J. 1921. "Some Features of Ovid's Style: III. Ovid's Methods of Ordering and Transition in the *Metamorphoses*." *CJ* 16: 464–76.

Morgan, L. 2003. "Child's Play: Ovid and His Critics." *JRS* 93: 66–91.

Myers, K.S. 1994. *Ovid's Causes: Cosmogony and Aetiology in the* Metamorphoses. Ann Arbor.

Nisetich, F. 2001. *The Poems of Callimachus*. Oxford.

O'Hara, J.J. 2007. *Inconsistency in Roman Epic: Studies in Catullus, Lucretius, Vergil, Ovid and Lucan*. Cambridge.

Reed, J.D. 2006. "New Verses on Adonis." *ZPE* 158: 76–82.

Roberts, D.H., F. Dunn, and D. Fowler, eds. 1997. *Classical Closure: Reading the End in Greek and Latin Literature*. Princeton.

Rosati, G. 2002. "Narrative Technique and Narrative Structures in the *Metamorphoses*." In Boyd 2002: 271–304.

Said, E. 1975. *Beginnings: Intention and Method*. New York.

Smith, B.H. 1968. *Poetic Closure: A Study of How Poems End*. Chicago and London.

Solodow, J.B. 1988. *The World of Ovid's* Metamorphoses. Chapel Hill, NC.

Tarrant, R.J., ed. 2004. *P. Ovidi Nasonis* Metamorphoses. Oxford.

Thomas, R.F. 1993. "Callimachus Back in Rome." In Harder, Regtuit, and Wakker 1993: 197–215.

Wheeler, S.M. 1999. *A Discourse of Wonders: Audience and Performance in Ovid's* Metamorphoses. Philadelphia.

Wilkinson, L.P. 1958. "The World of Ovid's *Metamorphoses*." In *Ovidiana, Recherches sur Ovid, publiées à l'occasion du bimillénnaire de la naissance du poète*, edited by N.I. Herescu, 431–44. Paris.

Ziogas, I. 2011. "Ovid as a Hesiodic Poet: Atalanta in the *Catalogue of Women* (fr. 72–6 M–W) and the *Metamorphoses* (10.560–707)." *Mnemosyne* 64.2: 249–70.

9

Elegy and Epic in Lucan's *Bellum Ciuile**

CEDRIC LITTLEWOOD

The private concerns of elegy are conventionally opposed in Latin literature to the public and political concerns of epic. To be a lover is to exchange the proud spoils of imperial glory for the private humiliations of a slave waiting at the door of his mistress. The lover prefers to be called idle and inactive than to be praised.[1] Tibullus in his first, programmatic poem reaches back to the funerary origins of the genre and progresses from the passivity of erotic subjection to ultimate *inertia* in the arms of his beloved on the "bed/bier destined to burn" (*arsuro ... lecto*, Tib. 1.61). The poetry of loss and the poetry of desire, combined in the genre of elegy, are two sides of the same coin: both aim to paper over the absence (the inevitable absence)[2] of the beloved with the illusion of presence. In this essay I construe elegy broadly as encompassing *elegos*, the poetry of mourning, as well as the amatory mode of Roman love elegy.[3] I discuss the destabilization of the familiar opposition of epic and elegiac modes in Lucan's *Bellum Ciuile*, an epic that mourns what it cannot praise: the death of the Roman Republic and the birth of autocracy.

Pompey the Elegiac Lover

Before the battle of Pharsalus Pompey parts from his wife, the last of many separations and estrangements in Book 5: the Senate from Rome (1–66); Caesar from his mutinous troops in Italy (237–73), then from Antony (476–503), and finally from his troops in Greece (504–677); Pompey from Cornelia (722–815). As Caesar mobilizes his forces for the climactic battle that will determine Rome's future, Pompey and Cornelia bid each other an emotional and personal farewell. Pompey is ashamed to lie safely with his wife while the world is shaken by war but does ultimately choose the battle line over the bed (5.749–52):

> ... nam me iam Marte parato
> securos cepisse pudet cum coniuge somnos,
> eque tuo, quatiunt miserum cum classica mundum,
> surrexisse sinu.

And, as for me, now that battle is near I am ashamed to have taken carefree slumbers with my wife, to have arisen from your embrace when the trumpets shake the troubled world.[4]

His characterization in this scene is markedly elegiac. Pompey is unmanned and sets his love above the fate of nations (5.727–31):

> ... heu, quantum mentes dominatur in aequas
> iusta Venus! dubium trepidumque ad proelia, Magne,
> te quoque fecit amor; quod nolles stare sub ictu
> fortunae quo mundus erat Romanaque fata,
> coniunx sola fuit.

O, how much power has lawful Venus over tranquil minds! Love has made even you, Magnus, hesitant and afraid of battle; the only thing you wished not to expose to the blow of Fortune which was waiting for the world and Roman destiny was your wife.

Pompey and Cornelia finally part (5.796–7), *uitamque per omnem | nulla fuit tam maesta dies* ("and through all their lives no day was so sad").

Lucan's literary models in this scene have been argued to reinforce the elegiac colour of the episode.[5] The dominant model is the Ceyx and Alcyone story from *Metamorphoses* 11, another elegiac modulation of an epic narrative.[6] Husband and wife, emotionally indivisible, are physically separated, as lovers so often are, by the cruel sea. Both wives deliver the "schetliastic propemptikon" of the elegiac lover; both will live to see a husband's corpse bobbing in the shallows. The influence of the Ceyx and Alcyone narrative is apparent also in the sequence of separations, storms, and shipwrecks of the opening poems of the *Tristia*.[7] Ovid, exiled from his wife and from Rome by the anger of Caesar, imagines himself dying at sea. This sequel, as Niall Rudd terms it, is significant for Lucan's narrative of the loss of Rome.[8] Lucan inherits the Ceyx and Alcyone story already politicized through its reworking in the *Tristia*. The storm and the separation of lovers are already related to the anger of Caesar when Lucan brings them into his epic.

The other major literary reference point is the *Aeneid*: Pompey's emotions have been compared to Dido's as she watches Aeneas depart.[9] The sad day that parts husband and wife (*uenit maesta dies*, 5.741) recalls the final day of Troy (*uenit summa dies, Aen.* 2.324–5) and is recalled when Rome dies (*uenit summa dies, BC* 7.195).[10] Aeneas would have preferred Troy and chooses Italy over Dido (*Aen.* 4.340–7), but for Pompey Cornelia is the world (8.133) and his very self (5.756–9):

> ... si numina nostras
> inpulerint acies, maneat pars optima Magni,
> sitque mihi, si fata prement uictorque cruentus,
> quo fugisse uelim.

If the gods drive back my troops, let the best part of Magnus survive; and if destiny and blood-stained victor chase me, let me have a welcome refuge.

Ovid describes himself similarly as surviving through his wife in *Tristia* 1.2.43 (*dimidia certe parte superstes ero*). Ariadne says the same thing to Theseus in *Heroides* 10.58 (*pars nostri ... maior*): it is how elegiac lovers talk.[11] In his biography of Pompey, Plutarch described him as being excessively devoted to his wife (*Pomp.* 48–55), and an obvious way of writing that criticism in political epic is to paint Pompey and Cornelia in elegiac colours. Pompey overcome by personal concerns is a poor imitation of a Vergilian Aeneas. To many he has seemed more sympathetic because of it: wars more than civil are a crime, and Pompey's lack of appetite for them may be read as an expression of *pietas*, however fatal to the Republic.[12] Pompey's desire to remain in Cornelia's arms and thereby delay the end of the epic is a desire of Lucan also in Masters' influential paradigm of the author's narrative technique.[13] Generic coding is significant in the programmatic conflict between enactment of and withdrawal from this epic of civil war. When at the Rubicon the ghost of Rome appears to Caesar "with unmistakable allusion to Propertius 4.1," we remember Propertius rebuked by Horos for his Roman historico-military ambitions and advised to write love-elegy instead.[14] The familiar opposition that Lucan inherits between public glory and ignoble self-absorption is complicated in an epic that can have no triumphs.

A different approach is to stress the continuity between public and private realms. We see Cato with Marcia, Pompey with Julia and Cornelia (and Caesar with Cleopatra – 10.53ff.[15]), and through these personal relationships the natures of the public men.[16] Marcia returns to Cato for a funereal remarriage and to write her epitaph (*BC* 2.343–4), a particularly elegiac act. He accepts her because her devotion to the empty name of their marriage (2.342–3) mirrors his devotion to the empty name of Liberty (2.302–3): he recognizes himself in her. More than that, he likens his grief for Rome to that of a father at the pyre of his son (2.297–302) in a passage that anticipates "the shock of Roman women at civil war" at the beginning of the book (3.21–8).[17] Expected oppositions between public and private worlds, masculine and feminine roles are thoroughly dismantled. One effect of Cato finding his image in Marcia and in the Roman women is to invest his devotion to the dead Republic with the emotional intensity of elegy.

Ulrich Hübner makes a similar argument for Pompey and Julia in a parallel scene at the beginning of Book 3.[18] Julia's angry ghost appears to Pompey as he sails away from Italy for the last time. The scene has drawn comparisons with the *Aeneid* – the Trojans' first sight of Italy in Book 3 and the departures from Troy in Books 2–3 and Carthage in Books 4–5[19] – but in Hübner's view there is much more of Cynthia in Julia than Dido or Creusa (3.23–35):[20]

"innupsit tepido paelex Cornelia busto.
haereat illa tuis bella per aequora signis,
dum non securos liceat mihi rumpere somnos
et nullum uestro uacuum sit tempus amori
sed teneat Caesarque dies et Iulia noctes.
me non Lethaeae, coniunx, obliuia ripae
inmemorem fecere tui, regesque silentum
permisere sequi. ueniam te bella gerente
in medias acies. numquam tibi, Magne, per umbras
perque meos manes genero non esse licebit;
abscidis frustra ferro tua pignora: bellum
te faciet ciuile meum." sic fata refugit
umbra per amplexus trepidi dilapsa mariti.

"That paramour Cornelia married into a warm tomb. Let her cling to your standards through warfare and through waters, provided that no time is free for love between you, but that Caesar occupies your days and Julia your nights. The oblivion of Lethe's bank has not made me forget you, husband; the kings of the dead have permitted me to chase you. When you are waging wars I shall come into the middle of the ranks. Never, Magnus, by the ghosts and by my shade, will you stop being his son-in-law; in vain you sever with the sword your pledges: civil war will make you mine." So spoke the ghost and fled away, melting through her trembling husband's embrace.

We may compare Propertius' report of the appearance of Cynthia's ghost to him in a dream (4.7.91–6):

"luce iubent leges Lethaea ad stagna reuerti:
  nos uehimur, uectum nauta recenset onus.

nunc te possideant aliae: mox sola tenebo:
    mecum eris, et mixtis ossibus ossa teram."
haec postquam querula mecum sub lite peregit,
    inter complexus excidit umbra meos.

"At dawn the law compels us to return to Lethe's waters: we board, the ferryman counts the cargo boarded. Other women may possess you now: soon I alone shall hold you: with me you will be, and my bones shall press yours in close entwining." When she had thus brought to an end her querulous indictment, the apparition vanished, baffling my embrace.

In her jealousy, and in the love which will not be forgotten even in death, Julia is emphatically elegiac.[21] Where Creusa encouraged Aeneas to set sail for a new life in Hesperia, Julia promises to possess Pompey in death: *bellum | te faciet ciuile meum* (3.33–4). Rome too will not long survive Pompey's defeat, and in this respect Lucan's negation of the *Aeneid* through contrast imitation is only to be expected; but what of the elegiac colouring and the strong erotic charge? Certainly one may speak of Lucan's taste for the macabre or the pathetic, but Alison Keith argues that phrasing Pompey's political alliances in personal and erotic terms "recasts the murderous confrontation of Roman strongmen in a civil war over the spoils of empire as a catfight between two women competing for Pompey's marital attention."[22] She concludes her article with a more serious affirmation of the prominence of women's lament in ancient Rome and in Lucan's epic, but there is certainly the potential for mischief[23] in a genre that devotes so much of its energy to appropriating and subverting the very matter from which it claims to distance itself: *militat omnis amans* (Ov. *Am.* 1.9.1) and so forth.[24] I too shall come to a serious conclusion, what it means to write a devotion to the Republic in the language of elegy; but first some mischief, perhaps surprisingly in the person of Caesar.

Caesar in Love

In many ways Caesar is defined in opposition to Pompey. In the famous introductory pair of character sketches (1.129–57) Pompey is a shadow and a tottering oak waiting to fall, Caesar the divine lighting. Pompey stands idle, Caesar cannot brook delay. Pompey is all too human, Caesar a fanatic. While Pompey and Cornelia lie in bed with the doom of Ceyx and Alcyone hanging over them, Caesar mobilizes his troops. More than that, Caesar has just faced and survived a storm modelled on the storm that destroyed Ceyx (and the storms of the *Tristia*) and presaged by signs that recall those from the end of *Georgics* 1.[25] Ceyx and Ovid suffer death and the loss of love. Caesar returns safe to land and regains his kingdoms and cities (5.676–7). This is a contrast not just of success and failure, but of characterization. Caesar wins the war because he is not an elegiac lover but a creature of the big genres: he entrusts himself to a storm on the high seas and to a chaos that threatens to unbind the cosmos and emerges unscathed. Nevertheless, Caesar does speak the language of love in this book. The reason for his dramatic voyage was Antony's failure to send reinforcements as requested. Caesar has been likened to the Vergilian Jupiter, frustrated that the Trojans are not proceeding to Italy as destined,[26] but Caesar's appeals sound unmistakably erotic (5.480–1, 484–5, 488–94):

> illum saepe **minis** Caesar **precibusqu**e morantem
> euocat. …
> … non rupta uadosis
> Syrtibus incerto Libye nos diuidit aestu.
> … prior ipse per hostes
> percussi medios alieni iuris harenas:
> tu mea castra times? pereuntia tempora fati
> conqueror, in uentos inpendo uota fretumque
> ne retine dubium cupientis ire per aequor:
> si bene nota mihi est, ad Caesaris arma iuuentus
> naufragio uenisse uolet.

As he delays, Caesar often summons him **with threats and prayers** ... Libya broken by the shallow Syrtes does not part us with its restless tide … Ahead of you myself, through the midst of enemies, I struck the sands in another's power: do you fear a camp that is mine? I bewail the loss of hours of destiny, on winds and sea I waste my prayers. Do not hold back men who are eager to go across the fickle water: if I know them right, the troops will want to join Caesar's army at the cost of shipwreck.

Compare Tarquin assailing a reluctant Lucretia: *instat amans hostis **precibus** pretioque **minis*** ("her lover foe is urgent with prayers, with bribes, with threats," Ov. *F.* 2.805) or the Ovidian *amator* on the door that bars him from his mistress (*Am.* 1.6.61–2): *nec te **precibusque minisque** | mouimus* ("we move you neither by prayers nor threats").[27] True lovers defy the seas to be together, like Hero and Leander – or Cynthia and Propertius (Prop. 2.26B.29–58) – even if this means facing Libya and the Syrtes (Ov. *Am.* 2.16.21): *cum domina Libycas ausim perrumpere Syrtes* ("with my mistress I would dare to burst through the Libyan shallows"). Lovers normally prefer the "true" camp of the mistress to the military camp of a mere general,[28] but sometimes love will drive the mistress either in imagination or in reality to the alien world of arms.[29] These are love's clichés, and *tu mea castra times?* (Luc. *BC*

5.490) shows the perverse contrivance of a lover's speech.[30] Caesar complains ("*conqueror*") that in pleading with Antony to join him he is wasting words on the winds and water. *Queror* and *querella* are elegiac markers, and it is lovers' words above all that disappear in the wind and water. Catullus 70.3–4 (*sed mulier cupido quod dicit amanti, | in uento et rapida scribere oportet aqua*) is perhaps the most famous expression, but note that Ovid employs the topos also in *Amores* 2.16 (discussed above, p. 164) as he shifts easily and in the same figure from the uncertainty of Fortune, which the lovers defy, to the inconstancy of the heart (*Am.* 2.16.45–6):[31] *uerba puellarum, foliis leuiora caducis, | inrita, qua uisum est, uentus et unda ferunt* ("Wind and wave carry unfulfilled where they wish the words of girls, lighter than falling leaves"). This is all of course very far from Caesar's own version of his communication (Caes. *B Civ.* 3.25): *Caesar Brundisium ad suos seuerius scripsit* ("Caesar wrote more sternly to his supporters in Brundisium").

Believing his troops are eager to play Leander, Lucan's Caesar slips unnoticed out of his own camp in the middle of the night while the guards are asleep – just like Nisus and Euryalus and/or just like a lover, depending on genre[32] – and sets sail for Italy and Antony. In putting himself in danger like this he does what slaves would barely dare to do (5.509). This is reckless behaviour certainly, and with perhaps a suggestion of *seruitium amoris*. So familiar is elegy's erotic refashioning of the military that once the epic integrity of a scene begins to fray, it is all too easy to unravel it completely. When Caesar returns to shore after his stormy voyage the soldiers cluster round him (5.680–2, 687–92):

> circumfusa duci fleuit gemituque suorum
> et non ingratis incessit turba **querellis**.
> "quo te, dure, tulit uirtus temeraria, Caesar ...?
> ... nullusne tuorum
> emeruit comitum fatis non posses superstes
> esse tuis? cum te raperet mare, corpora segnis
> nostra sopor tenuit. pudet, heu! tibi causa petendae
> haec fuit Hesperiae, uisum est quod mittere quemquam
> tam saeuo crudele mari."

A multitude of men surrounded their leader, wept, assailed him with groans and with **complaints** that did not displease him. "Pitiless Caesar, where has your reckless valour taken you ...? ... Is there none of your companions who did not deserve the chance not to survive your death? When the sea was sweeping you along, dull sleep held our bodies. O the shame! This was your reason for seeking Hesperia yourself, that it seemed cruel to send anyone on sea so fierce."

Note also Servius' comment on *Aeneid* 4.310–11 and his comparison of Dido to Caesar:

> et mediis properas Aquilonibus ire per altum | crudelis?
> CRUDELIS etiam in te odio mei. sic Lucanus de Caesare (5.687) ...
>
> And cruel, do you rush to cross the deep in the midst of the north winds?
> CRUEL even towards yourself in hatred of me. So Lucan on Caesar (5.687) ...

Caesar's relationship with his troops is tempestuous: they have only recently been reconciled after a mutiny in Italy. The lust for civil war had deserted the soldiers and Caesar addressed them in typically impassioned fashion (5.320–1): *miles, habes nudum promptumque ad uolnera pectus. | hic fuge, si bellis finis placet, ense relicto* ("soldiers ... you now have his [Caesar's] breast bare and ready for wounds. Here [i.e., in Caesar's breast] leave your sword and flee, if you want an end of war"). The Caesar of Dio Cassius, as one might expect, says nothing of the sort and assumes instead the calming role of a father who wants only the best for his children (41.27.1–2). No historical account of any mutiny among Caesar's men remotely resembles Lucan's in its passionate intensity. To find a parallel for this scene one has to turn to the poets: to the erotic, tragic deaths (attempted or achieved) of Phaedra and Dido, or to the trivial violence of the elegists.[33] Caesar's speech provokes an intense emotional reaction from his troops who prostrate themselves, as eager to die as to kill. The unholy bond between the general and his men is sealed by human sacrifice as they celebrate their submission in blood (5.371–3):

> nil magis adsuetas sceleri quam perdere mentis
> atque perire tenet. tam diri foederis ictu
> parta quies, poenaque redit placata iuuentus.

Nothing more binds minds which are familiar with crime than to destroy and be destroyed. By the stroke of pact so grim was order gained – the troops return to duty, calmed by the punishment.

Caesar's relationship both with Antony and with his soldiers incongruously recalls a lover's plaints before resolving emphatically in the heaviest of registers: the tragic criminality of the blood sacrifice that ends the mutiny and an epic storm to eclipse even those of the *Aeneid*.[34] Caesar's *furor* veers erratically between the erotic and the demonic. One may compare, very loosely, the fate of Dido whose burning desire, an elegiac figure of speech, is fatally literalized in tragic death on the pyre, whose literal and fatal wounding is prefigured by an earlier, figurative wound of love.[35] In the case of Dido the gap between the genres and their different narrative expectations creates tragic irony. Caesar's shifts of genre are altogether more unsettling and lacking in decorum.

The rhetoric of political invective offers one possible interpretation of the incongruous presence of the lover's voice in the midst of the epic of civil war. Cicero attacked both Catiline and Antony for being bound to their associates not by political *amicitia* but by something much more personal and shameful. Thus Catiline (*Cat.* 2.6):[36] *proficiscantur, ne patiantur desiderio sui Catilinam miserum tabescere* ("Let them go, so as not to let unhappy Catiline waste away in longing for them"). Similarly Antony (*Phil.* 2.44–5):[37]

sumpsisti uirilem, quam statim muliebrem togam reddidisti. primo uulgare scortum; certa flagiti merces nec ea parua; sed cito Curio interuenit, qui te a meretricio quaestu abduxit, et, tamquam stolam dedisset, in matrimonio stabili et certo collocauit.

You assumed the toga of manhood, which you immediately transformed into that of a prostitute. At first you were a common whore – a fixed price on your shame and no small one. But soon Curio arrived and took you away from your meretricious trade and, as if he had given you the robe of a married woman, established you in lasting and stable matrimony.

For Lucan to sneer at Caesar pining after Antony, particularly in contrast with the *iusta Venus* (5.728) of Cornelia and Pompey, would seem entirely conventional. But there is more than the familiar almost reflexive Roman dismissal of an enemy as a "girly-man." Caesar imposed a private voice on the Republic (3.105–9):

> ... non consule sacrae
> fulserunt sedes, non proxima lege potestas,
> praetor adest, uacuaeque loco cessere curules.
> omnia Caesar erat: priuatae curia uocis
> testis adest.

the sacred chairs were not resplendent with the consul, no praetor – by law the next in rank – is present, and the empty curule chairs are missing from their place. Caesar was everything: the Senate House listened to one man's voice.

One of the ways of representing this abomination is to characterize Caesar as an elegiac lover, to represent his alliances and his voice as personal. Distinctions between public and private collapse in a world in which Caesar is everything, in "the centripetal vortex of 'One-World' politics."[38] In the totalizing impetus of the *Bellum Ciuile* boundaries of literary genre together with social-political order are erased to leave only Caesar.[39]

It is of course not only by Caesar, but also by the defenders of the Republic that the boundaries of the public and the private are blurred. Cato's devotion to Rome is written in the elegiac mode. Pompey's dream of Julia at the beginning of Book 3 is clearly parallel to his dream of Rome's citizens at the beginning of Book 7 on which Morford writes: "Here Pompey and Rome are presented in a romantic light: their relationship can only be described by the vocabulary of love."[40] Is Pompey's bond with Rome disturbingly personal, as Caesar's is with his fanatical followers? Lucan claims that Pompey was of the senate's party, not vice versa (5.14), just as the consul Lentulus claimed that the senate remained the senate even exiled from its seat of power (5.17–22). But the day that demanded a pair of new names for the calendar (*nomina,* 5.5) ends with only one (*nomen* 5.47) (5.46–9):

> "**consul**ite in medium, patres, Magnumque iubete
> esse **ducem**." laeto nomen clamore senatus
> excipit et Magno fatum patriaeque suum
> inposuit.

"So, fathers, look to the common good and bid Magnus be your leader." With joyful shout the Senate greets his name and imposed on Magnus his country's fate and his own.

The last sentence of Lentulus' speech performs the transition from *consul* to *dux*. This accords with the view of Brutus, who described the senate as waging wars *duce priuato* (2.277–9), a charge Cato could only partially refute (2.319–22). Book 8 ends with the treachery of Ptolemy and begins with the exemplary loyalty of the people of Lesbos. Their loyalty to Pompey in defeat will be, he says, the measure by which he seeks out good and evil in the world. But just as Lesbos was Rome for Pompey because Cornelia was there (*hic mihi Roma fuit,* 8.133), so at his departure the Lesbians' grief for Pompey's fortune is far surpassed by their sorrow at being separated from Cornelia, *tanto deuinxit amore* (8.155).[41] Pompey's political ties are repeatedly coloured, even displaced by the personal and the erotic, and this is a manifestation of the disintegration of the Republic.

Memory's Different Voices

In this final section, I turn to elegiac mourning and epic praise as oppositional voices with which to remember Pompey and the Republic. Commemoration is a (arguably *the*) primary duty of epic. In Lucan's disjointed poem, "the ruin of Roman integrity" as Bartsch beautifully describes it,[42] Pompey is differently remembered, commemorated in different voices. The question of a suitable memorial for Pompey dominates the latter half of Book 8. Lucan inherits from the epic tradition a tension between public commemoration and private grief, which by the Augustan period has crystallized in a contra-posture of gender and genre. The *Aeneid* plays a crucial role in polarizing and gendering the poetics of private mourning and public commemoration.[43] Andromache at Buthrotum is a canonical figure. Mourning for Hector, she can only mistake the Trojan survivors for ghosts and Iulus for the *imago* of Astyanax (*Aen.* 3.310–12, 489–91). This is the paralyzing grip of the past, embodied in the grieving woman, that stands between the Trojans and their Roman future. In the figures of Dido and Amata the genres of tragedy and elegy and the passionate voices of lamentation and unsatisfied longing are aligned against the Roman destiny that Jupiter has prescribed as the goal of the epic.[44] One of the models for Lucan's Cornelia in Book 8 is the mother of Euryalus. Uniquely of the Trojan women she did not stay behind in Sicily (*Aen.* 9.216–18), but travelled to Italy. Cornelia similarly is the only Roman mother, as she significantly describes herself, to go to war (*BC* 8.648–9).[45] The grief of the unnamed mother for her lost son is an unwelcome voice in the *Aeneid*. She is swiftly bundled up and removed from the scene lest her lament upstage the authorized and authorial commemoration of Nisus and Euryalus, which inscribes them in the fabric of the Roman future (*Aen.* 9.446–9). The marginal and dissonant voices in the *Aeneid* become powerful, even dominant, voices in the *Bellum Ciuile* and also in the *Thebaid*.[46]

When Pompey faces the assassins' swords he not only veils his face, but also closes his eyes and silences his tongue so as not to mar his eternal fame with lamentation (8.613–17). The poet intervenes to supply the thoughts that the hero kept to himself,[47] in a speech that begins and ends with the knowledge that his wife, his child, and all posterity are watching the manner of his death (8.622–4):

> "saecula Romanos numquam tacitura labores
> attendunt, aeuumque sequens speculatur ab omni
> orbe ratem Phariamque fidem: nunc consule famae."

"Future ages which will never be silent about the toils of Rome are watching now, and time to come observes from all the world the boat and loyalty of Pharos: think now of your fame."

The serenity with which Pompey meets death and enters the memory of future ages contrasts sharply with the personal grief of Cornelia. Pompey sees himself becoming an exemplary figure not just for his family but for all those in the future who dare to break the silence of Rome's agony. Cornelia resents the separation from her husband and wishes to die with him (8.584–5, 651–2):

> "quo sine me crudelis abis? iterumne relinquor,
> Thessalicis summota malis? ...
> hoc merui, coniunx, in tuta puppe relinqui?
> perfide, parcebas? ..."

"Where are you going without me, cruel man? Am I deserted a second time, kept away from Thessaly's disaster? ... And this is my reward, my husband, to be left in the safety of the ship? Traitor, were you being kind?"

This is the rhetoric of elegy.[48] Cornelia carries in her heart an *imago* of Pompey (9.70–2) that differs from the vengeful soul that took up residence as an avenger in the hearts of Brutus and Cato (9.17–18) and differs again from the soul that ascended to the heavens and smiled from the perspective of eternity at the mockery done to his body (9.5–14).[49] The flight of Pompey's soul is modelled on the flight of Scipio's soul in Cicero *Republic* 6.[50] There is some irony that defeat in Africa awaits Cato and Pompey's avenging spirit, not the glorious victory and honorific cognomen that awaits Scipio, and in this irony there are significant questions: who will remember Pompey's name when Rome and liberty died for all time on the plains of Emathia, and how? In what voices? Cornelia lets go the memory of Pompey in military and political triumph – a memory that Lucan was at pains to recall (8.684–6) – and claims for herself Egypt and the grief and horror at the moment of his death (9.78–82). The future and the cause she entrusts, speaking not with her own words but with Pompey's, to their descendants (9.85–8):

> "... namque haec mandata reliquit
> Pompeius uobis in nostra condita cura:
> 'me cum fatalis leto damnauerit hora,
> excipite, o nati, bellum ciuile ...'"

"These orders Pompey left for you, stored up in my charge: 'When the fatal hour has condemned me to death, take up, O sons, the civil war ...'"

Having impersonated Pompey and delivered up the *bellum ciuile,* she then withdraws into private grief under the veil of mourning (9.110–16).[51]

In Book 9, when Pompey's insignia are burned in place of his body, Cornelia plays the focal and exemplary role. She is the pattern by which Roman soldiers remember the Thessalian dead (9.171–81):

sed magis, ut uisa est lacrimis exhausta, solutas
in uoltus effusa comas, Cornelia puppe
egrediens, rursus geminato uerbere plangunt.
ut primum in sociae peruenit litora terrae,
collegit uestes miserique insignia Magni
armaque et inpressas auro, quas gesserat olim.
exuuias pictasque togas, uelamina summo
ter conspecta Ioui, funestoque intulit igni.
ille fuit miserae Magni cinis. accipit omnis
exemplum pietas, et toto litore busta
surgunt Thessalicis reddentia manibus ignem.

But when Cornelia was seen as she left the ship, worn out by tears, with loosened tresses spread across her face, still more they wail, their blows redoubling. When first she came to the shores of allied land, she gathered Magnus' garments and his medals and his weapons and his armour stamped with gold, which he once had worn, and the embroidered toga, garments three times seen by highest Jupiter, and she put them on the funeral fire. In her sorrow those were Magnus' ashes. All devotion takes up her example and pyres rise on all the shore to offer fire to the shades of Thessaly.

The reference to *exuuiae* – the armour – is a Vergilian reminiscence (*Aen.* 4.651). David Kubiak comments: "Dido's '*dulces exuuiae*' are a sadly beautiful reminder of the love she and Aeneas shared; Cornelia possesses only the hollow emblems of Pompey's military glory: again Lucan glances sardonically at his great predecessor in recalling him."[52] What I would observe is not so much a sardonic glance, but the prominence of the elegiac mode in Lucan's scene of public commemoration and the blurring of the boundaries of the military and the erotic, the public and the private.

Tacitus offers another example of a grieving woman in a similarly focal role. When Germanicus died, Agrippina drew a similarly sympathetic and emotional response from the soldiers and citizens of Rome (*Ann.* 3.1–4). Tiberius himself made no public appearance and many noted the absence of a public funeral, of the family *imagines,* and of male relatives in attendance. They complained (*Ann.* 3.5):

non fratrem nisi unius diei uia, non patruum saltem porta tenus obuium. ubi illa ueterum instituta, propositam toro effigiem, meditata ad memoriam uirtutis carmina et laudationes et lacrimas uel doloris imitamenta?

No brother except for a single day's journey, no uncle to meet him not even as far as the gate. Where were those customs of the past, the effigy placed in front of the bier, the poems performed for the memory of virtue and the eulogies and the tears – or the imitations of grief?

It was Tiberius' poorly concealed intent to excise Germanicus from public memory by denying him the full ritual of a public funeral in Rome. Cato and Lucan attempt to avert a similar fate for Pompey. Cato delivers a eulogy for a dead citizen (*ciuis obit*, 9.190), which, Lucan says, could not have given greater honour had it been delivered in the Roman forum. But the mechanism that should transmute grief into Roman memory fails. The army is so geographically remote from Rome, and so morally dislocated from it, that its immediate response is to mutiny (9.215–17, 227–9):

uocibus his maior, quam si Romana sonarent
rostra ducis laudes, generosam uenit ad umbram
mortis honos. fremit interea discordia uolgi ...
"nos, Cato, da ueniam, Pompei duxit in arma,
non belli ciuilis amor, partesque fauore
fecimus. ..."

By these words greater honour in his death came to the noble ghost than if the Roman Rostrum had resounded with the general's praises. Meanwhile discord of the masses rumbled... "We – give pardon, Cato – were led to fight by love of Pompey, not of civil war; we turned partisan out of goodwill."

Cato wins them back to Rome's cause, albeit by appealing (9.276–8) to "the personal pleas for vengeance and curses enunciated in Cornelia's laments."[53] To some extent the republican army is loyal not to Rome or even to Pompey, but to Cornelia's impersonation of Pompey. This is potentially problematic in a similar way as are the ties that bind Pompey to Julia and to the past in Book 3 or Cato himself to the Republic in the funeral image of Book 2. Hershkowitz writes on this latter scene that Cato's "final statement echoes Dido's impassioned threat to become a Fury to Aeneas ... (*Aen.* 4.384–6). Will Cato similarly become a Fury to Caesar – and to Rome?"[54]

The slippage of *uirtus* in a broken world and the passion of the Republic's defenders is without doubt an important aspect of the poem (see, e.g., 9.147, *furens pietate*), but I wish to focus here not so much on *furor* as on the old Vergilian opposition of the eternal death of private grief to the immortality of public commemoration. In his pilgrim's progress through the deserts of Libya, Cato faces not only snaky madness, but also the erosion of foundational belief. Every year, to mark the beginning and end of the campaigning season, the Salii danced through Rome with the shield(s) that fell from heaven as a sign of the city's divine ancestry and the protection of Mars.[55] In the Libyan wasteland Lucan speculates that this was not a miracle but the act of a freak whirlwind (9.474–80). The ritual is empty, disconnected from reality and truth. Somewhat differently the book ends with the obliteration of the myths of Troy, origin of Rome and of epic, now ruined and deserted.[56] The *Bellum Ciuile* as a whole can be and arguably was read as a monument that did not allow the past to be erased.[57] The project is fraught with contradictions: to record the defeat of the Republic and the death of Pompey is to reify those events. Perhaps better that Pompey not be limited by a tomb (8.796–800):[58]

> cur obicis Magno tumulum manesque uagantis
> includis? situs ęst qua terra extrema refuso
> pendet in Oceano; Romanum nomen et omne
> imperium Magno tumuli est modus: obrue saxa
> crimine plena deum.

Why do you thrust a grave on Magnus and confine his roaming shade? He is buried where furthest earth floats on Ocean flowing back; the name of Rome and all its empire is the limit of the grave for Magnus; cover up the rock: it is brimming with reproach against the gods.

The end of Book 8 offers a series of conflicting memories and memorials: Lucan's image of Pompey's heroic face and the shrunken head on a stick fashioned by unspeakable Egyptian art (663–91);[59] the trunk that paradoxically identifies its owner by being headless (710–11); the humble and private burial performed by Cordus, which defines itself against the public funeral Pompey should have had (712–95); the absence of a containing tomb (795–805); Lucan's monument, which in concrete reality would not have the space for all Pompey's glories (806–816); the actual gravestone, defined against Pompey's public memorials real and imagined (820–2); Lucan's imagined pilgrimage to recover the ashes for Rome (843–50); Roman pilgrims in the sands of Egypt (851–60); the absence of the grave that would be more worthy of worship than the altars of the gods or of Caesar (860–4); the absence of a grave offering no evidence of Pompey's death (865–72). The sequence functions in a similar way as the sequence of seers at the end of Book 1

(584–695), where Lucan presents through a series of poet-surrogates (Arruns, Figulus, and the possessed *matrona*) the fractured poetics of a criminal epic, and in particular the conflict between the expression (and enactment) of *nefas* and the doubtful *pietas* of its repression.[60]

Here in Book 8 the choice for Lucan, as Martha Malamud sees it, is to weep or to thunder (175), to be "complicit in the victory of Caesar" or "obliterate ... Pompey ... and replace him with a divine but unreal hero."[61] The opposition of weeping to thundering corresponds very closely to the opposition between elegy and epic that is the subject of this essay. The quaestor Cordus[62] performs a pitiable, private funeral explicitly contrasted with the public funeral Pompey should have had (8.729–35) and, explicitly again, Cordus plays Cornelia's role in her absence (8.739–42). He recovers the corpse from the waves like Ovid's Alcyone (*Met.* 11.715–21), he embraces it, and weeps tears into the wounds like Ovid's Macareus (*Her.* 11.125–6). So far has Pompey fallen that Cordus can only cremate him by robbing another's funeral pyre (8.645–51). Only in the touch of a Roman hand (*Romana ... manu* 8.767) is the link with the Republic tenuously preserved. The absence of public honour is an indignity, to be sure, but elegiac mourning can also be seen as an appropriate commemorative mode when the Republic, in whose living fabric the memory of a Roman noble should be preserved, no longer exists. To weep for Pompey as if we were Cornelia and in the genre marginalized from public life is to acknowledge and complain of political impotence.[63] It is significant that Cordus plays the role of Cornelia as it is at the close of Book 1 that Lucan can be identified with an unnamed Roman *matrona* trapped in a cycle of grief and despair.[64]

Epic, Caesarian thundering offers an alternative, but not unproblematic voice with which to remember. A republican would have approved of Cato's qualified eulogy for Pompey at whose death not liberty, but the fiction of liberty, died (9.205–6). Compare Cicero's disapproval of Antony's uncritical memorializing of Julius Caesar (*Phil.* 2.110):[65] *O detestabilem hominem, siue quod Caesaris sacerdos es siue quod mortui!* ("O detestable man, whether because you are priest of Caesar or of a dead man!"). A similar charge can be levelled at Lucan, or at least at one of Lucan's voices. Repeatedly at the close of Book 8 Lucan, angered by the poor funeral on the Egyptian shore, complains of the worship of gods less worthy of honour than Pompey. Isis, Osiris, and Caesar have their temples in Rome while Pompey's ashes remain unrecovered (8.831–6). Perhaps in time of plague they will be recovered as sacred relics (8.846–50).[66] Roman travellers will worship Pompey in preference to Casian Jupiter (8.755–8), with whom Pompey is again compared in the final line of the book (8.872): ... *tam Magni mendax tumulo quam Creta Tonantis* ("... as false about the grave of Magnus as Crete about the Thunderer's"). The closest Lucan comes to making a god of Pompey is with his identification with Fortuna (8. 860–2):[67]

> ... nunc es pro numine summo.
> hoc tumulo Fortuna iaces? augustius aris
> uictoris Libyco pulsatur in aequore saxum.

Now you are like the highest deity. Fortune, do you lie in this grave? More majestic than the victor's altars is the sea-lashed rock beside the Libyan waters.

Augustus is not a common adjective. It appears only here in Lucan and twice in the *Aeneid,* where, with obvious implication, it describes the proto-Roman palace of King Latinus (7.153, 170). It appears three times, equally suggestively, in Ovid's *Metamorphoses*: of the gods in judgment depicted on the Minerva's tapestry in her competition with Arachne (6.73), of Hercules becoming a god on Mt Oeta (9.270), and of the divine mind that inspires the poet-surrogate Pythagoras (15.145). The process of making an imperial god of Pompey arguably begins earlier. When Cordus describes the funeral that Pompey should have had he borrows half a line from Claudius' funeral in the *Apocolocyntosis*: *resonet tristi clamore forum* (Sen. *Apoc.* 12) informs Lucan's *ut resonent tristi cantu fora* (8.734). Roland Mayer notes further that Lucan's plural, *fora,* is an anachronism if taken literally: there was only one forum in Pompey's time – not so in Lucan's imperial city.[68] A little later Lucan commits another anachronism (8.816–21):

> ... surgit miserabile bustum
> non ullis plenum titulis, non ordine tanto
> fastorum; solitumque legi super alta deorum
> culmina et extructos spoliis hostilibus arcus
> haud procul est ima Pompei nomen harena
> depressum tumulo.

A pitiable tomb arises, not full of any honours or the sequence of his annals so immense; and Pompey's name, which people were accustomed to read above the lofty rooftops of the gods and arches built with enemy's plunder, is not so far from the lowest sand.

There never were any triumphal arches with Pompey's name on them. Lucan speaks, to Mayer's exasperation, "from the point of view of his own age, when triumphal arches had become more common. Still, did he never use his eyes as he walked about the city?"[69] The anachronisms that Mayer so acutely notes are significant, not careless. In trying to rival imperial glorification, the Lucanian narrator comes to imitate it, to play Antony to Pompey's Caesar. This is of a piece with the irony that in the *Bellum Ciuile* the Republic is represented by one man.[70] Cato warned the mutinous soldiers at Pompey's funeral that if they fought for Pompey rather than for Rome, they fought for a master (9.256–8). To fabricate an alternative history in which Pompey's triumphal arches tower over the temples of the gods is to change the names on the arches but to surrender the ideological struggle.

Elegiac mourning betokens only political marginalization and extinction and enacts republican defeat. Writing the bond between Rome and her defenders as elegiac invests the relationship not just with an emotional charge but with a profound sense of helplessness: Cato goes to war in order to embrace dead Rome and the empty shade of a liberty already lost; at war, Pompey is still in the embrace of Julia's ghost; Rome exists only as a memory. The temptation of epic commemoration is altogether more sinister, for this republican history, fashioned to challenge the autocracy that succeeded it, is increasingly informed by its rival.[71] When Caesarism is the pattern for success Lethe has its attractions. The loss of republican ritual, and with it the memory of the past, is a concern of Lucan's poem, certainly, but it is not the only concern.[72] The endurance of Horace's lyric monument (*C.* 3.30) was tied to the endurance of Roman ritual,[73] but even the endurance of a community to practise that ritual does not guarantee immutability: as a community changes, so too do its memories.[74] Liberty of a kind survives in the very incoherence of Lucan's memorial: the oscillation between different commemorative voices, the dramatization of the struggle to reclaim what has been irrecoverably lost in an earlier age.[75]

NOTES

* My debt to Elaine Fantham's scholarship will be clear from the bibliography, where her work spans 1979 to 1999. I would like to acknowledge with gratitude particularly her 1992 commentary on *Bellum Ciuile* 2 for showing a student how to appreciate Lucan on his own terms.

1 I paraphrase Tib. 1.53–8. See usefully Murgatroyd 1980: 65, *ad loc.*, on the (un) military connotations of *laudare*, *segnis*, and *iners*.

2 On the inevitability of absence, see Kennedy 1993: 69–71.

3 In defence of this broad construction of elegy, see, e.g., Hinds 1987: 103–4; Hardie 2002: 62–5 and passim; Voigt 2004. Lowrie (1997: 77–93) discusses how Horatian lyric both defines itself in relation to the poles of epic and elegy and also "assimilates mourning song with the erotic concerns of elegy" (83).

4 Texts: OCT except Thilo and Hagen 1881 for Servius. Translations: Braund 1992 for Lucan; Goold 1990 for Propertius throughout.

5 For Ovidian influence on this passage of Lucan, see Bruère 1951: 224–30; Phillips 1962: 11–18; Viansino 1974: 121–4. For narrowly elegiac elements, see Rosati 1996: 151–2 and passim.

6 On elegiac elements in the Ceyx and Alcyone narrative, see Tränkle 1963; Fantham 1979: 336; Hardie 2002: 273–4. Cf. Otis 1970: 231–77, for whom this episode "is essentially an epic" (233). Both Hardie 2002 and Otis 1970 make comparisons with the *Heroides* to reach different conclusions. I find the common elements more persuasive than the differences. Against conjugal (as opposed to trivial and extramarital) love finding its higher dignity in a higher genre (so Otis 1970: 277), see Rosati 1991, on Protesilaus and Laodamia of the *Heroides* and a rapprochement between epic and elegy. More generally, on the complexity of interpreting Lucan's inheritance from the *Metamorphoses*, see Wheeler 2002 (esp. 365, where he observes that Ovid's *Metamorphoses*, "although identifiably epic in meter and extent, is famous for its mixing of generic modes").

7 See Ingleheart 2006.

8 Rudd 2008: 108.

9 Thompson 1984: 210.

10 Micozzi 1999: 352.

11 Barratt (1979: 251) notes these parallels and adds Hor. *C.* 1.3.8 and 2.17.5. *Odes* 1.3 is a propemptikon in which Vergil, leaving Horace behind, sails beyond the limits of lyric into the storms of high poetry (see Farrell 1991: 333–4). *Odes* 2.17 begins, *cur me querelis exanimas tuis?* Cf. Tib. 1.3 and Prop. 1.8. On *querel(l)a* as "a quasi-technical term for elegiac lament," see Keith 2008: 237, with further bibliography.

12 On Pompey's "human warmth," see Ahl 1976: 183; Viansino 1974: 125–6; Narducci 2002: 294–8. On Pompey denied the glory but importantly also (in comparison with Aeneas or Caesar) the guilt of winning a civil war, see Narducci 1979: 127–8. See also Thompson 1984: 212 on *BC* 6.303–5.

13 Masters 1992: 9–10.

14 Masters 1992: 8. The generic aspect is not developed here but see his later discussion of the *Bellum Ciuile* distinctively marked as "an epic of ... anti-Callimachean fatness" (145).

15 On the shameful love of Caesar and Cleopatra in marked contrast to the loves of the republicans, see Tucker 1990: 44.

16 So Armisen-Marchetti 2003.

17 See Fantham 1992: 143, 134–5, and 83–4 on all these passages.

18 Hübner 1984. On the parallelism, see also Finiello 2005: 169 and further 176, on Cornelia in turn coming to resemble Julia. Hübner (1984: 233–4) argues that

the dream of Alcyone and her *amor mortis* informs the Pompey-Julia scene (as well as the end of Book 5), which common intertext would again strengthen the connection. Feeney (1986: 242) connects Pompey, *magni nominis umbra* (1.135), with the *umbra* of Liberty, which Cato follows (2.303): "Pompeius is the played-out leader of a played-out cause: he and Libertas are both 'umbrae,' 'nomina'."

19 See Narducci 1979: 121–4; Rutz 1963: 340–4.

20 Hübner 1984: 236–7.

21 Finiello (2005: 170–1) accepts both Dido and Cynthia as models and stresses the elegiac colouring of Lucan's scene.

22 Keith 2008: 241.

23 Finiello (2005: 168–9) makes a calculating Cleopatra of Marcia with an allusion to Ov. *Ars am.* 3.431–2 and the charms of mourning widows.

24 For careful theorizing of the familiar point, see Davis 1983: 12–13.

25 For a summary of sources and correspondences, see Barratt 1979: 184–5; Morford 1967: 37–42. Of Lucan's many sources, I consider particularly important the storm warnings of *Georgics* 1 (351–514; cf. *BC* 5.540–56), because the eclipse of the sun foretells not just storms but civil war on the plains of Emathia (*G.* 1.491–2), and the storm of *Metamorphoses* 11 and its sequels in the *Tristia*. The influence of the storm of *Metamorphoses* 11 is all the more noticeable because of the clear traces of the Ceyx and Alcyone narrative on the Pompey and Cornelia scene that immediately follows (5.722–815).

26 Thompson and Bruère 1968: 11.

27 For the references above, see Barratt 1979: 158. The phrase (*precibus minisque*) is not confined to poetry. Cicero uses it of the threats and appeals Verres makes to Antiochus (*Verr.* 2.4.66). This context is not amatory, but Verres is a man at the mercy of his passions.

28 Compare, for example, Propertius' *uera ... castra puellae* (2.7.15) with his military *castra* (2.10.19).

29 E.g., Arethusa in fantasy (Prop. 4.3) and Lycoris in (literary) reality (Verg. *Buc.* 10.46–9).

30 If, as has been argued (see, e.g., Barratt 1979: 241–2), the influence of *Aeneid* 4 is strong in this scene, it is hard not to remember *mene fugis?* (*Aen.* 4.314).

31 See n. 12 above, on *querel(l)a*; cf. Prop. 2.9.33–6 on the Syrtes specifically as an image of feminine inconstancy.

32 For Nisus and Euryalus, see Thompson and Bruère 1968: 11–12. Lyne (1987: 229–30) notes that Vergil is here "radically extending the epic voice's scope" (230) through the admixture of elegiac material. For examples of a lover evading the guards, see Ov. *Am.* 1.9.27–30, 3.1.49–52.

33 Sen. *Hipp.* 704–12; Verg. *Aen.* 4.663–5; Prop. 3.8.1–8; Ov. *Am.* 1.7.

34 On Lucan's storm as aiming to surpass those of the *Aeneid,* see Thompson and Bruère 1968: 14.

35 The oscillation between generic codes in *Heroides* 7 has its origins in the generic plurality of the "epic" original: see Barchiesi 1987: 81–90 on both texts. For another example of this kind of generic trans-codification, as tragic death shows ominously through elegiac rewriting, see Casali 1995.

36 See Dyck 2008: 88 on "the application of amatory language to Catiline and his followers" (cf. 135).

37 On this and similar passages, in which political rivals are represented as effeminate, see Edwards 1993: 63–5, and 90–1 on Caesar specifically.

38 Henderson 1988: 124 and passim. Note also with Henderson 1988: 153 the entirety of history crushed into a single mass in Book 5 (*in unam | congeriem*, 5.175–6).

39 Cf. irresistibly, e.g., Champlin 2003: 208–9; Spencer 2005: 56–60: "By rearticulating Rome as domestic imperial space, Nero made explicit a process of slippage between public and private ..." (57).

40 Morford 1967: 82.

41 See also Keith 2008: 243: "Pompey's defeat is viewed in this passage primarily through the lens of Cornelia's personal grief, but her private lamentation provokes further (public) lamentation in the throng, with the poet privileging her private loss at the prospect of Pompey's death over his public calamity in the defeat at Pharsalus."

42 Bartsch 1997: 131.

43 See Panoussi 2009: 145–73. The gendering is not of course rigidly observed: see Panoussi 2009: 154–9 on Creusa's voice "assimilated to the voice of the state" (158); and Fantham 1999: 225, on the lament of Evander as closely resembling that of Euryalus' mother.

44 It is of course not that simple: see Hardie 1997. On the affiliation between tragedy and elegy, see, e.g., Conte 1986: 121n22. Of all divine messengers, it is Venus who delivers the prologue to the tragedy in Carthage (*Aen.* 1.314–68).

45 Compare Oliensis 1997: 305–8, on the "tangle of lovers and mothers" (306) in the *Aeneid*.

46 On the *Aeneid*, see, e.g., Perkell 1997: 271: "Her [Juturna's] lament temporarily halts the martial, forward-driving, male action of the poem." On the *Thebaid* as challenging Vergilian values through the rhetoric of lament, see Fantham 1999: 226–32; Henderson 1998: 247–54.

47 On the writer's power, see Malamud 1995: 175–80; cf. Bartsch 1997: 131–7, esp. for his duty to fabricate history, to "make our own meaning out of the rubble" (135).

48 *Crudelis* (584), Mayer comments (1981: 154), "echoes the cry of all abandoned heroines."

49 On the division of Pompey's spirit, see Hardie 1993: 42.

50 The influence of this passage on Lucan is mediated by its prior influence on the Elysium episode in the *Aeneid*. See Reed 2007: 165–6 in the context of this

discussion and, with reference to the fragile boundaries of public and private: "It is finally desire, *amor* (889), with which Anchises fires Aeneas with enthusiasm for his mission – a love that, from different perspectives, is both dishearteningly different from and unsettling close to the love he had for Dido" (166).

51 See Keith 2008: 249 on Cornelia's withdrawal, though compare her discussion of "*Cornelia's* call to renewed aggression" (my emphasis). Armisen-Marchetti (2003: 255) discusses "fides conjugale" transmuted into "fides politique" as Cornelia transmits a father's last wishes.

52 Kubiak 1990: 578.

53 Keith 2008: 253. On Cic. *Phil.* 2.68, cf. Dufallo 2007: 54–5, noting that Antony is represented as resembling "the Fury-driven murderers of tragedy incited to madness by the curse of their victims." Dufallo argues that the angry ghost of Pompey is the phantom that a worshipper of Caesar would create: it is to be understood as the fiction not of Cicero but of Antony, the delusional, fury-driven madman. The dissolution of republican culture is represented as a descent into histrionic madness. On the persistent anxiety in the first century CE (and with reference to Nero's reign particularly) that public life had been corrupted into mere theatre, see Bartsch 1994: 1–35.

54 Hershkowitz 1998: 236. See also Finiello 2005 on reiterated images of feminine fury in the poem. If Cato's "hardening gaze" in Book 9 is parallel to that of Medusa, as Bexley (2010: 143–9) suggests, this is surely far more problematic a parallelism than she allows.

55 See Ogilvie 1965: 98–9 on Livy 1.20.

56 Much discussed: see, e.g., Malamud 1995 and Spencer 2005.

57 Gowing 2005: 88–96; Malamud 1995: 180.

58 See Malamud 1995: 178–9 *ad loc.*; cf. Caesar's collection of Pompey's ashes within an urn at 9.1089–108, at once an image of closure (it also ends the book) and repression.

59 Even these polar oppositions are susceptible to deconstruction. With reference to Pompey's *caesaries* (8.681), cf. Henderson 1988: 140 on 1.188–9: "Lucan's *Patria* obtrusively collapses into a welter of signifiers, where her very 'hair', *cani* | *caesaries,* is already possessed by the 'name' Caesar."

60 On *uates* in Lucan, see O'Higgins 1988: 208–9n2, though the focus of her article, as of Masters 1992: 133–49 and 179–215, is Phemonoe and Erichtho in Books 5 and 6.

61 Malamud 1995: 179.

62 The quaestor Cordus is otherwise unknown and, Mayer (1981: 171) believes, an invention of Lucan. Having noticed that he shares a name with Cremutius Cordus, prosecuted under Tiberius for writing a history that praised Brutus and described Cassius as the last of the Romans (Tac. *Ann.* 4.34), I now cannot forget the fact.

63 On elegiac impotence in the public realm generally, see Voigt 2004: 202; and on Cornelia's love and the slow *passivity* of wasting away, Toohey 2004: 188.

64 See Hinds 1998: 8–10, on this scene as "a paradigm case of reflexive annotation" (9).

65 See Dufallo 2007: 59–60.

66 Mayer (1981: 187) compares "the recovery of the bones of Orestes by the Spartans or of Theseus by the Athenians." Lucan imagines a hero cult for Pompey.

67 This is not the text of Housman's OCT but of Shackleton-Bailey's Teubner, which Braund, rightly I think, translates in preference.

68 Mayer 1981: 174.

69 Mayer 1981: 183.

70 So Hardie 1993: 10–11.

71 Cf., e.g., Malamud 1995: 180–2, on Lucan as Caesar and as Alexander and "the dangerous proximity of Lucan's totalising vision to the totalitarian energy that propels his Caesar around the world and back to the origins of Rome" (182).

72 See Bartsch 1997: 133–5, on 7.389–99 and the Latin name disconnected from reality.

73 See Habinek 1998: 113–14, on this passage and the topos of monumentality.

74 So Gowing 2005: 94, on recovering the Republic in Neronian Rome: "(J)ust as all else has changed, so too has the seemingly simple act of remembering."

75 Cf. Masters 1992: 252, on 1.699–70 and resistance to closure.

WORKS CITED

Ahl, F. 1976. *Lucan: An Introduction*. New York.

Armisen-Marchetti, M. 2003. "Les liens familiaux dans le *Bellum Civile* de Lucain." In *Gli Annei*, edited by G. and G. Mazzoli, 245–58. Como.

Barchiesi, A. 1987. "Narratività e convenzione nelle *Heroides*." *MD* 19: 63–90.

Barratt, P. 1979. *M. Annaei Lucani Belli Civilis Liber V. A Commentary*. Amsterdam.

Bartsch, S. 1994. *Actors in the Audience: Theatricality and Doublespeak from Nero to Hadrian*. Cambridge.

– 1997. *Ideology in Cold Blood. A Reading of Lucan's Civil War*. Cambridge.

Bexley, E. 2010. "The Myth of the Republic: Medusa and Cato in Lucan, *Pharsalia* 9." In *Lucan's Bellum Civile: Between Epic Tradition and Aesthetic Innovation*, edited by N. Hömke and C. Reitz, 135–54. Berlin.

Braund, S.H. 1992. *Lucan: Civil War*. Oxford.

Bruère, R.T. 1951. "Lucan's Cornelia." *CP* 46: 221–36.

Casali, S. 1995. "Tragic Irony in Ovid, *Heroides* 9 and 11." *CQ* 45.2: 505–11.

Champlin, E. 2003. *Nero*. Cambridge.

Conte, G.-B. 1986. *The Rhetoric of Imitation: Genre and Poetic Memory in Virgil and Other Latin Poets*, edited by C. Segal. Ithaca.

Davis, G. 1983. *The Death of Procris: 'Amor' and the Hunt in Ovid's Metamorphoses*. Rome.

Dufallo, B. 2007. *The Ghosts of the Past: Latin Literature, the Dead and Rome's Transition to a Principate*. Columbus.

Dyck, A.R., ed. 2008. *Cicero:* Catilinarians. Cambridge.

Edwards, C. 1993. *The Politics of Immorality in Ancient Rome*. Cambridge.

Fantham, E. 1979. "Ovid's Ceyx and Alcyone: The Metamorphosis of a Myth." *Phoenix* 33.4: 330–45.

– ed. 1992. *Lucan,* De Bello Civili *Book II*. Cambridge.

– 1999. "The Role of Lament in the Growth and Eclipse of Roman Epic." In *Epic Traditions in the Contemporary World*, edited by M. Beissinger, J. Tylus, and S. Wofford, 221–35. Berkeley.

Farrell, J. 1991. *Vergil's* Georgics *and the Traditions of Ancient Epic: The Art of Allusion on Literary History*. Oxford.

Feeney, D.C. 1986. "'Stat magni nominis umbra.' Lucan on the Greatness of Pompeius Magnus." *CQ* 36.1: 239–43.

Finiello, C. 2005. "Der Bürgerkrieg: Reine Männersache? Keine Männersache! Erictho und die Frauengestalten im *Bellum Civile* Lucans." In *Lucan im 21. Jahrhundert*, edited by C. Walde, 155–85. Munich.

Goold, G.P., ed. 1990. *Propertius:* Elegies. Cambridge.

Gowing, A.M. 2005. *Empire and Memory: The Representation of the Roman Republic in Imperial Culture*. Cambridge.

Habinek, T.N. 1998. *The Politics of Latin Literature: Writing, Identity and Empire in Ancient Rome*. Princeton.

Hardie, P.R. 1993. *The Epic Successors of Virgil: A Study in the Dynamics of a Tradition*. Cambridge.

– 1997. "Virgil and Tragedy." In Martindale 1997: 312–26.

– 2002. *Ovid's Poetics of Illusion*. Cambridge.

Henderson, J. 1988. "Lucan: The Word at War." In *The Imperial Muse. Ramus Essays on Roman Literature of the Empire: to Juvenal through Ovid*, edited by A.J. Boyle, 122–64. Berwick and Victoria.

– 1998. "Statius' *Thebaid*: Form (P)re-made." In J. Henderson, *Fighting for Rome*, 212–54. Cambridge.

Hershkowitz, D. 1998. *The Madness of Epic: Reading Insanity from Homer to Statius*. Oxford.

Hinds, S. 1987. *The Metamorphosis of Persephone: Ovid and the Self-conscious Muse*. Cambridge.

– 1998. *Allusion and Intertext: The Dynamics of Appropriation in Roman Poetry*. Cambridge.

Hübner, U. 1984. "Episches und elegisches am Anfang des dritten Buches der 'Pharsalia'." *Hermes* 112: 227–39.

Ingleheart, J. 2006. "Ovid, *Tristia* 1.2: High Drama on the High Seas." *G&R* 53: 73–91.

Keith, A. 2008. "Lament in Lucan's *Bellum Civile*." In *Lament: Studies in the Ancient Mediterranean and Beyond*, edited by A. Suter, 233–57. Oxford.

Kennedy, D.F. 1993. *The Arts of Love*. Cambridge.

Kubiak, D.P. 1990. "Cornelia and Dido (Lucan 9.174–9)." *CQ* 40.2: 577–8.

Lowrie, M. 1997. *Horace's Narrative Odes*. Oxford.

Lyne, R.O.A.M. 1987. *Further Voices in Vergil's Aeneid*. Oxford.

Malamud, M.A. 1995. "Happy Birthday Dead Lucan: (P)raising the dead in *Silvae* 2.7." In *Roman Literature and Ideology: Ramus Essays for J.P. Sullivan*, edited by A.J. Boyle, 169–98. Bendigo and Victoria.

Martindale, C., ed. 1997. *The Cambridge Companion to Virgil*. Cambridge.

Masters, J. 1992. *Poetry and Civil War in Lucan's* Bellum Civile. Cambridge.

Mayer, R. 1981. *Lucan Civil War VIII*. Warminster.

Micozzi, L. 1999. "Aspetti dell' influenza di Lucano nella Thebaide." In *Interpretare Lucano*, edited by P. Esposito and L. Nicastri, 343–87. Naples.

Morford, M.P.O. 1967. *Lucan*. New York.

Murgatroyd, P., ed. 1980. *Tibullus 1*. Natal.

Narducci, E. 1979. *La provvidenza crudele: Lucano e la distruzione dei miti Augustei*. Pisa.

– 2002. *Lucano. Un'epica contro l'impero*. Rome.

Ogilvie, R.M. 1965. *A Commentary on Livy Books 1–5*. Oxford.

O'Higgins, D. 1988. "Lucan as 'Vates'." *CA* 7: 208–26.

Oliensis, E. 1997. "Sons and Lovers: Sexuality and Gender in Virgil's Poetry." In Martindale 1997: 294–311.

Otis, B. 1970. *Ovid as an Epic Poet*. Cambridge.

Panoussi, V. 2009. *Greek Tragedy in Vergil's* Aeneid. Cambridge.

Perkell, C. 1997. "The Lament of Juturna: Pathos and Interpretation in the *Aeneid*." *TAPA* 127: 257–86.

Phillips, O. 1962. The Influence of Ovid on Lucan's *Bellum Civile*. Chicago PhD dissertation.

Reed, J.D. 2007. *Virgil's Gaze. Nation and Poetry in the* Aeneid. Princeton.

Rosati, G. 1991. "Protesilao, Paride e l'amante elegiaco: un modello Omerico in Ovidio." *Maia* 43: 103–14.

– 1996. "The Arethusa Model (Propertius, 'Elegiae,' Book IV.3): Elegiac Traces in 1st-century Latin Epic." *Maia* 48: 139–55.

Rudd, N. 2008. "Ceyx and Alcyone: Ovid, *Metamorphoses* 11, 410–748." *G&R* 55: 103–10.

Rutz, W. 1963. "Die Traüme des Pompeius in Lucans *Pharsalia*." *Hermes* 91: 334–45.

Spencer, D. 2005. "Lucan's Follies: Memory and Ruin in a Civil–War Landscape." *G&R* 52: 46–69.

Thilo, G., and H. Hagen. 1881. *Servii Grammatici Qui Feruntur in Vergilii Carmina Commentarii*. Hildesheim.

Thompson, L. 1984. "A Lucanian Contradiction of Virgilian *Pietas*: Pompey's *Amor*." *CJ* 79: 207–15.

Thompson, L., and R.T. Bruère. 1968. "Lucan's Use of Vergilian Reminiscence." *CP* 63: 1–21.

Toohey, P. 2004. *Melancholy, Love and Time: Boundaries of the Self in Ancient Literature*. Ann Arbor.

Tränkle, H. 1963. "Elegisches in Ovids Metamorphosen." *Hermes* 91: 459–76.

Tucker, R.A. 1990. "Love in Lucan's 'Civil War'." *CB* 66: 43–6.

Viansino, G. 1974. *Studi sul Bellum Civile di Lucano*. Rome.

Voigt, A. 2004. *Female Lament in Greek and Roman Epic Poetry: Its Cultural Discourses and Narrative Presentation*. Oxford D.Phil. dissertation.

Wheeler, S. 2002. "Lucan's Reception of Ovid's *Metamorphoses*." *Arethusa* 35.3: 361–80.

10

Reading Aeneas through Hannibal: The Poetics of Revenge and the Repetitions of History*

ELIZABETH KENNEDY

The *Aeneid* and the *Punica* share the idea that, with the revolution of time, history repeats itself in new circumstances. The motivation of revenge carries through the cycles of history to produce its own revolutions. In the proem of the *Aeneid*, Juno desires revenge proleptically for the Romans' destruction of Carthage: *sic uoluere Parcas* ("the fates unroll in this way," *Aen.* 1.22).[1] This desire leads her to bring about the storm that shipwrecks Aeneas near Carthage and to encourage his relationship with Dido, which ends with Dido's curse. Dido calls for an avenger who will pursue Aeneas' descendants with fire and sword (*Aen.* 4.625–6).[2] In the *Punica*, Hannibal's oath to his father, which takes up the language of Dido's curse (*Pun.* 1.114–15), contains the promise to bring about another revolution in the cycle of history in order to achieve revenge: "*Rhoeteaque fata reuoluam*" ("'I will roll back the fate of Troy'," *Pun.* 1.115).[3] The idea of cycles of history and revenge underlies the literary practice of typology. Silius Italicus' characterization of Hannibal, the instrument of Dido's revenge, as an antitype of Aeneas,[4] draws attention to Aeneas as an instrument of revenge in the *Aeneid*. Much work has been done on how Silius imitated Vergil, and what light the earlier epic sheds on the *Punica*. I will take another direction, and read the *Aeneid* through the prism of Silius' epic. In particular, I will argue that Dido has reason to see Aeneas as a figure pursuing revenge in her dream vision of *Aeneid* 4 (465–73).

In portraying Hannibal as an antitype of Aeneas, Silius is activating a reading implicit in Vergil's text.[5] The Dido episode is an aetiology of the Punic Wars, showing how the love of the founder of Carthage for the future founder of the Roman people turns to hate. In *Aeneid* 4, Aeneas settles in Carthage, taking on a role different from his destined ktistic function in Italy. He dresses and acts the part of a Carthaginian.[6] Typologically, the reader can interpret Aeneas as mistakenly assuming the role of a Hannibal. By the end of the episode, however, Aeneas has become Dido's enemy (*Aen.* 4.424, 549; cf. 669). Aeneas tries on the role of Carthaginian, and then abandons it. Setting Aeneas in Carthage allows the reader to consider the possibility of a Punic Aeneas, a might-have-been alternative pleasing to Juno, a Trojan-Tyrian alliance[7] instead of the mix of Trojan and Italian that Juno eventually accepts (*Aen.* 12.818–28).

After playing the part of a Carthaginian, Aeneas sails to Italy and wages a war against its inhabitants, acting as Hannibal later does, but Aeneas is an antitype who would rather make peace. This war between the Trojans and Italians is compared to the war between the Carthaginians and Italians in Jupiter's speech at the opening of *Aeneid* 10 (6–15). Jupiter contrasts the forbidden (*abnueram,* 8) Trojan-Italian war with the lawful (*licebit,* 14) Carthaginian-Italian wars, and specifically (13) the Hannibalic war (*Aen.* 10.8–15):[8]

> "abnueram bello Italiam concurrere Teucris.
> quae contra uetitum discordia? quis metus aut hos
> aut hos arma sequi ferrumque lacessere suasit?
> adueniet iustum pugnae, ne arcessite, tempus,
> cum fera Karthago Romanis arcibus olim
> exitium magnum atque Alpis immittet apertas:
> tum certare odiis, tum res rapuisse licebit.
> nunc sinite et placitum laeti componite foedus."

"I had forbidden Italy to clash with the Trojans. Why is there discord against my express command? What has made them afraid and induced them to take up arms and make each other draw the sword? The time will come for war – there is no need to hasten it – when fierce Carthage will let destruction loose upon the citadels of Rome, opening up the Alps and sending them against Italy. That will be the time for pillaging, and for hate to vie with hate. But now let it be. A treaty has been decided upon. Accept it, and be content."

An implicit question in Jupiter's comparison, phrased typologically, is, since the Trojans are not the Carthaginians, and Aeneas is not Hannibal, why are they acting the part? In the second half of Vergil's epic, Aeneas looks forward to both Hannibal and Scipio, Italy's enemy and its champion: like Hannibal, Aeneas is the foreign attacker of Italians; he is also as essential to the founding of Rome as Scipio is to its defence in the Second Punic War. Silius' reception exploits these interpretive possibilities.

Silius sets out the revenge theme clearly in the opening sections of *Punica* 1. Because of Rome's dominance, Juno stirs the Carthaginians to wage the First Punic War (29–33), and when that effort fails, she turns to Hannibal to be her agent of vengeance (33–41).[9] Juno sees the Roman losses in the Second Punic War as an exchange for the founding of Rome, as she states in her first speech (42–54). Hannibal desires revenge for the Carthaginian defeat in the First Punic War (60–2); his father's injunction to carry on his efforts to correct this outcome (106–12) results in Hannibal's oath to Dido and the god of war to destroy Rome as Troy was destroyed (114–19).

The motivation of revenge, central to Hannibal's mission to destroy Rome, is part of an epic hero's role.[10] In the *Iliad,* desire for vengeance for Patroclus' death drives Achilles to return to battle in search of Hector. This private act of revenge leads to the fall of Troy.[11] In the second half of the *Aeneid,* desire for vengeance for Pallas' death drives Aeneas to seek out Turnus, whose death clears the way for the mix of Trojan and Italian blood, the founding of the Roman people.[12] In this Iliadic half of the epic, Aeneas, like Achilles, has a dual motivation for killing his adversary. Aeneas targets Turnus for revenge at first because he is standing in the way of his mission to establish his people in Italy. After Venus' portent of thunder, lightning, and weapons in the sky (*Aen.* 8.523–9), announcing, as Aeneas explains (*Aen.* 8.532–6), that she will bring armour made by Vulcan for the imminent war, Aeneas addresses the absent Turnus in the language of revenge (*Aen.* 8.538–40):[13]

> "quas poenas mihi, Turne, dabis! quam multa sub undas
> scuta uirum galeasque et fortia corpora uolues,
> Thybri pater! poscant acies et foedera rumpant."

"What a penalty, Turnus, you will pay me! How many shields and helmets and bodies of brave men you will roll beneath your waves, Father Tiber! Let them demand war and break treaties."

After the death of Pallas, it is the private motivation for revenge that drives Aeneas to accomplish the public act of conquest. As Achilles declares himself Patroclus' avenger when standing over the dying Hector (*Iliad* 22.331–6), so, too, as Aeneas kills Turnus, he tells him (*Aen.* 12.948–9): "*Pallas te hoc uulnere, Pallas | immolat et poenam scelerato ex sanguine sumit.*" ("'By this wound Pallas makes sacrifice of you, and Pallas exacts the penalty from your guilty blood'.") Aeneas becomes an instrument of revenge for Pallas.[14]

Like Aeneas, Hannibal speaks the language of revenge in the context of receiving his new armour.[15] Aeneas' words (*Aen.* 8.538–40, quoted above, p. 187) are echoed in Hannibal's exclamation after viewing the images of his father and Dido, among others, on his new shield (*Pun.* 2.455–6): "*heu quantum Ausonio sudabitis, arma, cruore! | quas, belli iudex, poenas mihi, Curia, pendes!*" ("'Ah, how much you will sweat with Ausonian blood, weapons! What a penalty you will pay me, Curia, decider of war!'") In addition to the repeated words ("*quas ... poenas mihi,*" *Pun.* 2.456; cf. *Aen.* 8.538), Silius' allusion to this passage is strengthened by the content of the exclamations, the vocatives midline, and the future tense of the verb for paying the penalty.[16] In keeping with his portrayal as a reverse Aeneas, Hannibal's shield depicts the past, with its motivation for revenge, while Aeneas' shield images the future history of Rome, which is part of Juno's motivation for revenge (*Aen.* 1.19–22). In *Punica* 2, Hannibal's threat of revenge shows his continued commitment to the cause during the Saguntum episode, but it is still early in the epic, in contrast to Aeneas' renewed enthusiasm for his purpose after receiving his shield in the last half of Vergil's epic.[17] Thus in the last half of the *Aeneid,* Aeneas fulfils the epic hero's role of avenger, killing the man who killed his protégé. In the *Punica,* Hannibal succeeds in acting as Dido's avenger, inflicting heavy losses on the Romans. These military successes also avenge Juno's hurt as a result of Carthage's loss of Mediterranean supremacy to Rome (cf. *Pun.* 1.42–54), and they are payback for Carthaginian losses in the First Punic War. Yet ultimately it is Scipio who fulfils the epic hero's role of avenger, defeating Carthage where Hannibal fails to defeat Rome, as I shall discuss below.

Aeneas is clearly an instrument of revenge in the second half of the epic, but why does Dido see him in this light before he takes on this role? I will argue that she has reason to fear revenge from him, first because he has already desired revenge on Helen and Dido is like Helen in some ways; second, because vengeance has a cyclic nature and she desires revenge on him; and last because her fear anticipates Rome's destruction of Carthage in the Punic wars. It is in considering this last point that reading Vergil through Silius is particularly enlightening: in different ways, the actions of both Hannibal, Dido's avenger, and Scipio, Rome's avenger, lead to the fall of Carthage.

In the first half of the *Aeneid,* if we take the Helen episode as authentic (*Aen.* 2.567–88),[18] then we can see Aeneas desiring revenge, but in an unheroic way. Aeneas sees Helen in the temple of Vesta in Troy (*Aen.* 2.571–6):

"illa sibi infestos euersa ob Pergama Teucros
et Danaum poenam et deserti coniugis iras
praemetuens, Troiae et patriae communis Erinys,
abdiderat sese atque aris inuisa sedebat.
exarsere ignes animo; subit ira cadentem
ulcisci patriam et sceleratas sumere poenas."

"She feared the Trojans, who were hostile to her because of the overthrow of Troy, the punishment of the Greeks, and the anger of the husband she had deserted. A fury both to Troy and her native country, she had hidden herself and was sitting by the altars, hated. Fires blazed in my spirit. Anger arises to avenge my falling country and to exact the penalty for her crimes."

There is verbal repetition between Aeneas' words in Books 2 and 12 ("***sceleratas sum***_ere poenas_," 2.576, quoted above; "***poenam scelerat***_o ex sanguine_ ***sum***_it_," 12.949).[19] Aeneas feels a desire to be an instrument of vengeance, first for his people in Troy, and, at the end of the epic, for Pallas.

Aeneas works himself up to annihilating Helen, the cause of suffering (*Aen.* 2.583–7):

"namque etsi nullum memorabile nomen
feminea in poena est, habet haec uictoria laudem;
exstinxisse nefas tamen et sumpsisse merentis
laudabor poenas, animumque explesse iuuabit
ultricis flammae[21] et cineres satiasse meorum."

"For although there is no fame worth remembering in punishing a woman, and such a victory holds no praise, nevertheless I will be praised for snuffing out this evil and exacting a deserved punishment. It will give pleasure to have filled my spirit with the avenging flame, and to have appeased the ashes of my people."

Aeneas is only deterred from exacting revenge by the intervention of his mother. Killing Helen will not change the fate of Troy, as Venus shows him (*Aen.* 2.601–3). Aeneas must look to the future, not the past. Killing Hector or Turnus looks to the immediate past, the deaths of Patroclus or Pallas, but also to the future conquest of the city. In this crucial moment of dispatching the city's main defender, neither Achilles nor Aeneas thinks of the woman who is the cause of the war, be it Helen or Lavinia. Aeneas will fulfil the role of epic hero in exacting punishment from the killer of his fallen comrade, not from a woman.

Helen and Dido are alike in being the causes of wars.[21] Aeneas calls Helen an Erinys (*Aen.* 2.573) because of the destruction she brings to both sides, to the Greeks who are exacting punishment for her theft and to the Trojans who pay the penalty with the fall of their city. Dido is also like a fury, calling for vengeance for Aeneas' abandonment of her and war between their descendants (*Aen.* 4.622–9):[22]

"tum uos, o Tyrii, stirpem et genus omne futurum
exercete odiis, cinerique haec mittite nostro
munera. nullus amor populis nec foedera sunto.
exoriare aliquis nostris ex ossibus ultor
qui face Dardanios ferroque sequare colonos,
nunc, olim, quocumque dabunt se tempore uires.
litora litoribus contraria, fluctibus undas
imprecor, arma armis: pugnent ipsique nepotesque."

"Then you, O Tyrians, harass with hatred their whole future stock and race, and send this offering to my ashes. Let there be no love or treaties between our peoples. Arise, some avenger from my bones, and pursue the Trojan colonists with fire and sword, now, in the future, at whatever time strength allows it. I pray that we may stand opposed, shore against shore, sea against sea, and sword against sword. Let both themselves and their descendants fight for ever."

Hannibal will be Dido's avenger (625), and ultimately, Dido, like Helen, will bring destruction to both sides, Roman and Carthaginian, through Hannibal.

Both Helen and Dido also fear retribution, partly because of their betrayal of their husbands, Menelaus and Sychaeus. Yet in her dreams it is not Sychaeus but Aeneas who pursues Dido, and it is his rejection of her that makes her call for revenge. Since Dido is the one calling for revenge, it is puzzling that in her dreams Dido sees Aeneas as a figure seeking revenge, pursuing her as furies pursue Pentheus and Orestes (*Aen.* 4.464–73):[23]

multaque praeterea uatum praedicta priorum
terribili monitu horrificant. agit ipse furentem
in somnis ferus Aeneas, semperque relinqui
sola sibi, semper longam incomitata uidetur
ire uiam et Tyrios deserta quaerere terra,
Eumenidum ueluti demens uidet agmina Pentheus
et solem geminum et duplices se ostendere Thebas,
aut Agamemnonius scaenis agitatus Orestes,
armatam facibus matrem et serpentibus atris
cum fugit ultricesque sedent in limine Dirae.

In addition, many prophecies of ancient seers alarm her with their terrifying warning. In dreams, Aeneas himself savagely drives her raving, and she seems to be always abandoned, by herself, alone, to go always unaccompanied on a long road, and to look for her Tyrians in a deserted land, just as Pentheus, out of his mind, sees columns of Eumenides, a double sun, and two cities of Thebes manifest themselves, or as Agamemnon's son Orestes was driven across the stage, when he flees his mother armed with torches and black snakes, and the avenging Dirae sit at the door.

On one level, this passage looks to the end of *Aeneid* 4 – the long, lonely road leads to Dido's death – and it may reveal Dido's feeling that she has abandoned her people. Her call for vengeance against the Aeneadae at the end of Book 4 is materialized in her use of Aeneas' sword to kill herself, to dramatize that he is the cause of her death, and the object of revenge. The passage also looks forward to the end of the epic, where Aeneas is acting as an instrument of revenge for Pallas. At the end of *Aeneid* 12, a *Dira* flies in the face of Turnus (*Dirae,* 12.869; 4.473); he is left *alone* by his sister Juturna to face Aeneas (12.869–86; 4.467); and he experiences a *dream* sensation of powerlessness (*in somnis,* 12.908; 4.466). Turnus is like Dido, feeling alone as he faces death at the hands of Aeneas. But in Book 4, Aeneas is *not* pursuing Dido for revenge, as he does Turnus in the second half of the epic.

One reason Dido has to fear Aeneas' revenge is the cyclic nature of vengeance, with one act of retribution calling for another. She had threatened Aeneas with revenge in their last conversation (*Aen.* 4.381–6):

"i, sequere Italiam uentis, pete regna per undas.
spero equidem mediis, si quid pia numina possunt,
supplicia hausurum scopulis et nomine Dido
saepe uocaturum. sequar atris ignibus absens
et, cum frigida mors anima seduxerit artus,
omnibus umbra locis adero. dabis, improbe, poenas."

"Go, pursue Italy with the winds; seek a kingdom over the waves. I, for my part, hope that you will drink a bitter cup of tortures among the ocean rocks, if the just gods have any power, and that you will often call on the name of Dido. Though absent, I will pursue you with obscuring fires, and when cold death has led life from limbs, I will be present in all places as a ghost. You, scoundrel, will pay the penalty."

Her dream is a reversal of her wish for him: she threatened to pursue him with black fires (*atris ignibus, Aen.* 4.384), and in her dreams Aeneas pursues her, as Orestes' mother pursues him with torches and black snakes (*facibus ... et serpentibus atris, Aen.* 4.472). Dido lets Aeneas know of her desire for vengeance, and then she also fears vengeance from him. She calls for revenge on Aeneas here in words that Aeneas uses later, calling for revenge on Turnus: Aeneas echoes Dido's words (*"dabis, improbe, poenas," Aen.* 4.386), when he addresses the absent Turnus (*"poenas mihi, Turne, dabis," Aen.* 8.538).[24] Yet Aeneas has no interest in punishing Dido, even though she sees him as pursuing revenge on her.

In light of the cycles of time and repetition of history, Dido does have reason to fear Aeneas as an instrument of revenge: Aeneas is an instrument of revenge in the Italian war; Aeneas has already desired revenge on Helen, who was the cause of the Trojan War, and Dido will be the cause of the Punic Wars; and the cyclic nature of revenge suggests that her desire to get him will eventually result in payback. With this long view, Dido and her call for revenge can be placed in the context of the cycle of wars. In the council of the gods that opens *Aeneid* 10, Jupiter compares the war in Italy to the future Punic Wars (11–15, quoted above, p. 186), and Venus replies by comparing it to the past Trojan War (26–30). It is this divine view that allows the reader to see the parallelism between Dido and Helen as causes of wars and so as possible targets of revenge. Yet Aeneas does not see with this divine view. He is as ignorant of the future (cf. *rerumque ignarus, Aen.* 8.730) as he is of the hurt he is causing Dido.[25] Dido's fear can be seen as partly proleptic: she will be the cause of a future war between her people and Aeneas', which ends in the obliteration of Carthage, matching her dream vision of Tyrians in a forsaken land (*Tyrios deserta quaerere terra, Aen.* 4.468, quoted above).[26] Aeneas' indirect destruction of Dido prefigures Rome's destruction of Carthage:[27] Dido stands for Carthage, and Aeneas stands for Rome. Aeneas causes Dido's suicide, in a symbolic, proleptic Roman destruction of Carthage. Dido's avenger, Hannibal, tries to destroy Rome, but ends by bringing destruction on his own city, Carthage. Dido's fear, manifested in her dreams, is shaped from her emerging hatred and desire for revenge that will result in self-destruction, literally in her suicide, and symbolically in the obliteration of her city after the Third Punic War.

Aeneas is not the instrument of revenge that Dido fears: he does not turn back after his delay in Carthage, but moves forward to Italy and accomplishes his mission of founding the Roman people. Dido calls for an avenger through her suicide, and this avenger, Hannibal, will cause fear and destruction for the Romans. Silius takes up Vergil's aetiology of the Punic Wars. Hannibal ironically brings destruction on Carthage by his fighting with the Romans, and he is an antitype of Aeneas. The portrayal of Hannibal as a reverse Aeneas creates a stable irony,[28] because while carrying out Dido's revenge he actually accomplishes the vengeance Dido feared from Aeneas. Ultimately the cycle of revenge will turn, and Rome's avenger will conquer Carthage. It is Scipio who is portrayed as Rome's avenger in Silius' epic.

In *Punica* 7, Proteus' prophecy heralds Scipio as the avenger of his father and uncle, as the conqueror of Hannibal and Africa, and as the one responsible even for Carthage's obliteration through his adopted grandson, Scipio Aemilianus (*Pun.* 7.487–93):

"hinc ille e furto genitus patruique piabit
idem ultor patrisque necem; tum litus Elissae
implebit flammis auelletque Itala Poenum
uiscera torrentem et propriis superabit in oris.
huic Carthago armis, huic Africa nomine cedet.
hic dabit ex sese, qui tertia bella fatiget
et cinerem Libyae ferat in Capitolia uictor."

"Then the man born from a secret love, the same avenger, will expiate the murder of both his uncle and father; then he will fill Dido's coast with flames and tear away the Carthaginian scorching the heart of Italy, and he will overcome him on his own shores. To this man Carthage will yield her weapons and Africa her name. This man will produce from himself one to carry on a third war and bring the ash of Libya to the Capitol as a victor."

Scipio is repeatedly named as the avenger later in the epic: in the underworld, the Sibyl tells Scipio that as a conqueror he will avenge his father in Spain ("*uictor patrem ulcisceris*," *Pun.* 13.507); after his father comes to him in a dream, Scipio tells his ancestral ghosts on waking, "I will be an avenger for you" ("*uobis ultor ego*," *Pun.* 15.205); and after Scipio holds funeral games for his father and uncle in Spain, "he returns to Italy, the avenger of both his country and his household, with all Carthaginians driven from the Western shore" (*pulsis de litore cunctis | Hesperio Poenis ultor patriaeque domusque | Ausoniam repetit, Pun.* 16.592–4). Scipio reappropriates the figure of Aeneas from Hannibal, and he also claims from him the role of avenger. This role goes back to Aeneas, who acted as an instrument of revenge against Turnus in order to establish his people in Italy. Aeneas does not act as an avenger in the context of Carthage, but his later types do. Silius takes the theme of revenge and highlights it in his epic of the Punic Wars, and so in turning back to the *Aeneid*, the place of revenge in Vergil's aetiology of the Punic wars emerges more clearly.

In sum, Aeneas acts as an avenger in the second half of Vergil's epic, and his potential as an avenger is seen in the first half, both in the Helen episode and in Dido's dream. Although in Book 4 Dido is the one calling for revenge, the *Aeneid* also looks forward to the Punic Wars, where Hannibal will be her avenger, and, I would argue, to their final outcome, the razing of Carthage.

Dido's dream vision of Aeneas as a figure of revenge fits with both his actions in Troy, where he desired to exact revenge from Helen, and in Italy, where he does exact revenge from Turnus. I suggest that in Dido's dream there is a symbolic adumbration of the end of the cycle of revenge arising from Aeneas' abandonment of her and leading ultimately to the destruction of Carthage. Aeneas himself never seeks revenge on Dido, but, in the sequel, both Aeneas' antitype, Hannibal, and his true type, Scipio, bring the cycle of revenge to this conclusion.

NOTES

* This paper is dedicated to Elaine Fantham, for her mentorship over many years and for providing an example to be imitated.

1 The text of Vergil used throughout is Mynors 1969, except where noted. Translations of Vergil are modified from West 1990.

2 Dido calls for an avenger to arise ("*exoriare*," *Aen*. 4.625), and, as Servius comments (ad *Aen*. 4.625), *exoriatur; et ostendit Hannibalem*.

3 For the text of Silius' *Punica* I have used throughout that of Delz 1987. Translations from the *Punica* are my own, in consultation with Duff 1934. Ganiban (2010: 96) comments that the figure of Dido "makes the *Punica* a poem of ancient revenge; Hannibal is her agent to achieve it."

4 I set out this point in Kennedy Klaassen 2010: 99–106, with further bibliography.

5 See Tipping 2010: 51 for how the *Aeneid* prepares the reader for the *Punica*.

6 Mercury sees Aeneas founding strongholds, building new homes, and dressed in clothes given to him by Dido (*Aen*. 4.260–4). For the reversal and transference of Punic stereotypes to Aeneas, see Starks 1999, especially 272–6.

7 In *Aeneid* 1, Dido invites the Trojans to settle with her (572–4); in *Aeneid* 4, Juno suggests that Trojans and Tyrians become one people ("*communem ... populum*," 102) and Venus wonders whether Jupiter would approve of the mix (110–12).

8 Jupiter's words recall Dido's curse (*odiis*, 10.14, 4.623; *foedus*, 10.15, *foedera*, 4.624; *olim*, 10.12, 4.627).

9 In the *Punica*, Hannibal is often simply referred to as *Poenus*, the Carthaginian, but its similarity in sound to *poenae* ("punishment," or even "the Avengers" or "Furies") may underline the association of Hannibal with revenge.

10 See, for example, Wilson 2002; cf. Jones 1941:195 noting: "The *Odyssey* has four main themes: the wanderings of Odysseus, his return home, the crimes of the suitors, and his vengeance upon them."

11 Quint (1989: 43) observes: "Revenge is, of course, a central Iliadic theme; Achilles' killing of Hector is a private act of vengeance for the death of Patroklos that also ensures the conquest of Troy."

12 Cf. Van Nortwick 1980: 308: "The anger of Aeneas at the death of Pallas, leading to a final confrontation with Turnus, is clearly based on the rage of Achilles over Patroclus' death and his subsequent duel with Hector."

13 Aeneas' apostrophe to father Tiber almost repeats part of Aeneas' exclamation during the storm in *Aeneid* 1, when he said about the Simois (*Aen.* 1.100–1), "*sub undis | scuta uirum galeasque et fortia corpora uoluit*!" ("'He rolled beneath his waves the shield, helmets, and strong bodies of men!'") Aeneas' descriptions of rivers filled with armour and men are echoed at the beginning and end of the *Punica*. Juno's apostrophe to the river Aufidus in the first speech of the *Punica* (1.42–54) is more of a threat (*Pun.* 1.52–4): "*teque uadi dubium coeuntibus, Aufide, ripis | per clipeos galeasque uirum caesosque per artus | uix iter Hadriaci rumpentem ad litora ponti*" ("'while you, Aufidus, doubtful of your course as your banks close in, can hardly force a passage to the Adriatic shore through the men's shields, helmets, and severed limbs'"). The context of a storm in both epics makes Aeneas' exclamation in *Aeneid* 1 a significant intertext for the description of Hannibal's shipwreck in *Punica* 17.279: *arma inter galeasque uirum cristasque rubentes* ("among the men's weapons, helmets, and red crests").

14 Nicoll 2001; Boyd 2002; Burnell 1987; Warde Fowler 1919; Galinsky 1988; Lyne 1983; Panoussi 2002.

15 Ganiban (2010: 84–91) highlights the theme of Dido's revenge on Hannibal's shield. See also Harrison 2010: 282–5, with bibliography; Frank 1974.

16 In *Punica* 4, Scipio's father uses similar revenge language when battling the Trebia river (*Pun.* 4.643–4): "*magnas, o Trebia, et meritas mihi, perfide, poenas | exsolues*" ("'O faithless Trebia, you shall pay the deserved penalty'"); and the river god replies with an echo of the passages discussed above, n. 14 (4.662–4): "*quot corpora porto | dextra fusa tua*! *clipeis galeisque uirorum, | quos mactas, artatus iter cursumque relinqui.*" ("'How many corpses I carry, slain by your right hand! So packed am I with the shields and helmets of your victims that I have left my proper channel'.") Compare also Dido's words to Aeneas (*Aen.* 4.386, discussed in the text below): "*dabis, improbe, poenas*" ("'You shall pay the penalty, rash man'"), echoed in Fabius' son's speech to his father about Minucius (*Pun.* 7.539–40): "*dabit improbus,*" *inquit* | "*quas dignum est, poenas.*" ("'That rash man,' he said, 'will suffer the penalty he deserves'.") At Cannae, Varro chastises Rome for electing him consul instead of Fabius (*Pun.* 9.646): "*das,*" *inquit*, "*patria, poenas.*" ("'Fatherland,' he said, 'you are paying the penalty'.")

17 See my fuller argument in Kennedy Klaassen 2010: 101. Stocks (2014: 225) notes that Jupiter striking Hannibal's shield "is a divine sweep at the Dido and Hamilcar motifs which drive Hannibal, and a response to the threats that he made in Book 2 to drench the shield with Ausonian blood (2.455–6), and in Book 6 to cast Jupiter down from the Tarpeian rock (6.713)."

18 I have included the Helen episode as part of my treatment of Aeneas as an instrument of revenge, but my argument does not hinge on its inclusion. The verbal echoes in the *Punica* of this scene are not strong enough to prove that they are not coincidental, and so are inconclusive for any argument about Silius' use of the episode (*furiata mente, Aen.* 2.588 = *furiata mente, Pun.* 2.210, in the same metrical position, and cf. *mentem furiata, Pun.* 6.514; *Pergama Teucros, Aen.* 2.571 ~ *Pergama Teucri, Pun.* 12.362, both at line end; *deserti coniugis, Aen.* 2.572 ~ *desertis coniuge, Pun.* 13.879, again in the same metrical position; *ulcisci patriam, Aen.* 2.576 ~ *patrem ulcisceris, Pun.* 13.507). There is extensive scholarly discussion debating the authenticity of the Helen episode: Austin 1961; Berres 1992, with the review of Gall 1995; Bleisch 1999; Bruère 1964; Clement 1958; Conte 1986; Egan 1996; Estevez 1981; Fairclough 1906; Gall 1993, with the review of Horsfall 1995; Garstang 1962; Geymonat 1995: 300–1; Goold 1970; Harrison 1970; Hatch 1959; Hedreen 1996; Körte 1916; Murgia 1971, 1974, and 2003; Reckford 1981; Rowell 1966: 211; Shipley 1925.

19 The phrase *sumere poenas* occurs ten times in the *Aeneid,* 2.103, 2.576, 2.585–6, 6.501, 7.766, 9.422, 10.617, 11.592, 11.720 (*inimico ex sanguine sumit*), 12.949; with the adjective *sceleratus,* the phrase occurs only twice.

20 Mynors 1969 reads †*famam*. I have chosen to read *flammae* with Hirtzel 1900. Austin 1964 reads *ultricis famam,* and notes ad 587, "the Servian manuscripts vary between *famam* and *famae*; the vulgate reading is *flammae*."

21 See Keith 2000: 68–9 on Helen and Dido as "*reginae* who instigate conflict in the poem" and who "work in association with the Furies" (68), and, for Silius' use of Dido's curse in setting out the origins of the second Punic war, see ibid. 90–2.

22 Adler 2003: 103–33, esp. 123–33; Monti 1981; Panoussi 2002.

23 Goldberg 2005. For revenge in tragedy and in Greek thought generally, see Burnett 1998, with the reviews of Halleran 2001, Lloyd 1999, and Pedrick 2000; cf. Foley 2001.

24 See above, n. 18, for Silian parallels to this language of revenge.

25 His ignorance of this hurt is suggested by the simile of the wounded doe (*Aen.* 4.68–73), where Aeneas corresponds to the *pastor... nescius* (71–2), and later by his exchange with Dido in the underworld, where he asks her (*Aen.* 6.458), "*funeris heu tibi causa fui?*" ("'Alas, was I the cause of your death?'")

26 Edgeworth (1976–7: 130) makes a similar connection: "certain particulars in Vergil's story of Dido, including her perishing amid the flames, are drawn from an episode which occurred at the fall of Carthage in 146 B.C.," namely, "the death scene of Carthage's nameless last queen" (133). The description of Dido's dream recalls Aeneas' narration of his wandering after the fall of Troy. Aeneas is driven (*agimur, Aen.* 3.5) to seek uninhabited lands (*desertas quaerere terras, Aen.* 3.4). In Dido's dreams, Aeneas drives her (*agit, Aen.* 4.465) and she seems to seek her Tyrians in a deserted land (*Tyrios deserta quaerere terra, Aen.* 4.468). The difference is that Aeneas looks for uninhabited lands in which to settle, while Dido looks for her people in a land that has been made empty (as happens in the razing of Carthage after the Third Punic War).

27 Cf. Bowie 1990: 479: "Aeneas' conflict with Dido prefigures the Punic Wars." Farrell (1997: 236) discusses the technique of temporal convergence, wherein Vergil links two time frames.

28 The term is from Booth 1974.

WORKS CITED

Adler, E. 2003. *Vergil's Empire: Political Thought in the* Aeneid. Lanham, MD.

Augoustakis, A. ed. 2010. *Brill's Companion to Silius Italicus.* Leiden.

Austin, R.G. 1961. "Virgil, *Aeneid* 2. 567–88." *CQ* 11.3–4: 185–98.

– ed. 1964. *P. Vergili Maronis Aeneidos Liber Secundus.* Oxford.

Berres, T. 1992. *Vergil und die Helenaszene.* Heidelberg.

Bleisch, P. 1999. "The Empty Tomb at Rhoeteum: Deiphobus and the Problem of the Past in *Aeneid* 6.494–547." *CA* 18: 187–226.

Booth, W. 1974. *A Rhetoric of Irony*. Chicago and London.

Bowie, A. 1990. "The Death of Priam: Allegory and History in the *Aeneid.*" *CQ* 40.2: 470–81.

Boyd, B.W. 2002. "'Tum Pectore Sensus Vertuntur Varii': Reading and Teaching the End of the *Aeneid.*" In *Approaches to Teaching Vergil's Aeneid,* edited by W.S. Anderson and L.N. Quartarone, 80–6. New York.

Bruère, R.T. 1964. "The Helen Episode in *Aeneid* 2 and Lucan." *CP* 59: 267–8.

Burnell, P. 1987. "The Death of Turnus and Roman Morality." *G&R* 34: 186–200.

Burnett, A.P. 1998. *Revenge in Attic and Later Tragedy*. Berkeley.

Clement, P.A. 1958. "The Recovery of Helen." *Hesperia* 27.1: 47–73.

Conte, G.B. 1986. "The Helen Episode in the Second Book of the *Aeneid*: Structural Models and a Question of Authenticity." In *The Rhetoric of Imitation: Genre and Poetic Memory in Virgil and Other Latin Poets,* edited by C. Segal, 196–207. Ithaca.

Delz, J., ed. 1987. *Silius Italicus:* Punica. Stuttgart.

Duff, J.D., ed. 1934. *Silius Italicus:* Punica. London.

Edgeworth, R.J. 1976–7. "The Death of Dido." *CJ* 72: 129–33.

Egan, R.B. 1996. "A Reading of the Helen-Venus Episode in *Aeneid* 2." *EMC/CV*, n.s. 15: 379–95.

Estevez, V.A. 1981. "*Aeneid* II 624–631 and the Helen and Venus Episodes." *CJ* 76: 318–35.

Fairclough, H.R. 1906. "The Helen Episode in Vergil's *Aeneid* II. 559-623." *CP* 1: 221–30.

Farrell, J. 1997. "The Virgilian Intertext." In *The Cambridge Companion to Virgil*, edited by C. Martindale, 222–38. Cambridge.

Foley, H. 2001. *Female Acts in Greek Tragedy*. Princeton.

Frank, E. 1974. "Works of Art in the Epics of Valerius Flaccus and Silius Italicus." *Rendiconti dell'Istituto Lombardo* 108: 837–44.

Galinsky, K. 1988. "The Anger of Aeneas." *AJP* 109: 321–48.

Gall, D. 1993. *Ipsius umbra Creusa: Creusa und Helena*. Stuttgart.

– 1995. Review of Berres 1992. *Gnomon* 67: 407–11.

Ganiban, R.T. 2010. "Virgil's Dido and the Heroism of Hannibal." In Augoustakis 2010: 73–98.

Garstang, J.B. 1962. "The Crime of Helen and the Concept of *Fatum* in the *Aeneid*." *CJ* 57: 337–45.

Geymonat, M. 1995. "The Transmission of Virgil's Works in Antiquity and the Middle Ages." In *A Companion to the Study of Virgil*, edited by N. Horsfall, 293–311. Leiden.

Goldberg, S. 2005. "Dido's Furies." In his *Constructing Literature in the Roman Republic: Poetry and Its Reception*, 115–43. Cambridge and New York.

Goold, G.P. 1970. "Servius and the Helen Episode." *HSCP* 74: 101–68.

Halleran, M.R. 2001. Review of Burnett 1998. *CJ* 96: 337–9.

Harrison, E.L. 1970. "Divine Action in *Aeneid* Book Two." *Phoenix* 24: 320–2.

Harrison, S.J. 2010. "Picturing the Future Again: Proleptic Ekphrasis in Silius' *Punica*." In Augoustakis 2010: 279–92.

Hatch, N.L. 1959. "The Time Element in Interpretation of *Aeneid* 2. 575–6 and 585–87." *CP* 54: 255–7.

Hedreen, G. 1996. "Image, Text, and Story in the Recovery of Helen." *CA* 15: 152–84.

Hirtzel, F.A., ed. 1900. *P. Vergili Maronis Opera*. Oxford.

Horsfall, N. 1995. Review of Gall 1993. *CR* 45: 162–3.

Jones, F.W. 1941. "The Formulation of the Revenge Motif in the Odyssey." *TAPA* 72: 195–202.

Keith, A.M. 2000. *Engendering Rome: Women in Latin Epic*. Cambridge.

Kennedy Klaassen, E. 2010. "Imitation and the Hero." In Augoustakis 2010: 99–126.

Körte, A. 1916. "Zum zweiten Buch von Vergils Aeneis." *Hermes* 51: 145–50.
Lloyd, M. 1999. Review of Burnett 1998. *CR* 49: 348–9.
Lyne, R.O.A.M. 1983. "Vergil and the Politics of War." *CQ* 33.1: 188–203.
Monti, R.C. 1981. *The Dido Episode and the* Aeneid. Leiden.
Murgia, C.E. 1971. "More on the Helen Episode." *CSCA* 4: 203–17.
– 1974. "The Donatian Life of Virgil, DS, and D." *CSCA* 7: 257–77.
– 2003. "The Date of the Helen Episode." *HSCP* 101: 405–26.
Mynors, R.A.B., ed. 1969. *P. Vergili Maronis Opera.* Oxford.
Nicoll, W.S.M. 2001. "The Death of Turnus." *CQ* 51.1: 190–200.
Panoussi, V. 2002. "Vergil's Ajax: Allusion, Tragedy, and Heroic Identity in the *Aeneid*." *CA* 21: 95–134.
Pedrick, V. 2000. Review of Burnett 1998. *CW* 93: 554–5.
Quint, D. 1989. "Repetition and Ideology in the *Aeneid*." *MD* 23: 9–54. [Reprinted in *Virgil: Critical Assessments of Classical Authors*, edited by P. Hardie, 117–57. London and New York, 1999].
Reckford, K.J. 1981. "Helen in *Aeneid* 2 and 6." *Arethusa* 14: 85–99.
Rowell, H.T. 1966. "The Ancient Evidence of the Helen Episode in *Aeneid* II." In *The Classical Tradition*, edited by L. Wallach, 210–21. Ithaca.
Shipley, F.W. 1925. "The Vergilian Authorship of the Helen Episode, *Aeneid* II, 567–88." *TAPA* 56: 172–84.
Starks, J.H., Jr. 1999. "*Fides Aeneia*: The Transference of Punic Stereotypes in the *Aeneid*." *CJ* 94: 255–83.
Stocks, C. 2014. *The Roman Hannibal: Remembering the Enemy in Silius Italicus'* Punica. Liverpool.
Tipping, B. 2010. *Exemplary Epic: Silius Italicus's* Punica. Oxford.
Van Nortwick, T. 1980. "Aeneas, Turnus, and Achilles." *TAPA* 110: 303–14.
Warde Fowler, W. 1919. *The Death of Turnus: Observations on the Twelfth Book of the* Aeneid. Oxford.
West, D., trans. 1990. *Virgil:* The Aeneid. London.
Wilson, D.F. 2002. *Ransom, Revenge, and Heroic Identity in the* Iliad. Cambridge.

PART III

Civic Spectacle

11

The Charms of an Older Lover: Afranius 378–82 Ribbeck[3*]

JARRETT WELSH

Fundamental, and fundamentally problematic, for our understanding of Roman social history in the second century BCE are the scripts of comedies penned by Plautus and Terence, whose adaptations of Greek New Comedy cast the domestic and civic relationships of that genre in a form recognizable and intelligible for Roman festival audiences. Except for the moments when Roman qualities obviously overrun the notionally Greek atmosphere of the comedies, however, the resulting pan-Mediterranean jumble of characters, behaviours, and relationships poses a challenge for those who would draw Roman social history out of the Latin comic text. Different problems face the interpreter of the fragmentary *fabulae togatae*. Although the civic situations of those comedies are ostensibly "closer to Rome" than what Plautus and Terence put on performance, their fragmentary preservation makes even more challenging the work of extracting from them useful information about comic performances of social and civic relationships. But fragmentation alone does not diminish the value of the evidence available in the fragments of Titinius, Afranius, and Atta, for these comic performances of Roman civic and social relationships offer important confirmation and correction to the impressions of those same relationships we gain from Plautus and Terence. Proper application of this evidence, however, requires that we have first properly understood the fragments themselves. As a contribution to that endeavour and as a tribute to Elaine Fantham's pioneering scholarship on Roman comedy and social history, then, this paper reopens some questions about a significant fragment of Afranius to probe afresh what it might tell us about the social roles and interpersonal relationships that Afranius' female comic characters might have performed.

Early in the first book of his *De compendiosa doctrina*, Nonius Marcellus quotes five verses from a complete script of Afranius' *Vopiscus* ("The Twin

Who Lived") in order to illustrate the expression *mala aetas* ("old age").[1] Since Otto Ribbeck brought forth his second edition of the fragments of light drama in 1873, a certain confidence in the text of these verses and in their sensibility has prevailed.[2] That such confidence is warranted, however, is far from certain. I begin from Ribbeck's text of Afranius 378–82, with a fresh apparatus:

si possent homines delenimentis capi,
omnes haberent nunc amatores anus.
aetas et corpus tenerum et morigeratio,
haec sunt uenena formosarum mulierum;
mala aetas nulla delenimenta inuenit.

378 si] in *F* : ni *Schoppe*
post **379** *quaedam excidisse suspicatus erat Ribbeck*[1]
ante **382** *personam mutauit Quicherat*
nulla] multa *olim coniecerat Quicherat* : alia *Madvig*

Ribbeck paid little attention to earlier discussions of this fragment, but he also did not indicate how he thought this fragment was to be understood, despite the pressing need for such guidance.[3] That silence has been problematic, for it has suggested, wrongly, that the difficulties in this fragment had been satisfactorily explained.[4] Before 1873, discussions of these verses centred on the contradiction that they present, which a literal, if inelegant, translation will help to highlight:

If men could be snared by "charms,"
every old woman would now have a lover.
Youthful age, a tender body, and compliance:
these are the weapons of beautiful women;
old age has no "charms."

The first two verses imply that old women have and are even experts in employing *delenimenta*, since they would have snared lovers, if men could be seduced by such things. The final verse of the fragment, however, expressly denies *delenimenta* to old age. This paradox presents a real challenge, for it is not clear how old women could both have and not have *delenimenta*.

One of the aims of this chapter is to reopen the questions about what this fragment means, whether the established text is correct, and how it was delivered on stage. The language of these verses will suggest that the common explanations of them cannot be accepted. A more precise reconstruction of how these verses were delivered is possible, but the arguments here presented also lead to the conclusion that we cannot know the identity of their speaker. With this discussion I want also to signal a destabilizing sociolinguistic feature that can sometimes be glimpsed in the Latin spoken by Afranius' female characters, which will make certainty about the delivery of these verses impossible. The result is a clearer understanding of the possibilities surrounding this fragment, and especially a better appreciation of how some of Afranius' female characters interacted with the domestic bourgeois society of the *fabulae togatae*.

The central contradiction in this fragment seems first to have been pointed out in 1596 by Caspar Schoppe, whose *Verisimilium Libri Quattuor* won their twenty-year-old author much attention, if not always admiration, in scholarly circles.[5] Scholars since Schoppe have followed one of four general approaches to resolving that problem: (1) adopting a conjecture at one of two places in the text; (2) arguing that Nonius was mistaken about the meaning of *mala aetas*; (3) translating around the paradox through heroic feats of interpretation; or (4) marking a lacuna or a change of speaker, so as to restore logic by distancing the conflicting statements from each other. Only the third approach enjoys any currency in scholarly discussions, although the fourth occasionally garners notice. The first two approaches, although unconvincing, still merit attention for the light they shed on the more popular solutions.

None of the conjectures that have been proposed – reading *ni* for *si* (378), or either *multa* or *alia* for *nulla* (382) – can now claim any adherents. Schoppe's *ni* ("if it weren't for the fact that men can be snared by charms…") would make the verses depend on a presumption that the men of Roman comedy naturally gravitated towards older women, only being seduced from that trajectory by the wiles of younger women.[6] Such a claim about comedy's lovers can scarcely be entertained, although the conjecture would have eliminated the paradox by making verses 378–9 claim that young women employ *delenimenta*, which their older counterparts cannot, thereby restoring harmony between those verses and verse 382. Similarly, Quicherat's *multa* and Madvig's *alia* strip the fragment of its contradictions by letting old women in the final verse keep the charms imputed to them earlier,[7] but those solutions are not completely happy, since the conjectures are bold, and render the second instance of the word *delenimenta* (382) flat and clumsy. That word would idly echo *delenimentis* (378) and make the same point as it. But the rhythm of the emphatic statement *mala aetas nulla delenimenta inuenit* calls attention to itself,[8] and it is difficult to attribute such a bland point to so striking a verse. Instead, the form of the sentence suggests that it pointedly contradicts the content of verses 378–9.[9] Such a contradiction, of course, is exactly what the transmitted text offers, and has for so long been deemed undesirable. Given the way that the final verse is phrased, any conjecture seeking to remove that contradiction would also need to provide a sound justification for the repetition of *delenimenta*, which no conjecture yet proposed has suitably explained.

Similarly problematic are the attempts to make *mala aetas* in this instance mean *iuuentas* or *adulescentia*, rather than, as Nonius claimed, *senectus*.[10] On this approach old women get to keep their charms, young women lose them, and comedy's men remain – against logic and comic tradition – unaffected by seduction. Whether or not Afranius' style of comedy made room for such a romantic constellation,[11] his Latin cannot, a point put beyond doubt by the substantial ancient evidence, most of it already assembled by Nonius, that *mala aetas* meant *senectus* to Latin-speaking audiences, while *bona aetas* was the comparable expression for *iuuentas*. Furthermore, Nonius read these verses in a complete script of the *Vopiscus* and could interpret them in their original context; his conviction about the meaning of *mala aetas* must not be discarded lightly.[12]

The third approach to this fragment's difficulties, namely, translating around its problems, has been by far the most common and remains the most tenacious. Yet for all its popularity, this kind of solution introduces grave problems of its own. Examples of it are offered by Jan van Broekhuizen, in his 1708 edition of Tibullus, who paraphrased:

dicit igitur Afranius delinimentis et ueneficiis amorem conciliari non posse: alioquin enim omnes uetulas habituras esse amatores. uera philtra adolescentarum, ac formosarum, esse aetatis florem, et corporis uenustatem, et mores ad omnem comitatem compositos. hisce rebus destitutas anus frustra sibi opem sperare a uenenis;[13]

by López López, quoting the annotated translation of Alfredo Adolfo Camús:[14]

El teatro representa un ambulacrum de casa romana; en el fondo una puerta que da al tocador, donde se estará poniendo la vieja como una imagen. Sale la ancillula con intención y señalando hacia la puerta.

Si pudieran los hombres prendarse de afeites,
Todas las viejas en el día tendrían cortejos.
(*Riendo y señalándose a sí misma.*)
La mocedad, el garbo y la zalamería,

Estos son los bebedizos de las buenas mozas,
(*con irisoria compasión y volviendo a señalar la puerta.*)
Pero la vejez no encuentra afeites que le cuadren;[15]

by Rosivach:[16]

If men could be caught by enticements, all the old women would now have lovers. Their age and tender body and compliance, these are the poisons of beautiful women; a bad age finds no such enticements;

and by Levée:[17]

S'il suffisait des caresses pour attirer les homes, nos vieilles ne manqueraient pas d'amoureux. Mais la jeunesse, la fraîcheur, la complaisance, voilà les moyens de séduction des jolies femmes. La vieillesse, sans attraits, ne saurait employer les mêmes artifices.[18]

In each instance, these solutions impose sense on the fragment by reading rather more into *nulla* (382) than that word in fact can support. Phrasing like "hisce rebus destitutas," "que le cuadren," "such," and "les mêmes" attributes to the final verse a logic that may be paraphrased in this way: "While old age has none of the *delenimenta* just mentioned, it in fact has other quite powerful weapons that would be effective at winning lovers, if only men could be swayed by such things." Such translations, which are in the end not so very different from Madvig's *alia*, restore logic to the fragment but go far beyond what the text itself suggests.[19]

It is not clear, and is in fact quite improbable, that *nulla* on its own could mean *quarum nulla*, or *cuius modi nulla*, or even *similia non (inuenit)*. Comparison with other instances of the word in republican comedy shows that *nulla* cannot on its own make the kind of distinctions that these translations extract from it. The phrasing with which Chremes addresses his workaholic neighbour Menedemus (Ter. *Heaut*. 67–70),

numquam tam mane egredior neque tam uesperi
domum reuortor quin te in fundo conspicer
fodere aut arare aut aliquid ferre. denique
nullum remittis tempus neque te respicis,

I never leave so early in the morning nor return home so late in the evening that I don't see you digging or plowing or carrying something around on your farm. In a word, you never take a break nor think about yourself;

or with which the prologue-speaker surveys the quiet audience before the successful performance of the *Hecyra* (Ter. *Hec.* 43), *nunc turba nulla est: otium et silentiumst* ("now there's no confusion: there's peace and quiet"), or with which Dauos reports how he uncovered the ruse of the *Andria* (Ter. *An.* 363–5),

> ... maneo. interea intro ire neminem
> uideo, exire neminem; matronam nullam in aedibus,
> nil ornati, nil tumulti,

I waited. In the meantime I saw nobody going in, nobody going out; not a wife in the house, no preparations, no confusion;

to select just three examples, shows quite clearly that Afranius' *nulla*, standing unqualified as it does, cannot support the interpretations so often imposed upon it.[20] Here, as elsewhere on the Roman stage, an unmodified "none" cannot mean "none, except for certain others." Had Chremes wished to tell Menedemus that he never takes a break from working, except when he takes a long and particularly restorative holiday, or had the prologue-speaker of the *Hecyra* meant that there was in fact some turmoil going on which threatened to derail the performance of that play yet again, they would have required more words to do so.[21] Only by explicit qualification could *nulla* convey such a sense, as in Terence, *Eun.* 840–2, where Chaerea speaks:

> apud Antiphonem uterque, mater et pater,
> quasi dedita opera domi erant, ut nullo modo
> intro ire possem quin uiderent me.[22]

At Antipho's house both his mother and father were at home as if they had made a concerted effort to be there, so that in no way could I go inside without their seeing me;

or in the prologue to the *Phormio*, where the words of an imagined interlocutor are brought forth by the *prologus* (Ter. *Phorm.* 13–15):

> "uetus si poeta non lacessisset prior,
> nullum inuenire prologum po[tui]sset nouos
> quem diceret, nisi haberet cui male diceret"

"If the old poet had not harmed him first, the new one could not have found any prologue to speak, unless he had someone to insult";

or in the famous *nullumst iam dictum quod non dictum sit prius* ("Nothing is said now which has not been said before," Ter. *Eun.* 41). There are therefore far greater difficulties with the most popular interpretation of the five verses of Afranius' *Vopiscus* than have been acknowledged.

We admittedly do not know what words were next uttered in Afranius' *Vopiscus*. It would be possible to argue that Nonius simply stopped copying from the script at an inopportune point, and that in the subsequent verses Afranius will have presented the kind of logical complement that would be necessary for *nulla* to convey the meaning attributed to it. The lexicographer's aims and habits would admittedly not obstruct such an argument. In order to provide context and support for the stated meaning of *mala aetas* in verse 382, Nonius also quoted the preceding verses where the common comic word for an old woman, *anus*, appeared; when he reached the verse containing *mala aetas*, the illustration of that expression was sufficient, and he did not need to transcribe any additional verses from the script. On that view, one could argue that the larger context of this fragment would have sanctioned the common interpretations of these verses. Yet such an argument would leave still unexplained the repetition of *delenimenta*, for this argument is in effect no different from Madvig's *alia* or Quicherat's *multa*; while restoring logic, it ignores the clear indications that *delenimenta* was a barbed utterance, not a bland restatement of the earlier point.[23]

The fourth and final approach that has won some degree of acceptance has been to circumvent the fragment's contradiction by marking a change of speaker within it. After his conjecture *multa* failed to convince, Quicherat proposed that verse 382 belonged to a different speaker.[24] This solution evades the contradiction by making the final verse reject the claim of the preceding four. In that respect it is attractive, but a cogent objection to it was signalled by Madvig, who pointed out that verses 380–2 cohere together so neatly, and verse 382 so plainly continues the thought of verses 380–1, that it is impossible to separate them and assign them to different speakers.[25]

A different division of this fragment, however, would be possible, since there is another point at which it could be broken into different speaking parts. Verses 378–9,

> si possent homines delenimentis capi,
> omnes haberent nunc amatores anus,

cohere together as neatly as do verses 380–1, whether they are taken on their own or in conjunction with the final verse, as:

> aetas et corpus tenerum et morigeratio,
> haec sunt uenena formosarum mulierum.
> mala aetas nulla delenimenta inuenit.

It is therefore worth considering whether the division between those two parts of the fragment is starker than the established text would suggest. Here we are nearer to an old suggestion that never attracted much attention, namely, the young Ribbeck's tentative proposal, put forward in the apparatus of his first edition, to mark a lacuna between verses 379 and 380.[26] The loss of one or more verses in the interior of a long fragment is indeed possible, but it is only a slightly less invasive way of restoring order than emending the text. A simpler explanation presents itself, which shall have to be given in two stages, the second retreating somewhat from the conclusions of the first.

Positing a change of speaker, rather than a lacuna, after verse 379 restores sense to the repetition of *delenimenta* and the apparent contradiction. The confident claim of the first two verses ("If men could be snared by charms, every old woman would have a lover!") would be answered with an emphatic denial ("Youth, a tender body, and compliance: these are the weapons of beautiful women. Old age has no charms!"). On this arrangement, *delenimenta* (382) would therefore not clumsily restate the claim of verses 378–9; it would simultaneously offer a neat variation on the same speaker's *venena,* while echoing and refuting, with the same language, the first speaker's partisan claims. Such an interpretation is supported by verses 380–1, for the speaker there points out that men can, in fact, be snared by the charms of youth, nubility, and compliance, a list of potential weapons rendered more emphatic still by *haec;* in verses 378–9 it had been claimed that men could not be snared by any charms whatsoever. Assigning verses 380–2 to a different speaker than the one whose words are contained in verses 378–9 thus would restore coherent logic to the fragment and a point to the repetition of *delenimenta.*

There is, however, at least one significant stumbling block that ultimately will prompt a modification of the solution just outlined. Who, it must be asked, would have spoken these verses in Afranius' play? Verses 380–2 will have been spoken by someone who rejects the idea of seductive old women and trumpets instead the attractions of a young woman; many of the stylized character types of Roman comedy could plausibly be given such words.[27] The logic of verses 378–9, which make old women supreme in the arts of snaring lovers, is so markedly partisan that the thought could only plausibly have been spoken by an old woman; she will have been confident that her inability to seduce a young lover is owed not to the fact that she has no seductive charms, but that men just cannot be seduced at all.[28]

Yet it is on that conclusion that we run afoul of a problem in the diction of this fragment that has never received the full attention it demands.[29] The problem arises in the use of the word *anus* (379), which is not a polite term for old women in the language of comedy, except in the case of women in one particular and circumscribed situation.[30] It is, furthermore, not a word that, in its usual sense, old women ever use to describe themselves or their comrades.[31] Given the usual tone of *anus* in Roman comedy, it is difficult to accept a solution that makes an old woman herself speak verses 378–9, while the partisan content of those verses pointed to exactly that conclusion. The word *anus* therefore poses an obstacle to marking a change of speaker after those verses, which solution I have so far been adumbrating.

A further instance of the word *anus* in the remains of Roman comedy may show the way to make sense of the delivery of Afranius' great fragment; here I proceed to the second stage of my explanation of these verses. In the first of the passages of Caecilius Statius' *Plocium* that Gellius set against the passages of Menander's Πλόκιον that inspired them, a *senex* complains that he has had to sell a slave-girl whom his wife suspected was his mistress (Caecilius 150–7 Ribbeck):

ita plorando orando instando atque obiurgando me optudit,
eam uti uenderem. nunc credo inter suas
aequalis, cognates sermonem serit:
"Quis uostrarum fuit integra aetatula
quae hoc idem a uiro
impetrarit suo, quod ego anus modo
effeci, paelice ut meum priuarem uirum?"
haec erunt concilia hocedie: differar sermone misere.

She so wore me down by weeping, begging, insisting, and quarrelling that I sold the girl. Now I guess she's sowing this kind of conversation among her friends and equals: "Who of you, in the fullness of youth, could win from her husband the same thing that I, an old *hag*, just now accomplished, namely depriving my husband of his mistress?" That's the coven they'll have today: their conversation will absolutely rip me to shreds.

The old man, *per prosopopoeiam*, imagines what his wife will be saying at that moment to her friends, but he allows his own attitudes to intrude into "her" words; she calls herself an *anus* (155), but the attitude that that word implies more accurately belongs to her husband than it does to the wife herself.[32]

In explaining Afranius' fragment, we have seen that positing a change of speaker offers the best way of making sense out of a difficult text, but that that same solution runs afoul of the word *anus*. I would suggest that in the *prosopopoeia* in Caecilius' *Plocium* is to be found the way forward in explaining Afranius' text. Verses 378–9 will not have been spoken by an old woman herself, but by another character imitating the logic and words of the old woman; the speaker's animus towards that character will have intruded in the word *anus*. The following paraphrase, which expands on the translation given earlier, represents the second stage of this interpretation of Afranius' verses:

> (*Mimicking the voice of an old woman*)
> "If men could be snared by charms, every old *hag* would have a lover."
> (*Dropping the imitation, and now scornful of the thought*)
> "Youth, a supple body, and obedience – these are the seductive weapons of beautiful women. Old women have no charms!"

This interpretation makes sense of the apparent contradiction in the first and last verses of the fragment, restores a point to the repetition of *delenimenta*, and explains how the partisan claim of the first two verses may be reconciled with the use of the impolite term *anus* to describe an old woman and her coevals, without relying on emendation of a text whose components are themselves sensible.[33]

In order to make sense of these five verses of Afranius' *Vopiscus*, it will therefore be necessary to understand a "change of speaker," of one sort or another, after verse 379. The solution that best respects the words with which these thoughts are expressed gives all five verses to a single speaker, who is not an old woman; that character will have imitated the speech and logic of an old lover in verses 378–9, but allowed his or her own prejudices to intrude at the end of the old woman's words, and will have presented his or her own refutation, in verses 380–2, of the old woman's position. Whether one prefers that explanation, or instead prefers to mark a true change of speaker after verse 379 and attribute the first two verses to an old woman in the flesh, it is clear that in any case the old guesses that made these five verses offer an old cougar's manifesto must be abandoned.

As I signalled earlier, though, there is still more to the story of the language of these verses. At least a modicum of doubt must remain about my prosopopoetic solution because of an important and neglected feature of the language that Afranius' women sometimes spoke. The speech patterns of women in Roman comedy have attracted considerable attention. It is well known that certain stylistic features mark the language that male comic dramatists wrote for their female characters, and that the style of that language is as likely to represent male stereotypes about female speech as the actual traits of their speech.[34] Furthermore, the stereotypes of how women speak and the prescriptions for how they should speak are as likely to be observed as they are to be violated, whether the speaker is unaware of the rule, indifferent to it, or even intentionally breaking it.[35]

However much stock we may wish to place in the conviction that an old woman in comedy would never willingly have called herself by the impolite term *anus*, we must also consider the possibility that Afranius intentionally represented a character as breaking with those conventions, reclaiming a "male" word for her own purposes.[36] It is striking that clear evidence of this pattern survives even in the fragments of his comedies. Afranius' *Diuortium* provides two indisputable instances where a female character violates the conventions of "female" comic speech and appropriates for herself words and characteristics that are otherwise marked as belonging to male speakers. The first occurs in Afranius 61–3:

uigilans ac sollers, sicca sana sobria
uirosa non sum, ac si sum, non desunt mihi
qui ultro dent: aetas integra est, formae satis.

Watchful and skillful, solid, sound, and sober: I don't lust after men, and if I did, there are no lack of people who would gladly give me (what I asked for?); I'm in the flower of youth, and pretty enough.

The adjective *uirosus* is in second-century BCE Latin otherwise used, markedly, as a negative quality that men apply to other men, or that men apply to their wives; this speaker in the *Diuortium*, however, claims it for herself, making the absence of that quality one of her own positive traits.[37] In the same way, a female character indirectly attributes to herself the virtue of *fortitudo* by remarking that it is faltering (Afranius 65): *disperii, perturbata sum, iam flaccet fortitudo*[38] ("I'm done for! I'm such a wreck! Now my boldness is drooping"). But *fortitudo* and the more common adjective *fortis* are almost exclusively the domain of men in Roman comedy, and it is striking to find a woman attributing that characteristic to herself.[39] In each instance, words that are markedly "male" are used and reinterpreted by a female character, who would have seemed to Afranius' audiences, or at least to other characters on stage, to talk like a man.[40]

In Afranius' *Epistula*, a similar but less markedly gendered expression is given to a woman whose husband is thought to be dead. She explains her decision not to take a second husband and to tend to her own affairs in language drawn from moralizing discourse, language that would probably have seemed to Afranius' audience incongruous and even highfalutin' in the mouth of a woman talking about her own circumstances (Afranius 116–17):

nam proba et pudica quod sum, consulo et parco mihi,
quoniam comparatum est, uno ut simus contentae uiro.

For since I am virtuous and chaste, I am tending to my own interests and looking after myself, since it has been established that we [women] be content with just one man.

The collocation *consulo et parco* does not occur elsewhere in the remains of Roman comedy, although *consulere* is common and *parcere* not unknown in the *sermo comicus* in the sense here required, indicating that the speaker is tending to her own affairs and needs no help from anyone else. Her language is nearer to that found in elevated religious and moralizing contexts than it is to that of the *palliata*.[41] Much like her counterpart in the *Diuortium,* this woman, thinking herself to be widowed, uses an expression that is commonly but not exclusively "male" in order to defend her decision not to take a new husband.

In at least a few instances, therefore, Afranius gave to his female characters who were describing their own circumstances words that would have seemed more appropriate if spoken by men. It is perhaps especially significant for the shape of Afranius' comedies and for the way his characters were represented, that the women who used "manly" language to describe themselves had apparently been or were thought to be widowed or divorced, and had not taken a second husband.

That feature of women's speech also raises the possibility of doubting the conclusion reached earlier, where *anus* was taken as an indication that an old woman could not herself have spoken Afranius 378–9, for even in the fragments of Afranius' comedies there are clear signs of women appropriating and reclaiming men's words (in which category *anus* most certainly belongs). It therefore remains possible to doubt the need for the second stage of my interpretation of this fragment. On the whole, lacking specific evidence that Afranius scripted this speech pattern for any of the female characters in the *Vopiscus,* it is perhaps best to make sense of these verses through imitation, satire, and prosopopoeia. Yet the subtle ways in which Afranius characterized some women in his plays by giving them "reclaimed" words mean that marking a true change of speaker after verse 379, and thereby making an old woman proudly imply that she is a sexy "hag," would not beyond the realm of possibility.

NOTES

* It is a pleasure to record my gratitude to the editors of this volume for their labours over it, and especially to Elaine Fantham, whose cheerful presence, wit, and erudition continue to shine in Toronto. This work was supported by a grant from the Social Sciences and Humanities Research Council of Canada.

1 Nonius p. 1.6 *nam* AETATEM MALAM *senectutem ueteres dixerunt*. For Nonius' sources, see Lindsay 1901; White 1980.

2 The text as given in Ribbeck 1873 is printed without change by Ribbeck 1898; Onions 1895; Lindsay 1903; Daviault 1981; López López 1983.

3 In his sketch of the plot of the *Vopiscus*, Ribbeck (1898: 250) wrote "anusque adulescentis amorem captans (XX, XXI) inducitur" (citing these verses and Afranius 383–5, respectively, where an old woman is faintly indicated only by emendation). Ribbeck's *inducitur* seems intentionally vague.

4 Ribbeck, as often, was more focused on heaping scorn on Lucian Müller, whose *tenerumst* (380) had already been rightly rejected by Bergk (1884: 398 [an article first published in 1870]). Müller is a frequent target of Ribbeck's abuse; see, e.g., Ribbeck 1873: LXXVII on this fragment.

5 Schoppe 1596: 130–2. On Schoppe, his teacher Rittershausen, the *Verisimilium Libri*, and Justus Lipsius, see Papy 1998: 277–80.

6 Schoppe paraphrased his emended text as *nisi homines delenimentis caperentur, etiam uetulae amari solerent. nunc autem senectus nulla delenimenta habet… quare nec amatores habent*. The paraphrase, especially *etiam*, changes the point considerably. The conjecture was soon consigned to the dustbin, enjoying only a brief resurrection when J.H. Onions (1888: 161), the ill-starred young editor of Nonius Marcellus, drew attention to the reading *in possent* (F^1).

7 Quicherat in Miguel and de Morante 1864a: 49–55; Madvig 1873: 653.

8 The first two metra of verse 382 scan *aBCDaBCD*, a pattern remarkably avoided by both Plautus and Terence, on which see Gratwick 1993: 257–60 and 1999: 233–7. Instructive are the rhythmically comparable verses (to be taken in their fuller context) at Ter. *Ad.* 430 *inepta haec esse nos quae facimus sentio*; *Ad.* 514 *si est facturus ut sit officium suom*.

9 Quicherat in Miguel and de Morante (1864a: 50) pointed out that the repetition of *delenimenta* rendered the contradiction "encore plus flappante," which he took to support his conjecture eliminating the paradox. The resulting verses present a simpler logic but give little point to that striking repetition of *delenimenta*.

10 Theil in Miguel and de Morante 1864b: 85–9, 94–106; Miguel and de Morante 1864a, 1864b.

11 I have argued that Quintilian's famous judgment of Afranius (*Inst.* 10.1.100) refers not to the inclusion of pederasty in his comedies, but rather to the (in Quintilian's view) unhappy and unimproving representation of wasteful love affairs, known best to us from the *palliata*, in Roman and Italian contexts; see Welsh 2010. While the *togata* also presents a broader view of love and marriage, including especially divorces and second marriages, there seems to be no evidence for anything like a pairing of Benjamin Braddock and Mrs. Robinson in the genre.

12 Although ultimately not compelling, this argument is of substantial independent historical interest. It came to the fore in an *annus mirabilis*, between April 1863 and April 1864, which saw no fewer than fifteen discussions of these verses appear in print. The contributions to that debate can be traced in the pages of Miguel and de Morante 1864a and 1864b, who reprinted the francophone contributions in their appendices; the numerous hispanophone contributions are summarized and excerpted in Menéndez y Pelayo 1902: 23–53. The only contribution of that year known to me which is not signalled in those compendia is the unsigned article Auctor Anon. 1864. For all the ink spilled, there is little to be gained from this rapid-fire debate; most of the points made in it were summarily dispatched by Auctor Anon. 1864, whose own suggestion, however, similarly misses the mark.

13 "Afranius therefore says that love cannot be produced with charms and sorcery: for otherwise all old women would have lovers. The true seductive potions of young and beautiful women are the flower of youth, the charming appearance of the body, and good behaviour arranged with a view towards being entirely courteous. Old women, bereft of these same things, hope in vain that help will come to them from potions." The paraphrase is quoted with approbation by Neukirch (1833: 263), and could not be improved upon by either Hermann (1834) or Bothe (1834: 193; 1837: 283–4).

14 López López 1983: 260–1.

15 Camús scripted several scenes to provide a full, imaginative context for the fragment; for his discussion, see most conveniently Menéndez y Pelayo 1902: 29–42. A French version is provided by Quicherat in Miguel and de Morante 1864b: 112–13. Camús' annotations are essential for understanding how he read the scene.

16 Rosivach 1998: 197.

17 Levée 1823: 229.

18 Further attempts in the same vein are offered by Rocca in Miguel and de Morante 1864a: 53–8; Smith 1913: 164; Panchón Cabañeros 1996: 74n35.

19 Auctor Anon. (1864: 135) rejected such attempts: "Ils donnent au passage un sens raisonnable; mais ce sens ils le mettent eux-mêmes, car il n'y est pas."

20 Cf. further, Plaut. *Bacch*. 214–15, *Capt*. 998–1000, *Epid*. 306–7, *Men*. 226–8; Ter. *Eun*. 240, *Ad*. 188–9.

21 Further examples at Titinius 106 and Afranius 268.

22 Cf. Ter. *Heaut*. 805–6, 1006–7; *Hec*. 240; Afranius 170–2.

23 Despite the tidy parallel of Ter. *Phorm*. 14–15, the verb *inuenire* requires no such complement to make sense, and so the thought need not have continued in a subsequent verse. Afranius' *nulla delenimenta inuenit* plays off the common collocation *aurum* or *argentum inuenire* (e.g., Ter. *Heaut*. 329, *Phorm*. 534); whereas the young men of comedy win their lovers with silver, Afranius' women use, or would use, *delenimenta* or *uenena* to seduce a man.

24 Quicherat 1872. This solution was accepted by Bardon (1952: 142n3) and signalled by Daviault (1981: 240n15).

25 Madvig 1873: 653: "personae novae aperta eiusdem sententiae continuatio tribui nequit."

26 Ribbeck 1855: 181; the suggestion is not mentioned in his second or third editions and has not, it seems, been taken up by any other defender.

27 On speculation, the thought suits comedy's old men as well as its young men, and it would perhaps be even neater to give these verses to a young woman.

28 Indeed, those scholars who ventured to identify the speaker of this little manifesto most often suggested that an old woman delivered it.

29 It was perhaps signalled by the perceptive anonymous author (1864: 136) at the end of that contribution, who noted in passing "la raillerie qui perce dans le second vers," in order to suggest that a young woman spoke all five verses.

30 For the different situation where the pathetic circumstances of the old abandoned woman are more prominent, see Rosivach 1994: 108, 115. Sophrona's words at Ter. *Phorm.* 751–3 (*ego autem, quae essem anus deserta egens ignota, | ut potui nuptum uirginem locaui huic adulescenti | harum qui est dominus aedium*) are informative. A character in so dire a situation, however, can scarcely be imagined to concern herself with snaring a young lover, which makes this usage of the word irrelevant here.

31 Donatus, Ter. *Hec.* 231, *<ut illam> "puellam" blande dixit, ita hanc cum amaritudine "anum,"* indicates the tone of the word; cf. Afranius 276; Jocelyn 1969: 317. Rosivach 1994 surveys the characteristics that are attributed to old women identified by this term.

32 Whether or not one accepts my attribution of Com. inc. 51–5 Ribbeck[3] to Afranius' *Priuignus*, precisely the same strategy occurs in the use of *miser* in that fragment (55), where someone else's perspective makes itself felt in the imagined words of the deceased *pater*; see Welsh 2012.

33 Dübner in Miguel and de Morante 1864a: 59 thought of a similar effect, but had an old woman speak all five verses, borrowing *formosarum* from the language of younger women and in the final verse imitating them through *prosopopoeia*. This solution, however, leaves *anus* unexplained and the emphatic *haec* without a point, and *delenimenta* would remain somewhat weak.

34 For discussion, see Adams 1984; Dutsch 2008.

35 Adams' formulation (1984: 44) is neat: "For every individual or group which is subservient to such a rule, there is another which is either unaware of or indifferent to it." I am here interested in what are perhaps intentional breaches of such conventions, which the male dramatist wrote into the script as a means of characterization.

36 In thinking about these patterns, I have benefited especially from the discussions of linguistic reclamation in Moon 1995 and Sutton 1995.

37 Scipio Aemilianus, *ORF* 21.17; Lucilius 287 Krenkel. On this fragment see further Welsh 2015.

38 Admittedly, *sum* is the conjecture of Junius (1565: 139; anticipating Gulielmus [1583: 84]), but there seems no reason, even in view of *fortitudo*, to doubt it. Both *disperii* and *flaccet fortitudo* point to personal emotional turmoil, rather than a confused situation, while *perturbata sunt* would be a remarkably ineffective utterance between *disperii* and *iam flaccet fortitudo*.

39 The only exceptions are Plaut. *Bacch*. 216 and *Mil*. 1106, where *fortis* is used to describe a woman's hearty constitution. At Afranius 158, in a fragment of the *Fratriae*, Nonius makes *fortis* mean *diues*; see Welsh 2015.

40 Another possible instance, although supported by insufficient evidence, occurs in Afranius 52–4, which opens *o <in>dignum* (Del Rio) *facinus*. The eight instances of that cry in the *palliata* are spoken by men (admittedly not guaranteeing that the expression was exclusively "male"), but it is nevertheless attractive to assign the fragment to one of the *adulescentes optumae* (itself is an uncommon descriptor of young married women) whose divorces it laments.

41 Cf. Accius 136–7: [probably Ismene speaking] *quanto magis te isti modi esse intellego, | tanto, Antigona, magis me par est tibi consulere et parcere*; Plin. *HN* 7.122.5: [attributed to Ti. Sempronius Gracchus, father of the Gracchi] *hoc erat uxori parcere et rei publicae consulere*; [Caes.] *B Alex*. 24.2: *itaque regem cohortatus ut consuleret regno paterno, parceret praeclarissimae patriae*; Livy 37.45.9; Val. Max. 3.2.6; [Sen.] *Oct*. 473. None of these instances show someone directing the action of *consulere et parcere* at him- or herself.

WORKS CITED

Adams, J.N. 1984. "Female Speech in Latin Comedy." *Antichthon* 18: 43–77.

Auctor Anon. 1864. "Interprétation d'un passage d'Afranius." *Revue de l'instruction publique en Belgique* 7: 134–6.

Bardon, H. 1952. *La littérature latine inconnue*. 1. Paris.

Bergk, T. 1884. *Kleine philologische Schriften*. 1. Halle-an-der-Saale.

Bothe, F., ed. 1834. *Poetarum Latii Scenicorum Fragmenta* 5.2. Leipzig.

– 1837. "Emendationes Nonianae." *RhM* 5: 250–300.

Daviault, A., ed. 1981. *Comoedia Togata: Fragments*. Paris.

Dutsch, D. 2008. *Feminine Discourse in Roman Comedy: On Echoes and Voices*. Oxford.

Gratwick, A.S., ed. 1993. *Plautus:* Menaechmi. Cambridge.

– 1999. *Terence:* The Brothers. Warminster.

Gulielmus, J. 1583. *Plautinarum quaestionum commentarius*. Paris.

Hermann, G. 1834. "Adnotationes ad Io. Henr. Neukirchii librum *de fabula togata Romanorum*, editum Lipsiae a. 1833." In his *Opuscula* 5. 254–88. Leipzig.

Jocelyn, H.D., ed. 1969. *The Tragedies of Ennius*. Ed. corr. Cambridge.

Junius, H., ed. 1565. *Nonius Marcellus:* De Proprietate Sermonum. Antwerp.

Levée, J.B. 1823. *Théâtre complet des latins* XV. *Fragments des tragiques et des comiques latins*. Paris.

Lindsay, W.M. 1901. *Nonius Marcellus' Dictionary of Republican Latin*. Oxford.

– ed. 1903. *Nonii Marcelli* De Conpendiosa Doctrina *Libros XX*. Leipzig.

López López, A., ed. 1983. *Fabularum Togatarum Fragmenta: edición crítica*. Salamanca.

Madvig, J.N. 1873. *Adversaria Critica*. 2. Copenhagen.

Menéndez y Pelayo, M., ed. 1902. *Bibliografía hispano-latina clásica*. Madrid.

Miguel, R. de, and El Marqués de Morante. 1864a. *Cuestión filológica. Un fragmento de Afranio*. Madrid.

– 1864b. *Nueva disertación acerca de un fragmento de Afranio*. Madrid.

Moon, D. 1995. "Insult and Inclusion: The Term Fag Hag and Gay Male 'Community'." *Social Forces* 74.2: 487–510.

Neukirch, J.H., ed. 1833. *De Fabula Togata Romanorum. Accedunt fabularum togatarum reliquiae*. Leipzig.

Onions, J.H. 1888. "Noniana Quaedam." *JPh* 16: 161–82.

Onions, J.H., ed. 1895. *Nonius Marcellus:* De Conpendiosa Doctrina *I–III*. Oxford.

Panchón Cabañeros, F. 1996. "La expresión *Mala Aetas*." *Voces* 7: 63–74.

Papy, J. 1998. "*Manus manum lavat*. Die Briefkontakte zwischen Kaspar Schoppe und Justus Lipsius als Quelle für die Kenntnis der sozialen Verhältnisse in der Respublica litteraria." In *Kaspar Schoppe (1576–1649), Philologe im Dienste der Gegenreformation. Beiträge zur Gelehrtenkultur des europäischen Späthumanismus* [= *Zeitsprünge: Forschungen zur Frühen Neuzeit* 2.3–4], edited by H. Jaumann, 276–97. Frankfurt.

Quicherat, L., ed. 1872. *Nonii Marcelli* De Compendiosa Doctrina ad Filium. Paris.

Ribbeck, O., ed. 1855. *Scaenicae Romanorum Poesis Fragmenta. 2. Comicorum Romanorum praeter Plautum et Terentium fragmenta*. Leipzig.

– 1873. *Scaenicae Romanorum Poesis Fragmenta. 2. Comicorum Romanorum praeter Plautum et Terentium fragmenta*. 2nd ed., Leipzig.

– 1898. *Scaenicae Romanorum Poesis Fragmenta. 2. Comicorum Romanorum praeter Plautum et Syri quae feruntur sententias fragmenta*. 3rd ed., Leipzig.

Rosivach, V.J. 1994. "*Anus*: Some Older Women in Latin Literature." *CW* 88: 107–17.

– 1998. *When a Young Man Falls in Love: The Sexual Exploitation of Women in New Comedy*. London.

Schoppe, C. 1596. *Verisimilium Libri Quattuor*. Nuremberg.

Smith, K.F. 1913. "Notes on Satyros, Life of Euripides, Oxyr. Pap. 9, 157–8." *AJP* 34: 62–73.

Sutton, L.A. 1995. "Bitches and Skankly Hobags: The Place of Women in Contemporary Slang." In *Gender Articulated: Language and the Socially Constructed Self*, edited by K. Hall and M. Bucholtz, 279–96. New York.

Welsh, J.T. 2010. "Quintilian's Judgement of Afranius." *CQ* 60.1: 118–26.
– 2012. "Com. inc. 51–5 Ribbeck[3]: A Fragment of Afranius' *Privignus?*" *CQ* 62.1: 201–10.
– 2015. "Roman Women in the *Fabula Togata.*" In *Women in Roman Republican Drama*, edited by D. Dutsch, S.L. James, and D. Konstan, 155–70. Madison, WI.
White, D.C. 1980. "The Method of Composition and Sources of Nonius Marcellus." *Studi Noniani* 8: 111–211.

12

Knowledge, Power, and Republicanism in Lucan*

JONATHAN TRACY

In the age of WikiLeaks and Edward Snowden, the degree of government control that can or should be exercised over the flow of information to the general public is a burning issue, as is the related question of whether education should be designed to create broadly enlightened citizens of the world or narrow specialists within the various professions demanded by the global economy. These same questions (*mutatis mutandis*) also exercised ancient Greek and Roman authors from Homer to Procopius and were of particular concern during the turbulent years of the end of the Roman Republic and the establishment of the Principate, with the painful transition from a comparatively democratic form of government[1] to a thinly veiled autocracy.

The Roman Consensus

As a leading prophet of the new world order, Vergil promotes a vision of society in which all spheres of knowledge are placed strictly under elite control. This is especially apparent in the *Aeneid*, where Aeneas is shown to enjoy uniquely privileged access to information about the universe. Aeneas thus premises his request for clear oracular enlightenment from the Sibyl upon his status as his people's ruler, who is capable of erecting temples, appointing national feast days, and establishing public priesthoods in honour of her and of her master Apollo (*Aen.* 6.69–74).[2] Similarly, Aeneas craves access to the additional enlightenment of a journey to the underworld on the basis of his membership within a very select circle of heroes (6.119–24):[3]

si potuit Manis accersere coniugis Orpheus
Threicia fretus cithara fidibusque canoris,
si fratrem Pollux alterna morte redemit

itque reditque uiam totiens. quid Thesea, magnum
quid memorem Alciden? et mi genus ab Ioue summo.

If Orpheus availed to summon his wife's shade, strong in his Thracian lyre and tuneful strings; if Pollux, dying in turn, ransomed his brother and so many times comes and goes his way – why speak of Theseus, why of Hercules the mighty – I, too, have descent from Jove most high!

Aeneas' eligibility on these grounds is then confirmed in the Sibyl's response (6.129–31): ***pauci***, *quos aequus amauit | Iuppiter aut ardens euexit ad aethera uirtus, | dis geniti potuere* ("Some **few**, whom kindly Jupiter has loved, or shining worth uplifted to heaven, sons of the gods, have availed"). Indeed, according to the analysis of Adler,[4] the entire *Aeneid*, and especially Book 6, is itself an embodiment and illustration of a two-tier access to knowledge: the average reader is presented with the edifying picture of a morally appropriate afterlife (with rewards for the virtuous and punishment for the wicked), whereas the enlightened few can read between the lines to grasp Vergil's true Epicurean sentiments (socially dangerous for mass consumption).

Not only are the ordinary Trojan people denied access to the sources of information available to Aeneas, but they are also excluded from Aeneas' counsels. Aeneas may (like any monarch) take advice from individual counsellors or from Anchises (the only human to whom he owes any kind of obedience), but he never consults his people (or their representatives) as a group on crucial decisions, for instance the choice to seek alliance with Evander in Pallanteum. An illuminating example of Aeneas' decision-making process occurs near the end of Book 5, in the aftermath of the near-destruction of all his people's hopes with the burning of their ships by the Trojan women. Wrestling with dismay at yet another obstacle to his quest, Aeneas receives solace, together with a proposal for leaving the disaffected women behind in Sicily, from his aged counsellor Nautes (5.704–18). Nautes, however, is in fact conveying not his own opinion to Aeneas but rather the advice of the very gods and the injunctions of Fate, since he has been personally instructed in such matters by the goddess Minerva (5.704–7). Consequently, Aeneas is here, in effect, accepting counsel from those above him in the cosmic hierarchy, not from a mere mortal. What is more, Aeneas does not even resolve to follow Nautes' advice until it is confirmed by the apparition of Anchises in a dream, who assures him that this message comes all the way from Jupiter himself (5.721–39). Aeneas then summons his comrades (*socios*), but not to a council of equals (5.746–9). Rather than inviting a general discussion on the matter, he "instructs" them (*edocet*, 748) in Jupiter's (and Anchises') command and his own determination to follow Jupiter's lead (*quae nunc animo sententia constet,* "the resolve now settled in his soul"). What follows (5.749) is precisely a total absence of any kind of open debate or discussion (*haud mora consiliis,* "there is not at all a delay for debate") and a thoroughgoing deference to Aeneas' heaven-mandated commands (*nec iussa recusat Acestes,* "nor does Acestes refuse his bidding"). This is very far removed from a spirit of public consultation, and, over the entire course of the poem, there is no Trojan council to rival the turbulent council of the Latins depicted at 11.234–446.[5] The Trojans are in fact portrayed throughout the poem as behaving with remarkable unanimity, united in blind obedience to their all-wise, all-knowing, benevolent leader.

In his extreme elitism on the question of access to information and discourse, Vergil stands firmly planted within the orthodox consensus of antiquity. For one thing, the *Aeneid*'s genre, heroic epic, was by definition a celebration of elite achievements from Homer onwards, in which the lower orders were expected to know and keep to their place. The Thersites episode of *Iliad* 2.211–64 thus constitutes a vivid warning against the baser sort interfering in the counsels of their betters, and the *Aeneid* goes even further in promoting caste exclusivity and purity. Vergil has clearly modelled his character of Drances on Homer's Thersites as a spiteful and meddlesome social inferior hurling slander at his betters.[6] Thersites, however, is merely and vaguely designated as "inferior" (*Il.* 2.248), as opposed to the kings he insults, and is easily swatted aside by Odysseus. Drances, on the other hand, poses a much more serious threat to the Latins' social order through his high-born mother, who has granted him a dangerous foothold within the elite that, because of the obscurity of his paternal lineage, he does not truly deserve (*Aen.* 11.341–2).

The issue of epic audiences is more complex, especially for the period of oral epic, but, by the time of Aristotle, epic was regarded by some critics as designed for the most refined sort of audience (*Poet.* 1462a), in contrast to tragedy, appreciated by the comparatively "base" (φαύλους). At any rate, the first reported audience for the *Aeneid* (in Donatus' report) was of the most elite quality imaginable, consisting of Augustus himself and his sister Octavia. An intensification of elitism over time can also be observed in regard to didactic epic: whereas, in the Archaic age, Hesiod deliberately casts his *Works and Days* as a humble alternative to Homeric epic, designed to express the values and address the needs of ordinary farmers and merchants like himself, both of the great didactic poems of the late Roman Republic, Lucretius' *De Rerum Natura* and Vergil's *Georgics*, are dedicated to high-born and illustrious individuals, Memmius and Maecenas, respectively.[7]

As for Adler's thesis that Vergil covertly endorses the elite suppression or distortion of truth within the religious sphere, this is supported by a host of examples from ancient, and especially Roman, literature. There is of course Plato, who authorizes rulers to deceive the ruled for the common good, in particular through the celebrated "noble lie" about the divinely ordained stratification of the human race (*Rep.* 3.414–15). In his analysis of the Roman constitution, Polybius likewise praises the Roman governing class for imposing an array of edifying superstitions upon the credulous masses and thereby encouraging popular discipline and morality (6.56). Livy offers specific instances of such elite manipulation. For instance, he reports the story of Proculus Iulius' timely intervention during the chaos following the mysterious disappearance of Romulus, when he assuaged the people's mounting panic and discontent with a fable of Romulus' immortality (1.16); he also describes, with approval, how Numa instilled pious discipline into the hearts of the Roman people by inventing the story of his personal instruction from the goddess Egeria (1.19).

Nor can Vergil, propagandist for one-man rule, be distinguished from the arch-republican Cicero on this issue, for the cynical exploitation and cultivation of popular religious beliefs are nowhere more flagrant than in the latter's writings. For his elite readership, Cicero can voice personal scepticism about traditional religion (e.g., in his *De Natura Deorum*) and the art of divination (in the *De Divinatione*), but in his *De Legibus* he insists on the political utility and necessity of a strong state religion (2.7), prescribes aristocratic supervision of all religious rites as a guarantee of political stability (2.12), and celebrates the power of augurs to dismiss popular assemblies and nullify popular legislation (2.12). Cicero can be observed putting this principle of statecraft into practice with his four Catilinarian speeches, for the orations addressed to the people (2 and 3) display a markedly greater religious emphasis than those directed at the Senate (1 and 4). In particular, the third speech incorporates a long account of the gods' pre-eminent role in foiling the conspiracy, including a catalogue of the sort of omens that Cicero dismisses as empty superstition in the *De Divinatione*, as well as an attack on sceptics who are so "turned away from the truth, so reckless, so insane" as to deny the fact of Rome's government by the gods (*Cat.* 3.18–23). In the fourth oration, by contrast, although he does insert a brief, throwaway reference to the divine will (*Cat.* 4.2), Cicero offers, at considerably greater length, a sceptical critique of traditional beliefs in the afterlife, along with a reference to the political utility of promoting such views among the masses (4.7–8).

Cicero also exploits religion in suppressing the people's awareness of their own power of action. Where, in the fourth Catilinarian, Cicero seeks to impress upon the Senate their awesome responsibility in safeguarding the commonwealth through their choice of punishment for the conspirators, his exhortation to the people in the second and third speeches is merely to pray and go home,[8] leaving the actual work of combating the conspiracy in Cicero's capable hands (under divine leadership, of course): all that is required of the Roman plebs, as of Aeneas' Trojans, is passive, pious, unquestioning trust in their leader. Cicero also conceals certain inconvenient facts from the people that he deems suitable for his senatorial audience, such as Catiline's (at least ostensibly) conciliatory offer to place himself in Cicero's custody (or that of some other leading senator), as reported in the first (1.19) and omitted from the second oration. It should be noted that, although the Catilinarian speeches were delivered orally to two separate audiences, the readership for the subsequent published version of all four was presumably restricted to (relatively) elite circles. Taken together, they accordingly function as a model (for use by the elite) of careful management of information during a time of potential revolution, whereby the democratic component of the famously "mixed-constitution" Roman Republic can be kept firmly in check.

Both Vergil's Aeneas and Cicero (as he represents himself in his speeches) are shown exercising their control over public knowledge purely in altruistic service of the common welfare. In Lucan's *Bellum Ciuile*, on the other hand, autocrats (especially Caesar) repeatedly and cynically exploit their monopoly on information (religious, scientific, and political) as a means of maintaining and increasing their own power. Lucan thereby reveals popular ignorance to be a necessary precondition not for social stability but rather for tyranny. The fundamentally anti-elitist tenor of this perspective sets Lucan not only against Vergil (along with the entire epic tradition), and not only against the imperial system, but also against the mainstream current of Roman republicanism. It is true that Lucan displays the deep reverence for the Senate typical of nostalgic republicans, and on occasion he even gives voice to an aristocratic contempt for the rabble, as with his bitter reference to Caesar's purchase of popular favour through cheap grain (3.52–6), which can be compared to Cicero's similar complaint against the easy bribery of the "ignorant multitude" in the second *Philippic* (2.116). It is also true that, amid all the horrors of Lucan's self-destructing cosmos, we can more easily discern what Lucan abominates than any positive designs he may have for a future, better world. Understandably, then, scholars have paid little attention to the type of republic that Lucan might have envisaged as his ideal society; instead, scholarly debate has focused on the question of whether Lucan was a republican at all, rather than merely an advocate of a benevolent, constitutional Principate (or even a cheerleader for Nero).[9] In the following pages, however, I will adopt a different approach, by assuming Lucan's republicanism as the beginning rather than the endpoint for my investigations. After all, it is a simple and inarguable truth of history that the Roman Republic did fail spectacularly as a system of government. If Lucan in fact hoped for a restoration of the Republic (as assumed by my investigation), it would therefore have been natural for him to ask how a similar collapse could be prevented in the future. I will argue, particularly on the evidence of his portrayal of the contrasting interactions of Caesar and Cato with their respective armies (republics in microcosm) in Books 5 and 9, as well as his idealized depiction of the state of Massilia in Book 3, that Lucan represents a Republic's freedom as dependent on the freedom of access to information enjoyed by its citizens. Lucan may not have been a democrat in the purest sense of that term (was any Roman?), but he certainly seems to have credited the common people with enough sense to believe that, if placed in full command of the facts, they could be trusted to make moral and rational decisions on that basis.

Caesar

Book 5 offers Lucan's clearest picture of the techniques for maintaining authoritarian rule, particularly in the field of public information. It is perhaps no coincidence that this book was (probably) composed shortly after Lucan himself had experienced imperial censorship first-hand with the publication ban imposed on him by Nero.[10] Indeed, Lucan explicitly laments contemporary censorship with his statement that, not content with monopolizing access to oracles, the ruling powers of his own time have shut down Delphi altogether in order to prevent the spread of accurate knowledge about the future (5.111–14), *postquam reges timuere futura | et superos uetuere loqui* ("ever since kings feared the future and forbade the gods to speak").[11] This is a disaster not just to privileged individuals but to the human race as a whole, since Lucan emphasizes that the oracle, when in operation, was equally accessible to all mortals except the wicked, with no apparent distinction of rank (5.102–4): *hoc tamen expositum cunctis nullique negatum | numen ab humani solum se labe furoris | uindicat* ("This power, though available to all and denied to none, yet alone keeps itself free from stain of human wickedness").

Although Lucan's lines on the closure of the oracle refer to rulers in general (with perhaps a specific dig at Nero, as suggested by the *Commenta Bernensia* ad loc.), Caesar is the most egregious culprit in the acts of censorship and misinformation scattered through Book 5 (and the poem as a whole). On the issue of public accountability, for instance, Book 5 begins with an open meeting of the exiled republican senators in Epirus. Lucan underscores the transparency as well as the anti-monarchical thrust of the senate's acts with his introductory statement that the senate thereby "instructed the peoples" (*docuit populos*) in its own primacy over Pompey (5.13–14). The republican decision-making process is shown to be a matter of public, not private, business and consultation, above all with regard to the most important decision of the entire war, namely, the vesting of formal command in Pompey (5.45–9). The didactic phrase *docuit populos* also suggests the importance of disseminating political enlightenment about the true nature of the republican constitution among the broad masses. This council is, however, balanced near the end of Book 5 by Caesar's reckless attempt to cross the Adriatic on a stormy night, which he undertakes in secret (note the verb *fallere*, "to deceive," at 5.512, and *fefellit*, "he deceived," at 5.679), without consulting the men who would be most affected by his loss; they accordingly chastise his inconsiderateness at 5.682–99. Fantham shows that Lucan models the soldiers' reproach on a similar scene from the Alexander tradition, which follows Alexander's near-fatal wounding during a reckless attempt to climb the walls of an enemy town (Curt. 9.4–6); she notes, however, the crucial distinction that, "whereas Alexander's comrades have passed days afraid for his life, Caesar's men in Lucan have slept all night to be confronted at reveille by a wet but healthy commander, so that they have to imagine the dangers he might have succumbed to."[12] In other words, the episodes are differentiated by the secrecy of the commander's plight. After all, according to Curtius Rufus, Alexander's impulsive act of daring at the siege occurred *in conspectu tanti exercitus* ("in sight of so great an army," 9.4–33), while Caesar, with cold premeditation, takes great pains to conceal his venture from his soldiers. This refusal to engage in public consultation (maintained by Caesar throughout Lucan's poem) harks back to Vergil's Aeneas, but Caesar is shown exercising his untrammelled freedom of decision and action far less responsibly than the Augustan hero.

Caesar also practises deception in matters far more central to the welfare of the Republic than his own foolhardy escapades. For instance, he foreshadows the hypocritical Principate through a pretence of republicanism during a brief visit to Rome, holding sham elections and assuming lying titles of constitutional office to mask the ugly face of despotism (5.381–94). This all amounts to a monstrous lie, directed at both the Roman people and the world at large, but Caesar also specifically impedes the flow of accurate information to the people, since he imposes a gag on the augurs and prevents them from reporting evil omens for the elections, extorting favourable (i.e., lying) reports from them instead (5.395–6). The augurs' authority is thereby exploited not to safeguard the Republic's stability (as in Cicero's theorizing) but rather as a prop for tyranny.

The Mutiny

Caesar's disingenuousness comes most to the fore in his dealings with the specific individuals or groups on whom he relies as his instruments for the pursuance of his political and military goals. This is apparent from three episodes in Book 5 that, as Fantham demonstrates, are closely linked by shared themes and imagery: the mutiny, the crossing of the Adriatic, and the violent sea storm.[13] During the first two incidents, Caesar is shown unabashedly deceiving and misleading his own soldiers, in marked contrast with the image of an intimate bond between general and army cultivated by Caesar's own *Commentaries*. With the mutiny scene, Lucan also subverts a respectable Vergilian *exemplum* of responsible leadership. In his first address to his followers (which follows a near-disastrous storm, where Lucan's mutiny scene precedes a storm), Aeneas is careful to repress his true feelings and conceal his despondency (expressed by *simulat*, a verb of artifice and deception), in order to give them heart to pursue their divinely sanctioned mission and fill them with a confidence that he does not himself share (1.208–9): *talia uoce refert, curisque ingentibus aeger | spem uultu simulat, premit altum corde dolorem* ("Such words he spoke, while sick with deep distress he feigns hope on his face, and deep in his heart he stifles his anguish").

How does this compare with Caesar's address to his troops during the mutiny of Book 5? Like Aeneas, Lucan's Caesar is filled with anxiety (denoted by the fearing verbs *timetur*, 5.309, and *pauet*, 5.368). Also like Aeneas, Caesar buries his fears, at least as far as facial expression is concerned (*intrepidus uultu*, "with face undaunted," recalls Vergil's *spem uultu*) as he browbeats his men into continuing with their campaign (5.316–18): *stetit aggere fulti | caespitis intrepidus uoltu meruitque timeri | non metuens* ("On a mound of piled turf he stood with face undaunted, and his fearlessness deserved to be feared"). Nevertheless, the psychological goal and effect of the two speeches are diametrically opposed. Aeneas is afraid *for* his folk, but Caesar is afraid *of* his troops, of their new mental clarity and freedom of will (5.309): *militis indomiti tantum mens sana timetur* ("Only the sanity of his unbridled troops makes him afraid"). Consequently, where Aeneas engages in a pardonable act of self-restraint with a view to making his people stronger and more confident in their destiny (*durate, et uosmet rebus seruate secundis*, "endure, and live for a happier day," 1.207), Caesar deceives his men precisely in order to render them powerless.

What Caesar must achieve in his speech to the mutineers is the eradication of their newfound awareness of one of the great secrets of government, namely, the total dependence of all rulers upon the ruled. Caesar himself perceives the lesson of the mutiny clearly, namely, that he will instantly forfeit his lofty eminence if he can no longer exploit the people beneath him as appendages, *manus* ("hands"),[14] devoid of independent thought and will (5.249–54):

haud magis expertus discrimine Caesar in ullo est
quam non e stabili tremulo sed culmine cuncta
despiceret staretque super titubantia fultus.
tot raptis truncus manibus gladioque relictus
paene suo, qui tot gentis in bella trahebat,
scit non esse ducis strictos sed militis enses.

In no crisis did Caesar learn more clearly
how he looked down on everything from a height which was
not firm but shaking and how he stood supported on a rocking platform.
Maimed by the loss of so many hands and almost left
to his own sword, the man who drew to war so many nations
knows that unsheathed swords are not the general's but the soldier's.

More importantly, his soldiers have come to the same conclusion about their indispensability to Caesar's fortunes (5.293–95): *nos fatum sciat esse suum. licet omne deorum | obsequium speres, irato milite, Caesar, | pax erit* ("He must know that we are his destiny: Caesar, though you hope for absolute compliance of the gods, if your troops are angered, there will be peace"). This is the dangerous truth that all subjects must unlearn (or be kept from learning in the first place) if they are to serve as pliable instruments of tyranny (or of a Cicero). Caesar accordingly proceeds, through a forceful and brilliant oration, to reduce his men once more to a state of total ignorance concerning their real power over events (a power of which he himself is only too keenly aware, as revealed by *scit*, "he knows," at 5.254 – hence the deception inherent in his speech). In particular, Caesar encapsulates the whole elitist-religious vision of the *Aeneid* within a few short lines of breathtaking arrogance (5.339–43):

… an uos momenta putatis
ulla dedisse mihi? numquam sic cura deorum
se premet, ut uestrae morti uestraeque saluti
fata uacent: procerum motus haec cuncta secuntur:
humanum paucis uiuit genus.

… Do you think that you have turned
the scales for me? Never will the gods' concern

so lower itself that Fate has time for *your* death
and *your* safety: all such events ensue from actions of the chieftains;
for a few does humankind live.

Caesar's confidence trick succeeds beyond his wildest expectations. By the close of his speech, his men have once more degenerated into mere extensions of his will, forgetting that they are themselves potentially autonomous and even influential historical agents who hold Caesar's fortune ("a man they could depose") in their hands (5.364–7):

... tremuit saeua sub uoce minantis
uolgus iners, unumqe caput tam magna iuuentus
priuatum factura timet, uelut ensibus ipsis
imperet inuito moturus milite ferrum.

... Under his fierce and threatening voice
the spiritless crowd quaked, and an army so enormous fears a single
man – a man they could depose – as if he commanded their very
swords and could move the blade against the soldier's will.

Lucan has already complained of the Caesarian soldiers' inability (or refusal) to perceive their own power over their commander at 4.185–8. Clearly, effective resistance to dictatorship demands a political education sufficiently deep and solid to withstand a demagogue's rhetoric.[15]

This is amply illustrated by the contrast with the tribune Metellus, as presented in Lucan's Book 3. A member of Rome's governing class, educated in the traditions of that class and in the sacrosanctity of his tribunician office, Metellus, although alone and unarmed, can dare to face down Caesar at the gates of the Treasury of Saturn, which Caesar is preparing to loot (3.112–33). An infuriated Caesar tries to cow Metellus with precisely the same rhetoric that he will go on to deploy successfully against his mutinous soldiers, namely, by convincing Metellus, in words dripping with contempt, of his utter insignificance compared with Caesar (3.134–40):

... uanam spem mortis honestae
concipis: haud ... iugulo se polluet isto
nostra, Metelle, manus; dignum te Caesaris ira
nullus honor faciet. te uindice tuta relicta est
libertas? non usque adeo permiscuit imis
longus summa dies ut non, si uoce Metelli
seruantur leges, malint a Caesare tolli.

... Empty are the hopes of honourable death
which you conceive: my hand will not pollute itself
with your slaughter, Metellus; no office you hold will make you
deserving of Caesar's wrath. Are you the champion to whose safe keeping
Freedom has been left? The length of time has not confused the highest
and the lowest to this extent, that, if by Metellus' voice
the laws are saved, they would not rather be destroyed by Caesar.

Caesar here insists on the sharp divide between "highest" and "lowest" that informs all Roman elitism (whether republican or Caesarian). It should be noted that Lucan has earlier praised the tribune Curio for daring to bridge this divide in the service of liberty and equality, until he sold his soul to Caesar (1.270–1): *uox quondam populi libertatemque tueri | ausus et armatos plebi miscere potentes* ("Once the people's voice, he dared to champion liberty, to level with the people armed grandees"). Resistance against Caesar is therefore equated with a rejection of Caesar's (and Vergil's) extremely hierarchical conception of society and cosmos: Lucan casts this struggle not merely as Caesar vs. the Senate but also as Caesar vs. the common people. Impressionable and naive, Caesar's soldiers prove incapable of such resistance in Book 5 and end up uncritically embracing Caesar's elitist world view. Unlike the troops, however, the politically sophisticated Metellus is unimpressed with Caesar's bullying histrionics and makes no move from the doorway (3.141): he obviously considers himself Caesar's equal. Instead, Metellus must be dissuaded from his rash defiance by the equally sophisticated, cynical *suasoria* (rhetorical exercise in persuasion) of his friend Cotta (3.145–52). A whole people raised up to think and feel like Metellus would never have succumbed to Caesar's wiles.

The Calm

The two further deceptions of subordinates by Caesar in Book 5, which both nearly end in disaster for all concerned, likewise result from Caesar's talent at imposing upon the ignorance and naivety of those below him in the social order. In his *Bellum Gallicum* (1.40), Caesar reports a speech in which he firmly instructs his disputatious subordinates to place unquestioning trust in his own judgment as commander on such matters as the army's provisioning and route of march, but such trust is shown to be decidedly misplaced by Lucan's narrative. First is Caesar's speech urging his soldiers to make a dangerous winter crossing from Brundisium (5.413–23). Now, Appian also reports an address by Caesar at this juncture (*B Civ.* 2.53). In Appian's version, Caesar emphasizes, naturally enough, the advantages of speed and surprise for the current campaign. He certainly does not contend that winter weather will be safe or reliable for sailing, merely presenting it as an obstacle to be overcome in pursuit of victory, like the smallness of his forces. The speech of encouragement summarized by Caesar himself at this point in his commentaries is similarly reasonable and straightforward, appealing to realistic prospects of victory and to his own record of sound generalship (*B Civ.* 3.6). The address by Lucan's Caesar, however, does not hinge at all on considerations of strategy, with which his soldiers might have been expected to enjoy a certain familiarity. Rather, it is concerned exclusively with meteorology. Flying in the face of a millennium of accumulated Greek and Roman nautical experience and lore, as reflected, for example, in Hesiod's *Works and Days* (619–29), Caesar argues paradoxically that, at least for the short crossing from Brundisium to Epirus, winter will actually provide more dependable sailing than other seasons, because the violent winter winds are constant and unidirectional.

It is true that Caesar's speech in Lucan does bear a superficial resemblance to a subsequent stage in the narrative of Caesar's own *Civil War* (3.25). Having successfully crossed to Epirus himself with a part of his army (at 3.6), Caesar now grows increasingly impatient at the failure of the forces left behind in Brundisium to follow him there, because favourable winds have often blown in the interim (3.25.1), and because his Pompeian adversaries at least believe that the gentler winds of the coming spring will make the crossing more difficult, with the result that they are applying their blockade with increasing rigour and enthusiasm (3.25.2). Caesar consequently instructs his dilatory commanders to seize the first opportunity of a suitable wind (3.25.3, corresponding loosely to the plaintive letter addressed from Caesar to Antony at Lucan 5.476–98). Nevertheless, there are two key divergences between this episode of the *Commentaries* and the exhortation to the troops at Brundisium in Lucan's poem. First, Caesar here makes no meteorological assurances to tempt his forces across the Adriatic: whatever his own prior reasoning on the topic, his message as such merely enjoins his officers to make the crossing by the first favourable wind, without any reflections on the relative merits of winter and spring weather. Next, unlike Lucan's Caesar, the Caesar of the *Commentaries*, in his own thoughts, does not associate the key, specific quality of steadiness and reliability with winter winds,[16] and even a general belief in the greater difficulty of a spring crossing is attributed to the Pompeians, not to Caesar himself. Indeed, it would be ludicrous for Caesar to portray winter winds as steadfast when in the very next section of the *Commentaries*, 3.26, he goes out of his way to emphasize the vagaries of meteorological chance at this time of year, whereby the south wind (the Auster) first carries Caesar's fleet part of the way across from Brundisium, then fails, then picks up again, bringing them to the little port of Nymphaeum, and finally, by an amazing stroke of luck, shifts from the south to the southwest (the Africus), allowing them to find shelter in a harbour that is exposed to the Auster but protected from the Africus. Caesar's *Commentaries* can thus in no way be read as recommending dependence on winter winds, and so the speech that Lucan attributes to him in Book 5 is a matter of Lucan's own authorial choice, invention, and colouring.

Lucan introduces this speech with a significant comment (5.412): *expertes animos pelagi sic robore conplet* ("Like this he fills with confidence minds inexperienced in the sea"). On first reading, the natural interpretation of this line would be as an account of the process of benign enlightenment: Caesar is making a noble effort to encourage his troops by assuaging their irrational fears about a sphere beyond their normal ken. In other words, where Caesar's speech to the mutineers is designed to foster weakness through ignorance, here at least he seeks to impart strength to his men (*robore conplet*), who are ignorant of the sea, by *removing* their ignorance through a sophisticated analysis of winter weather and its implications for navigation. As a responsible commander, Caesar is sharing his superior (and celebrated) knowledge of geography and natural phenomena with his less fortunate subordinates in order to improve their military effectiveness.[17]

This is precisely the image of Caesar cultivated by his own propaganda (although not with respect to the specific instance of the crossing from Brundisium). For instance, the Caesarian *Bellum Alexandrinum* tells how panic spread among Caesar's men, besieged in Alexandria, when their water supply was poisoned with salt water through the Alexandrians' contrivances (*B Alex.* 5–7), just as Lucan's Caesar finds his forces at Brundisium paralysed by their fear of winter weather (*pauidas ... classes*, "his fleets afraid," 5.408). Caesar immediately responds with a speech of rational encouragement (*B Alex.* 8):[18] *Caesar suorum timorem consolatione et ratione minuebat* ("Caesar diminished the fear of his men through comforting and reasoning"). Among other reasonable grounds for hope, he enlightens his men, ignorant of the facts of physical geography, on the availability of underground fresh water in coastal areas: *puteis fossis aquam dulcem reperiri posse adfirmabat: omnia enim litora naturaliter aquae dulcis uenas habere* ("He asserted that fresh water could be found if wells were dug, for all coastal regions naturally possessed veins of fresh water"). When his men, thus encouraged, proceed to dig the wells, a great quantity of fresh water is indeed promptly uncovered (*B Alex.* 9).

Caesar also casts himself as the standard-bearer of cool-headed rationality in Lucan's Book 3, when he rebukes his soldiers' superstitious fear of violating the sacred grove outside Massilia by striking the first axe blow himself

(3.432–7). This he does with apparent impunity, unpunished or unnoticed by the gods (3.448–9). It is one thing to flout primitive Gallic superstition, however, but the basic, scientific facts of seasonal weather patterns are quite another matter. The oddness of Caesar's insistence on the reliability of winter winds (as compared with spring) is suggested by a comparison of this passage, with its reference to *perfida nubiferi ... inconstantia ueris* ("the treacherous fickleness of cloud-bearing spring," 5.415), to Statius' more conventional use of the winter sea as a paradigm for wild changefulness, *hiberno par inconstantia ponto* ("fickleness equal to the winter sea," *Theb.* 6.306).[19] It is rather to the winds of summer that Hesiod attributes the virtues of regularity and trustworthiness (*Op.* 670–3). It is also in the summer that the so-called Etesian winds were understood to blow reliably for forty days from the north or northwest. Indeed, Pliny the Elder (*HN* 2.124) explicitly identifies these summer Etesian winds with the north wind (Aquilo), which features in the exhortation by Lucan's Caesar as the wind that will bear his army reliably across the Adriatic in *winter* (5.417); Aristotle makes a point of contrasting the constant northern Etesian winds of summer with the winds that blow much less continuously and reliably from the south during winter (*Mete.* 362A).[20] The constancy of winter winds is also called into question by the famous phenomenon of the so-called halcyon days, according to which the sea was said to enjoy perfect calm around midwinter, as in the aetiological myth reported by Ovid (*Met.* 11.745–8), as well as by Caesar's own narrative of the many fluctuations in the wind during the second crossing of his forces from Brundisium (*B Civ.* 3.26, discussed above, p. 232).

Nevertheless, where his men are *expertes ... pelagi* ("inexperienced in the sea"), Caesar is anything but unfamiliar with nautical matters, having famously mastered the outer Ocean itself in the form of the English Channel. Appian thus portrays Caesar as one celebrated for his conquests of the seas (*B Civ.* 2.150). Caesar also enjoys a reputation for scientific and geographical enquiry (as in the ethnographic sections of his *Bellum Gallicum*). His landlubber soldiers must therefore, against their better judgment, accept his ostensibly scientific arguments. Grounded in ignorance and a lack of self-confidence, such blind acceptance brings them close to disaster: Caesar's speech of encouragement is immediately belied by actual events when the "reliable" winter winds suddenly abandon Caesar's fleet midway on the crossing to Epirus (5.430–55). This is in signal contrast to the praise lavished by Appian, who lists the crossing of the Adriatic from Brundisium among Caesar's marine successes and remarks on Caesar's good fortune in enjoying unseasonably navigable and quiet seas during winter (*B Civ.* 2.150).[21] As the soldiers face the prospect of starvation or capture, the orderly sequence of the edifying story from the Alexandrian campaign is brutally interrupted.

As in the *Bellum Alexandrinum*, Caesar offers a plausible, scientific exhortation to spur on men temporarily paralysed by fear of some natural phenomenon, and his troops are swayed to act by his apparent expertise. Unlike the *Bellum Alexandrinum*, however, Lucan's narrative shows the outcome entirely and immediately contradicting Caesar's words of reassurance.

On the basis of this gap between prediction and outcome, Radicke declares that Caesar has lied to his soldiers, but in fact the gap by itself only shows Caesar to be mistaken, not actually deceptive.[22] Caesar's lie as such is exposed by Lucan's report of the state of mind in which he made his speech to the soldiers (*BC* 5.409–11): *turpe duci uisum rapiendi tempora belli | in segnes exisse moras, portuqe teneri | dum pateat tutum uel non felicibus aequor* ("To the leader it seemed disgraceful that the moment for hastening war had extended into slow delays, disgraceful to be kept in harbour until the sea would be safely open to others, even the unlucky").[23] The meteorological certainty of Caesar's actual address to his soldiers is nowhere evident in these lines. Rather, Caesar's eagerness to make the crossing is premised on his belief that winter seas are only dangerous for those who are not *felices* ("lucky"), in other words, for those who are not Caesar. Interestingly, in the speech attributed to him by Appian, Caesar makes exactly this argument to his soldiers, exhorting them to oppose their "good fortune," τύχην ἀγαθήν, to the perils of winter weather. Lucan, however, has introduced a disjunction between Caesar's true beliefs and his words, such that Caesar appeals to his troops not as *felix* but as an expert in natural science addressing men ignorant of the sea. The gap in scientific expertise between the ruling elite (as embodied in the especially learned Caesar) and the common soldiery allows the former cynically to manipulate the latter. Now the true significance of line 5.412, *expertes animos pelagi sic robore conplet* ("Like this he fills with confidence minds inexperienced in the sea"), stands starkly revealed: rather than filling his men with well-grounded confidence through the removal of their ignorant fears about the winter sea, Caesar lulls them into a false sense of security by *exploiting* their inexperience in order to spin them a plausible yarn.

The Storm

By contrast, there is another character in Book 5, the skipper Amyclas, who can in no way be described as "inexperienced in the sea." Although he is a "poor man" (5.539), he is also an undisputed master of nautical lore, skilled in reading the signs of sea, sky, and marine fauna. This expertise allows him confidently to predict a violent storm on the night that Caesar comes banging on his door to demand passage to Italy (5.540–56).[24]

Up to this point, Amyclas has enjoyed a life of Epicurean isolation and tranquillity, pursuing his own craft in humble poverty, remote from the world's upheavals.[25] He is *securus*, "free from anxiety," upon hearing Caesar's peremptory knocks, for *praedam ciuilibus armis | scit non esse casas* ("well he knows that in civil warfare huts are not the loot," 5.526–7), a fact that elicits a glowing celebration of poverty from Lucan (5.527–31). The remoteness of war from Amyclas' thoughts is also apparent from his initial assumption that his nocturnal visitor is only some shipwrecked sailor (5.521–2), a normal phenomenon of his everyday existence. Like all other characters of Lucan's poem, however, Amyclas is about to be violently dragged into the political-military realm of civil strife (as he is into the storm itself). The fragility of Amyclas' Epicurean bubble is exposed by the conclusion to his speech of admonition against the crossing to Italy, where, after cataloguing all the weather signs that presage a dangerous storm, he meekly casts aside his expertise and, like Caesar's troops, places himself unreservedly at Caesar's disposal (5.557–9):

sed si magnarum poscunt discrimina rerum,
haud dubitem praebere manus: uel litora tangam
iussa, uel hoc potius pelagus flatusque negabunt.

Yet if the crisis of immense events demands, I cannot
hesitate to offer my hands: either I shall touch the shores
which you command or this will be refused by sea and squalls, not me.

It is noteworthy that, in his acquiescence, Amyclas does not seem tempted by Caesar's offer of untold wealth (5.532–7).[26] His Epicurean morality is proof against such vulgar allurements. Rather, he is overwhelmed by the impression, conveyed in Caesar's imperious speech and bearing (note Lucan's characterization of Caesar here as *indocilis priuata loqui* ("untrained to speak as an ordinary man," 5.539), of Caesar as a very important man on a very important mission. It is simply not for Amyclas, a mere humble seaman, to deny passage to a great man of Rome amidst a world-shattering crisis. For all his craft-scientific expertise, Amyclas is therefore extremely naive, inexperienced in the domains of war and politics, from which his tranquil existence has hitherto sheltered him completely. He lacks the political awareness and sophistication to question Caesar's self-importance or the value of Caesar's mission in the manner of a Metellus.

Unlike Caesar's own confident prediction of steady wind to his soldiers at Brundisium, which was refuted by the ensuing calm, Amyclas' dire, expert forebodings are immediately corroborated by additional signs observed once the crossing is begun (5.561–7), for these point even more obviously towards an imminent catastrophic storm. Once again, Amyclas lays his expertise at Caesar's feet, begging Caesar to allow him to return to shore on the basis of his skilled observations, just as Palinurus offers his expert advice to Aeneas at *Aen.* 5.17–25. Where Aeneas, however, confirms and acts upon Palinurus' counsel,[27] Lucan's Caesar turns the tables on Amyclas by instructing him in turn on what he portrays as a higher order of cosmic, spiritual, and political truth, which takes precedence over the merely scientific lore of Amyclas (5.578–93). Caesar cannot exploit the appearance of scientific learning to bamboozle Amyclas as he did with his soldiers at Brundisium, since Amyclas' meteorological expertise is greater than his own. Instead, he must prey upon Amyclas' political naivety, to persuade Amyclas to discard scientific rationality altogether in favour of a religious faith in Caesar's higher purpose. He represents himself as privy to an inner knowledge of the workings of the universe hidden from Amyclas, repeatedly emphasizing that his untutored hearer fails to comprehend Caesar's true importance to the cosmos: *sola tibi causa est haec iusta timoris,* | *uectorem non* ***nosse*** *tuum* ("The sole legitimate cause of fear for you is this: **ignorance** of who your passenger is," 5.580–1), and *quid tanta strage paretur* | ***ignoras*** ("You do not **know** what is made ready in such vast destruction," 5.591–2).[28] Caesar urges Amyclas to disregard the natural warnings of phenomena in the heavens, just as the augurs were compelled to ignore the supernatural warnings of ill-omened birds during the sham elections earlier in Book 5, and to place his trust in Caesar instead (5.579–80). Essentially, Caesar aims to impress upon Amyclas, as upon the mutinous soldiers, the basic ideology of the *Aeneid*, albeit in a cruder form than Vergil would have preferred: the presence of Caesar, a favoured child of destiny (like Aeneas), will protect Amyclas' ship from the storm until it can safely reach Italy, just as Aeneas' fleet eventually succeeded in doing under Neptune's protection. No further words are uttered by Amyclas after this piece of Caesarian-Vergilian propaganda: he has entirely subsumed himself within Caesar's will, just as did the mutineers earlier in Book 5. Amyclas' *ars*, his science, is subsequently said to be overwhelmed by the terrors of the storm (5.645–6), but it has already been nullified by Caesar's megalomaniacal ideology.

Nevertheless, as with Caesar's previous assurances to the soldiers at Brundisium, Lucan takes pains to illustrate the hollowness and falsity of this ideology over the entire course of the storm. Like the soldiers, Amyclas has been cruelly deceived, although in this case Caesar himself seems actually to believe his own propaganda.[29] First of all, Caesar's rousing proclamation of his centrality to the cosmos, along with the consequent safety of any ship lucky enough to enjoy his presence on board, is immediately followed (indeed, interrupted) by the ship's near-destruction through violent winds as the predicted storm is fully unleashed (5.593–6). Later, when death seems imminent, Caesar adjusts his spin-doctoring of events, but without sacrificing the narcissistic core of his ideology, for he now boasts of the titanic forces that have needed to be brought into play with the sole purpose of accomplishing his destruction (5.654–71). Once again, his vainglorious words are immediately (almost comically) contradicted by events, as his ship unexpectedly emerges safe from the waves (5.672–6).

The universe has therefore conspicuously failed to bring about either of the ends that, according to Caesar, were guaranteed by his supreme importance: either his safe arrival in Italy (to pursue his political-military destiny) or his cataclysmic death amid the world's ruin. On both counts, Caesar has quite simply got it wrong, for this is not the cosmos of the *Aeneid*. He has deceived Amyclas (and perhaps himself) through a political-religious lie, just as he deceived his soldiers at Brundisium through a scientific lie. Where the soldiers were "inexperienced in the sea," Amyclas is ignorant of the wider political domain, unused (in contrast with Metellus) to the self-serving, deluded rhetoric of megalomaniacs. What is more, in spite of his specific scientific expertise, Amyclas also lacks the broad cosmic-philosophical education of men like Lucan's uncle Seneca the Younger, who (as emerges from his *Naturales Quaestiones*) can read in the phenomena of the natural universe precisely a series of lessons against the monstrous egotism displayed by Caesar in this episode. Whether in the political, the philosophical, or the scientific spheres, ignorance and naivety are invariably shown to provide easy dupes for Lucan's Caesar to exploit.

Cato

In Book 9, on the other hand, Lucan shows the republican leader Cato trying to build a more democratic army of resistance by spreading moral, religious, political, and even scientific enlightenment as widely as possible. Cato's anti-elitism is most apparent in the episode staged by Lucan at the famous oracle of Ammon. When Cato's forces arrive there, his comrade Labienus beseeches him to consult the oracle, on the grounds that the virtuous Cato will enjoy a uniquely privileged access to its lore (9.554–5): *nam cui crediderim superos arcana daturos | dicturosque magis, quam sancto, uera, Catoni?* ("For I cannot believe the gods would grant their secrets and speak the truth to any more than sacred Cato"). In response, however, Cato vehemently rejects such epistemological elitism (9.566–84). In opposition to the ethos espoused by Caesar in Book 5 (and also 10),[30] as well as to the ideology of the *Aeneid*, Cato insists that the important truths of nature are already freely available to all men, implanted at birth by a benevolent providence. Where Caesar asserts that the human race lives for the sake of a few men, *paucis* (5.343), Cato refuses to accept the idea of an elite monopoly on knowledge whereby the oracle imparts wisdom only to a fortunate few (*paucis*, 9.577).

If there is any crucial information of which his men are currently unaware, Cato is happy to enlighten them. In quelling the mutiny of Book 5, for instance, Caesar intimidates his men into believing themselves less powerful than they in fact are, but Cato adopts exactly the opposite approach when he comes to address his own mutinous soldiers, who are ready to desert him upon hearing the news of their commander Pompey's death (9.256–83). Ahl comments that Cato's goal in this speech is not intimidation or compulsion but rather a kind of elevating moral education designed to produce men capable of appreciating and fighting for *libertas* alongside him: "Cato draws men up to his own level; he invites them to emulate him; he ennobles them. Caesar reduces them to the level of minions."[31] The emphasis on enlightenment is apparent from the verbs of ignorance (*nescis*, 9.262) and knowledge (*sciat*, 9.280) employed by Cato, while the content of Cato's message is fundamentally a lesson in empowerment: Cato instructs his men on their own true power and interests and persuades them that, with Pompey now out of the way, they have an opportunity to take their destiny in their own hands and fight for their own freedom instead of the ambitions of warlords (9.256–67). As Wick observes, Cato's declaration that now *tibi, non ducibus, uiuis morerisque* ("you live and die not for your leaders but yourselves") is an answer to Caesar's arrogant dismissal of the mutineers' claim to autonomy with the elitist maxim, *humanum paucis uiuit genus* ("for a few does humankind live," 5.343).[32] Cato points out that his men also have the power, if they choose, to ingratiate themselves with Caesar further by surrendering Cato himself as well as Pompey's wife and children (9.275–83). Unlike Caesar, Cato increases his soldiers' awareness of their freedom of action and of the real consequences of their different possible choices, so that they can make a mature, informed decision rather than rushing off impulsively. It is not his purpose to reduce his soldiers to mere instruments of his will, but instead to transform them into autonomous citizens: they should consider themselves not as Pompeians (9.257), nor as Caesarians, and certainly not as "Catonians," but rather as *Romans* (9.258).

In a subsequent speech, eschewing the kind of misinformation supplied by Caesar at Brundisium, Cato refuses to mislead his men about the dangers of the proposed march through the deserts of Libya (9.379–406).[33] He embraces this principle of transparency explicitly at 9.388–9 (*neque enim mihi fallere quemquam | est animus tectoque metu perducere uolgus*, "For it is not my intention to deceive anyone or onwards lead the mass by concealing the risk"), dissociating himself from the action of *fallere* ("to deceive") that is twice applied to Caesar's dealings with his own troops in Book 5 (5.512 and 679). It would have been entirely feasible for Cato to emulate Caesar in contriving some pseudo-scientific piece of spin and persuading his soldiers that Africa is not nearly so frightful as popular legend has made it out. After all, Cato's men are as ignorant of exotic geography as are Caesar's of the finer points of seasonal meteorology: this is evident from the soldiers' complaint at 9.848–80, where they wrongly imagine themselves to be already in the antipodes of the southern hemisphere, with Rome below their feet, and where they indulge in wild speculation on what awaits them as they journey further west. Nonetheless, Cato clearly and repeatedly lays out the perils of snakes, thirst, and heat that will dog the men's steps if they follow his plan (9.382–4 and 394–403). He also suggests the alternative of an easy surrender to Caesar (9.392–4): *at, qui sponsore salutis | miles eget capiturque animae dulcedine, uadat | ad dominum meliore uia* ("But the soldier who requires a guarantee of safety and is captivated by life's sweetness, let him take the fairer path to be his master's slave"). Once again, Cato is implementing a democratic model whereby the body of ordinary members of the community (in this case, the common soldiers) are given full access to information and freedom of choice to act on that information.

It is also noteworthy that, both on the occasion of this address and in the previous mutiny, Cato absolutely refrains from making any appeal to his soldiers' religious sensibilities, even though their subsequent complaint on the march reveals their firm belief in divine providence (e.g., at 9.860–5). This is in contrast with Caesar's speeches to the mutineers and to Amyclas, where he insists on his all-importance within the divine plan for the cosmos. Lucan's Cato is, at best, doubtful of the gods' benevolence and of the stable government of the cosmos (as shown by his pessimistic words to Brutus at 2.288–92), and he makes no attempt to instill in his men a faith in the gods' protection that he does not, in fact, feel himself (unlike Aeneas' deceptive encouragement of his followers after the storm of *Aeneid* 1). Instead, Cato inspires his soldiers with the only truth that he still trusts absolutely, which he sums up at 9.566–84: the value of pursuing virtue and liberty, regardless of material success or failure. What is more, Cato's faith in the ability of ordinary citizens to respond rationally and virtuously to a clear, accurate statement of the facts is rewarded by their voluntary cooperation after each of his speeches. Obedient Caesarian soldiers may be created by misinformation and intimidation, but if the goal is to cultivate instead true champions of the Republic, empowerment through education is needed. A free Republic cannot be constituted or defended by an army of brainwashed slaves.

Nor does the process of enlightenment stop there, for Cato disseminates accurate scientific knowledge to his men in order to lead them as safely as possible through the dangers of their march. When the thirsty soldiers come to a pool of water infested by venomous snakes (9.607–12), Cato persuades them to drink by explaining that snake venom is only dangerous when it enters the bloodstream, and that it can be safely ingested (9.612–16).[34] He then backs up speech with action and drinks first from the pool: by the mere fact that he and his soldiers survive to embark on the next stage of their journey, Lucan vividly demonstrates Cato's teaching of zoology to be more reliable than Caesar's meteorological instruction. On the march, Cato also maintains the role of empowering moral educator that he originally displayed in his address to the mutineers, teaching (*docet*, 9.889) his men to despise the power of death through his fortifying presence.

Massilia vs. Rome

Especially within Books 5 and 9, democracy is shown to depend on the combined dissemination of accurate political, religious, and scientific knowledge among the mass body of citizens, but this is borne out elsewhere in the poem as well. Book 3, for example, witnesses a heroic act of defiance in Lucan's story of Massilia (Marseilles), which dared to resist and delay Caesar's inexorable advance with far more constancy than was displayed by the panicked citizens of Rome itself in Book 1. The defiance begins with an embassy to Caesar expressing both a desire for peace and a willingness to fight to the death to preserve the Massilians' neutrality in this unholy conflict (3.303–57). Now, Caesar also reports such an embassy, but with a significant difference. According to Caesar (*B Civ.* 1.35), the legation was composed of the fifteen "first" men of Massilia (*primos*), in other words the super-elite presiding over the six hundred aristocrats who governed Massilia. Indeed, Massilia was generally regarded, for instance by Cicero, as an ideal specimen of the aristocratic form of government.[35] Lucan, however, identifies the ambassadors simply as the collective body of young Massilian citizen-soldiers, *iuuentus* ("body of youth," 3.355), which is also the word employed by Lucan at the start of this section in describing the Massilian people's heroic resistance (3.301), and which is applied to the Massilians on several occasions during the subsequent siege (at 3.446, 3.461, 3.499, and 3.516).[36] In other words, the same common people who do the fighting for Massilia are also those who conduct its diplomatic relations and, by implication, all its other affairs. This is a striking democratization of Massilia, whose famously aristocratic-oligarchic constitution would have remained a total secret to us if Lucan's narrative had been our only source for the ancient city. Through its reference to youth, the term *iuuentus* also serves to throw the spotlight on the education of these bold citizen-warriors. The latter are in fact portrayed as deeply steeped in political, military, and religious education, and they resist Caesar's bullying on this basis. Their speech to Caesar thus cites Roman and Massilian history, the Gigantomachy, the fall of Saguntum at the start of the Second Punic War, and considerations of global strategy (3.307–55). Furthermore, the accuracy of the Massilians' strategic understanding is confirmed by actual events: they emphasize their own relative insignificance to Caesar's war effort (3.336–42), and, although Caesar rejects this argument in his angry speech of response (3.358–60), his actions belie his words, for he soon loses patience with the siege, passing command over to a subordinate in order to free himself for the more important campaign in Spain (3.453–5). In other words, unlike Amyclas, the ordinary citizens who (by Lucan's account) appear to govern Massilia are far from sheltered or naive in the fields of war and politics.

In addition to their "humanistic" education, Lucan's Massilians also enjoy a surprising degree of scientific literacy. After the siege begins, at 3.455–61, the defenders of Massilia, witnessing the mighty Roman siege towers moving along the ground without any apparent means of propulsion, suspect an earthquake, which, on eminently respectable ancient scientific-philosophical grounds,[37] they ascribe to the movement of wind underground. Schrijvers criticizes this incorporation of scientific learning into Lucan's narrative as[38]

> not entirely satisfying from a psychological or situational point of view. It is rather improbable that the Massilian soldiers, feeling the trembling of the earth under the towers, expressed this experience by a scientific explanation of an earthquake ... Lucan projected his own erudition into the minds of the soldiers.

Is this, however, a mere display of Lucan's "own erudition?" By stressing once more the youth of the Massilian soldiery (*iuuentus*, 3.461), Lucan again hints at the breadth of their education.[39] They have been instructed not only in the political and historical learning evidenced by the envoys' speech but also in scientific knowledge. These are the kind of people, Lucan suggests, who can constitute a free citizenry, indeed, the only truly free nation of the entire poem (since the Romans themselves are already halfway to slavery). The earthquake passage also leads directly into a portrayal of Massilian technological superiority over Caesar's forces (3.463–73), a recurrent theme in the siege narrative: compare 3.553–60, on the naval battle, which is cast as a conflict between Massilian technological *ars* and Caesarian brute force. Political education, scientific education, and technological proficiency are thus woven intimately together into a blueprint for freedom.

If Massilia's (at least temporarily) successful resistance to Caesar is premised on the twin pillars of democracy and education, it should be noted that, in Lucan's previous, contrasting story of the pathetic collapse of the Roman people's morale and their consequent abandonment of their city in the face of Caesar's approach in Book 1, popular ignorance and elite control are both prominent themes. With their panicked flight, the common people merely imitate their supposed betters in the Senate (1.486–9), who in turn are following the shameful example of their leader, Pompey (1.521–2). In contrast, moreover, with the Massilians' accurate appraisal of the strategic situation, the Roman people are beset by ignorant and exaggerated or false rumours about Caesar's movements and forces (1.469–86). The implication is that Rome would have stood up more stoutly against Caesar's onslaught if, like Lucan's Massilians, the Roman people had both been better enlightened and enjoyed a greater share of control over their own Republic.

Lesbos vs. Egypt

Lucan's "democratization" of the republican support base continues after the disastrous Battle of Pharsalus, when loyalty to Pompey and his cause is put to the test as never before. Larisa, the first town encountered by Pompey in the wake of his defeat, vociferously proclaims its continued allegiance (7.713–16): *omnibus illa | ciuibus effudit totas per moenia uires | obuia ceu laeto: promittunt munera flentes, | pandunt templa, domos, socios se cladibus optant* ("With all her citizens she [Larisa] poured forth her entire strength through her walls, to meet you as in victory: with tears they promise gifts, open up their homes and temples, long to be your partners in defeat"). Larisa's loyalty in adversity is thus manifested through the mass of ordinary citizens who make up its polity, *omnibus ... ciuibus* ("all her citizens"). When Lucan described the betrayal of Pompey by the inhabitants of Brundisium during his flight from Italy at the end of Book 2, by contrast, he was careful to attribute fair-weather friendship not to the citizens as such but rather to the personified town itself (2.704–5): *portis, quas omnis soluerat* ***urbis*** *| cum fato conuersa fides* ("Then all the gates are opened by the **city's** loyalty reversed along with destiny").

The faithfulness of a politically educated citizen body then emerges with even greater force during Pompey's visit to Lesbos in Book 8. When Pompey has retrieved his wife Cornelia (whom he deposited on the island for safe keeping) and is about to depart again, the people of the capital Mytilene flock shoreward with a collective plea for him to remain and honour their island by choosing it as his base of operations for a renewed campaign against Caesar (8.109–10): *tunc Mytilenaeum pleno iam litore uolgus | adfatur*

Magnum ("Then the throng of Mytilene speaks to Magnus on the shore now full"). Lucan's use here of the loaded term *uolgus/uulgus*, "common people, crowd," is particularly significant, for this word is fraught with elitist overtones, often being employed to voice contempt for the unwashed masses (hence the English "vulgar").[40] It appears, for instance, in the ideologically crucial riot simile of *Aeneid* 1, which depicts the imposition of elite order on political chaos (1.148–50): *ac ueluti magno in populo cum saepe coorta est | seditio saeuitque animis ignobile* ***uulgus*** *| iamque faces et saxa uolant, furor arma ministrat ...* ("And as, when often in a great nation tumult has risen, the base **rabble** rage angrily, and now brands and stones fly, madness lending arms ...").[41] The most vehement expression of fidelity to Pompey over the course of Lucan's entire poem therefore arises from the same common folk despised by Vergil et al., who have come together in sufficient numbers to fill the shore of Lesbos. The degree of Lucan's authorial choice in this matter can be gauged by a comparison with Plutarch's account of the same episode in his life of Pompey: Plutarch merely speaks of "the Mytilenaeans," οἱ Μυτιληναῖοι, in general protesting their loyalty to Pompey, not the "Mytilenaean masses," and his focus is not on Pompey's interaction with the common people of Lesbos but rather on an elite-level personal exchange between Pompey and the leading Peripatetic philosopher Cratippus of Pergamum (Plut. *Pomp*. 75.2–4).

What is more, the address to Pompey by this loyal "rabble" in Lucan displays the same strategic, geopolitical savvy that characterized the Massilians in their opposition to Caesar during Book 3 (8.118–20): *quid, quod iacet insula ponto, | Caesar eget ratibus? procerum pars magna coibit | certa loci; noto reparandum est litore fatum* ("And what is more, our island lies upon the sea, and Caesar has no ships. A large part of your chieftains, certain of the place, will gather here; on this familiar shore your fate must be restored"). In their judgment of both these key points, the Mytilenaeans are vindicated by events within and beyond Lucan's text. Pompey's superiority in naval power was one of the central strategic facts of the civil war[42] and the reason why Caesar could only pursue him to Egypt with a small body of ships and troops, while the bulk of Caesar's forces followed along by foot down from Asia Minor. Likewise, Lesbos did actually serve as a rallying point for Pompey's scattered forces, as attested, for example, by Caesar (*B Civ.* 3.102.5) and by Lucan himself a little later in Book 8. Lucan records that, when Pompey reached the Ionian coast after leaving Mytilene, *primus ... a litore Lesbi | occurrit gnatus, procerum mox turba fidelis* ("his son came to meet him first after leaving Lesbos' shore; soon came the loyal band of chieftains," 8.204–5), which suggests that at least Sextus Pompey and probably the "chieftains" (senators) as well stopped first at Lesbos before effecting a reunion with their fugitive leader.[43] The Mytilenaean people are no ignorant mob, since they enjoy precisely that enlightened grasp of the wider military-political situation lacked by Lucan's narrowly educated Amyclas.

In addition to their strategic insight, the Mytilenaeans display a profoundly democratic, egalitarian ethos. Lucan explains their passionate devotion to Pompey's wife thus (8.150–6):

> Pompeiumque minus, cuius fortuna dolorem
> mouerat, ast illam, quam toto tempore belli
> ut **ciuem** uidere suam, discedere cernens
> ingemuit populus... tanto deuinxit amore
> hos pudor, hos probitas castique modestia uoltus,
> quod summissa animis, nulla grauis hospita turba,
> stantis adhuc fati uixit quasi coniuge uicto,

And as they saw them leave, the people groaned, less for Pompey, whose fortune had aroused their sorrow, than for her, whom in all the time of war they regarded as a fellow **citizen** ... with such deep love her purity had bound some to her, her goodness others and the modesty of her virtuous face, because in spirit she was humble, a guest irksome with no retinue, because she lived as if her husband had been conquered when his destiny was still intact.

In other words, the common citizens of Mytilene adored Cornelia not as some great lady, noble-born, bride of Rome's most illustrious commander, but rather because they could regard her as one of their own number in her old-fashioned virtue and freedom from aristocratic airs and graces.

In spite of such obvious, heartfelt attachment to his cause, however, Pompey rejects the Lesbians' proffered help, casting his gaze instead beyond the Graeco-Roman world entirely, and also beyond the zone where citizen bodies hold political sway. To the republican senators assembled at Syhedra to debate the prospects for continued struggle against Caesar, Pompey proposes the following choice of allies (8.276–8): *uos pendite **regna** | uiribus atque fide, Libyam Parthosque Pharonque, | quemnam Romanis deceat succurrere rebus* ("You must weigh for strength and loyalty the **kingdoms**: Libya and the Parthians and Pharos [i.e., Egypt], which ruler can most appropriately help the Roman state"). In order to prevent Caesar from establishing a kingship over Rome itself, Pompey (with no apparent sense of incongruity) is ready to beg assistance from foreign kings. His own first choice among these three alternatives, namely, Parthia, was particularly notorious as a tyrannical regime and enemy to the very *libertas* for which Pompey claims to be fighting, a contradiction stressed by the senator Lentulus in dissuading

Pompey from the Parthian option (8.339–441). Lentulus' preferred choice of Ptolemaic Egypt, however, which carries the day among the senators at Syhedra, was no less of a tyranny than Parthia in Roman eyes, as is fully borne out by Lucan's subsequent narrative.[44] It is after all not members of a *res publica* but the courtiers of a private royal *domus* ("house," 8.475) whom Lucan shows meeting to decide Pompey's reception in Egypt, and this corrupt group (with the boy-king Ptolemy XIII at their head) is persuaded to Pompey's murder through a speech that combines glorification of the absolute, unbridled, violent exercise of royal power (8.489–95) with contempt for the ordinary Egyptian people ruled by the Ptolemies (8.525–6). There is nothing "seemly" (*deceat,* 8.278) in vesting the hopes of the republican commonwealth on such a thuggish regime. Clearly, one of the central lessons of Lucan's eighth book is that, instead of courting the precarious favour of despots, Pompey would have done far better to entrust himself to the enlightened and egalitarian citizens of Mytilene.

The Medium Is the Message?

On a more speculative note, Lucan's poem can even be seen as embodying this ideal of broad, democratic enlightenment through its very generic structure, as compared with other ancient epics, both narrative and didactic. For all Lucretius' undoubted debts to the heroic epic tradition, for instance, the domain of political and military history is kept firmly subordinated throughout his poem to his scientific-didactic purpose, with only an occasional, brief episode from myth or history inserted to illustrate or flesh out some point of Epicurean philosophy. Lucretius also urges his readers to abandon all political concerns to the ambitious, cultivating instead their own private Epicurean gardens (5.1131–2):[45] *proinde sine incassum defessi sanguine sudent, | angustum per iter luctantes ambitionis* ("Leave them then to be weary to no purpose, and to sweat blood in struggling along the narrow path of ambition"). Political awareness is thereby sharply distinguished from and subordinated to the study of nature.

As for Vergil, his conception of an ordered, hierarchical society finds perfect reflection in a highly separatist and hierarchical approach to genres. In the *Georgics,* he carefully distinguishes agricultural didactic poetry both from scientific didactic poetry, with which the happy rural poet need not concern himself (2.475–94),[46] and from political-military epic, which is portrayed as a future, culminating stage in Vergil's career (3.10–48). This is in keeping with the ethos found throughout the *Georgics* of narrow, apolitical craft specialization. Farmers should know what they need to know in order to practise their craft within the blessedly self-sufficient communities of the countryside, but they should leave war and politics to those concerned with such activities: such a view emerges from the praise of the farming lifestyle at 2.495–502. This is the essential life philosophy of Lucan's Amyclas, in his exclusive preoccupation with his own specialized craft to the exclusion of wider political considerations – a philosophy that leaves him dangerously exposed to Caesar's manipulations.[47]

A Berlin Wall between the realms of technical craft and of statecraft is also maintained faithfully in Vergil's *Aeneid*. Although it contains many references to scientific and technical lore, these are narrowly confined within their political-military context, and there is no attempt to present the lore directly and in detail (as with the extremely brief summary of the scientific song of Iopas at 1.742–6). It is true that, as a member of the governing class, Aeneas is shown to be master of all useful branches of learning. He thus commands the steersman's art, taking the helm himself after Palinurus' demise (5.867–8). The specialist helmsman Palinurus, however, is uninterested in anything beyond the rudder that he grips so tenaciously (6.350–1). He deploys his skill unquestioningly at Aeneas' discretion, presenting his expert findings to Aeneas alone (5.17–25); nor is it the business of the Trojan people as a whole to concern themselves with the navigational *ars*, any more than with the *ars* of divination (the seer Helenus communicates his counsel to a solitary Aeneas in Book 3). As a scion of the elite and the prospective ruler of Pallanteum, Pallas receives a privileged education from Aeneas on the science of celestial navigation as well as on Aeneas' political and military experiences (10.160–2). No such broad-based insight or knowledge is required of the mass of Trojans, however, merely an unquestioning devotion to their ruler (who always knows best), in narrow performance of their own specific duties for the common welfare. Similarly, the new generation of ordinary Romans does not require any comprehensive education to play their parts within the Augustan world order, and they receive none from Vergil in the *Aeneid*, the new core text of the Roman school curriculum. In Dido's Carthage, on the other hand, the people as a whole are depicted receiving a dangerously comprehensive, Epicurean-flavoured instruction in the principles of natural science by the song of Iopas (1.740–6).[48]

On the other hand, more (I think) than any other surviving poem from antiquity, Lucan's *Bellum Ciuile* straddles the generic line between scientific didactic epic and heroic epic. Every book of this poem is heavily loaded with detailed scientific learning (which unfortunately tends to be removed from the excerpted highlights of Lucan taught to undergraduates), as Lucan traverses the diverse realms of astrology, astronomy, geography, herpetology, hydrology, meteorology, etc., in the course of his military-political narrative. Clearly, Lucan possessed the requisite knowledge and interest to have composed a separate scientific-didactic poem as a preliminary to his great Roman-historical epic, in imitation of the trajectory of Vergil's career, if he had so wished.[49] Instead, Lucan has chosen to blend the two genres in a way that cannot simply be blamed on either his subject matter or his time period, since the historical epic of his contemporary Silius Italicus (born before Lucan but writing after him) is far less scientifically curious or literate. In my view, at least one possible explanation for this surprising generic fusion is Lucan's desire to illustrate the fusion of scientific and political learning that, according to him, is a prerequisite for a healthy, free Republic.

Even the manner in which Lucan presents scientific, philosophical, and religious lore can be seen as a reflection of his democratic ideals. As Schrijvers notes, Lucan is very fond of offering multiple explanations for scientific and cosmic phenomena and refusing to choose between them, for example on the tides (1.409–19) or on the Nile's flood (10.209–67).[50] Although this approach is rooted in Epicurean epistemology and the model of Lucretius, Schrijvers observes that Lucan takes it far beyond the Lucretian precedent into realms undreamt of by an "orthodox Epicurean." At 2.7–13, Lucan even refuses to commit himself, in a way that would have utterly horrified Lucretius, on the fundamental constitution of the cosmos: is it governed by random chance or by providence? Perhaps Lucan's goal with this device is to present his readers with all the available information and options and then leave them to decide for themselves, as Cato does with his soldiers in Book 9. Lucan also resembles the Cato of Book 9 in his scrupulous refusal to propagate among his readers ideas about the gods that he no longer accepts for himself, by way of contrast with the pious fictions embodied in the *Aeneid* or in Cicero's second and third *Catilinarians*: this is signalled through his famous exclusion of the traditional Homeric-Vergilian divine machinery from the action of his epic. Once again, Lucan seeks to enhance his readers' freedom of choice, instead of manipulating them with deliberate falsehoods designed to prop up the political *status quo*.

In itself, of course, Lucan's poem is a work neither of historiography nor of scientific-philosophical writing, nor would he have intended it to be relied on as a factual source in either domain. If, however, it had succeeded in supplanting the *Aeneid* at the heart of the Roman curriculum (as Lucan must surely have hoped), the *Bellum Ciuile* would have provided an ideological foundation for the spread of enlightenment to each new generation of Roman citizens, encouraging students to expand their mental horizons, to learn their own powers, and to claim their birthright of freedom. The *Aeneid*, by contrast, like the *Catilinarians*, amounts to a charter document for a system of elite suppression of popular knowledge (along with the people's self-confidence) through manipulation, misinformation, and the segregation of disciplines, the same system that had condemned Lucan himself to silence under Nero. The purpose of Lucan's revolutionary approach to epic poetry was not only to highlight his own erudition and artistic brilliance but also, more importantly, to encourage a political and educational revolution in the world around him, towards a more enlightened, democratic society.

NOTES

* I am very grateful for the comments and suggestions offered by the editorial team, Alison Keith and Jonathan Edmondson, as well as for their combined efforts in assembling this volume and shepherding it through to press. I would also like to express my heartfelt thanks to Elaine Fantham, who has (through the length of my adult career in Classics) inspired me with her wide-ranging scholarship, guided me by her sage counsels, and supported me tirelessly in both the professional and personal domains.

1 See, e.g., Millar 1998 on the democratic qualities of the Roman Republic.

2 Compare Augustus' assumption of personal control and editorship over the Sibylline oracles, although this occurred after Vergil's death (Suet. *Aug.* 31.1 and Cass. Dio 54.17.2).

3 All translations of Vergil are by Fairclough 1999 (revised by Goold), with a few slight alterations. The Latin text of Vergil is that of Mynors 1969.

4 See especially Adler 2003: 222–6 and 291–9.

5 In Aeneas' absence from the camp in Book 9, the Trojan *ductores* do hold a nocturnal council, *consilium* (9.226–8), but there is no mention of any debate, and the only point at issue seems to be the best means of informing Aeneas of their predicament so that he can resume his natural leadership over them.

6 See, e.g., Gransden 1991: 13–14.

7 Lucretius underscores Memmius' splendid ancestry with the patronymic *Memmiadae* at 1.26.

8 See, e.g., *Cat.* 2.26, 2.29, 3.29.

9 The spectrum of scholarly opinion is nicely covered by Ahl 1976, on Lucan as a staunch republican; Brisset 1964, on Lucan as a moderate supporter of the Principate; and Masters 1994, on Lucan as a subtle propagandist for Nero.

10 This assumes that the books of the epic were written in the order in which they now stand, with the first three being the only ones published during Lucan's lifetime, before Nero's ban took effect, and the fourth and fifth being composed soon afterwards. See Brisset 1964: 181–2; Ahl 1976: 346n22.

11 All translations of Lucan are by Braund 1992, with occasional, slight alterations. The Latin text of Lucan is that of Housman 1926.

12 Fantham 1985: 130.

13 Fantham 1985: 121–2.

14 Fantham (1985: 124) comments on 1.388 that *manus* is "a recurring term used to treat the soldiers as a mere weapon or instrument of Caesar's warfare." Cf. the findings of Blake in this volume (above, ch. 5).

15 The susceptibility of Caesar's troops to such rhetoric is further suggested by their enthusiastic response to the speech of the centurion Laelius at 1.359–86, which, although ostensibly addressed to Caesar himself, is in fact designed to remind Caesar's men, hesitating on the terrible brink of civil war, that they are (or should be) mere unthinking instruments of Caesar's will and ambitions (see especially 1.372 and 376–8). The links between the Laelius and the mutiny scenes, including the theme of the soldiers' submissiveness, are explored by Fantham 1985: 123–6.

16 This is especially true if the original manuscript reading of *certe* ("surely, certainly") is accepted for 3.25.1 (as it is by Du Pontet 1901); but even if Gronov's (in my opinion unnecessary) emendation *certi* ("sure, certain" as an adjective modifying *venti*) were to be adopted, Caesar would not be claiming that winter winds are *more* reliable than spring winds, merely that usefully reliable winds have in fact occurred over the past months and been squandered by his laggard subordinates.

17 Compare Cicero's approving account of the use of superior scientific knowledge by Greek and Roman commanders to combat their soldiers' irrational, superstitious fears (*Rep.* 1.15–16).

18 The text I have used of the *Bellum Alexandrinum* is Du Pontet 1901.

19 This comparandum is offered by Barratt 1979: 133 *ad loc.*, although she offers no comment on Statius' implied contradiction of Lucan (or of Lucan's Caesar).

20 See also Sen. *Q Nat.* 5.10. At *BC* 10.239–41, Lucan identifies the Etesian winds of summer as coming from the west rather than from the north, but a west wind would have been even more useful than a north wind for Caesar's project of crossing the Adriatic from Brundisium to Corcyra.

21 In characteristically tendentious fashion, Lucan has perhaps distorted this historical tradition of a mere quiet crossing into an episode of dangerous becalming.

22 Radicke 2004: 335.

23 I here side with Duff's translation (1928) against Braund's (1992) in rendering *dum* with the subjunctive as "until" rather than "while" ("disgraceful to be kept in harbour *while* the sea *is* safely open to others, even the unlucky"), with "until" referring to the onset of the traditional season for safe sailing in summer, whereas Braund's "while" would make the time for universal safe sailing contemporary with Caesar's current situation, namely, during winter. For one thing, the winter seas would never have been regarded by any ancient as safely open for the *unlucky*: seafaring was dangerous enough at the best of

times, let alone in winter, without the benefit of divine protection. Even Caesar, in his speech to his men, does not suggest that navigation is universally safe during winter, merely that the (supposedly) reliable seasonal winds will help speed their specific journey from Brundisium to Epirus. For another, it is much more in keeping with Lucan's general characterization of Caesar to show the latter egotistically braving a voyage at a moment that would be dangerous for all those not specially favoured by fortune (as he believes himself to be), i.e., in winter, rather than to show Caesar merely desiring to join the crowd of the unlucky and obtain the same access to the sea enjoyed by everyone else (as Braund's translation suggests). Lucan's Caesar always craves the extraordinary, for instance with his attempted recrossing of the Adriatic through the storm later in Book 5.

24 For the erudition of Amyclas' catalogue of weather signs, see, e.g., Barratt 1979: 178.

25 See Nehrkorn (1960: 155–7) for the "idyllic" character of Amyclas' lifestyle prior to Caesar's intrusion.

26 Narducci (2002: 253) thus comments, "Amicla sa resistere alla tentazione."

27 See Quint (1993: 137–8) for the Amyclas scene as a "rewriting" of Aeneas' exchange with Palinurus.

28 Matthews (2008: 151) comments on this speech that "[w]e are left with the impression of a man with a more privileged knowledge of the 'wider picture' than ordinary men."

29 On Caesar's megalomania in the storm episode, see, e.g., Ahl 1976: 205–9.

30 Compare Caesar's boastful address to Acoreus at Lucan 10.181–7, where he claims privileged access to Egypt's mysteries.

31 Ahl 1976: 256–7.

32 Wick 2004: 2.98.

33 This contrast between Caesar and Cato is briefly noted by Radicke 2004: 335–6.

34 Cato is in fact quite correct on this point, according to the University of Florida's Department of Wildlife Ecology & Conservation (http://ufwildlife.ifas.ufl.edu/venomous_snake_faqs.shtml), although the ingestion of snake venom is not recommended.

35 See, e.g., Cic. *Flac.* 63 and *Rep.* 1.27; Strabo 4.1.5.

36 See also Delarue (2010: 126) for the importance of collective speech and action at Massilia (in Book 3) and Mytilene (in Book 8).

37 On earthquakes, see Sen. *Q Nat.* 6.12–26.

38 Schrijvers 2005: 29.

39 Note that Lucan has placed the word *iuuentus* emphatically at the end of the entire earthquake passage. The potential association of this term with educational techniques is illustrated by, for instance, Caesar's contemptuous reference to *Grais delecta iuuentus | gymnasiis* at 7.270–1.

40 See the *OLD* s.v. (2a) for the derogatory implications of *vulgus*.

41 Compare Verg. *Aen.* 11.451, on the disorderly behaviour of the Latin *vulgus*.

42 See, e.g., Plut. *Pomp.* 76.2–3.

43 See Mayer 1981 *ad loc.* on the arguments for reading *a litore Lesbi* as a reference to the movements of Sextus rather than of Pompey.

44 See, e.g., Cic. *Rab. Post.* 22–4 for the tyrannical reputation of the Ptolemies.

45 The translation is by Rouse 1992; the text is by Bailey 1921.

46 On Vergil's rejection of Lucretius' scientific didactic poetry, see, e.g., Adler 2003: 9–16.

47 See Narducci (2002: 252) for Amyclas' affinity with the ethos of the *Georgics* in his *otium*, "leisure," and *paupertas*, "poverty."

48 See Adler (2003: 17–40) on the "Carthaginian Enlightenment."

49 See Suetonius' *Vita Lucani* for Lucan's spirit of *aemulatio* with regard to Vergil's career.

50 Schrijvers 2005: 36–9.

WORKS CITED

Adler, E. 2003. *Vergil's Empire: Political Thought in the* Aeneid. New York.

Ahl, F.M. 1976. *Lucan: An Introduction.* Ithaca.

Barratt, P. 1979. *M. Annaei Lucani Belli Civilis Liber V: A Commentary.* Amsterdam.

Bailey, C., ed. 1921. *Lucretii De Rerum Natura Libri Sex.* Oxford.

Braund, S.H., ed. 1992. *Lucan:* Civil War. Oxford.

Brisset, J. 1964. *Les idées politiques de Lucain.* Paris.

Delarue, F. 2010. "Les foules de Lucain: émergence du collectif." In *Lucain en débat: rhétorique, poétique et histoire,* edited by O. Devillers and S. Franchet D'Espèry, 125–36. Paris.

Du Pontet, R., ed. 1901. *Libri III De Bello Civili Cum Libris Incertorum Auctorum De Bello Alexandrino, Africo, Hispaniensi.* Oxford.

Fairclough, H.R., ed. 1999. *Virgil, Eclogues; Georgics; Aeneid 1–VI.* Revised by G.P. Goold. Cambridge, MA.

Fantham, E. 1985. "Caesar and the Mutiny: Lucan's Reshaping of the Historical Tradition in *De Bello Civili* 5. 237–373." *CP* 80: 119–31.

Gransden, K.W., ed. 1991. *Virgil:* Aeneid, *Book XI.* Cambridge.

Housman, A.E., ed. 1926. *Belli Civilis Libri Decem.* Oxford.

Masters, J. 1994. "Deceiving the Reader: The Political Mission of Lucan *Bellum Civile* 7." In *Reflections of Nero: Culture, History and Representation,* edited by J. Elsner and J. Masters, 151–77. London.

Matthews, M. 2008. *Caesar and the Storm: A Commentary on Lucan* De Bello Civili *Book 5, Lines 476–721*. Oxford.

Mayer, R. ed. 1981. *Lucan: Civil War VIII*. Warminster.

Millar, F. 1998. *The Crowd in Rome in the Late Republic*. Ann Arbor.

Mynors, R.A.B., ed. 1969. *Virgilii Opera*. Oxford.

Narducci, E. 2002. *Lucano: Un'epica contro l'impero*. Rome.

Nehrkorn, H. 1960. *Die Darstellung und Funktion der Nebencharaktere in Lucans* Bellum Civile. PhD Diss., Baltimore.

Quint, D. 1993. *Epic and Empire: Politics and Generic Form from Virgil to Milton*. Princeton.

Radicke, J. 2004. *Lucans poetische Technik: Studien zum historischen Epos*. Leiden.

Rouse, W.H.D., ed. 1992. *Lucretius De Rerum Natura*. Revised by M.F. Smith Cambridge, MA.

Schrijvers, P. 2005. "The 'Two Cultures' in Lucan. Some Remarks on Lucan's Pharsalia and Ancient Sciences of Nature." In *Lucan im 21. Jahrhundert*, edited by C. Walde, 26–39. Munich.

Wick, C. 2004. *M. Annaeus Lucanus: Bellum Civile Liber IX*. 2 vols. Munich.

13

The Rites of Others*

CLIFFORD ANDO

Introduction: Diversity and Empire

The remarkable diversity of the religious landscape of the Roman Empire has been the object of scholarly scrutiny since the Renaissance. Unsurprisingly, it was often the *fact* of diversity that drew the most attention, under two rubrics above all. First, the sheer number of cults – the sheer number of gods – was taken to confirm an understanding of polytheist systems as essentially additive. This understanding was further consolidated by the twin factors that scholars gradually identified more and more cults of the Roman period, largely through epigraphic and archaeological discovery, and that these discoveries themselves indicated a surge across time in the number of cults in which Roman linguistic and material cultural forms were practised.

The second rubric under which diversity was studied was tolerance: assuming that Romans conceived religion as a concern of government even as they did, namely, as interested in the confessional status of individuals, Enlightenment philosophers and historians identified the Roman Empire as tolerant because, it was assumed, the fact of diversity must indicate willingness on the part of Romans that subordinate populations should worship their own gods. In all this, early modern scholars were aided and abetted by Christian polemics of the high and late Empire, nor were they always misled. To the nature of the distortion worked by the Christian apologists in this arena, I shall return in closing.

In part in consequence of this understanding, in recent years it has been Roman interference in cult that has been taken as the explanandum.[1] In this literature it seems to be assumed that the default position at Rome in regard to foreign cults in foreign places was tolerance, or perhaps even ignorance (perhaps in consequence of another empirically falsifiable assumption, namely, that polytheist systems are inherently tolerant).[2] But that assumption, it seems to me, is neither helpful to historical or comparative understanding nor even accurate as a characterization of the evidence. The object of this chapter is, therefore, to explore precisely the policies held or practices exercised by Rome in respect to foreign cults, and the understanding of religion that those policies and practices presupposed. In so doing, I build upon arguments that I have laid out piecemeal over the last few years. Allow me to rehearse briefly two strands in that work of relevance to my argument here.

First, in an essay on so-called *interpretatio romana*, I drew attention to a discrepancy between provincial and metropolitan evidence in respect to that phenomenon.[3] As I see it, the evidence for practice is nearly wholly provincial. The evidence from Rome, by contrast, is meagre at best and largely theoretical, but if it tells us anything, it is that the nature of the identification performed by acts of epiclesis is terribly elusive.

Second, in a set of essays on epistemology and social theory in Roman philosophies of religion and law, I have argued for three interrelated conclusions: first, that Romans regarded religion as properly the object of knowledge rather than belief; second, that partly because communication with gods at Rome was so indirect – it was, for example, never oral – the Romans regarded religious knowledge as fraught and hence in constant need of verification; and third, in consequence of the first two, the Romans regarded practice in the worship of gods as no more and no less than the purely contingent product of human institution building. As such, the institutions of Roman religion had no greater claim to validity or ontological security than those of other societies: those of any given society must be assessed autonomously, in light at once of the epistemic resources on which they rested and the durability of the social orders they secured.[4]

The evidence that I shall consider here is of two kinds: some documents attest injunctions that particular communities should continue the same cult practices as they had before conquest or annexation; others offer normative statements, whether of principle or law, or systematizing claims in respect to historical practice. These I read against and alongside such accounts as we have of Roman administration in respect to local legal systems. I take it as axiomatic that the conceptual frameworks of law and religion at Rome were highly interdependent, and I hope that the arguments advanced in this chapter will work to support that claim.

Bracketing specific analyses of evidence, my argument in brief is as follows. First, the evidence from legal literature for a practice and theory of legal pluralism before the Antonine Constitution may usefully and legitimately stand in hermeneutic relation to the evidence for religious pluralism as a problem of government in the late Republic and high Empire. Second,

Roman statements of policy in respect to provincial religion do amount, as such statements often do, to post-eventum efforts at systematization; but in this case, I believe that these statements in fact condense the earlier evidence for practice, such as it was, and further that they give useful articulation to postulates of social theory essential to Roman government, broadly construed. Third and last, the metropolitan evidence for actions of government in respect to provincial religion concentrates overwhelmingly on rites (hence my title) or, perhaps, on the institutionalization of cult. Specific gods are not named, much less subjected to an *interpretatio*. The number and diversity of gods comes to figure as a prominent index of analysis – such that gods are potentially each the object of a religion – only in Christian Roman literature. This is perhaps not a surprising conclusion, but I suspect that we have not adequately addressed the consequences for our understanding of classical Roman thought of imagining a world without that assumption.

Surrender, Restoration, and the Status Quo Ante

Perhaps the most famous Roman statement regarding practice in respect to the rites of others is the definition offered by Festus under the lemma "municipal rites" (146L):

MUNICIPALIA SACRA: municipalia sacra uocantur, quae ab initio habuerunt ante ciuitatem Romanam acceptam; quae obseruare eos uoluerunt pontifices, et **eo more** facere, **quo adsuessent antiquitus**.

Those *sacra* are called *municipalia* that a people had from its origin, before receiving Roman citizenship, and which the *pontifices* wanted them to continue to observe and perform in the way in which they had been accustomed to perform them from antiquity.

I want you to resist the urge, to which I have myself in the past succumbed, to dismiss this statement as an anachronistic invention of the antiquarian tradition. Allow me instead to focus your attention on a number of its aspects: (i) the focus on *sacra*, rites; (ii) the identification of a turning point, in this case, a communal grant of Roman citizenship; and (iii) the command by Roman authorities that the community should maintain its practices after the turning point even as they had before, indeed, from antiquity.

So described, the situation imagined by Festus has important analogues and precedents in the formal legal acts that comprised surrender and restoration in Roman foreign relations.[5] The fullest account of a *deditio in fidem* – and it must be stressed that we have no fully elaborated account, to say nothing of one contemporaneous with the action it describes – is provided by Livy (1.38.1–2).

Deditosque Collatinos ita accipio eamque deditionis formulam esse: rex interrogauit: "Estisne uos legati oratoresque missi a populo Collatino ut uos populumque Collatinum dederetis?" – "Sumus." – "Estne populus Collatinus in sua potestate?" – "Est." – "Deditisne uos populumque Collatinum urbem agros aquam terminos **delubra utensilia diuina humanaque omnia** in meam populique Romani dicionem?" – "Dedimus." – "At ego recipio."

I find that the Collatini surrendered and that the formula of surrender was as follows. The king asked, "Are you the envoys and spokesmen sent by the Collatine people to surrender yourselves and the Collatine people?" – "We are." – "Is the Collatine people in your power?" – "It is." – "Do you give yourselves and the Collatine people and their city and fields and water and boundaries and temples and utensils and all divine and human properties into my judgment and that of the Roman people?" – "We give." – "And I receive."

There is much about this text that has the air of late second-century BCE legal religious antiquarianism, not least the emphatic insistence on the act of acceptance. But I draw your attention for now simply to the enumerative definition of the totality of Collatine property that is surrendered to Rome: "yourselves and the Collatine people and their city and fields and water and boundaries and temples and utensils and all divine and human properties."

Livy so concentrates on the so-called formula of surrender that he elides altogether the aspect of these exchanges that so interested Festus, namely, the exhortation to continue as before. This, however, is the very feature of formal processes of surrender that received precise and lasting commemoration in the epigraphic record. For example, in two separate inscriptions recording legal actions in second-century Spain, the one analogous to a restoration, the other a full-blown surrender, stress is laid upon two aspects: first, in one or more respects there should be an exact correspondence between the situations before and after the act commemorated on the tablet, articulated above all in the correlatives *dare – reddere*; and second, the restoration of some status quo ante was realized through a sovereign act of the Roman people, together with Senate or magistrate (I translate the sections in bold type only):

1. A decree of L. Aemilius Paulus as governor of Hispania Ulterior in 189 BCE (*CIL* I[2] 614 = *CIL* II 5041 = *ILS* 15 = Bruns[7] 70 = *FIRA* I 51 = *ILLRP* 514 = *ELRH* U1; Fig. 13.1)

Figure 13.1 A decree of L. Aemilius Paulus as governor of Hispania Ulterior in 189 BCE. The Louvre, Paris. Photo: © RMN-Grand Palais / Art Resource, NY.

L(ucius) Aimilius L(uci) f(ilius) inpeirator decreiuit
utei quei Hastensium seruei
in turri Lascutana habitarent
leiberei essent; **agrum oppidumqu(e)**
quod ea tempestate posedisent,
item possidere habereque
iousit, dum poplus senatusque
Romanus uelet. Act(um) in castreis
a(nte) d(iem) XII k(alendas) Febr(uarias)

The land and city that they possessed at that time, he ordered them to possess and to hold exactly those things, so long as the Roman People and Senate wish.

2. The *deditio* from Alcántara, 104 BCE (*AE* 1984, 495 = 1986, 304 = *ELRH* U2; Fig. 13.2)

C(aio) Mario C(aio) Flauio [co(n)s(ulibus)]
L(ucio) Caesio C(aii) f(ilio) imperatore populus Seano+[- - - se (?)]
dedit L(ucius) Caesius C(aii) f(ilius) imperator postquam [eos - - -]

Figure 13.2 The *deditio* from Alcántara, 104 BCE. Museo Provincial de Cáceres. Photo: © Museo Provincial de Cáceres, reproduced with permission.

accepit ad consilium retolit quid eis im[perare (?)]
censerent de consili(i) sententia inperau[it (?) - - -]
captiuos equos equas quas cepisent [- - - (?)]
omnia dederunt **deinde eos L(ucius) Caesius C(aii) [f(ilius) imp(erator) liberos(?)]**
esse iussit agros et aedificia leges cete[**raque omnia**]
quae sua fuissent pridie quam se dedid[**erunt - - - (?)**]
extarent (*vacat*) **eis redidit dum populu**[**s senatusque**]
Roomanus (!) uellet (*vacat*) deque ea re eos [- - -]
eire iussit (*vacat*) legatos Cren[- - -]
Arco Cantoni f(ilius) (*vacat*) legates

Then Lucius Caesius son of Gaius, imperator, ordered them to be free and the lands and buildings and laws and all other things which were theirs on the day before they surrendered themselves ... he gave back to them so long as the Roman People and Senate might wish.

These abbreviated texts mention neither sacred properties nor rites. But divine properties figure again and again in Livy, which might of course indicate no more than that Livy echoes on each occasion the formula he "found" for the surrender of the Collatini to Tarquin.[6] But the details provided in Livy's other accounts of surrenders that represent accretions to the framework at 1.38 are by and large just those corroborated by the epigraphic texts, not least the act of restoration and the sovereignty of the people in authorizing that restoration.

Finally, there existed a strong formal similarity between the restoration of a people to freedom and property after surrender and the release to freedom of political communities that existed in friendly relations with Rome but found themselves within the borders of a province. One such community was the Thermitani of Sicily, who figure prominently in Cicero's account of the misdeeds of Verres. What concerns me here is the description, placed by Cicero in the mouth of a citizen of that city, of the act by which that city received the right to use its own laws (Cic. *Verr.* 2.2.90; see also Livy 9.43.22–4, quoted below, p. 263):

Sthenius postulat ut, cum secum sui ciues agant de litteris publicis corruptis, eiusque rei legibus Thermitanorum actio sit; **senatusque et populus Romanus Thermitanis, quod semper in amicitia fideque mansissent, urbem agros legesque suas reddidisset** ...

Because the Thermitani had always persisted in friendship and loyalty, the Senate and Roman People gave back to them their city, lands, and laws ...

The language used by Cicero also suggests a degree of similarity between his conception of the granting of autonomy – the right of a community to use its ancestral laws – and the order by the *pontifices* that a community should practise its ancestral cults. What more might we say of the legal evidence, and what aid does it offer in the evaluation of religion?

Legal Pluralism in Roman Practice and Theory[7]

As in the religious evidence, so in respect to law, we might first examine the chronologically prior evidence arising from specific cases. In the case of Sicily, Cicero also provides a schematic description of the legal landscape of the province in the aftermath of its reduction to the form of a province (Cic. *Verr.* 2.2.32):

Siculi hoc iure sunt ut, quod ciuis cum ciue agat, domi certet suis legibus, quod Siculus cum Siculo non eiusdem ciuitatis ... sortiatur. quod priuatus a populo petit aut populus a priuato, senatus ex aliqua ciuitate qui iudicet datur, cum alternae ciuitates reiectae sunt.

> The Sicilians are subjects of law as follows: actions of a citizen with a fellow citizen are tried at home, according to their own laws. To adjudicate actions of a Sicilian with a Sicilian not of the same citizenship ... the praetor should appoint a judge by lot. To adjudicate suits brought by an individual against a community, or by a community against an individual, the senate of another *ciuitas* should be assigned, granting the possibility that a *ciuitas* might be rejected by each side.

In other words, the landscape of Sicily – and, I might add, of all Roman provinces – was legally pluralist. Not only was the landscape tesselated into multiple jurisdictions, in each of which a different code of law applied; but multiple, non-interlocking logics were used to assign cases to *fora*: determinations were made by geography but also by citizenship of the parties to the dispute, and so forth.

Reflection on a world so ordered subsequently produced among Roman legal philosophers a remarkable theoretical and normative apparatus to account for this pluralism. The most concise formulation to be found in a classical text is that which opens the *Institutes* of Gaius (1.1; the opening lines are missing in the manuscript and are quoted from the *Dig.* 1.1.9; translation after de Zulueta):

> Omnes populi qui legibus et moribus reguntur partim suo proprio, partim communi omnium hominum iure utuntur: nam quod **quisque populus ipse sibi** ius constituit, id ipsius proprium est uocaturque ius ciuile, quasi ius proprium civitatis; quod uero naturalis ratio inter omnes homines constituit, id apud omnes populos peraeque custoditur uocaturque ius gentium, quasi quo iure omnes gentes utuntur. populus itaque Romanus partim suo proprio, partim communi omnium hominum iure utitur.

> All peoples who are governed by statutes and customs observe partly their own peculiar law and partly the common law of all human beings. The law that a people establishes for itself is peculiar to it, and is called *ius ciuile*, being, as it were, the special law of that *ciuitas*, that community of citizens, while the law that natural reason establishes among all human beings is followed by all peoples alike, and is called *ius gentium*, being, as it were, the law observed by all peoples. Therefore the Roman People uses partly its own peculiar law and partly the common law of all human beings.

The heart of Gaius' claim is contained in the distributive and reflexive pronouns *quisque* and *sibi*: *ius ciuile* denotes those bodies of law that *every* political community makes *for itself*. No evaluative framework is offered to adjudge between these, neither moral nor ontological, because one adheres more closely to some transcendent norm or is authorized by a source of such; nor is any robust interest expressed here or elsewhere in texts before the Antonine Constitution in the positive law content of these separate *iura ciuilia*.

The operative assumption would seem to be that local social orders are best secured by adherence to locally generated norms; and, as a corollary, Rome has neither an epistemic basis nor any deontological obligation to override those. Late ancient texts do in fact say nearly this much. For the classical period, perhaps it will do to point out the affinity between the philosophical and practical systems laid out by the jurists and the most characteristic structure of empire as a political form, which is to say, that ancient empires govern through the management and cultivation of difference and not, that is, through the universalization of some national culture, with all that that entails.[8]

Enjoining Pre-Roman Practice

If we turn now to the texts that I denominate loosely injunctions requiring the continuance of local rites, they exhibit a number of structural similarities to both formulae of surrender and to the sovereign grants of autonomy that we have examined so far. Particularly notable are those historical accounts that focus on Roman efforts to organize local social, economic, political, and religious life in the aftermath of war or some similar turning point. There is, first, the shorthand used of favoured parties, as in the case of the Lanuvini in settlement of Latium in 338 BCE (Livy 8.14.2):

> relatum igitur de singulis decretumque. Lanuuinis ciuitas data **sacraque sua reddita**, cum eo ut aedes lucusque Sospitae Iunonis communis Lanuuinis municipibus cum populo Romano esset.

Motions were therefore made and passed concerning each individually. To the Lanuvini citizenship was given and their *sacra* were returned, with the proviso that the shrine and grove of Juno Sospita should be shared between the townspeople of Lanuvium and the Roman people.

We are naturally at a loss to say with certainty what the referent for *sacra* is, whether sacred objects or the right to perform certain rites, or both. This much at least seems certain: the concision of the language bespeaks a common understanding; the return of the *sacra* arises from a sovereign act of the Roman people; and the return is intended at some level to restore in some new guise the status quo ante, else it would not be labelled a return.

The act described by Livy and the language he uses should also be understood against a wider evidentiary backdrop in which two patterns stand out: first, the right and perhaps the obligation to continue to perform ancestral rites was restored to *defeated* parties, in acts in which political and religious authority was disaggregated in remarkably sophisticated ways;[9] and second, the situation of any one party was assimilated to some wider framework for dealing with provincial cults in general. Let me discuss examples of each of these two patterns in turn.

As regards defeated parties, one might name both Fregellae and the Hernici, the former described by Strabo (5.3.10) and the latter by Livy (9.43.22–4):

ἔτι δὲ Φρεγέλλαι ... νῦν μὲν κώμη, πόλις δέ ποτε γεγονυῖα ἀξιόλογος καὶ τὰς πολλὰς τῶν ἄντι λεχθεισῶν περιοικίδας πρότερον ἐσχηκυῖα, αἳ νῦν εἰς αὐτὴν συνέρχονται, **ἀγοράς τε ποιούμεναι καὶ ἱεροποιΐας τινάς**· κατασκάφη δ᾽ ὑπὸ Ῥωμαίων ἀποστᾶσα.

There also is Fregellae ... It is now a village but was once a noteworthy city, which held in subordination many of the communities just mentioned situated around it; they still come together at Fregellae to hold markets and perform sacred rites. The city was destroyed by the Romans after it revolved.

Cornelius in Samnio relictus: Marcius de Hernicis triumphans in urbem rediit statuaque equestris in foro decreta est, quae ante templum Castoris posita est. Hernicorum tribus populis, Aletrinati Verulano Ferentinati, quia maluerunt quam ciuitatem, **suae leges redditae** conubiumque inter ipsos, quod aliquamdiu soli Hernicorum habuerunt, permissum. Anagninis quique arma Romanis intulerant ciuitas sine suffragii latione data: concilia conubiaque adempta et magistratibus **praeter quam sacrorum curatione** interdictum.

Cornelius was left behind in Samnium. Marcius returned to the city in triumph over the Hernici and an equestrian statue in the forum was decreed, which was placed before the temple of Castor. To three polities of the Hernici [who had sided with Rome in the war] – the Aletrinati, Verulani, and Ferentinati – because they preferred this to Roman citizenship, it was permitted that their laws should be returned to them and rights of intermarriage granted, which for a time they alone of the Hernici possessed. To the Anagnini who had borne arms against the Romans, citizenship was given without the power of the vote; their rights of common deliberation and intermarriage were taken away and their magistrates forbidden all functions other than looking after rites.

These descriptions of the continuance of cult upon the forced dissolution of political communities should be compared to Cicero's account of the dissolution of Capua in the aftermath of the Hannibalic war (*Leg. agr.* 2.88):

Those wise men decided that if they deprived the Campanians of land and removed from that city its magistrates, senate, and public council, if, that is, they left there not even the image of a civic community (*si agrum Campanis ademissent, magistratus, senatum, publicum ex illa urbe consilium sustulissent, imaginem rei publicae nullam reliquissent*), there would be no reason for us to fear Capua. Therefore, you will find this written in our ancient records, that an *urbs* can exist to supply whatever is needed to cultivate the *ager Campanus*, that there should be a place where crops might be collected and stored; that farmers, exhausted from the cultivation of the fields, should make use of urban dwellings.

As with literary and epigraphic records of surrenders, so it was possible to describe the punishment of Capua without reference to matters of religion. But the pattern of our evidence suggests that contingent interests governed the selection of material to be included in any given summary, rather than that an act of silence correlates with an actual historical lack of attention to the continuance of rites.

These acts of restoration and orders to maintain ancestral rites were furthermore cast even in legislation as actualizing principles that could be or were in fact being generalized. Perhaps the most tantalizing case of this kind is the famous decree of Augustus and Agrippa from 27 BCE, which seeks to establish legal safeguards against the profanation of sacred properties, and a governor's letter implementing that decree in respect to Kyme, 27 BCE (*SEG* XVIII 555 = *RDGE* 61, trans. after Sherk 1988: no. 2):[10]

[Α]ὐτοκράτωρ Καῖσαρ Θεοῦ υἱός Σεβαστὸς [- - -]
[Μ]ᾶρκος Ἀγρίπας Λευκίου υἱὸς ὕπατοι ἐ[κέλευσαν]·
[Εἴ] τινες δημόσιοι τόποι ἢ ἱεροὶ ἐν πόλεσ[ιν ἢ ἐν χώρᾳ]
[π]όλεως **ἑκάστης** ἐπαρχείας εἰσὶν εἴτε τι[νὰ ἀναθή]-
ματα τούτων τῶν τόπων εἰσὶν ἔσονταί τ[ε, μηδεὶς]
[τ]αῦτα αἱρέτω μηδὲ ἀγοραζέτω μηδὲ ἀπο[τίμημα]
[ἢ] δῶρον λαμβανέτω. ὃ ἂν ἐκεῖθεν ἀπενη[νεγμένον ἢ]
[ἠ]γορασμένον ἔν τε δώρῳ δεδομένον ῆ̣, [ὃς ἂν ἐπὶ τῆς]
[ἐ]παρχείας ῆ̣ ἀποκατασταθῆναι εἰς τὸν δημ[όσιον λόγον]
ἢ ἱερὸν τῆς πόλεως φροντιζέτω, καὶ ὃ ἂν χρ[ῆμα ἐνεχύρι]-
[ο]ν δοθῇ, τοῦτο μὴ δικαιοδοτείτω{ι}. (*vacat*)

Imperator Caesar, son of the god, Augustus ... and Marcus Agrippa son of Lucius consuls. [- - -] If there are any public or sacred places in the cities or in the territory of (?) city of each province (?), and if there are or will be any dedications belonging to these places, no one is to remove them or buy them or take them as collateral property or gift. Whatever has been taken away from those places or bought or given as a gift, whoever may be in charge of the province is to see to it that these are restored to the public or sacred account of the city, and whatever may have been given as security, he is not to use this in his administration of justice.

[L(ucius) (?)] Vinicius proc(onsul) s(alutem) d(at) mag(istratibus) Cumas. Apollonides L(uci) f(ilius) No[race(us)] [c(iuis) u(ester)] me adeit et demo(n)strauit Liberei Patris fanum nom[ine] [uen]ditiones possiderei ab Lusia Diogenis f(ilio) Tucalleus c(iue) [u(estro)], [et c]um uellent thiaseitae sacra deo restituere iussu Au[gus]-[t]i Caesaris pretio soluto quod est inscreiptum fano [Patris] [Li]berei ab Lusia, e(go) u(olo) u(os) c(urare), sei ea ita sunt, utei Lusias quod [est] positum pretium fano recipiat et restituat deo fa-[num e]t in eo inscreibatur Imp(erator) Caesar Deivei f(ilius) Augustu[s] re[sti]-[tuit. Sei] autem Lusia contradeicit quae Apollonides pos[tu]-[lat, uadi]monium ei satis dato ubi ego ero. Lusiam pr[o]m[it]-[tere -6-7-]s probo.

[L.(?)] Vinicius, proconsul, sends greetings to the magistrates of Cyme. Apollonides, son of Lucius, from Norace, your citizen, came to me and showed that the temple of Liber Pater was by title of sale possessed by Lysias, son of Diogenes, of Tucalla (?), your citizen, and that when the worshippers wished to restore to their god the sacred property, according to the order of Augustus Caesar, by paying the price that is inscribed on the temple of Liber Pater by Lysias, I wish you to see to it that, if such is the case, Lysias accepts the price that has been placed on the temple and restores to the god the temple and that there be inscribed on it, "Imperator Caesar *diui filius* Augustus restored (this)." But if Lysias denies what Apollonides stipulates, let him give sufficient security to appear where I will be. That Lysias promises [?] ... I approve.

Alas, the present condition of the text does not permit precise conclusions in regard to the scope of the legislation. Although some have suggested the distributive "each" in line 4 could be construed either with πόλεως ("each city of the province") or ἐπαρχείας (" - - - city of each province"), it seems to me unlikely that it should construe with "city," as that would leave "province" without an article.[11] We are, therefore, dealing with an edict of general application to all provinces.[12] To my mind, the singular "city" that opens line 4 is overwhelmingly likely to have been characterized with a distributive as well: "each city of each province." As importantly, no specification or restriction in respect to the identity of the gods who were honoured by and, indeed, formally owners of those properties is made. The proconsul whose letter actualizes the edict in respect to the specific case at Kyme makes clear, however, that an inscription was to record the piety, beneficence, and agency of Augustus in any restoration.

Similar in kind are the language of two edicts directed at the situation of eastern Jews preserved by Philo and Josephus.[13] The fuller, addressed by

Claudius to the Alexandrians, attributes to Augustus a desire "that each party [namely, the Macedonians and the Jews] should abide by its own customs and not be compelled to violate its ancestral *religio*" (Jos. *AJ* 19.282–3: βουλόμενον ὑποτετάχθαι ἑκάστους ἐμμένοντας τοῖς ἰδίοις ἔθεσιν καὶ μὴ παραβαίνειν ἀναγκαζομένους τὴν πάτριον θρησκείαν).[14] ("*Religio*" I adopt as a translation for θρησκεία, although that term could also translate *cultus*: Greek and Latin terms of art in religious discourse notoriously did not map each other closely.) Once again, the principle is generalized by means of a distributive pronoun: the concentration on the situation of the Jews is merely an expression of the contingent facts that motivated the edict. Similarly, in a letter to the Ephesians, Agrippa urges that those who steal the temple tax of the Jews "and flee to places of asylum, I want them to be dragged away and handed over to the Jews, on the same legal principle under which temple-robbers are dragged away" (Jos. *AJ* 16.168: τούς τε κλέπτοντας ἱερὰ χρήματα τῶν Ἰουδαίων καταφεύγοντάς τε εἰς τὰς ἀσυλίας βούλομαι ἀποσπᾶσθαι καὶ παραδίδοσθαι τοῖς Ἰουδαίοις, ᾧ δικαίῳ ἀποσπῶνται οἱ ἱερόσυλοι). Again, please observe the assimilation performed by the relative clause specifying the legal principle at stake: any particularity of the Jewish case is elided in favour of an act of construal by which the religious properties of the Jews are assimilated to sacred properties more generally.

As a final matter regarding these specific injunctions, the text of Festus, in which parties are told to continue in the future their religious practice in the past, and the legal instruments from Spain, in which surrendering parties are restored to the condition in which they found themselves the day before their surrender, draw our attention to the language in these texts that often explicitly, sometimes implicitly, urges that religious practice in the future should continue that of the past: in the *senatus consultum* on the Serapeion at Delos, Demetrius is to be allowed to administer the shrine "just as formerly he administered it" (*SIG*^{3} 664 = *RDGE* 5: καθὼς τὸ πρότερον ἐθεράπευεν); the acts enjoined by Augustus and Agrippa in the decree of 27 BCE are ones of restoration, as is the specific demand of Vinicius the proconsul; according to Claudius, the cult practice that Augustus was keen to protect was *patrion*; and the same term is unsurprisingly used by Josephus in his translation of a decree of Augustus on the privileges of the Jews of Asia (Jos. *AJ* 16.163: γνώμῃ δήμου Ῥωμαίων τοὺς Ἰουδαίους χρῆσθαι τοῖς ἰδίοις ἐθισμοῖς κατὰ τὸν πάτριον αὐτῶν νόμον).

One piece of information is conspicuous for its absence from many of these texts, and that is the name – indeed, any identification – of the god or gods to whose honour the local rites in question are directed. I will return to this issue in the final section of this essay, when I turn to normative accounts of the Roman Empire's religious pluralism, in the discourses of law and theology, classical and Christian. To anticipate one of the conclusions I shall there draw, metropolitan discourse on religion exhibits a stunning lack of interest in the identity of the gods worshipped in provincial communities. This came about for at least two reasons. First, I suspect that in their view, the Romans lacked the information one would want in order to adjudicate the question whether any given recipient of worship was in fact a god. Second, their express interests lay elsewhere, namely, in the maintenance of social order, and towards that end the customary practices of any given locality were as a matter of principle deemed those best able to secure its continuance. This was true, as we have seen, of law, and it was likewise true of religion: hence the insistence by Augustus and Claudius that the Jews (and all other peoples) should "use their own customs" (τοῖς ἰδίοις ἔθεσιν), as well as practise their own rites. I shall return again to the assumption that lies behind this insistence, namely, the assumption that communities worthy of the name have rites, customs, and a religion.

Theology at the Centre: Practice

Before I turn to those more explicitly generalizing statements in the discourses of law and theology, allow me to consider two examples only of Roman confrontations with individual cults. The first is perhaps the most famous instance in which the Romans *did* concern themselves directly with the question of whether the recipient of worship at a provincial site was in fact a god. I refer, of course, to the trial conducted before a board of senators to determine the tax status of the Amphiareion at Oropus. The young Cicero served on the board that heard the case, and in his amused reflection it turned on the wording of the law: "Since by law of the censor lands in Boeotia that belong to immortal gods are tax-exempt, our publicans denied that any were immortal who had once been human" (*Nat. D.* 3.49: *nostri quidem publicani, cum essent agri in Boeotia deorum inmortalium excepti lege censoria, negabant inmortalis esse ullos qui aliquando homines fuissent*). The wording of the consuls' cover letter, which forwarded the Senate's decree and which is available, as I have said, only in the Greek translation erected at the shrine, suggests an eagerness to dispose of the issue altogether: they declare that the Senate has reached a decision "regarding the dispute between the god Amphiaraus and the publicans." They will have none of this "immortal gods" nonsense (*SIG*[3] 747 = *RDGE* 23, ll. 1–5: περὶ ἀντιλογιῶν τῶν ἀνὰ μ[έσον] θεῷ Ἀμφιαράῳ καὶ τῶν δημοσιωνῶν γεγονότων).

As a second example, I turn to the most famous injunction against a cult other than Christianity issued by the Roman authorities, namely, the assault on the worship of Dionysus of the early second century BCE. I cite relevant clauses from the Senate's decree (*CIL* I[2] 581 = *ILS* 18 = *ILLRP* 511 = *AE* 2006, 21, lines 10–18):

sacerdos nequis uir eset; magister neque uir neque mulier quisquam eset;
neue pecuniam quisquam eorum comoine[m h]abuise ue[l]et; neue magistratum
neue pro magistratu[d] neque uirum [neque mul]ierem quiquam fecise uelet;
neue post hac inter sed conioura[se neu]e comuouise neue conspondise
neue conpromesise uelet, neue quisquam fidem inter sed dedise uelet.
sacra in [o]quoltod ne quisquam fecise uelet; neue in poplicod neue in
preiuatod neue extrad urbem sacra quisquam fecise uelet, nisei
pr(aitorem) urbanum adieset, isque de senatuos sententiad dum ne minus
senatoribus C adesent quom ea res cosoleretur, iousiset. censuere.

Let no man be a priest. Let no man or woman be a master. Let none of them want to have money in common. Let no one want to make either a man or a woman a master, or make a man or a woman serve in the place of a master; let no one after this want to swear oaths in common or make vows in common or pledge things in common or promise in common, nor let anyone swear loyalty to another among them. Let no one want to perform [Bacchic] rites in secret; let no one want to perform [Bacchic] rites in public or private or outside the City, unless he approaches the urban praetor and the urban praetor permits it, in accordance with the will of the Senate, provided that not less than a hundred senators are present when the matter is deliberated. Decreed.

What requires stress about this famous incident in this context is not simply that the Senate permitted the worship of Bacchus to continue. Rather, it is that the Senate eschewed any effort to regulate the forms that Bacchic worship might take, concentrating instead on the institutionalization of the cult and the financial and legal relationships among its members: no secular officials are permitted; no common swearing of oaths; no common property. The rites may take place unchanged, but not in secret. The major exception to this characterization, to wit, the injunction against male priests, can perhaps be explained by Livy's insistence that it had been a recent innovation, one not authorized by the god (Livy 39.13.8–10). It is loyalty to other members of the cult, and not loyalty to Bacchus, that is the Senate's province. To describe the suppression of the Bacchanalia in terms kindred to those employed by Livy elsewhere: once the Senate had conceded the divinity of Bacchus, it was no longer the Senate's place to decide "by what prayers and supplications" he wished to be worshipped (cf. Livy 22.57.5).

Theology at the Centre: Theory

I should like now to conclude with two reflections, the first placing this Roman discourse within a broader historical and theoretical framework of a post-colonial nature, and the second, as promised earlier, on ancient normative accounts of the Empire's religious pluralism.

The assumption on the part of Romans that each community has its own customs, laws, and religion is at some level unsurprising. It finds particularly potent articulation in Livy's description of the permission granted to the Aletrinates, Verulani, and Ferentinates that they should not be compelled to accept Roman citizenship: "their laws were given back, because they preferred this to [Roman] citizenship" (Livy 9.43.23: *quia maluerunt quam ciuitatem, suae leges redditae*). But insofar as this assumption shaped practice, it is likely to have had important effects in the provinces. No doubt there were communities that were then for the first time constituted as unitary communities through their interpellation by Roman agents, and there are important historical parallels for the discovery – which is to say the invention – by colonized populations of "customs, laws, and religion" in the light of such imperial epistemes.[15] What is more, as Josephus' remarks on Alexandria make clear, the challenge to Roman government lay not in those cases where the assumption held, but in those where it failed.

Turning now to normative accounts of the Empire's religious pluralism, these reveal again the indifference of an official, metropolitan discourse regarding the identity or the names of provincial gods, to say nothing of their potential identification with Roman ones. This is not to say that official documents exhibit *no* interest in the diversity of gods. The letter of M. Valerius Messala to Teos in 193 BCE is a case in point (*SIG*[3] 601 = *RDGE* 34, lines 11–17):

καὶ ὅτι μὲν διόλου πλεῖστον λόγον ποιούμενοι διατελοῦμεν τῆς πρὸς τοὺς θεοὺς εὐσεβείας, μάλιστ᾽ ἄν τις στοχάζοιτο ἐκ τῆς συναντωμένης ἡμεῖν εὐμενείας διὰ ταῦτα **παρὰ τοῦ δαιμονίου**· οὐ μὴν ἀλλὰ καὶ ἄλλων πλειόνων πεπείσμεθα συμφανῆ πᾶσι γεγονέναι τὴν ἡμετέραν **εἰς τὸ θεῖον** προτιμίαν.

That we have wholly and constantly attached the highest importance to piety toward the gods one can estimate particularly from the goodwill that we have experienced on this account from the divine. Not only that, but for many other reasons we are convinced that our own high respect for the godhead has become manifest to everyone.

But despite the one reference to plural "gods," Messala's other references to the divine take the form of radically underdetermined singulars: τὸ δαιμόνιον and τὸ θεῖον.

Of greater interest are those texts that explicitly or implicitly focus attention on religion as a socio-cultural institution and, what is more, do so through universalizing distributives. Among these I include both Cicero's famous dictum, *sua cuique ciuitati religio, Laeli, est, nostra nobis* ("every political community has its own *religio*, Laelius, even as we do," Cic. *Flac.* 69, who like Gaius employs both a distributive and a reflexive possessorial), as well as Livy's description of the conduct of the Albans at the signing of a treaty with Rome (1.24.8): "The Albans completed their own *carmen* and swore their own oath through their own *dictator* and their own priests." I have written elsewhere at some length about Livy's assumption of a homology between the religious institutions of the Albans and Romans.[16] What I would emphasize here are rather two observations. First, the institutions of the Albans are their own: ***sua** carmina, **suum** ius iurandum, **suum** dictatorem, **suos** sacerdotes.* Second, no record is made – nor is any interest expressed – to whom they swore their oath.

To understand why this was so, we might consider a much later text, an aside by Ammianus Marcellinus on the oath-swearing of the Sarmatians (Amm. Marc. 17.12.21): *eductisque mucronibus, quos pro numinibus colunt, iurauere se permansuros in fide* ("and, having drawn their swords, which they worship as gods, they swore that they would abide in loyalty").[17] How does Ammianus know that the Sarmatians worship their swords as gods? It is presumably an inference from the form taken by their ritual. That said, at the event depicted here, no Roman invited the Sarmatians to swear by a Roman god, or even a real god: if the oath was to be effective, it had to be their oath, made before whatever they held divine.

Roman indifference to the content of cult and especially to the identity of gods should not, of course, be taken for a lack of interest in religion in provincial communities writ large. On the contrary, as the very notion of municipal rites suggests, imperial, which is to say, metropolitan commitment to localism in matters of religion was understood to conduce both a local and an imperial order. This is visible even in Roman regulations directed at colonies of Roman citizens, which were conceived as in some sense constituent parts of the Roman state.[18] Even there, the pre-eminent concern at the centre is that the communal *sacra* should be properly constituted and performed, as laid down in chapter 64 of the *Lex coloniae Genetivae Iuliae* (*RS* 25):

> Whoever shall be *IIviri* after the foundation of the colony, they, within the ten days next after that on which they shall have begun to hold that magistracy, are to raise with the decurions when not less than two-thirds shall be present, which and how many days it may be agreed shall be festivals and which sacrifices shall be publicly performed and who shall perform those sacrifices (*quos et quot dies festos esse et quae sacra fieri publice placeat et quos ea sacra facere placeat*).

The magistrates are likewise ordered to look after the maintenance of the material fabric of religious observance, most importantly the *fana templa delubra*, but also the games and *puluinaria* (*Lex coloniae Genetivae Iuliae* ch. 128). That said, the colony is expected to pay due worship to the Capitoline triad (*Lex coloniae Genetivae Iuliae* ch. 70), but also to gods and goddesses whose worship will develop out of purely local processes of discovery and decision making. Concern at Rome is restricted to the problem that, gods having been selected, the institutions of their worship should be properly funded and respected (*Lex coloniae Genetivae Iuliae* ch. 72):

quotcumque pecuniae stipis nomine in aedis sacras datum inlatum erit, quot eius pecuniae eis sacri{i}s superfuerit, quae sacra, uti h(ac) l(ege) <f(ieri)> oportebit, **ei deo deaeue, cuius ea aedes erit**, facta <fuer>i<n>t, ne quis facito neue curato neue intercedito, quo minus in aede consumatur ...

Whatever sum shall have been given or brought in to the sacred temples under the character of an offering, whatever of that sum shall be left over from those sacrifices, which sacrifices shall have been performed as it shall be appropriate for them to be performed according to this statute, for that god or goddess whose temple it shall be, no one is to act or see or intercede to the effect that it may not be spent in that temple ...

A nearly identical understanding is visible in the claims made more than two centuries later by the land surveyor Agennius Urbicus and the jurist Ulpian, to the effect that a paramount duty of governors was religious scruple and the custodial care attached to sacred places (Agennius Urbicus 44.14–23 Campbell):

locorum autem sacrorum secundum legem populi Romani magna religio et custodia haberi debet: nihil enim magis in mandatis etiam legati prouinciarum accipere solent, quam ut haec loca quae sacra sunt custodiantur.

According to a law of the Roman people, great religious scruple and protection must be maintained in respect to sacred places. Indeed, the governors of provinces customarily receive no greater injunction among their instructions than that those places that are sacred must be protected.

As was the case with the Augustan edict from Kyme that these echo (*SEG* XVIII 555 = *RDGE* 61, quoted above on pp. 264–5), no interest is expressed in the identity of the gods worshipped in these buildings. The concern of government, such as it is, lies in the integrity of the urban fabric, the maintaining of public properties, and the contribution of religious scruple to provincial social orders. Hence it is that in Ulpian's text, a further obligation of the governor is to grant whatever holidays "accord with ancestral practice and the custom that has obtained in the past" (Ulpian, *De officio proconsulis* bk. 2 fr. 2147 Lenel = *Dig.* 1.16.7.*pr.*–1: *et ferias secundum mores et consuetudinem quae retro optinuit dare*). Imperial practice, therefore, seeks an alignment between local and imperial pieties, one that exists altogether to one side of any speculative identification of local and Roman manifestations of any one godhead. One might have labelled the Roman interest cynical or functionalist, did it not so clearly exemplify the attitude that the Romans denominated piety.

In their profound lack of interest in the identity of gods, the radical indeterminacy of the language of all these texts in respect to the manifestation of the divine might usefully be compared to the opening clauses of Cicero's code of law in *De legibus* (Cic. *Leg.* 2.19; trans. Zetzel, lightly adapted):

separatim nemo habessit deos, neue nouos neue aduenas, nisi publice adscitos. priuatim colunto quos rite a patribus <cultos acceperint.> ... ritus familiae patrumque seruanto. diuos et eos qui caelestes semper habiti sunt colunto, et ollos quos endo caelo merita locauerunt, Herculem, Liberum ... sacra sollemnia obeunto.

Let no one have gods separately, neither new nor foreign, unless they have been taken up publicly. Privately let them worship those whose worship they have duly received from their fathers ... Let them preserve the rituals of their family and ancestors. Let them worship both those who have always been considered heavenly gods and those whose deeds have placed them in heaven: Hercules, Liber ... Let them take part in established rites.

It is only when Cicero names those humans whose deeds have earned them a place in heaven that he provides a list. Otherwise, his interest is solely in the social values that religious affiliation both echoes and sustains: respect for public authority; identification with communal values; adherence to tradition. It is here that the affinity between Cicero speaking *in propria persona* in *De legibus* and Cotta of Cicero's *De natura deorum* emerges most clearly.

I have elsewhere deplored the tendency in scholarship to index the state of affairs in religious history by counting gods, or religions, for that matter.[19] Indeed, the adoption of such indices is perhaps the most significant practice the discipline of Religious Studies owes to Christian late antiquity. The distortions worked upon religious thought by Christianity – the occlusion Christian texts have performed – in persuading us not to recognize what is most distinctive about Roman religious texts, may thus be expressed in shorthand by contrasting Cicero's formulation in *Pro Flacco* with the formulations offered by Tertullian and Minucius Felix:

Superest gentile illud <genus> inter populos deorum quos libidine sumptos, non pro n<ec>ess<itate> ueritatis, docet priuata notitia. (Tert. *Ad nat.* 2.8.1)

It remains to discuss the national or political type of gods: these are taken up among the nations according to their whim, not from the constraint of truth, as the records of each people reveals.

Satis rideo etiam **deos decuriones cuiusque municipii**, quibus honor intra muros suos determinatur. (Tert. *Ad nat.* 2.8.7)

I laugh enough at the city-councillor gods of each little town, whose honour is delimited by their city's walls.

Inde adeo per uniuersa imperia, prouincias oppida uidemus **singulos sacrorum ritus gentiles habere et deos colere municipes**, ut Eleusinios Cererem, Phrygas Matrem, Epidaurios Aesculapium, Chaldaeos Belum, Astarten Syros, Dianam Tauros, Gallos Mercurium, uniuersa Romanos. (Min. Fel. *Oct.* 6.1)

Hence we see that throughout all empires, provinces, and towns, nations have their own rites and city dwellers worship their own gods, such that the Eleusinians worship Ceres, the Phrygians Mother, the Epidaurians Aesculapius, the Chaldaeans Belus, the Syrians Astartes, the Taurians Diana, the Gauls Mercury, the Romans all gods.

We are again confronted with distributive pronouns (*cuiusque; populi sibi quique*) or, occasionally, semantic equivalents (*inter populos; singulos*). But it is neither rites nor scruples – things constructed by human societies for themselves – that exist in correlation with the communities the Christian authors map, but gods.

NOTES

* Elaine Fantham taught me in two courses at Princeton, in which we read Livy Book 5 and selections from Ovid; she also served as second reader for my junior paper on Plutarch's life of Camillus. This essay is intended to complement the studies she has made of Roman literary culture and, more recently, the engagements of Latin poetry with the religious landscapes of Roman Italy (Fantham 1996, 2009). This essay focuses rather on Roman practice in respect to the religion of others and especially on the understanding of religion that this practice presupposes, an understanding that finds articulation also in

Varro, Cicero, Livy, and Festus. I hope that something of the distinctiveness of poetic discourse in this field is thereby revealed, kindred, perhaps, to the work performed by poets in the imagining of a unified Italy: cf. Ando 2002.

1 In very different ways, Beard, North, and Price 1998: 228–44 and Baudy 2006 well illustrate the modern consensus; see also Cancik 2009. North 1979 represents a turning point in the literature. Frend (1965: 104–26) presents an invaluable survey but operates, it seems to me, with largely insupportable analytic presuppositions. Garnsey 1984 is widely cited, but in surveying nineteen hundred years in twenty-seven pages can scarcely describe even the evidence, let alone offer meaningful historical analysis.

2 On this theme, see also Rüpke 2001.

3 Ando 2005, revised in Ando 2008: 43–58.

4 Ando 2008: 1–18 and 59–92; see also Ando 2010 and 2015: 53–86.

5 Rüpke 1990: 209–10 is the only discussion of surrender and restoration as a problem in religious history known to me, and his focus is altogether different than my own.

6 Livy 7.31.3–4: *itaque populum Campanum urbemque Capuam agros* ***delubra deum diuina humanaque omnia*** *in uestram, patres conscripti, populique Romani dicionem dedimus, quidquid deinde patiemur deditici uestri passuri*; 26.33.12–13: *omnes Campani Atellani Calatini Sabatini qui se dediderunt in arbitrium dicionemque populi Romani <Q.> Fuluio proconsuli, quosque una secum dedidere quaeque una secum dedidere agrum urbemque* ***diuina humanaque utensiliaque*** *siue quid aliud dediderunt, de iis rebus quid fieri uelitis uos rogo, Quirites*; 34.5, 12; 28.34.7: *omnia diuina humanaque.*

7 On legal pluralism as a practical and theoretical issue in Roman legal history, see Ando 2011a: 1–36 and 2014.

8 Barfield 2001: 29; Maier 2006: 5–7, 29–36.

9 On punishment as revealing commonplace assumptions at the moment of their disarticulation, see Ando 2011b. The fire-walking Hirpi constitute a distant analogue to such cases: after their incorporation into the Roman state, so long as they continued to perform their gentilician rites, they were excused from the *munera* of citizenship (Plin. *NH* 7.19): *haut procul urbe Roma in Faliscorum agro familiae sunt paucae quae uocantur Hirpi; hae sacrificio anno quod fit ad montem Soractem Apollini super ambustam ligni struem ambulantes non aduruntur, et ob id perpetuo senatus consulto militiae omniumque aliorum munerum uacationem habent.*

10 For this complex text, I have in the main followed the text given in *SEG* XVIII 555 (on-line), but I have adopted alternative restorations for the right margins of lines 1, 6, 9, and 10.

11 Sherk 1988: 6n4.

12 What is more, I believe that *IG* II 1035 should be read as responding to this command. That is so, even if we accept Culley's dating to the last decade of the first century. It seems to me that lines 8–9 of the conjoined fragments A–C do correspond very precisely to the wording of lines 5–7 of the edict from Kyme. On this topic, see Oliver 1972; Culley 1975, 1977.

13 On these documents, see Pucci Ben Zeev 1998, esp. 262–72, 295–326.

14 Observe, too, the very similar language employed by Philo to describe the attitude of Augustus, which also involves a distributive (Philo, *Leg.* 153, trans. Colson in the Loeb Classical Library): ἤδεσαν αὐτου τὴν ἐπιμέλειαν καὶ ὅτι τοσαύτην ποιεῖται τῆς βεβαιώσεως τῶν παρ' ἑκάστοις πατρίων, ὅσην καὶ τῶν Ῥωμαικῶν ... ("They knew his carefulness and that he showed it in maintaining firmly the native customs of each particular nation no less than those of the Romans…").

15 In respect of colonial law in comparative perspective, Merry (2000) is a deservedly famous study of one such situation, though this invocation scarcely does justice to the richness of her account; see also Ando forthcoming. In ancient contexts, it merits observation that experts in local law are largely a phenomenon of the high Empire: this is true of Phrygia (Kantor 2013). Likewise in Egypt, references to "the laws of the Egyptians" are largely a feature of the high Empire, and not a phenomenon of the first generations under Roman rule, clinging to the norms of the pre-Roman past.

16 Ando 2011a: 37–63.

17 I have adopted the neutral translation "as gods," although *pro numinibus* could also mean "in the place of gods": on the use of *pro* in legal and religious discourse, see Ando 2011a: 1–18.

18 The religious content of Roman municipal and colonial charters has been subjected to searching enquiry in two splendid essays: Scheid 1999; Rüpke 2006. Cf. Scheid 2006.

19 Ando 2013.

WORKS CITED

Ando, C. 2002. "Vergil's Italy: Ethnography and Politics in First-Century Rome." In *Clio and the Poets: Augustan Poetry and the Traditions of Ancient Historiography*, edited by D.S. Levene and D. Nelis, 123–42. Leiden.

– 2005. "Interpretatio Romana." *CP* 100: 41–51.

– 2008. *The Matter of the Gods*. Berkeley.

– 2010. "The Ontology of Religious Institutions." *History of Religions* 50.1: 54–79.

– 2011a. *Law, Language, and Empire in the Roman Tradition*. Philadelphia.

– 2011b. "Law and the Landscape of Empire." In *Figures d'empire, fragments de mémoire. Pouvoirs et identités dans le monde romain impérial (IIe s. av. n.è. – VIe s. de n.è.*, edited by S. Benoist, A. Daguey-Gagey, and C. Hoët-van Cauwenberghe, 25–47. Paris.

– 2013. "Subjects, Gods and Empire, or Monarchism as a Theological Problem." In *The Individual in the Religions of the Ancient Mediterranean*, edited by J. Rüpke, 85–111. Oxford.

– 2014. "Pluralism and Empire, from Rome to Robert Cover." *Critical Analysis of Law: An International & Interdisciplinary Law Review* 1: 1–22.

– 2015. *Roman Social Imaginaries: Language and Thought in Contexts of Empire.* Toronto.

– forthcoming. "Colonialism, Colonization: Roman Perspectives." In *The Oxford Handbook of Literatures of the Roman Empire*, edited by D.L. Selden and P. Vasunia. Oxford.

Ando, C., and J. Rüpke, eds. 2006. *Religion and Law in Classical and Christian Rome.* Stuttgart.

Barfield, T.J. 2001. "The Shadow Empires: Imperial State Formation along the Chinese-Nomad Frontier." In *Empires. Perspectives from Archaeology and History*, edited by K.D. Morrison and C.M. Sinopoli, 10–41. Cambridge.

Baudy, D. 2006. "Prohibitions of Religion in Antiquity: Setting the Course of Europe's Religious History." In Ando and Rüpke 2006: 100–14.

Beard, M., J. North, and S. Price. 1998. *Religions of Rome. 1. A History*. Cambridge.

Cancik, H. 2009. "Religionsfreiheit und Toleranz in der späteren römischen Religionsgeschichte (zweites bis viertes Jahrundert n. Chr.)." In *Die Religion des Imperium Romanum*, edited by H. Cancik and J. Rüpke, 365–79. Tübingen.

Culley, G.R. 1975. "The Restoration of Sanctuaries in Attica, *IG* II^2, 1035." *Hesperia* 44.2: 207–23.

– 1977. "The Restoration of Sanctuaries in Attica, II." *Hesperia* 46.3: 282–98.

de Zulueta, F. ed. 1946. *The* Institutes *of Gaius. 1. Text with critical notes and translation.* Oxford.

Fantham, E. 1996. *Roman Literary Culture from Cicero to Apuleius.* Baltimore.

– 2009. *Latin Poets and Italian Gods.* Toronto.

Frend, W.H.C. 1965. *Martyrdom and Persecution in the Early Church: A Study of a Conflict from the Maccabees to Donatus.* Oxford.

Garnsey, P. 1984. "Religious Toleration in Classical Antiquity." In *Persecution and Toleration*, edited by W.J. Sheils, 1–27. Oxford.

Kantor, G. 2013. "Law in Roman Phrygia: Rules and Jurisdictions." In *Roman Phrygia: Culture and Society*, edited by P. Thonemann, 143–67. Cambridge.

Maier, C. 2006. *Among Empires: American Ascendancy and Its Predecessors.* Cambridge.

Merry, S.E. 2000. *Colonizing Hawai'i: The Cultural Power of Law.* Princeton.

North, J.A. 1979. "Religious Toleration in Republican Rome." *PCPS* 25: 85–103.

Oliver, J.H. 1972. "On the Hellenic Policy of Augustus and Agrippa in 27 BC." *AJP* 93: 190–7.

Pucci Ben Zeev, M. 1998. *Jewish Rights in the Roman World.* Tübingen.

Rüpke, J. 1990. Domi militiae. *Die religiöse Konstruktion des Krieges in Rom.* Stuttgart.

– 2001. "Polytheismus und Pluralismus." In *Pluralismus in der europäischen Religionsgeschichte*, edited by A. Gotzmann, V.N. Makrides, J. Malik, and J. Rüpke, 17–34. Marburg.

– 2006. "Religion in the lex Ursonensis." In Ando and Rüpke 2006: 34–46.

Scheid, J. 1999. "Aspects religieux de la municipalisation. Quelques réflexions générales." In *Cités, municipes, colonies. Les processus de municipalisation en Gaule et en Germanie sous le Haut Empire romain,* edited by M. Dondin-Payre and M.-T. Raepsaet-Charlier, 381–423. Paris.

– 2006. "Les dévotions en Germanie inférieure: divinités, lieux de culte, fidèles." In *Sanctuaires, pratiques cultuelles et territoires civiques dans l'Occident romain,* edited by M. Dondin-Payre and M.-T. Raepsaet-Charlier, 298–346. Brussels.

Sherk, R.K., ed. 1988. *The Roman Empire: Augustus to Hadrian.* Translated Documents of Greece and Rome 6. Cambridge.

Zetzel, J.E.G., ed. 1999. *Cicero:* On the Commonwealth *and* On the Laws. Cambridge.

14

Rituals of Reciprocity: Staging Gladiatorial *munera* in Apuleius' *Metamorphoses*[*]

JONATHAN EDMONDSON

In his novel *The Metamorphoses* (more commonly known as *The Golden Ass*) Apuleius of Madauros worked up two memorable episodes in which members of the local elite of Roman Greece sponsored gladiatorial *munera* in their respective cities. In Book 4 a local notable, punningly named Demochares ("crowd pleaser"), in an act of civic euergetism put on *munera gladiatoria* at Plataea in Boeotia (4.13–21), while in Book 10 a local chief magistrate with censorial powers, a *IIvir quinquennalis* called Thiasus, as part of the requirements of his office, staged an even more elaborate three-day *munus* at Corinth, chief city of the Roman province of Achaea. The novel's unfortunate hero Lucius the ass was to perform at this *munus* in what Kathleen Coleman has so aptly and memorably termed a "fatal charade" that was to climax with the ass engaging in sexual intercourse with a female criminal, forced to play the role of Pasiphae (10.16–35).[1] (Another *munus* is briefly mentioned in Book 1, when Socrates relates how "[he] was pursuing the pleasure of a particularly fame-inducing gladiatorial spectacle" to be put on at Larissa in Thessaly on his return from a business trip to Macedonia when he was violently accosted by brigands (1.7.5: *voluptatem gladiatorii spectaculi satis famigerabilis consector*), but this assault forced him to seek refuge in an inn run by the witch Meroe and we never get to hear anything more about the spectacle in Larissa.) Even though the demands of the plot mean that we never receive a full description of either the *munus* at Plataea or the spectacle at Corinth from start to finish, Apuleius' narratives do allow us to glimpse an otherwise neglected aspect of gladiatorial *munera* in the cities of the Roman Empire: that is, the complex rituals of reciprocity between sponsor and local citizenry that any gladiatorial *munus* entailed. It is the aim of this study to explore some of the rich detail of this socio-political dialogue that Apuleius' narrative allows us to reconstruct.

It might be argued that any attempt to use Apuleius' novel to throw light on the social conditions of the Roman Empire in the second century CE is vitiated by the distorting effects that the literary tradition of the Greek novel may have had on Apuleius' work. The latter was clearly based on a Greek original, the *Metamorphoses,* of which a summary version in Greek (*Onos,* "The Ass") survives, preserved in the manuscripts of Lucian of Samosata. Apuleius clearly took the now lost Greek novel as his basic framework.[2] In some places, he followed his source fairly closely; but even so, there is no question that the resultant work, *The Golden Ass,* is very much more Roman. It was written for a Roman audience – Roman in a broad sense to include Roman citizens and provincial subjects of Rome – and it owed much to Apuleius' own personal experiences as an educated rhetorician, sophist, and philosopher who had lived in several parts of the Roman world: his native North Africa, Greece, and also Rome.[3] As Fergus Millar argued in his now classic study on the "world of Apuleius" and as Keith Bradley has developed in greater depth in a series of more recent articles, Apuleius' novel evokes a very real sense of place, a cultural milieu: that is, the world of a Greek province under Roman rule.[4]

Second, it might be objected that the novel's exuberantly fantastic elements reduce its value as a historical source. Of course the plot is an imaginative fantasy, but its world is populated by vivid, realistic individuals of a whole range of social statuses. We encounter Roman proconsuls and local magistrates; members of the leisured elite and the labouring poor; Roman soldiers and a range of priests (travelling or otherwise); humble millers, gardeners, doctors, and cooks, not to mention a whole array of bandits and slaves. Within many of these social categories, Apuleius also conjures up a rich variety of types: among the *domi nobiles* the miserly Milo (1.21–3.28) and the rich Corinthian *matrona* who is more than willing to pay large sums of money for some very rough and intense sex (10.19–23); the slaves portrayed range from the perfumed and seductive domestic Photis (1.22–6; 2.6–10, 16–18, 32; 3.13–26) to the wretched, welt-covered specimens who chained, branded, and half-naked are forced to work the grain mill day after day after day (9.12.3–4).[5] Even if the novel is shot through with all sorts of intertextual references to earlier Greek and Latin literature, and even if these intertexts often determine how Apuleius constructs his narrative, there is no question that the novel reveals much of the social mentality of this provincial world, in some ways remote, bandit-ridden, and dangerous (especially outside the *cordon sanitaire* of the cities), but at the same time a world in which the processes of Roman law and order were at least sometimes enforced.[6] Many of the characters have distinctly Roman values: the bandits have a rather Roman sense of honour and prestige, and even the overtly mythical tale of Cupid and Psyche (4.28–6.24) has a remarkably Roman feel to it. Venus is furious at Cupid's desire to marry a woman of a lower social rank: his *sordidi amores*, as she describes them (5.29.2); she simply cannot allow her son to marry Psyche, since this would contravene the terms of the *lex Iulia de maritandis ordinibus*.[7] Similarly, Juno rejects Psyche's request to harbour her, fearful of the shame she would incur if she disregarded the wishes of a close relative, her daughter-in-law Venus, and unwilling to contravene the Roman law (the *lex Fabia*) whereby it was illegal to harbour the fugitive slaves of another slave owner (6.4.5).[8]

Apuleius himself was the wealthy son of a *IIvir* of the colony of Madauros in North Africa, from whom he and his brother came to inherit no less than two million sesterces. By 158–9 he was launched on a local public career (*Apol.* 24.9). According to a tradition preserved in one of the letters of St Augustine, he was also high priest (*flamen*) of the imperial cult of the province of Africa, a position of considerable social eminence, in which capacity he sponsored gladiatorial *munera* and wild-beast hunts at Carthage (August. *Ep.* 138.19).[9] In short, he was unusually well placed to understand the social context of such spectacles and, in particular, the motivations that lay behind the local elite's sponsorship of them. From his narratives of the *munera* put on by Demochares at Plataea in Book 4 and, in particular, by Thiasus at Corinth in Book 10, written arguably in the 170s or 180s, we can reconstruct the elaborate sequence of communicative acts that took place between the sponsor of such spectacles and his fellow citizens.[10] Others have explored the literary function of spectacle within the novel and the manner in which spectators often become the spectacle.[11] My purposes in this essay are more historical. With Apuleius as our guide, we may probe the civic context in which gladiatorial spectacles were staged in Roman Achaea and isolate in a more vivid way than is possible from any other surviving source material the various stages of the reciprocal dialogue that took place between civic benefactors and the grateful recipients of their generosity whenever a gladiatorial *munus* was put on in a Roman provincial setting.

The Local Civic Context

The two communities in the Roman province of Achaea in which the *munera* are to be staged were rather divergent in terms of their status and local histories. Plataea was a relatively small community in southern Boeotia, but one granted the honoured status of a *civitas libera et immunis* within the

Roman province of Achaea. It had survived many vicissitudes throughout its long history both at the hands of its powerful neighbour Thebes and as the site of pitched battles or the target of sieges during a series of wars from the Persian invasion of 481–479 BCE through to the Sulla's campaigns in Greece in 86 BCE. Its fame in the Roman period was mainly based on the crucial battle fought outside its walls in which the combined land forces of the Greeks had defeated the much larger Persian army of Xerxes in 479 BCE. Various cults were still active in the second century CE that commemorated the famous battle, as well as Panhellenic games known as the Eleutheria.[12] Corinth, on the other hand, was a Roman colony, chief city (*caput*) of the Roman province of Achaea and seat of the Roman governor.[13] Refounded by Julius Caesar as a colony in 44 BCE for freedmen sent out from the city of Rome and for army veterans a century after its destruction by L. Mummius in 146, it could boast some impressive Roman monuments, including a stone-built amphitheatre as well as a theatre and an odeion.[14] Very few amphitheatres were built in the Greek world; other examples can be found at Knossos (a veteran colony in Crete), Gortyn (provincial capital of Crete and Cyrenaica), Antioch (capital of the province of Syria), Pergamum (a *conventus* centre in the province of Asia), and Pisidian Antioch (another Roman colony). The presence of an amphitheatre very much symbolized Corinth's status as the focal point of Roman power in Achaea.[15]

A first point to note is that the two *munera* in Apuleius' narrative were staged at very different times of the year. The one at Plataea was to take place in high summer, as we can infer from the fact that most of the bears that had been mustered for the show died of starvation and heat exhaustion in the hottest part of the Greek year (4.14.2). The arena spectacles at Corinth, on the other hand, were staged in February or March, since at the festival of Isis at Cenchreae, Corinth's port on the Saronic Gulf, which in Apuleius' narrative occurs immediately after the ass's transformation back into human form after his performance in the arena, the scribe pronounces a prayer for the start of the navigation season (11.17.3). Just as the painted advertisements for such *munera* that have survived on the walls of Pompeii suggest, there was no set season nor fixed calendar for such spectacles.[16] It appears that their sponsors chose the most opportune moment at which they would be held.

More significantly, the socio-political context for each of the two respective *munera* is distinct. At Plataea, Demochares appears to have been a member of the local aristocracy engaging in act of civic euergetism for the benefit of his native *polis*. He was, according to Apuleius, a "man of high birth and great wealth and noted for his liberality"; his aim was to provide "pleasures for the people with a brilliance worthy of his fortune" (4.13.2: *vir et genere primarius et opibus plurimus et liberalitate praecipuus digno fortunae suae splendore publicas voluptates instruebat*). To underline the civic-mindedness of his benefactions, Apuleius, as so often, gives him a punningly significant name: Demochares, old "crowd-pleaser" himself.[17] In his essay *Politika Parangelmata* giving advice to young members of the local elite on the difficulties of engaging in local political life now that Greece was firmly under Roman rule, Plutarch criticizes those members of the elite who felt obliged to provide gladiatorial combats to gain popular support.[18] He was obviously hostile to the introduction of gladiators into the Greek cultural milieu, and the fact that he returns to the point no fewer than three times in his essay suggests that he might have been fighting a losing battle.[19]

The surviving epigraphic evidence for *munera* suggests that it was rare in both the Greek East and the Roman West for private citizens to sponsor them; more normally, it was the concern of magistrates or, especially in the Greek East, local priests or regional high priests of the imperial cult.[20] But this focus on magistrates and priests may be somewhat exaggerated: the result more of the nature of our surviving evidence – often inscriptions carved on the bases of honorific statues that listed the public careers of the honorands – than of actual social practice. Given the precision with which Apuleius describes his *munerarii* in both Book 4 and Book 10, his narrative of the events at Plataea assumes that private, spontaneous acts of euergetism did continue into the second century CE.[21] Parallels, though rare, can be found from Italian municipalities and occasionally from the Greek East. Pliny's friend Maximus had promised to sponsor a *munus* in Verona out of his own private generosity (Plin. *Ep.* 6.34). In the end, it was ruined by the fact that the African wild-beasts he had purchased did not arrive in time.[22] At Thessalonica, a notable gladiatorial centre in the Roman province of Macedonia, a private citizen bequeathed funds in his will to the community to allow a *venatio* and gladiatorial combats to be staged in 141 CE over a three-day period in his memory.[23]

At Corinth, the sponsor is also a member of the local elite, but someone obliged to provide the entertainment for his fellow citizens in return for their bestowal on him of local political office. Thiasus (another significant name alluding to the Dionysiac revels to follow) had held "all the local magistracies at Corinth" and had now been nominated *IIvir quinquennalis*, i.e., local censor, the highest office in the *cursus honorum* in the Roman colony and chief city of Roman Achaea.[24] In return for this nomination, he had promised a three-day *munus gladiatorium* (10.18.1). If we were dealing with a real Corinthian magistrate, Thiasus would not be his full name. Since Corinth was a Roman colony, its magistrates would have been Roman citizens and hence borne the full *tria nomina*, as was the case with M. Antonius Orestes, *IIvir quinqu(ennalis)* of Corinth in 40 BCE, or P. Memmius

Cleander, *IIvir quinqu(ennalis)* in 66–7 CE.[25] So in the real world Thiasus' full name would have been something like C. Iulius C.f. Thiasus. Local magistrates took up office on 1 January and so Thiasus' *munus*, although promised before he took up office, as we shall see (see below, p. 284), actually took place in February or March (see above, p. 281), that is, early in his year in office as local censor. As we shall see, the preparations for it were elaborate and would have taken several months to carry out.

Corinth had since the establishment of the Roman colony there in 44 BCE become one of the main centres of gladiatorial spectacle in the Greek world.[26] Indeed a number of Greek writers of the imperial period specifically attack the Corinthians for their love of this quintessentially Roman cultural practice. Both Dio Chrysostom (*Or.* 31.121) and Philostratus (*V S* 4.22) criticize the Athenians for even thinking of putting on gladiatorial spectacles in their city "in emulation of those bloodthirsty Corinthians." At the opposite end of the Mediterranean, the charter of another Caesarian colonial foundation, the Colonia Genetiva Iulia (formerly Urso) in Hispania Ulterior (later Baetica), clearly shows that the senior magistrates of a Roman colony, both the *IIviri* and aediles, were required to put on gladiatorial *munera* at some point during their tenure of office and to fund these at least partially at their own expense.[27] It is possible that a similar requirement was enforced in the Roman colonies of the Greek East as well. So at the *colonia* of Antioch in Pisidia, the aedile and *IIvir* Maximianus (whose *praenomen* and *nomen* are missing at the start of the inscription) was honoured because "during his duumvirate he had put on a two-day *munus* of beast-hunts and gladiators."[28] There is another possible case from Dyrrachium in Epirus, where a *IIvir quinquennalis* put on a gladiatorial *munus* at the dedication of a public library that he had funded; he was also *pontifex* and patron of the colony, but it is not clear at what point of his public career this Roman equestrian undertook the construction project and its concomitant munificent spectacle.[29] The best parallels, however, come from Roman Italy and the western provinces, where exactly the same process as Apuleius describes for Thiasus is attested on honorific inscriptions. At Paestum, for example, the decurions voted a statue be erected for a local *IIvir quinquennalis* "in return for his munificence in being the first to put on a gladiatorial troupe through his own liberality in return for holding office as *quinquennalis*."[30] At Corfinium in Samnium, an interesting hierarchy is revealed of the kind of public entertainments local politicians would put on at the various stages of their political career. In the later second century, Q. Avelius Priscus was honoured for a whole series of munificent acts that included games for the goddess Vetidina when he was aedile, *ludi scaenici* when he was *quattuorvir* (the equivalent in a *municipium* of a *IIvir* in a colony), and a gladiatorial *munus* "to mark his holding of quinquennial power."[31] And this same hierarchy of spectacles seems to have been observed at Pompeii in the first century CE by A. Clodius Flaccus. He held the duumvirate twice and was *IIvir quinquennalis* once; it was only when he was *quinquennalis* that he included gladiators among the entertainments that he sponsored.[32] It would appear, therefore, that Thiasus, as *IIvir quinquennalis* of Corinth, was putting on his spectacle as a direct consequence of his holding of public office.

So Apuleius' narrative, if we are correct in our precise reading of it, underlines the role the local elite played in the sponsorship of public entertainments, but highlights that it was not just magistrates who felt the need to expend some of their considerable wealth for the public good. On occasion, private acts of munificence were also possible and may well have been the norm in smaller centres such as Plataea. More interestingly, Apuleius' narrative allows us to reconstruct something of the reciprocal dialogue that took place between the sponsors of gladiatorial spectacles in provincial cities and their fellow citizens. It is possible to isolate five acts in this social drama.

Act 1: *Pollicitatio*

The sequence began when the sponsor made a formal promise (*pollicitatio*) to put on the *munus*. In Thiasus' case, this occurred at the assembly at which the citizens of Corinth gathered to "nominate" him to the highest magistracy in the Roman colony, the duovirate. Apuleius describes this formal act in the following terms (10.18.1): *ut splendori capessendorum responderet fascium, munus gladiatorium triduani spectaculi pollicitus latius munificentiam suam porrigebat* ("To respond to the honour of receiving the *fasces,* he promised a *munus gladiatorium* comprising a three-day spectacle in a generous sharing of his munificence"). Thiasus' promise is explicitly represented as a direct response to the people's act of nomination. Such a *pollicitatio* was a legally binding form of contract between the magistrate-elect and the community and could be the object of litigation, if the magistrate tried to renege on his word.[33] Apuleius' use of the formal legal term *pollicitatio* helps us understand the solemn and binding nature of the promise.[34] Its importance is underlined in a number of commemorative inscriptions honouring benefactors for their munificence: for example, at Pisidian Antioch the local *pontifex* L. Calpurnius Longus was enthusiastically praised on the base of the statue erected in his honour for the beast hunts, the thirty-six pairs of gladiators, and the *sparsiones* ("sprinklings") that he provided during an eight-day celebration; but the formal *pollicitatio* is explicitly recalled at the start of the text: "he was the first to promise a gladiatorial *munus* ... and within two months built a wooden amphitheatre."[35] In one case from

Carthage, dated to 133 CE, the inscription on the base of an honorific statue outlines very precisely the details of the *pollicitatio* made by a local *IIvir quinquennalis*: Q. Voltedius Optatus Aurelianus made a concrete promise of HS 200,000, which he paid into the local treasury and then supplemented by another HS 38,000, to allow him to stage four days of gladiators and wild-beast hunts in return for his holding of the office (*ob honorem*).[36] The *pollicitatio* was a formal act, a very public ritual, in which magistrate-elect and local citizenry sealed a social contract, as it were, with pledges made on both sides to guarantee how the magistracy would be performed.

Act 2: Preparing for the *munus*

Apuleius pays considerable attention to the elaborate preparations that Thiasus then made for his *munus*. These include a heavily publicized expedition to Thessaly to procure "the most renowned wild beasts" and the "most famous gladiators" (10.18.2: *tunc Thessaliam etiam accesserat, nobilissimas feras et famosos inde gladiatores comparaturus*). Thessaly could boast at least one relatively important gladiatorial centre, Larissa, from where some gladiators' epitaphs have survived and which Apuleius mentions (1.7.6) as the site of an upcoming *munus gladiatorium* in Book I, as we have seen (above, p. 278).[37] Perhaps this was where Thiasus was planning to acquire his gladiators and wild beasts.

He made this journey, Apuleius explicitly tells us, "through a desire to win public glory" (10.18.2: *gloriae publicae studio*). The care taken over preparations bore a direct relationship to the renown he would gain for sponsoring such a spectacle. Furthermore, by the size and splendour of his entourage for this mission, Thiasus ensured that popular attention focused on his upcoming act of munificence well before its staging. Apuleius spares nothing in his detailed and highly visual description of the expedition, in particular the splendid carriages and wagons (both covered and uncovered) and the thoroughbred horses (Thessalian and Gallic) that were involved. We hear about all these in Apuleius' description of the return leg of the trip, when Thiasus rather paradoxically elects to ride back home on the ass (10.18.3):

> spretis luculentis illis suis vehiculis ac posthabitis decoris raedarum carpentis, quae partim contecta, partim revelata frustra novissimis trahebantur consequiis, equis etiam Thessalicis et aliis iumentis Gallicanis, quibus generosa suboles perhibet pretiosam dignitatem.

He spurned those splendid carriages of his and relegated the decorous four-wheeled wagons, which followed behind unused, some covered, others open, at the very end of the retinue. Likewise he spurned his Thessalian horses and other Gallic beasts, whose noble breeding ensure their high-priced esteem.

Even though Thiasus preferred to ride on a humble ass, the ass was decked out with all sorts of precious decorations, as Lucius/the ass himself relates (10.18.4): *me phaleris aureis et fucatis ephippiis et purpureis tapetis et frenis argenteis et pictilibus balteis et tintinnabulis perargutis exornatum* ("I was decked out with gold discs and dyed caparisons and crimson tapestries and silvered bridle and decorated halter and shrill tinkling bells"). These "shrill tinkling" bells helped further to ensure that no one could avoid hearing and noticing the splendid procession as it wended its way back to Corinth. It served to publicize Thiasus' upcoming *munus*, but also in the process enhanced his reputation for generosity well beyond the confines of his hometown.

So too in describing Demochares' ill-fated *munus* at Plataea, Apuleius lingers over the preparations and the generosity that his presentation involved (4.13.2): *nam vir et genere primarius et opibus plurimus et liberalitate praecipuus digno fortunae suae splendore publicas voluptates instruebat* ("A man of high birth, great wealth and liberality, he was preparing pleasures for the people of a brilliance to match his own fortune"). Apuleius then makes sure his readers are concentrating by pausing to interject a rhetorical question before enumerating more specifically what Demochares provided (4.13.3): *quis tantus ingenii, quis facundiae, qui singulas species apparatus multiiugi verbis idoneis posset explicare?* ("Who has sufficient talent, sufficient eloquence to find the right words to describe each element of the multi-faceted show?"). And then the three types of performers Demochares enlisted are carefully delineated (4.13.4): *gladiatores isti famosae manus, venatores illi probatae pernicitatis, alibi noxii perdita securitate suis epulis bestiarum saginas instruentes* ("There were gladiators of renowned strength, beast-hunters of proven agility, and criminals [*noxii*] too without hope of reprieve, who were to provide a banquet of themselves to fatten the beasts"); or, in other words, the performers needed to put on a full *munus iustum atque legitimum*, which since the mid-first century CE had crystallized in form to comprise beast hunts in the morning, executions of criminals in the middle of the day, and gladiators in the afternoon.[38] In his carefully chosen phraseology Apuleius emphasizes the quality of the performers: gladiators of "renowned" fighting prowess and physical strength, but also perhaps from a renowned troupe of gladiators (with a rhetorical play on the sense of *manus*);[39] beast hunters of "proven agility"; and criminals "without any hope of reprieve" (*perdida securitate*) and so able to have the worst sorts of physical atrocities inflicted upon them.

We then get a detailed and very complicated description of the stage machinery that was to be used in the arena, essential apparatus to make a show memorable (4.13.5): some sort of wooden contraptions (*confixilis machinae sublicae*), towers of scaffolding that functioned like a house on wheels (*turres tabularum nexibus ad instar circumforaneae domus*), colourful paintings (*floridae picturae*), and decorated "receptacles for the upcoming beast hunt" (*decora futurae venationis receptacula*) – perhaps cages from which the wild beasts would be released into the arena at Demochares' *venatio*.[40] Here Apuleius stresses the wondrously artful design and elaborate decoration of these elements, which would certainly have enhanced the effect of the spectacle. Preparations for the physical staging of the *munus* were just as important, it would appear, as supplying the necessary performers.

Similarly, the scenery and staging details for the pantomime "The Judgment of Paris" that formed part of Thiasus' *munus* in Corinth are lovingly described in Book 10: a wooden mountain was constructed "with supreme craftsmanship" to resemble Mt Ida, planted with bushes and trees, and with a man-made fountain pouring water down its slopes (10.30.1: *mons ligneus ... sublimi instructus fabrica, consitus virectis et vivis arboribus, summo cacumine de minibus fabri fonti manante fluviales aquas eliquans*).[41] In a number of the laudatory texts carved on the bases of statues honouring them for their spectacles, sponsors of municipal *munera* in Italy were praised for the quality of the *apparatus* (i.e., stage machinery, scenery, and the overall *mise-en-scène*) they had provided.[42] Apuleius' rich descriptions in both Book 4 and Book 10 allow us to flesh out more clearly the rather anodyne praise for the quality of the *apparatus* found in these honorific inscriptions.

In his account of Demochares' preparations in Book 4, Apuleius saves the wild beasts till last. Interjected exclamations help to focus the reader's attention (4.13.6): *qui praeterea numerus, quae facies ferarum!* ("What a quantity, what a fine look did the wild beasts have!").[43] Using a portentously mock-solemn periphrasis to describe them (*generosa illa damnatorum capitum funera*, "those noble sepulchres of the condemned individuals"),[44] Apuleius goes on to explore (4.13.6) the "exceptional pains" (*praecipuo studio*) that Demochares had taken to acquire them "from abroad" (*foris*). In particular, he emphasizes the enormous cost and socially competitive outlay that this *munus* required (4.13.7): *praeter ceteram speciosi muneris supellectilem totis utcumque patrimonii viribus immanis ursae comparabat numerum copiosum* ("Besides the other furnishings of this sparkling spectacle, he used the total resources of his inheritance (*patrimonii*) to acquire a large band of enormous bears"). Some of these bears were hunted down by his household staff (*domesticis venationibus captas*), we are told, others purchased on the open market at very high prices (*largis emptionibus partas*), while still more were acquired from friends, who competed to provide the best gifts for his show (*amicorum etiam donationibus variis certatim oblatas*) (4.13.8).

Later in the story the robbers who are the narrators of this particular tale admit that they had managed to discover the name of one of Demochares' closest friends, Nicanor from Thrace, and forged a letter from him to accompany a special cage containing one of their robber band, Thrasyleon, dressed up in a bearskin to resemble a huge bear. Their aim was to convince Demochares that Nicanor "as a good friend of his was, it appeared, presenting him with the first fruits of his own hunt to embellish his *munus*" (4.16.1: *venationis suae primitias bonus amicus videretur ornando muneri dedicasse*). Demochares exulted in his friend's apparent generosity (4.16.3: *suique contubernalis opportuna liberalitate laetatus*) and reciprocated by rewarding the supposed attendants 10 *aurei* for escorting Nicanor's "gift."

This partial reliance on the generosity of friends echoes the well-known case of M. Caelius Rufus, who as aedile elect in 51 BCE pestered Cicero with a string of letters, asking the then proconsul of Cilicia to acquire panthers for the games that he would be required to sponsor during his aedileship in 50 BCE.[45] The same process was still in place in the late fourth century CE when Symmachus contacted various friends in the provinces to request they contribute various types of wild beast for his son's quaestorian games in Rome.[46] Apuleius' remarks provide some insight into the logistical difficulties that any local sponsor of such *munera* had to confront. At a higher level, the Roman emperor had a whole infrastructure, involving the Roman army, to ensure a sufficient supply of wild beasts for his presentations in the city of Rome. If needs be, a provincial governor could be instructed to use detachments from the Roman army to help muster the animals needed, as an altar set up in 147 CE at the sanctuary of Diana and Apollo at Montana in Moesia Inferior illustrates. It was dedicated to Diana by a military tribune of an auxiliary cohort operating with the support of vexillations from two legions and the Black Sea fleet (the *classis Flavia Moesica*) "after bears and bison had been successfully captured for the purposes of an imperial *venatio* (*ob venationem Caesarianam*) as enjoined by Cl(audius) Saturninus, *leg(atus) Aug(usti) pr(o) pr(aetore)*," i.e., the provincial governor of Moesia Inferior.[47] And sometimes private connections were relied upon to request *venatores* for provincial spectacles, as when Libanius used his influence with Andronicus, governor of Phoenicia, to assist his cousin acquire hunters in 360 CE for the wild-beast shows the latter had to put on in Antioch in his capacity as Syriarch (*Ep.* 217).[48]

The painted announcements of upcoming *munera* from the walls of Pompeii allow us to capture something of the excitement and gratitude expressed by the local citizenry in advance of their actual staging. For in addition to the details of the date and place of the *munus*, they often include a brief acclamation of the sponsor. For example, the following notice was painted on a wall in the so-called Via della Fortuna near the Nola Gate:[49]

Thirty pairs of gladiators and substitutes for them, the property of Cn. Alleius Nigidius Maius, *quinquennalis*, will fight at Pompeii on 24, 25, and 26 November. There will be a *venatio* and Ellios (?? [Gav]ellius) will be present. Good luck to Maius, *quinquennalis*. Paris [painted (this notice).] Martialis greets Maius.

The preparations for such a *munus* were thus not just an opportunity for the elite to demonstrate its economic and social power to citizens of lower rank, but they also involved public gestures of the giving and receiving of gifts between social peers.[50] The distinctions of the social hierarchy were reinforced, it is clear, but so too was the social solidarity of the elite and the importance of bonds of friendship within it.

Act 3: *Adventus* of the *munerarius*

For insights into the next act, we must return to Corinth. When Thiasus' entourage reaches the outskirts of the colony on its return from Thessaly with its supply of gladiators and wild beasts in tow, a large crowd gathers to welcome their benefactor home: a local analogue of an imperial *adventus*.[51] The arrival of the procession provided another occasion for advertising the "most renowned" wild beasts and the "most famous" gladiators that Thiasus had procured on his trip, but also for further acclamations of the local benefactor. Apuleius hints at this when he has the narrator Lucius/the ass remark – with a touch of immodesty – that the crowds had turned out not just to honour Thiasus, but in a desire to gain a sighting of the now famous ass (10.19.1: *magnae civium turbae confluebant ... non tantum Thiasi studentes honori quam mei conspectus cupientes*). Some of them, no doubt, were anxious to see the gladiators and wild beasts too. We may here recall that the ass has already commented a few chapters earlier that his almost human exploits as an entertainment at dinner parties had already made his owner "illustrious and famous" (10.17.6: *conspectum atque famigerabilem meis miris artibus effeceram dominum*). The quality and skills of performers clearly enhanced the prestige of the *munerarius*; and this was often expressed in the form of very public, very audible acclamations.

Apuleius conveys this graphically in his account of the *munus* at Plataea, when he reports on the reaction of the townspeople once Demochares acquires the gift of a huge bear, or so it would appear, from a close friend to replace those that had been wiped out through heat, exhaustion, and disease: "By the unanimous voice of the citizenry," we are told, "Demochares was more than once pronounced quite lucky and blessed (*felix ac beatus*) because after so great a disaster to his wild-beasts with this new arrival he had somehow managed to thwart Fortune" (4.16.5: *consonaque civium voce satis felix ac beatus Demochares ille saepe celebratus, quod post tantam cladem ferarum novo proventu quoquo modo fortunae resisteret*). The language Apuleius uses here – especially the rhetorical conceit of the "unanimous voice of the people" (*consona civium voce*), the use of the terms *felix* and *beatus*, and the idea of overcoming fortune – is highly reminiscent of the language of acclamations in general and those connected with the arena in particular. Thus Martial claims that the crowd at the inauguration of the Flavian Amphitheatre in 80 CE, although made up people of many diverse languages, nevertheless chanted in unison (*vox una*) when acclaiming Titus as *pater patriae* (*Spect.* 3.11–12: *vox diversa sonat populorum, tum tamen una est, | cum verus patriae diceris esse pater*).[52] The notion of "felicity" (*felicitas*) is amply represented in the acclamations for Commodus that were recorded on a marble plaque set up in Rome in the meeting place of the college of Silvanus Augustus, whose membership included a large number of gladiators (*CIL* VI 632 = *ILS* 5084a = *EAOR* I 46): *felici imperatori omnia felicia! salvo Commodo felix familia*! ("All felicities to our felicitous emperor! So long as Commodus is healthy our gladiatorial troupe will be felicitous!").

Act 4: The Performances in the Arena

Enough can be gleaned from the incomplete treatments of the *munera* at Plataea and Corinth to allow us to reconstruct something of the elaborate program of events that Demochares and Thiasus respectively devised on each of these occasions. In Apuleius' mind and in actual practice, *munera gladiatoria* (the specific phrase is used at 4.13.2 and 10.18.1) involved more than gladiators. As we have seen (above, p. 286), at Plataea Demochares lined up not just gladiators, but also beast hunters and criminals to be executed in the arena; in other words, a standard program for a full-scale *munus legitimum* comprising morning beast hunts and midday executions, with gladiatorial combats in the afternoon. The heat exhaustion and subsequent epidemic that caused the death of all the bears – or, to use Apuleius' memorable formulation, "the animal wreckage of their moribund carcasses lying scattered all over the place in most of the streets" (4.14.3: *passim per plateas plurimas cerneres iacere semivivorum corporum ferina naufragia*) – prevented Demochares' *venatio* and gladiatorial combats from taking place, but a clever novelistic device provides Apuleius' readers with a substitute *munus*.[53] First, the ordinary people, "forced by ignorant poverty with no taste in their choice of food to seek the filthiest supplements and free meals for their shrunken bellies" (4.14.3: *vulgus ignobile, quos inculta pauperies sine delectu ciborum tenuato ventri cogit sordentia supplementa et dapes gratuitas conquirere*), get to feast off the dead bears' carcasses rather than through gifts scattered among the audience at an actual spectacle (*missilia*).[54] Second, Thrasyleon's dressing up as a bear results in a large crowd streaming in to marvel at this fine specimen (4.16.4: *multi numero mirabundi bestiam confluebant*) and then to acclaim their civic benefactor Demochares, as we have seen (above, p. 290). Third, when one of his household slaves sees the supposed bear running loose in the yard of Demochares' house at night and summons a group of slaves to round it up, this leads to a sort of *venatio*, with Thrasyleon eventually surrounded by packs of savage dogs to be lacerated by their bites (4.19–20). And then a kind of gladiatorial combat ensures, in which Thrasyleon fights bravely against human and animal foes to the end, despite being transfixed by a lance and torn apart by the dogs, winning "glory" (4.21.6: *a gloria non perivit*) for his stout efforts before being put out of his misery by a butcher, who uses his knife to cut open his belly (4.21.5: *lanius Paulo fidentior, utero bestiae resecto, ursae magnificum despoliavit latronem*). So in the end the novel's readers get to experience, if only vicariously, a *venatio*, gladiatorial combat, and public execution, even if the actual denizens of Plataea were frustrated in this regard.

At Corinth, Thiasus' three-day presentation (10.18.1: *munus gladiatorium triduani spectaculi*) was much more elaborate. The first day began with a parade through the streets to the theatre where the spectacle was to take place. So the ass was "led to the outside wall of the auditorium in a ceremonial procession escorted by an enthusiastic crowd of onlookers" (10.29.3: *ad consaeptum caveae prosequente pompatico favore deducor*). The *pompaticus favor* clearly alludes to the parade (*pompa*) of gladiators with which most *munera gladiatoria* began, and we must presume that the other performers also formed part of this procession. The parade of the gladiators is explicitly mentioned in the pseudo-Quintilianic declamation concerning a rich man's son ransomed from a gladiatorial school, but disowned by his father (ps.-Quint. *Decl.* 9.6), while a relief panel from a funerary monument of a local benefactor from the necropolis near the Stabian Gate at Pompeii shows in its upper register this very kind of parade. It is led off by two lictors who, together with musicians, precede the local magistrate, commemorated as the *editor* of the *munus*, and he is immediately followed by gladiators carrying their shields or helmets. Scenes from the gladiatorial combats and beast hunts were represented in the central and lower registers below. For this local magistrate's family, the parade was seen as an integral part of the spectacle that he sponsored and worthy of commemoration on the monument that was designed to allow his act of munificence to live on in the community's memory long after his death.[55]

Apuleius then provides a vivid account of the complex program of events staged on the opening day alone of Thiasus' three-day *munus*. The spectacle opens with a Pyrrhic dance, in which antiphonal choruses of boys and girls perform an elaborately choreographed dance to the accompaniment of horns (10.29.4–5). Apuleius is careful to describe it as a Pyrrhic dance performed "in the Greek style" (10.29.4: *Graecanicam saltaturi pyrricam*). This "dance in armour" had originated in Crete and was then adopted by the Spartans, for whom it became something approaching a national dance before being introduced to Athens, where it was integrated into the Panathenaic festival. During the fourth century BCE it lost its military character altogether, and once it had been introduced at Rome it gradually became more and more lascivious, often approaching a pantomime. It was also transformed into a spectacle of public execution at Rome, with the "performers" being whipped and wounded and even cremated to death for the edification of the spectators.[56] This, however, is not what Apuleius is describing; the executions would come later in the day. Thiasus, it seems, put on a traditional Greek Pyrrhic, performed by freeborn boys and girls, a dance similar to those staged by Roman emperors in Rome: for example, at the Ludi Palatini at which Caligula was murdered in 41 CE or at Claudius' victory games after his British triumph in 44, where youths were summoned from Asia Minor to perform.[57]

The Pyrrhic dance was followed by a very elaborately staged pantomime, "The Judgment of Paris" (10.30.1–34.1).[58] As we have seen, Apuleius goes into luxuriant detail in describing the scenery (see above, p. 287), and he loses no opportunity to linger – in almost voyeuristic tones – over the physical charms and rich costumes of the performers: not just the protagonists Paris and Venus, but even the attendants of the main characters: the "radiantly beautiful boy" playing Mercury, "naked except for his ephebic *chlamys* covering his left shoulder" with his eye-catching blond curls (10.30.3–4: *adest luculentus puer, nudus nisi quod ephebica chlamida sinistrum tegebat umerum, flavis crinibus usquequaque conspicuus*) or the "crowd of very happy little boys" playing Cupids, "those soft, round, milky-skinned little boys" who surrounded Venus (10.32.1: *circumfuso populo laetissimorum parvulorum; ... illos teretes et lacteos puellos ... Cupidines*). He also conveys a sense of the rich variety and quality of the musical accompaniment: the martial tones in Dorian mode of the pipe, modulating "deep growls with shrill whistles like a war-trumpet," which intensified the energy level of the rapid dance (10.31.5: *tibicen Dorium canebat bellicosum et, permiscens bombis gravibus tinnitus acutos in modum tubae, saltationis agilis vigorem suscitabat*), or the Lydian modes of the flutes "in sweet harmony ... charming the spectators' hearts" (10.32.2–3: *tibiae multiforabiles cantus Lydios dulciter consonant. quibus spectatorum pectora suave mulcentibus*). Apuleius is also keen to describe several dramatic stage effects with which the performance ended: pipes hidden within the mountain spurted "saffron dissolved in wine" (*vino crocus diluta*) over the animals grazing on the mountainside, transforming the white goats into golden ones and filling the whole theatre with a "delightful fragrance." Visual, aural, and olfactory pleasures all contribute to the overall impact of the spectacle. And then – as a final *coup de théâtre* – the stage floor suddenly opened up to swallow the entire mountain (10.34.2: *tota suave fraglante cavea montem illum ligneum terrae vorago decepit*). The picture Apuleius conveys is of a pantomime of superb quality and striking stage effects. The *munerarius* Thiasus would have gained still more plaudits for the "amazing," "spectacular" nature of this part of his show and Apuleius does pause to comment on the loud applause – the *magnus favor* – that rang out from the audience, when the star pantomime made her entrance as Venus (10.32.1: *Venus ecce cum magno favore caveae in ipso meditullio scaenae ... dulce surridens constitit amoene*).

The auditorium is then prepared for the third element of the day's entertainment: the *venatio*, which is to open with the striking "fatal charade" of a condemned woman forced to undergo sexual intercourse with the now famous performing ass in, once again, a lavish stage setting. Just before this fatal drama is to begin, the ass makes his escape for Cenchreae, and so we do not actually hear anything more of the details of the day's program. But two points are worth emphasizing: first, the crowd is becoming impatient and it is in response to their requests that a Roman soldier runs across the stage floor in front of the crowd and goes off to fetch the condemned criminal from the "public prison" (10.34.3: *ecce quidam miles per mediam plateam dirigit cursum, petiturus iam populo postulante illam de publico carcere mulierem, quam dixi propter multiforme scelus bestiis esse damnatam*). In the gladiatorial arena at Rome, the crowd could occasionally demand the appearance of a particular gladiator or condemned criminal, as when during the reign of Caligula they demanded that a particular bandit called Tetrinius be brought into the arena for punishment or when under

Claudius they called for a particular gladiator to appear and fight.[59] Hence Apuleius confirms that the arena crowd could help to accelerate or sometimes modify even a well-planned program. The second point is the luxuriant and emphatic way in which Apuleius describes the stage setting for the woman's execution (10.34.4): *et iam torus genialis scilicet noster futurus accuratissime disternebatur lectus Indica testudine perlucidus, plumea congerie tumidus, veste serica floridus* ("a bed, evidently meant to serve as our marriage bed (*torus genialis*) was being very carefully prepared: it shone with Indian tortoiseshell, bulging with feather cushions and brightly decorated with silk covers"). Just as the scenery was crucial for the overall effect of the "Judgment of Paris" pantomime, so too was the *apparatus* for public executions and connected *venationes*.[60] And it is clear from the narrative that the execution is to be just one part of a more complex *venatio*. For not only does Apuleius remark that some of the attendants were "occupied with preparations for the *venatio*" (10.35.1: *tota familia partim ministerio venationis occupata, partim voluptario spectaculo attonita*), but the ass is terrified that when he and the condemned criminal are locked together in their potentially fatal coital embrace, the wild beasts are not going to be able to differentiate quickly enough between the criminal, whom they are supposed to devour, and the innocent performing ass, whom they should, strictly speaking, be careful to spare (10.34.5). So it appears that two possible means of execution are envisaged: either the condemned woman will die in the act of intercourse with the ass – and here readers will recall the ass's worries just before having sex with the Corinthian matron that he is going to rupture the noble lady (10.22.1) and as an ironic result get thrown to the wild beasts himself in Thiasus' upcoming *munus gladiatorium* (10.22.2) – or she will be mangled to death once the wild beasts have been unleashed into the arena.

It might be thought that the "passion of Pasiphae" act is so over the top as to be simply an exuberant fictional element taken over by Apuleius from the original Greek version of the novel to embellish his narrative: just another outlandish tale in a work full of well-told, if often bizarre, stories.[61] But, as Kathleen Coleman has so persuasively shown, public executions were frequently staged at Rome in which the condemned were required to take on roles from myth: to borrow her memorable term, "fatal charades." And we know of at least two other occasions on which female criminals were forced to play the role of Pasiphae being penetrated by a bull during executions in the arena at Rome, first under Nero and then at the games that inaugurated the Flavian Amphitheatre in 80 CE.[62] And executions of all sorts were frequently staged as part of *munera gladiatoria* in the city of Rome, where they often occupied the middle part of the day after the completion of the *venatio* and before the start of the afternoon's gladiatorial combats; it was these lunchtime executions, the so-called *meridianum spectaculum*, that elicited the disgust of the younger Seneca (*Ep.* 7.3–5). Sponsors of municipal *munera* were sometimes able to add executions to their programs, increasingly, it seems, during the second century CE.[63] The *senatus consultum* of 177 limiting expenditures on gladiatorial spectacles mentions as if it were a regular practice the fact that imperial procurators sold condemned prisoners to local *lanistae*, who in turn could furnish local *munerarii* with such performers for their spectacles; the senatorial resolution sets a maximum price of six *aurei* per criminal.[64] And, as we have seen, earlier in the novel Demochares was planning to stage the execution of a number of criminals who had been condemned *ad bestias* as part of his *munus* at Plataea (4.13.4; see above, p. 286).[65]

So even though we are denied a description of the execution, the *venatio* proper, or the gladiatorial combats that must have followed, Apuleius' account as it stands provides a rich picture of the complexity of the program of the *munus* staged by the local magistrate at Corinth. The interweaving of dance, pantomime, wild-beast hunts, executions, and gladiators formed a varied program of entertainments, and Apuleius' narrative allows us to see the importance of the stage effects and scenery for each of the given events. Thiasus would have received the applause of the crowd as many points during his three-day *munus*. Of this, we hear mere snippets. First, we are told that the opening parade (or *pompa*) in which the ass (and, we must presume, the other performers including the gladiators) took part was very enthusiastically received by the crowd (10.29.3: *ad consaeptum caveae prosequente populo pompatico favore deducor*). Acclamations on his entry into the arena, acclamations at certain key moments of the entertainment, and most of all the interplay between him and the crowd when he was called upon to preside during the gladiatorial combats would have conveyed once again the crowd's gratitude and enhanced Thiasus' social and political position. An early third-century mosaic from Smirat near Thysdrus in the province of Africa [Figure 14.1] that commemorates a *munus gladiatorium* put on by a certain Magerius brings out the vigour and liveliness of this dialogue between the crowd and a generous sponsor. The *munerarius* is addressed twice by name in the vocative, *Mageri* ("Magerius!"), at the left and right side of the mosaic, and the acclamations he received from the crowd are recorded right next to the image of an attendant carrying a tray with four bags of prize money for the wild-beast hunters, each marked with the symbol for 1,000 (∞) (*AE* 1967, 549):[66]

Figure 14.1 Mosaic from a villa at Smirat, near Thysdrus, Africa Proconsularis, showing elements from a *munus* involving a wild-beast hunt (*venatio*), with (in the centre) lengthy acclamations for Magerius, the sponsor of the public spectacle and most probably the owner of the villa. Sousse Museum. Photo: © Vanni Archive / Art Resource, NY.

adclamatum est. | exemplo tuo mu|nus sic discant | futuri! audiant | praeteriti! unde | tale? quando tale? | exemplo quaesto|rum munus edes! | de re tua mu|nus edes! (i) sta dies! | Magerius do|nat. hoc est habe|re! hoc est posse! | hoc est! ia(m) nox est. | ia(m) munere tuo | saccis missos.

The acclamations were: By your example let future generations learn that a *munus* was staged like this! Let past generations hear about it! From where did such a show originate? When did such a show take place? You will put on a *munus* as an example for the quaestors (sc., in Rome)! You will put it on at your own expense! This is your day! Magerius donates! This is what it is to possess wealth! This is what it is to have power! This is it! Now it is night. Now they have been dismissed from your *munus* with their bags (of money).

The relationship of course could turn hostile, and at Thiasus' *munus* the crowd, as we have seen (above, p. 293) urgently demanded (10.34.3: *populo postulante*) the appearance of the condemned criminal. But usually the *munerarius* would preside enjoying the general good cheer (*hilaritas*) and acclaim of the crowd.

Act 5: Expressions of Gratitude

Following the *munus*, further rituals would have taken place, as the citizen body and the local town council expressed their thanks to the *munerarius* for the splendour of his show. In fact, much of our evidence for *munera* in the municipalities of Italy and the Roman provinces stems directly from this phase of the reciprocal discourse: that is, the texts inscribed on the bases of commemorative statues honouring worthy *munerarii*, which are often replete with expressions of thanks.[67] A particularly fulsome example of this genre, an inscription of ca. 150 CE from Palermo in Sicily, illustrates the very vocal expression of the community's gratitude and the modest response of the benefactor:[68]

...... [- - - l]ạudabili munerario qui indulgentia | [sacra cum munus - - - ex]hibuit illut meruit optando quod voluit | [et universis civibus - - - ed]itionem gratissimam reddidit quod die|[bus - - - populum per multa]s horas theatri voluptas tenuit et hilaris | [totus in harenam - - - inde a] meridie transiit, in qua miratus honestissimum | [apparatum instructum - - - omni] genere herbariarum et numerosas orientales | [feras versatusque - - - inde a] meridie in utriusque caveis varis missionibus | [delectatus est idemque ex indulg]entia sacra specialiter meruit at cultum | [epulum instructumque - - - a]mplissimo apparatu cives suos universos | [ut vocaret. cui cum populus propter] voluptates honeste exhibitas ad augendum |[optimi viri honorificentiam freq]uentissimis vocibus bigas centuriatim | [postulasset motus - - - verec]undia quod esset duabus bigiis et equestrib(us) | [statuis tribus ? contentus - - -] ...

... (in honour of) a praiseworthy *munerarius* who thanks to the sacred indulgence (sc., of the emperor) exhibited [a ... *munus*] which lived up to all expectations [and for all the citizens] he gave back a most pleasing production (*editio*), at which over [...] days the pleasure of the theatre occupied [the people for many] hours and the people in total good cheer crossed [from there to the arena at] midday; in that (arena), the people marvelled at the very distinguished [apparatus that had been prepared ... with every] kind of herbivores and numerous oriental [wild beasts and ... from] midday onwards in both auditoria [they took delight] in the various acts put on. [And thanks to] the sacred [indulgence (sc., of the emperor)] he proved particularly worthy [in summoning] all his fellow citizens to an elegant [banquet, prepared] with most ample accoutrements (*apparatus*). [And when the people demanded] with most frequent requests that statues of him in a two-horse chariot (*biga*) be set up by centuries (i.e., in all the districts of the city) in his honour to increase the dignity of this excellent man on account of the pleasures that he had splendidly provided, in modesty he was content with two two-horse-chariot statues and [?three] equestrian statues ...

The day on which such statues were publicly dedicated marked the final stage of this ritual sequence. It provided yet another occasion for the community to gather and recall the benefactor's munificence and to thank him very publicly for it; and of course the *munerarius* would take the chance to respond yet again with his own speech of thanks. Apuleius was perfectly familiar with this discourse. He himself received honorific statues in several cities of the province of Africa and excerpts from the speech he made in the 160s to thank the local elite of Carthage for the statue they voted in his honour is preserved in his collection of speeches, the *Florida* (*Flor.* 16).[69] So it is not surprising that his ear is well attuned to the rhetorical rituals involved in the sponsoring of *munera gladiatoria* and he gives them a prominent place in his narratives of the fictional *munera* incorporated within his novel.

Conclusion

The gladiatorial narratives of Apuleius' *Metamorphoses*, therefore, allow us to piece together, if sometimes only partially, the sequence of highly ritualized, but potent, acts of reciprocal communication that took place between members of the local elite and the ordinary citizenry during the preparations for, the celebration of, and the subsequent paying of thanks for *munera gladiatoria* staged in provincial towns across the Roman Empire. More than any other source, Apuleius' novel emphasizes the social motivation that lay behind such acts of generosity by the local elite and illustrates the important role that ordinary citizens played in the manner in which *munera* were received and remembered in the communities of the Roman Empire. Reading between the lines of the carnivalesque representations of arena spectacles helps us to enter, at least partially, into the real world of local productions in the amphitheatres of the Roman provinces and to gain some conceptual understanding of how the local elite and the ordinary citizens experienced these often lavish entertainments. Without Apuleius' vivid arena narratives, even if they are interrupted, abruptly truncated, and fail to cover any *munus* in its entirety, we would have a much poorer appreciation of the reciprocal discourse that followed a ritualized pattern and that lay at the very heart of the *munera* put on in the Roman provinces.

NOTES

* Throughout her distinguished career Elaine Fantham has explored the intersection between Latin literature and Roman social and cultural life across a wide variety of genres and periods. This study (in part inspired by Fantham

1995; 1996: 252–63; 2013: 237–46) is offered by a fellow Liverpudlian émigré to Canada as a small token of gratitude for the inspiration she has provided to countless Latinists and Roman social and cultural historians over many years on both sides of the Atlantic. A briefer version of this paper was presented at the Annual Meeting of the American Philological Association in New Orleans in 2003, and I am grateful to the audience for their comments on that occasion, especially Ewen Bowie, Erich Gruen, Stephen Harrison, and Maaike Zimmerman. The text used throughout is Zimmerman 2012; the translations are taken from the Loeb edition of Hanson 1989, though sometimes with some slight modifications of my own.

1 For "fatal charades," Coleman 1990.

2 On the relationship between Apuleius' text and its Greek predecessors, see Mason 1978, 1994, 1999; Holzberg 1984; Zimmerman 2002; Finkelpearl 2007.

3 For the Roman provincial contexts in which Apuleius lived and wrote, see Harrison 2000: 1–38; Sandy 1997; Graverini 2002; Bradley 2004. For a broad Roman audience, including provincials, see Graverini 2002; cf. Dowden 1994 (arguing for an audience in the city of Rome).

4 Millar 1981; Mason 1983; Bradley 1998, 2000a, 2000b, 2012; for contemporary culture and ideology in the novel, Harrison 2000: 235–59; for Apuleius' treatment of Corinth and for allusions to real prominent families in contemporary Greece, Jones 2014.

5 For further discussion of Apuleius' treatment of slaves in the novel, see Bradley 2000a; Vasconcelos 2009.

6 For some examples of the burgeoning literature on intertextuality in Apuleius, see Shumate 1996; Finkelpearl 1998; Graverini 2001 and 2003; Pasetti 2007; Riess 2008; Tordoff 2008; De Trane 2009. For the social mentality of this provincial world, see Millar 1981, developed by Riess 2001, with the review by Shaw 2002.

7 For this aspect, see Osgood 2006. For the *lex Iulia de maritandis ordinibus*, Treggiari 1991: 60–80.

8 For the law against harbouring fugitive slaves, cf. *Coll.* 14.3.5 (Ulpian); *Dig.* 11.4.1.1–8a (Ulpian); *CJ* 6.1.1–8; Watson 1987: 64–6, 131–2. On elements of Roman law in the *Met.*, see Norden 1912; Summers 1970; Elster 1991.

9 On the provincial flaminate in Africa, see Bassignano 1974; Fishwick 2002: 187–204. For an attempt to argue that Apuleius' priesthood was not the provincial flaminate, but perhaps a priesthood of Aesculapius, see Rives 1994.

10 For the difficulties in dating the *Metamorphoses* and for arguments that it was composed in the 170s or 180s, see Harrison 2000: 9–10.

11 Most notably Slater 2003; more briefly Connors 2008: 178. See also Freudenburg 2007 on scopophiliac elements in the novel.

12 Prandi 1988; for the Eleutheria, see *IG* VII 49.

13 Apuleius, significantly, switched the setting of the gladiatorial *munus* in Book X at the novel's *dénouement* from Thessalonica in Macedonia, the setting in the Greek version of the story (ps.-Lucian *Onos* 49), to Corinth; for the significance of this, Mason 1971.

14 On Roman Corinth, see Wiseman 1979: esp. 497–548; Hoskins Walbank 1997; Romano 2000.

15 See further Plut. *Caes.* 57; Welch 1999: 133–40 and 2007: 178–83.

16 For the dates of *munera* at Pompeii, see Tuck 2008; Cooley and Cooley 2004: 51 (Fig. 4.1), 218–19 (Appendix 1). For the announcements from Pompeii in general, see Sabbatini Tumolesi 1980.

17 For discussion of this "significant name," with parallels, see Hijmans et al. 1977: 102–4, *ad loc.* On significant names in Apuleius, see further Keulen 2000.

18 Plut. *Politika Parangelmata* 5, 29, 31 (= *Mor.* 802d, 821f, 823f).

19 On this issue, see Robert 1940: 248–53; Woolf 1994; Mann 2009, 2011: 111–25; Carter 2009.

20 For the Roman west, see Ville 1981: 175–225. For the Greek East, Robert 1940: esp. 267–80; Mann 2011: 57–64.

21 Robert (1940: 276–80) emphasizes how the local and provincial priests of the imperial cult often stressed how *philotimia* (equivalent to the Latin *liberalitas*) was involved in their acts of munificence.

22 For examples from other municipalities in Italy, see Fora 1996: 35–6, with instances from Praeneste (*CIL* XIV 3015 = *ILS* 6256 = *EAOR* IV 26), Verona (*CIL* V 3222 = *ILS* 3264 = *EAOR* II 28; *EAOR* II 29), Formiae (*AE* 1927, 124 = *EAOR* IV 19), Abella (*CIL* X 1211 = *ILS* 5058), and Puteoli (*EE* VIII 369 = *ILS* 5186 = *AE* 2005, 337).

23 Robert 1940: 78–9, no. 11, an announcement of a spectacle to be held on 16, 17, and 18 March 141 CE. In the Greek version of the novel, Thessalonica is in fact the setting for the gladiatorial *munus* at the novel's climax: ps-Lucian *Onos* 49–54.

24 For the name, Zimmerman 2000: 249–50, *ad loc.* For the local elite in Roman Corinth, see Spawforth 1996; Rizakis 2001: esp. 41–6.

25 M. Antonius Orestes and P. Memmius Cleander are two of the numerous *IIviri* (some of whom are *quinquennales*) who appear on Corinth's local coinage: see *RPC* I, nos. 1122–3 and nos. 1203–6, respectively. For these and more examples, see Spawforth 1996: 175–82.

26 For gladiatorial *munera* at Corinth, see Dio Chrys. *Or.* 31.121; Lucian *Demon.* 57; Robert 1940: 36, 38–9, 42, 117–18, nos. 60–1; *SEG* XXIX 328; Welch 1999 and 2007: 178–83.

27 *Lex col. Gen. Iul.* chs. 70–71 (*CIL* II 5439 = II^2/5, 1022 = *RS* 25): *IIviri* are to sponsor a *munus* or *ludi scaenici* for Jupiter, Juno, Minerva, and "the gods and goddesses" for four days, with each spending not less than HS 2,000 from their

own funds; aediles are to sponsor either a *munus* or *ludi scaenici* for Jupiter, Juno, and Minerva over three days, plus one day of *ludi circenses* or gladiators for Venus in the forum, with each spending no less than HS 2,000.

28 Robert 1940: 141, no. 94 (2nd – 3rd c. CE), lines 2–6: ... *qui IIv[i]|ratu suo munus v[e]|nationum et gladia[torum] | ex liberalit(ate) sua bidu[um] | dedit* ... For a possible example from the colony at Patrae (modern Patras), see Rizakis 1990: 205–8, no. 4 & pl. VIII (photo) = *AE* 1990, 888; cf. Kleijwegt 1995 = *AE* 1995, 1408.

29 *CIL* III 607 = Robert 1940: 75, no. 2 (1st half of 2nd c. CE), lines 5–8: ... *qui in comparat(ione) soli oper(i) byblio[th(ecae) sestertium] | CLXX m(ilibus) f(aciundo) | rem p(ublicam) impend(io) levavit et ob [ded(icationem) e]ius | [munus d(e)] s(ua) p(ecunia) gladiatorib(us) p(aribus) XII edi[dit - - -].*

30 *AE* 1975, 252 = *EAOR* III 9 = Fora 1996: 148, no. 156 (late 1st c. CE), lines 5–8: ... *ob munificentiam eius quot | familiam gladiatorum ex sua | liberalitate ob honorem q(uin)q(uennalitatis) | primus ediderit ...*

31 *AE* 1961, 190 = *EAOR* III 40 = Fora 1996: 151–2, no. 168 (late 2nd c. CE), lines 6–8: ... *hic ob honorem quinq(uennalitatis) munus gladiatorum edidit et ob | honorem IIIIvir(atus) ludos scaenicos dedit et ob honor(em) aedilit(atis) ludos deae Vetidinae | fecit ...*

32 *CIL* X 1074d = *ILS* 5053,4 = Sabbatini Tumolesi 1980: 17–21, no. 1 = Fora 1996: 122, no. 24 (Augustan period, after 3/2 BCE).

33 *Dig.* 50.12.1.1 (Ulpian): *si quidem ob honorem promiserit decretum sibi vel decernendum vel ob aliam iustam causam, tenebitur ex pollicitatione: sin vero sine causa promiserit, non erit obligatus* ("if someone has made a promise in return for an office granted to him or to be granted or for any other just cause, he will be bound by that promise; but if he has made a promise for no reason, he will not be obligated"); cf. 50.12.6.2 (Ulpian): *non tantum masculos, sed etiam feminas, si quid ob honores pollicitatae sunt, debere implere sciendum est* ("one must realize that not only men but also women must fulfil an undertaking if they have promised it on account of an office").

34 A similar *pollicitatio* is alluded to by Pliny in discussing his friend Maximus' *munus* at Verona: Plin. *Ep.* 6.34: *gladiatorium munus Veronensibus nostris promisisti.*

35 *CIL* III 6832 = Robert 1940: 140, no. 92 (2nd half of 2nd c. CE), lines 3–9: ...*[q]ui primus omn[ium] | [[- - - - - -]]|i messe p[op]u[lo Ant(iochensi)] | [m]unus promisit [et] | [in]tra duos men[ses] | [a]mphitheatrum ligne|[u]m fecit*; cf. Levick 1967: 83: "from the profits of the harvest (?)." For further discussion, see Ramsay 1924: 178, no. 5; Robinson 1925: 254. On *sparsiones*, see further Ville 1981: 428–30.

36 *ILS* 9406 = *AE* 1910, 78: *Q(uinto) Voltedio L(uci) [f(ilio) - - -] | Optato Aurelian[o fl(amini)] | divi Ner(vae) equo pub(lico) adle[cto a divo] | Traiano*

et in quinq(ue) dec(urias) ab [Imp(eratore)] | Caes(are) Hadriano Aug(usto) trib(uno) mi[l(itum) leg(ionis)] | VI Victricis P(iae) F(idelis) aed(ili) praef(ecto) i(ure) [d(icundo) sacerdoti] | Cer(erum) sacror(um) ann(o) CLXXVII [IIvir(o)] | IIvir(o) quinq(uennali) qui ob honorem | cum HS CC mil(ia) promisisset inla[tis] | aerar(ium) HS XXXVIII mil(ibus) leg(atis) am[pliata] | pec(unia) spectaculum in amphi[theatro] | gladiatorum et Africanaru[m] | quadriduo dedit d(ecreto) d(ecurionum) p(ecunia) p(ublica).

37 Robert 1940, 115–16, nos. 56–7; *SEG* XXXII 605, with photo at Catlin 1984: 36, fig. 56.

38 For the term *munus iustum atque legitimum,* see Suet. *Cl.* 21.4. See further Ville 1981: 129–73; Edmondson 1996: 77, with references. For means of acquiring gladiators in a provincial setting, see Carter 2003: 103–8.

39 This play on the double sense of *manus* is acknowledged by Hijmans et al. 1977: 105, *ad loc.*

40 For discussion of this complex passage, Hijmans et al. 1977: 106–7, *ad loc.;* Coleman 1990: 52–3.

41 For further discussion of the setting and its identification as a *locus amoenus,* Zimmerman 1993: 146–7 and 2000: 366–8, pointing out how Apuleius emphasizes the artifice/artificiality of the setting and scenery.

42 For instance, *CIL* X 3704 = *ILS* 5054 = Fora 1996: 136–7, no. 114 (Neapolis, late 2nd/early 3rd c. CE): ... *ceteroq(ue) honestissim(o) apparatu largiter exhibui[t]; CIL* X 1211 = *ILS* 5058 = Fora 1996: 136, no. 111 (Abella, 170 CE): ... *diem gladiatorum et omne apparatum pecunia sua edidit; CIL* IX 2237 = *ILS* 5060 = *EAOR* III 28 = Fora 1996: 149, no. 161 (Telesia, Samnium, late 1st/early 2nd c. CE): ... *su[mptu pr]oprio quinque fer[as Libyca]s cum familia [glad(iatoria) Arr]ianorum et adpa[ratu m]agnifico dederit.*

43 I here prefer Hanson's interpretation of *facies* (1989 ad loc.) to "how many species!" of Hijmans et al. 1977: 107.

44 For a similar expression, cf. Cicero's description (*De prov. cons.* 1.2) of A. Gabinius and L. Calpurnius Piso in 56 BCE as "those two agents of doom and destruction of the Republic" (*duo rei publicae portenta ac paene funera*).

45 Cic. *ad Fam.* 8.2.2 (SB 78); 8.4.5 (SB 81); 8.6.5 (SB 88); 8.9.3 (SB 82); 2.11.2 (SB 90); cf. *ad Att.* 6.1.21 (SB 115).

46 For example, Symm. *Ep.* 2.77 (*Scottici canes,* 393 CE), 6.43 (crocodiles, 401 CE), 7.59 (leopards, 401 CE), 9.141 (crocodiles, 401 CE), 151 (crocodiles, 398–401 CE), 142 (Dalmatian bears, 400–1 CE); cf. 5.62, 65 for his complaints in 397–8 CE about exactions of *portorium* dues on wild beasts being sent from the provinces to Rome for the games.

47 Bérard 1989 = *AE* 1987, 867; Knoepfler 1999 = *AE* 1999, 1327: *Dianae | Ti(berius) Claudius Ulpianu[s] | trib(unus) coh(ortis) I Cili(cum) cum vexilla|tionib(us) leg(ionum) I Ital(icae) XI Cl(audiae) class(is) | Fl(aviae) Mo(esicae) ob venationem | Caesarianam iniunc|tam a Cl(audio) Saturnino*

leg(ato) | Aug(usti) pr(o) pr(aetore) ursis et vison|tibus prospere captis | aram consecra|vit Largo et Mes|sallino co(n)s(ulibus). For *venatores* of the Legio XI Claudia, see also *CIL* III 7449 (Montana), dated to 155 CE.

48 For the position of Syriarch, Liebeschuetz 1959.

49 *CIL* IV 1179 = *ILS* 5143 = Sabbatini Tumolesi 1980: 36–7, no. 10: *[C]n(aei) Allei Nigidi | Mai quinq(uennalis) gl(adiatorum) par(ia) XXX et eor(um) supp(ositicii) pugn(abunt) Pompeis VIII VII VI k(alendas) Dec(embres). Ellios [et] ven(atio) erit. Maio quin(quennali) feliciter. Paris [scr(ipsit)?]. | Marti[alis M]aio [salutem?]*. For other acclamations from Pompeii of this *munerarius*, see Sabbatini Tumolesi 1980: nos. 8, 11, 17–20, 25.

50 On the continued importance of gift-giving in the Roman economy, see Verboven 2002.

51 On imperial *adventus* rituals, see Lehnen 1997.

52 I continue to believe that Martial's *Liber Spectaculorum* was composed for the opening of the Flavian Amphitheatre under Titus in 80 CE: see Edmondson 2008; cf. Coleman 2006: xlv–lxiv. On acclamations at public spectacles, see Roueché 1984; Potter 1996.

53 For this line of interpretation of the Thrasyleon episode, see Frangoulidis 1999; Slater 2003: 94–6.

54 For *missilia*, see Stat. *Silv.* 1.6.9–27; Dio 66.25.5; Suet. *Dom.* 4.5; and for legal issues when spectators sold the gifts distributed as *missilia*, *Dig.* 18.1.8.1 (Pomponius); note also Ville 1981: 429–30.

55 On the *pompa*, Ville 1981: 399–401. For the relief from Pompeii, see Maiuri 1947; Jacobelli 2003: 95–7 and fig. 77.

56 On the Pyrrhic dance, see briefly Sabbatini Tumolesi 1970; in detail Ceccarelli 1998.

57 Dio 60.7.2 (Ludi Palatini); 60.23.5 (Claudius' triumph); cf. Suet. *DJ* 39.1, *Nero* 12.1.

58 On which there has been much discussion: e.g., Fick 1990; Zimmerman 1993; Freudenburg 2007: 253–6; and especially the rich, detailed commentary of Zimmerman 2000: 375–410.

59 Suet. *Cal.* 30.2; *Cl.* 21.5; cf. *Dom.* 4. On arena crowds and executions, see Fagan 2011: 174–88.

60 For this in real life, see Coleman 1990: 51–4 and 2006: 97–9, 212–17, 249–59.

61 This "fatal charade" with a female criminal is taken over from the Greek version of the story, where it takes place in the arena at Thessalonica: see ps.-Lucian *Onos* 52–53.

62 Suet. *Nero* 12.2; Mart. *Spect.* 5 (= SB 6), with Coleman 1990: 63–4 and 2006: 62–8, *ad loc.*

63 For examples from Gades (Cadiz) in 43 BCE, see Cic. *ad Fam.* 10.32.3 (SB 415) and from Cumae from the 70s CE (announced at Pompeii), see *CIL* IV 9983a = Sabbatini Tumolesi 1980: 107–9, no. 79; for general discussion, Sabbatini Tumolesi 1980: 143–5.

64 *CIL* II 6278 = *ILS* 5163 = Oliver and Palmer 1955, lines 57–8 = *EAOR* VII 3, with Carter 2003.
65 For attestations of executions at *munera gladiatoria* in the Greek East, see Robert 1940: 320–1.
66 Beschaouch 1966; Dunbabin 1978: 67–9 and pls. 52–3; Hanoune 2000; Fagan 2011: 128–32 and fig. 9.
67 For texts see *EAOR* I, VI (Rome), II–IV (Italy, Sicily, Sardinia, and Corsica), V (Alpine provinces, the Gallic provinces, Upper and Lower Germany, and Britain), VII (the Hispanic provinces), VIII (Campania outside Pompeii); Sabbatini Tumolesi 1980 (Pompeii); Fora 1996 (Italy); Robert 1940 and Mann 2011 (the Greek East).
68 *CIL* X 7295 = *ILS* 5055 = *EAOR* III 53 (with photo), lines 3–15 quoted.
69 On the *Florida*, see Bradley 2004; Lee 2005; Harrison 2000: 89–135. On *Flor*. 16, Harrison 2000: 116–20; Lee 2005: 145–58.

WORKS CITED

Bassignano, M.S. 1974. *Il flaminato nelle provincie dell'Africa*. Rome.
Bérard, F. 1989. "La cohorte *I a Cilicum*, la *classis Flavia Moesica* et les vexillations de l'armée de Mésie inférieure: à propos d'une inscription de Montana." *ZPE* 79: 129–38.
Beschaouch, A. 1966. "La mosaïque de chasse à l'amphithéâtre découverte à Smirat en Tunisie." *CRAI* 110.1: 134–57.
Bradley, K.R. 1998. "Contending with Conversion: Reflections on the Reformation of Lucius the Ass." *Phoenix* 52.3–4: 315–34. [Revised version in Bradley 2012: 23–40.]
– 2000a. "Animalizing the Slave: the Truth of Fiction." *JRS* 90: 110–25. [Revised version in Bradley 2012: 59–78.]
– 2000b. "Fictive Families: Family and Household in the *Metamorphoses* of Apuleius." *Phoenix* 54.3–4: 282–308. [Revised version in Bradley 2012: 79–103.]
– 2004. "Apuleius and Carthage." *Ancient Narrative* 4: 1–29. [Revised version in Bradley 2012: 126–46.]
– 2012. *Apuleius and Antonine Rome: Historical Essays. Phoenix* Suppl. 50. Toronto, Buffalo, and London.
Carter, M.J. 2003. "Gladiatorial Ranking and the *SC de Pretiis Gladiatorum Minuendis* (*CIL* II 6278 = *ILS* 5163)." *Phoenix* 57.1–2: 83–114.
– 2009. "Gladiators and *Monomachoi:* Greek Attitudes to a Roman 'Cultural Performance'." *International Journal of the History of Sport* 26.2: 298–322.
Catlin, H.W. 1984. "Archaeology in Greece, 1983–84." *Archaeological Reports for 1983–84*, 3–70. *JHS* Suppl. 30. London.

Ceccarelli, P. 1998. *La pirrica nell'antichità greco-romana. Studi sulla danza armata.* Pisa and Rome.

Coleman, K.M. 1990. "Fatal Charades: Roman Executions Staged as Mythological Enactments." *JRS* 80: 44–73.

Coleman, K.M., ed. 2006. *Martial: Liber Spectaculorum.* Oxford.

Connors, C. 2008. "Politics and Spectacle." In *The Cambridge Companion to the Greek and Roman Novel,* edited by T. Whitmarsh, 162–82. Cambridge.

Cooley, A.E., and M.G.L. Cooley, eds. 2004. *Pompeii: A Sourcebook.* London and New York.

De Trane, G. 2009. *Scrittura e intertestualità nelle* Metamorfosi *di Apuleio.* Lecce.

Dowden, K. 1994. "The Roman Audience of the *Golden Ass.*" In *The Search for the Ancient Novel,* edited by J. Tatum, 419–34. Baltimore.

Dunbabin, K.M.D. 1978. *The Mosaics of Roman North Africa: Studies in Iconography and Patronage.* Oxford.

Edmondson, J. 1996. "Dynamic Arenas: Gladiatorial Presentations in the City of Rome and the Construction of Roman Society during the Early Empire." In Slater 1996: 69–112.

– 2008. "Celebrating the Inauguration of the Flavian Amphitheatre in A.D. 80? Or 'An Untitled Collection of Uncertain Length Celebrating a Series of Unspecified Occasions in Honour of an Unnamed Caesar'." *JRA* 21: 465–70.

Elster, M. 1991. "Römisches Strafrecht in den *Metamorphosen* des Apuleius." In *Groningen Colloquia on the Novel* IV, edited by H. Hofmann, 135–54. Groningen.

Fagan, G.G. 2011. *The Lure of the Arena: Social Psychology and the Crowd at the Roman Games.* Cambridge.

Fantham, E. 1995. "Aemilia Pudentilla: or The Wealthy Widow's Choice." In *Women in Antiquity: New Assessments,* edited by R. Hawley and B.M. Levick, 221–32. London.

– 1996. *Roman Literary Culture from Cicero to Apuleius.* Baltimore.

– 2013. *Roman Literary Culture from Plautus to Macrobius.* 2nd ed. Baltimore.

Fick, N. 1990. "Die Pantomime des Apuleius (Met. X,30–43.3)." In *Theater und Gesellschaft im Imperium Romanum. Théâtre et société dans l'empire romain,* edited by J. Blänsdorf, J. André, and N. Fick, 223–32. Tübingen.

Finkelpearl, E. 1998. *Metamorphosis of Language in Apuleius: A Study of Allusion in the Novel.* Ann Arbor.

– 2007. "Apuleius, the *Onos,* and Rome." In Paschalis et al. 2007: 263–76.

Fishwick, D. 2002. *The Imperial Cult in the Latin West: Studies in the Ruler Cult of the Western Provinces.* III. *Provincial cult.* 2. *The Provincial Priesthood.* Leiden, Boston, and Cologne.

Fora, M. 1996. *I* munera gladiatoria *in Italia: Considerazioni sulla loro documentazione epigrafica.* Naples.

Frangoulidis, S.A. 1999. "Theatre and Spectacle in Apuleius' Tale of the Robber Thrasyleon (*Met.* 4.13–21)." In *Griechisch-römische Komödie und Tragödie III* (Drama: Beiträge zum antiken Drama und seiner Rezeption 8), edited by B. Zimmermann, 113–35. Stuttgart and Weimar.

Freudenburg, K. 2007. "Leering for the Plot: Visual Curiosity in Apuleius and Others." In Paschalis et al. 2007: 238–62.

Graverini, L. 2001. "L'incontro di Lucio e Fotide. Stratificazioni intertestuali in Apul. Met. II.6–7." *Athenaeum* 89: 425–46.

– 2002. "Corinth, Rome, and Africa: A Cultural Background for the Tale of the Ass." In *Space in the Ancient Novel*, edited by M. Paschalis and S. Frangoulidis, 58–77. *Ancient Narrative* Suppl. 1. Groningen.

– 2003. "The Winged Ass. Intertextuality and Narration in Apuleius' *Metamorphoses*." In Panayotakis, Zimmerman, and Keulen 2003: 207–18.

Hanson, J.A. tr. 1989. *Apuleius, Metamorphoses (The Golden Ass)*. 2 vols. Cambridge, MA.

Hanoune, R. 2000. "Encore les *Telegenii*, encore la mosaïque de Smirat!" *L'Africa romana* 13: 2.1565–76.

Harrison, S.J., ed. 1999. *Oxford Readings in the Roman Novel*. Oxford.

– 2000. *Apuleius: A Latin Sophist*. Oxford.

Hijmans, B.L., Jr, et al., eds. 1977. *Apuleius Madaurensis. Metamorphoses. Book IV. 1–27: Text, Introduction and Commentary*. Groningen.

Holzberg, N. 1984. "Apuleius und der Verfassen des griechischen Eselromans." *WJA* 10: 161–78.

Hoskins Walbank, M.E. 1997. "The Foundation and Planning of Early Roman Corinth." *JRA* 10: 95–130.

Jacobelli, L. 2003. *Gladiators at Pompeii*. Los Angeles and Rome.

Jones, C.P. 2014. "Apuleius, Corinth, and Two Epigrams from Nemea." *ZPE* 192: 115–20.

Keulen, W. 2000. "Significant Names in Apuleius: A 'Good Contriver' and His Rival in the Cheese Trade (*Met.* 1, 5) (*Apuleiana Groningana X*)." *Mnemosyne* 53.3: 310–21.

Kleijwegt, M. 1995. "A Presumptuous Quaestor from Patras?" *Epigraphica* 57: 39–43.

Knoepfler, D. 1999. "Pausanias à Rome en l'an 148?" *REG* 112.2: 485–509.

Lee, B.T., ed. 2005. *Apuleius'* Florida*: A Commentary*. Berlin.

Lehnen, J. 1997. *Adventus principis. Untersuchungen zu Sinngehalt und Zeremoniell des Kaiserankunft in den Städten des Imperium Romanum*. Prismata 7. Frankfurt.

Levick, B.M. 1967. *Roman Colonies in Southern Asia Minor*. Oxford.

Liebeschuetz, J.W.H.G. 1959. "The Syriarch in the Fourth Century." *Historia* 9: 113–26.

Maiuri, B. 1947. "Rilievo gladiatorio di Pompei." *RAL* ser. viii 2: 491–510.

Mann, C. 2009. "Gladiators in the Greek East: A Case Study of Romanization." *International Journal of the History of Sport* 26.2: 272–97.
– 2011. *"Um keinen Kranz, um das Leben kämpfen wir!" Gladiatoren im Osten des römischen Reiches und die Frage der Romanisierung*. Berlin.
Mason, H.J. 1971. "Lucius at Corinth." *Phoenix* 25: 160–5.
– 1978. "*Fabula graecanica*: Apuleius and his Greek Sources." In *Aspects of Apuleius' Golden Ass*, edited by B.L. Hijmans, Jr, and R.T. van der Paardt, 1–15. Groningen. [Reprinted in Harrison 1999: 217–36.]
– 1983. "The Distinction of Lucius in Apuleius' *Metamorphoses*." *Phoenix* 37: 135–43.
– 1994. "Greek and Latin Versions of the Ass-Story." *ANRW* II.34.2: 1665–707.
– 1999. "The *Metamorphoses* of Apuleius and Its Greek Sources." In *Latin Fiction. The Latin Novel in Context*, edited by H. Hofmann, 103–12. London and New York.
Millar, F.G.B. 1981. "The World of the *Golden Ass*." *JRS* 71: 63–75. [Reprinted in Harrison 1999: 247–68 and in F. Millar, *Government, Society, and Culture in the Roman Empire*, edited by H.M. Cotton and G.M. Rogers, 313–35. Chapel Hill, 2004.]
Norden, F. 1912. *Apulejus von Madaura und das römische Privatrecht*. Leipzig.
Oliver, J.H., and R.E.A. Palmer. 1955. "Minutes of an Act of the Roman Senate." *Hesperia* 24.4: 320–49.
Osgood, J.W. 2006. "*Nuptiae iure civili congruae*: Apuleius's Story of Cupid and Psyche and the Roman Law of Marriage." *TAPA* 136: 415–41.
Panayotakis, S., M. Zimmerman, and W. Keulen, eds. 2003. *The Ancient Novel and Beyond. Mnemosyne* Suppl. 241. Leiden.
Paschalis, M., S. Frangoulidis, S.J. Harrison, and M. Zimmerman, eds. 2007. *The Greek and the Roman Novel: Parallel Readings. Ancient Narrative* Suppl. 8. Groningen.
Pasetti, L. 2007. *Plauto in Apuleio*. Bologna.
Potter, D.S. 1996. "Performance, Power, and Justice in the High Empire." In Slater 1996: 129–59.
Prandi, L. 1988. *Platea: momenti e problemi della storia di una polis*. Padua.
Ramsay, W.M. 1924. "Studies in the Roman Province Galatia. VI. Some Inscriptions of Colonia Caesarea Antiochea." *JRS* 14: 172–205.
Riess, W. 2001. *Apuleius und die Räuber. Ein Beitrag zur historischen Kriminalitätsforschung*. Heidelberger Althistorische Beiträge und Epigraphische Studien 35. Stuttgart.
Riess, W., ed. 2008. *Paideia at Play: Learning and Wit in Apuleius. Ancient Narrative* Suppl. 11. Groningen.
Rives, J.B. 1994. "The Priesthood of Apuleius." *AJP* 115: 273–90.
Rizakis, A.D. 1990. "*Munera gladiatoria* à Patras, II." *ZPE* 82: 201–8.

– 2001. "La constitution des élites municipales dans les colonies romaines de la province d'Achaïe." In *The Greek East in the Roman Context: Proceedings of a Colloquium Organized by the Finnish Institute at Athens, May 21 and 22, 1999*, edited by O. Salomies, 37–49. Papers and Monographs of the Finnish Institute at Athens 7. Helsinki.

Robert, L. 1940. *Les gladiateurs dans l'Orient grec*. Paris. [Reprinted Amsterdam, 1971.]

Robinson, D.M. 1925. "Notes on Inscriptions from Antioch in Pisidia." *JRS* 15: 253–62.

Romano, D.G. 2000. "A Tale of Two Cities: Roman Colonies at Corinth." In *Romanization and the City: Creations, Transformations, and Failures*, edited by E. Fentress, 83–104. *JRA* Suppl. 38. Ann Arbor.

Roueché, C. 1984. "Acclamations in the Later Roman Empire: New Evidence from Aphrodisias." *JRS* 74: 181–99.

Sabbatini Tumolesi, P. 1970. "Pyrricharii." *La Parola del Passato* 134: 328–38.

– 1980. *Gladiatorum Paria: Annunci di spettacoli gladiatorii a Pompei*. Tituli 1. Rome.

Sandy, G.N. 1997. *The Greek World of Apuleius: Apuleius and the Second Sophistic*. Leiden.

Shaw, B.D. 2002. Review of Riess 2001. *Ancient Narrative* 2: 268–79.

Shumate, N. 1996. "'Darkness Visible': Apuleius Reads Virgil." *Groningen Colloquia on the Novel* VII, edited by H. Hofmann and M. Zimmerman, 103–16. Groningen.

Slater, N.W. 2003. "Spectators and Spectacle in Apuleius." In Panayotakis, Zimmerman, and Keulen 2003: 85–100.

Slater, W.J., ed. 1996. *Roman Theater and Society: E. Togo Salmon Papers* I. Ann Arbor.

Spawforth, A.J.S. 1996. "Roman Corinth: The Formation of a Colonial Elite." In *Roman Onomastics in the Greek East: Social and Political Aspects*, edited by A.D. Rizakis, 167–82. Meletemata 21. Athens.

Summers, R.J. 1970. "Roman Justice and Apuleius' *Metamorphoses*." *TAPA* 101: 511–31.

Tordoff, R.L.S. 2008. "A Note on Echo in Apuleius, *Metamorphoses* 5.25." *CQ* 58.2: 711–12.

Treggiari, S. 1991. *Roman Marriage:* Iusti Coniuges *from the Time of Cicero to the Time of Ulpian*. Oxford.

Tuck, S.L. 2008. "Scheduling Spectacle: Factors Contributing to the Dates of Pompeian *munera*." *CJ* 104: 123–43.

Vasconcelos, B. Ávila. 2009. *Bilder der Sklaverei in den Metamorphosen des Apuleius*. Vertumnus. Berliner Beiträge zur Klassischen Philologie und zu ihren Nachbargebieten 7. Göttingen.

Verboven, K. 2002. *The Economy of Friends: Economic Aspects of* Amicitia *and Patronage in the Late Republic.* Collection *Latomus* 269. Brussels.

Ville, G. 1981. *La gladiature en Occident des origines à la mort de Domitien.* BEFAR 245. Rome.

Watson, A. 1987. *Roman Slave Law.* Baltimore.

Welch, K.E. 1999. "Negotiating Roman Spectacle Architecture in the Greek World: Athens and Corinth." In *The Art of Ancient Spectacle,* edited by B. Bergmann and C. Kondoleon, 125–45. CASVA Symposium Papers 34. Washington.

– 2007. *The Roman Amphitheatre: From its Origins to the Colosseum.* Cambridge.

Wiseman, J. 1979. "Corinth and Rome I: 228 B.C.–A.D. 267." *ANRW* II.7.1: 438–548.

Woolf, G. 1994. "Becoming Roman, Staying Greek: Culture, Identity and the Civilizing Process in the Roman East." *PCPS* 40: 116–43.

Zimmerman, M. 1993. "Narrative Judgment and Reader Response in Apuleius' *Metamorphoses* 10, 29–34. The Pantomime of the Judgment of Paris." In *Groningen Colloquia on the Novel* V, edited by H. Hoffmann, 143–61. Groningen.

– ed. 2000. *Apuleius Madaurensis: Metamorphoses. Book X. Text, Introduction and Commentary.* Groningen.

– 2002. "Latinising the Novel: Scholarship since Perry on Greek 'Models' and Roman (Re-)Creations." *Ancient Narrative* 2: 123–42.

– 2012. *Apulei Metamorphoseon libri XI.* Oxford.

CONTRIBUTORS

Clifford Ando, David B. and Clara E. Stern Professor of Classics, History and Law and in the College, University of Chicago

Sarah Blake, Associate Professor of Classical Studies, York University

Barbara Weiden Boyd, Henry Winkley Professor of Latin and Greek, Bowdoin College

Christer Bruun, Professor and Chair of Classics, University of Toronto

Fanny Dolansky, Associate Professor of Classics, Brock University

Jonathan Edmondson, Professor of History and Classical Studies, York University

Alison Keith, Professor of Classics and Women's Studies, University of Toronto

Elizabeth Kennedy, Instructor in Greek and Roman Studies, Carleton University

Cedric Littlewood, Associate Professor of Greek and Roman Studies, University of Victoria

C.W. Marshall, Professor of Classics, University of British Columbia

Sarah L. McCallum, Postdoctoral Fellow, Department of the Classics, Harvard University

Jonathan Tracy, Lecturer in Classical Studies, School of Humanities, Massey University

Jarrett Welsh, Associate Professor of Classics, University of Toronto

INDEX LOCORUM

INSCRIPTIONS

GENERAL INDEX

PHOENIX SUPPLEMENTARY VOLUMES

1 *Studies in Honour of Gilbert Norwood* edited by Mary E. White

2 *Arbiter of Elegance: A Study of the Life and Works of C. Petronius* Gilbert Bagnani

3 *Sophocles the Playwright* S.M. Adams

4 *A Greek Critic: Demetrius on Style* G.M.A. Grube

5 *Coastal Demes of Attika: A Study of the Policy of Kleisthenes* C.W.J. Eliot

6 *Eros and Psyche: Studies in Plato, Plotinus, and Origen* John M. Rist

7 *Pythagoras and Early Pythagoreanism* J.A. Philip

8 *Plato's Psychology* T.M. Robinson

9 *Greek Fortifications* F.E. Winter

10 *Comparative Studies in Republican Latin Imagery* Elaine Fantham

11 *The Orators in Cicero's* Brutus: *Prosopography and Chronology* G.V. Sumner

12 Caput *and Colonate: Towards a History of Late Roman Taxation* Walter Goffart

13 *A Concordance to the Works of Ammianus Marcellinus* Geoffrey Archbold

14 *Fallax opus: Poet and Reader in the Elegies of Propertius* John Warden

15 *Pindar's* Olympian One: *A Commentary* Douglas E. Gerber

16 *Greek and Roman Mechanical Water-Lifting Devices: The History of a Technology* John Peter Oleson

17 *The Manuscript Tradition of Propertius* James L. Butrica

18 Parmenides of Elea *Fragments: A Text and Translation with an Introduction* edited by David Gallop

19 *The Phonological Interpretation of Ancient Greek: A Pandialectal Analysis* Vít Bubeník

20 *Studies in the Textual Tradition of Terence* John N. Grant

21 *The Nature of Early Greek Lyric: Three Preliminary Studies* R.L. Fowler

22 Heraclitus *Fragments: A Text and Translation with a Commentary* edited by T.M. Robinson

23 *The Historical Method of Herodotus* Donald Lateiner

24 *Near Eastern Royalty and Rome, 100–30 BC* Richard D. Sullivan

25 *The Mind of Aristotle: A Study in Philosophical Growth* John M. Rist

26 *Trials in the Late Roman Republic, 149 BC to 50 BC* Michael Alexander

27 *Monumental Tombs of the Hellenistic Age: A Study of Selected Tombs from the Pre-Classical to the Early Imperial Era* Janos Fedak

28 *The Local Magistrates of Roman Spain* Leonard A. Curchin

29 Empedocles *The Poem of Empedocles: A Text and Translation with an Introduction* edited by Brad Inwood

30 Xenophanes of Colophon *Fragments: A Text and Translation with a Commentary* edited by J.H. Lesher

31 *Festivals and Legends: The Formation of Greek Cities in the Light of Public Ritual* Noel Robertson

32 *Reading and Variant in Petronius: Studies in the French Humanists and Their Manuscript Sources* Wade Richardson

33 *The Excavations of San Giovanni di Ruoti, Volume I: The Villas and Their Environment* Alastair Small and Robert J. Buck

34 *Catullus Edited with a Textual and Interpretative Commentary* D.F.S. Thomson

35 *The Excavations of San Giovanni di Ruoti, Volume 2: The Small Finds* C.J. Simpson, with contributions by R. Reece and J.J. Rossiter

36 The Atomists: Leucippus and Democritus *Fragments: A Text and Translation with a Commentary* C.C.W. Taylor

37 *Imagination of a Monarchy: Studies in Ptolemaic Propaganda* R.A. Hazzard

38 *Aristotle's Theory of the Unity of Science* Malcolm Wilson

39 *Empedocles The Poem of Empedocles: A Text and Translation with an Introduction, Revised Edition* edited by Brad Inwood

40 *The Excavations of San Giovanni di Ruoti, Volume 3: The Faunal and Plant Remains* M.R. McKinnon, with contributions by A. Eastham, S.G. Monckton, D.S. Reese, and D.G. Steele

41 *Justin and Pompeius Trogus: A Study of the Language of Justin's* Epitome *of Trogus* J.C. Yardley

42 *Studies in Hellenistic Architecture* F.E. Winter

43 *Mortuary Landscapes of North Africa* edited by David L. Stone and Lea M. Stirling

44 Anaxagoras of Clazomenae *Fragments and Testimonia: A Text and Translation with Notes and Essays* by Patricia Curd

45 *Virginity Revisited: Configurations of the Unpossessed Body* edited by Bonnie MacLachlan and Judith Fletcher

46 *Roman Dress and the Fabrics of Roman Culture* edited by Jonathan Edmondson and Alison Keith

47 *Epigraphy and the Greek Historian* edited by Craig Cooper

48 *In the Image of the Ancestors: Narratives of Kinship in Flavian Epic* Neil W. Bernstein

49 *Perceptions of the Second Sophistic and Its Times – Regards sur la Seconde Sophistique et son époque* edited by Thomas Schmidt and Pascale Fleury

50 *Apuleius and Antonine Rome: Historical Essays* Keith Bradley

51 *Belonging and Isolation in the Hellenistic World* edited by Sheila L. Ager and Riemer A. Faber

52 *Roman Slavery and Roman Material Culture* edited by Michele George

53 *Thalia Delighting in Song: Essays on Ancient Greek Poetry* Emmet I. Robbins

54 *Stymphalos: The Acropolis Sanctuary, Volume 1* Gerald Schaus with contributions by Sandra Garvie-Lok, Christopher Hagerman, Monica Munaretto, Deborah Ruscillo, Peter Stone, Mary Sturgeon, Laura Surtees, Robert Weir, Hector Williams, Alexis Young

55 *Roman Literary Cultures: Domestic Politics, Revolutionary Poetics, Civic Spectacle* edited by Alison Keith and Jonathan Edmondson

www.ingramcontent.com/pod-product-compliance
Lightning Source LLC
LaVergne TN
LVHW040153080826
844660LV00014B/942/J

* 9 7 8 1 4 4 2 6 2 9 6 7 7 *